INTELLECTUAL FOUNDERS OF THE REPUBLIC

Intellectual Founders of the Republic

Five Studies in Nineteenth-Century French Republican Political Thought

Sudhir Hazareesingh

OXFORD
UNIVERSITY PRESS

OXFORD

UNIVERSITY PRESS

Great Clarendon Street, Oxford OX2 6DP

Oxford University Press is a department of the University of Oxford.
It furthers the University's objective of excellence in research, scholarship,
and education by publishing worldwide in

Oxford New York

Athens Auckland Bangkok Bogotá Buenos Aires Cape Town
Chennai Dar es Salaam Delhi Florence Hong Kong Istanbul Karachi
Kolkata Kuala Lumpur Madrid Melbourne Mexico City Mumbai Nairobi
Paris São Paulo Shanghai Singapore Taipei Tokyo Toronto Warsaw

with associated companies in Berlin Ibadan

Oxford is a registered trade mark of Oxford University Press
in the UK and in certain other countries

Published in the United States
by Oxford University Press Inc., New York

© Sudhir Hazareesingh 2001

The moral rights of the author have been asserted
Database right Oxford University Press (maker)

First published 2001

British Library Cataloguing in Publication Data
Data available

Library of Congress Cataloging in Publication Data
Hazareesingh, Sudhir.
Intellectual founders of the Republic: five studies in nineteenth-century
French republican political thought / Sudhir Hazareesingh.
p. cm
Includes bibliographical references and index.
1. French—Politics and government—1870–1940.
2. Republicanism—France—History—19th century.
3. Intellectuals—France—Political activity.   I. Title.
JN2562.H39 2001   321.8'6'09034—dc21   2001036397
ISBN 0–19–924794–3

1 3 5 7 9 10 8 6 4 2

Typeset by Hope Services (Abingdon) Ltd
Printed in Great Britain
T. J. International Ltd
Padstow, Cornwall

For
Karma
A true republican spirit

PREFACE

THIS book got off to an unpromising start. When, having drafted what I thought was an alluring proposal, I approached a major publishing house to add this project to its forthcoming titles, I was told that the series in which I had hoped to include the book was being wound up. When an Oxford colleague—a historian—asked me about my next project after *From Subject to Citizen*, I replied that I was hoping to revisit the intellectual origins of the Third Republic. 'Vaste programme' he retorted sarcastically. Another Oxonian friend—a political scientist this time—after being informed of my cast of characters, tartly declared that the book would be an exercise in 'self-indulgence'. Most of my colleagues, both in the Anglo-American world and in France, freely confessed that the names of Barni, Dupont-White, Pelletan, and Vacherot meant nothing to them. As for Littré, everyone knew his Dictionary, but little else. When I mentioned to one of my French colleagues that I was reading Littré's voluminous political writings, he looked startled: 'il est vraiment très ennuyeux, tu ne trouves pas?'

Such was my challenge: to write about the founding of the Third Republic in France but to narrate it through the eyes of a group of largely unknown thinkers, and in such a way as to open up the rich treasures of the republican political theory to which they subscribed—all the while keeping my French colleague awake. Of whether I have succeeded all the way my readers will be the judge. For my part, I have found the exercise illuminating in many respects, three of which especially stand out. The first was to see through the lives of five intellectuals how political theory and political practice could be indissociably linked: an uplifting experience in these days when political theory is all too often free-floating or else completely instrumentalized, and political practice grounded in little except expediency—perhaps there is a connection.

Just as enriching was having to face the multiple challenges of biographical research: hunting down the relics of particular individuals in public and private archives and coming to terms with the seemingly impossible task of trying to provide unity and coherence to lives which constantly appeared to subvert such logics. I came away with a wonderful sense of the complexities of human inspiration and an even greater resolve to ignore the mindless theorizing which seeks to reduce what we do—and who we are—to mere expressions of 'interest'.

Above all I have benefited from the support of my peers. Thanks to them, and to the patience, the generosity, and the collective wisdom of a large number of friends and colleagues in Britain, France, and the United States, this is now a much better book than it would otherwise have been. I would like to express my warmest gratitude to those who took the time to read all or part of the draft manuscript: Ceri Crossley, always ready to share his infectious enthusiasm for the French nineteenth century; Michael Freeden, providing invaluable help in thinking about the properties of ideologies, and spurring me to reformulate my concluding thoughts; Robert Gildea, as ever encouraging, lucid, and discerning in his comments; John Goldthorpe, offering up his insights on the origins of sociological thought and the writing of intellectual history, as well as his own copies of Comte's *Cours de Philosophie Positive* and *Catéchisme Positiviste*; Patrick Harismendy, volunteering his expertise on Sadi Carnot and his robust appreciation of the eccentricities of the latter's father-in-law Charles Dupont-White; Ruth Harris, polishing my introduction and encouraging me in my theoretical and historical revisionism; Patrice Higonnet, providing incisive and erudite comments, and extremely pertinent suggestions; Stanley Hoffmann, warm and consistent in his encouragement, and insightful and wise in his observations; Olivier Ihl, *force de la nature*, urging me to aim higher and wider than I had thought necessary, desirable, or possible; Lucien Jaume, sharing his expertise of nineteenth-century French liberal thinking, and offering helpfully sceptical comments on my interpretation of Dupont-White; Stuart Jones, for his Comtian expertise, his penetrating observations, and also for helping to weed out my conceptual anachronisms; Karma Nabulsi, for being an inspiration, understanding everything, and patiently reading successive drafts of the book; Quentin Skinner, for combing through my prose with his eagle eye, and helping through his scholarship to frame my approach to this book; Marc Stears, for being a true spirit, perceptive critic, and good friend—all three for the price of one; Judy Stone, for introducing me to Eugène Pelletan and offering constructive suggestions about the French republican tradition; and the late Vincent Wright, who loved the French nineteenth century and encouraged me to follow him up its dizzying heights.

I am also extremely grateful to the staff at the following institutions, all of whom greatly facilitated my quest for primary and secondary material and did everything to make my visits both pleasant and productive: the Bibliothèque Nationale, Archives Nationales, Bibliothèque de l'Arsenal, Bibliothèque du Protestantisme, Archives de la Préfecture de Police, Bibliothèque Historique de la Ville de Paris, Fondation Thiers, Musée et Bibliothèque Victor Hugo, Bibliothèque du Grand-Orient, and Bibliothèque de l'Institut de France (all in Paris); the Archives Départementales of the Somme (Amiens), Rhône (Lyon), and Bouches-du-Rhône (Marseilles); and the Archives d'État and Bibliothèque Publique et Universitaire (Geneva). I would especially like to thank Mme. Béatrice Denuit of the Académie Royale (Brussels) for her invaluable assistance in locating the correspondence of Émile de Laveleye to Charles Dupont-White; Monsieur Lucien Debary (Auberchicourt) for providing me with the letters sent to his forebear Frédéric Petit by Jules Barni; Thierry and Caroline Carnot, for welcoming me into the sumptuous Chateau de Presles, and allowing me to consult the papers of Cécile Carnot, daughter of Charles Dupont-

White; and finally Paul Baquiast, the dynamic President of the Association des Amis d'Eugène et Camille Pelletan, for inviting me to participate in the association's scholarly activities and thus enabling me to meet other devotees of the Pelletan cult, notably Ceri Crossley, Phil Nord, and Judy Stone.

Equally invaluable has been the institutional support I have received from a variety of sources: the British Academy, for enabling me through its Small Grants scheme to travel to many of the above locations; Balliol College, Oxford, for the regular support provided through my academic support allowance; the Research and Equipment Committee of the Department of Politics and International Relations at Oxford, for lavishing me with the appropriate hardware and software—thank you, Clive Payne; the Maison Française of Oxford, for its willingness to provide hospitality to colleagues who have helped me with this project—my gratitude goes here to Jean-Claude Vatin; and the quatrième section of the École Pratique des Hautes Études (Paris), for welcoming me as a visiting Maître de Conférences in the spring of 2000; I am especially grateful to François Monnier and Jean-Pierre Machelon for their friendship and support for all my endeavours.

Early versions of some parts of this book were presented to seminars and conferences organized by the Maison Française, Oxford; Royal Holloway College, London University; the Centre for European Studies, Harvard University; the History Department, University of Illinois; and the Association des Amis d'Eugène et Camille Pelletan. I am most grateful to all those who attended these gatherings and helped and encouraged me through their questions and comments. For their kind invitations to speak at these different venues—and, in the non-Oxonian cases, their wonderful hospitality—I would like to thank Robert Gildea, Karma Nabulsi, Katharine Ellis, Brendan Dooley, Patrice Higonnet, Nils Jacobsen, and Paul Baquiast.

I would also wish to record my deepest gratitude to a number of people for various kindnesses: Dominic Byatt, my Oxford University Press editor, for welcoming this book under his wing, and for his friendship, his unceasing encouragement, and his generous support; Amanda Watkins, for her invaluable help in steering it through production; Michael James, for his copyediting expertise; Frank Pert, for completing the index with his usual thoroughness and dedication; Patrick Harismendy, for sharing information gathered in his perusal of the Sadi Carnot papers, and retrieving a letter of Dupont-White; Stephanie Wright, for her typically prompt and effective handling of assorted requests for information; Karma Nabulsi, for being willing to talk to me about nineteenth century France at all hours of the day and night, and enlightening me with the experiences of 'her' *républicains de guerre*; Colin Lucas, for the extended loan of some superb books culled from the drawing room of the Master's Lodgings in Balliol; Ceri Crossley, for providing me with his copy of Du Pasquier's wonderful work on Quinet's years in exile—so wonderful indeed that I have not returned it to him; Basil Smith, for his generous gift of an 1877 edition of Littré's *Dictionnaire de la langue française*—carrying the five volumes across the road was a physical endurance test; Hikmat and

Mary Ellen Nabulsi, Martha Dewell and Bob Himoff, for their hospitality in a variety of settings; Thara Hazareesingh, for enabling me on numerous occasions to retreat to the tropical beaches of Mauritius; and Jo Whitfield, my former secretary at Balliol, who handled business out of term on the home front with efficiency and aplomb while the Senior Tutor chased archives abroad.

One metaphorical description of this book is 'finding a home': it is the story of how five intellectuals strove to build a just political order in nineteenth century France, and in so doing helped to define for their political community new ways of thinking about the relationship between identity and citizenship. A home was not for them a purely 'private' institution: it had to be enriched by incorporating values which were collective and public-oriented. They believed that a sense of 'patriotism' could be shared across space, and that one could feel at home in more places than one. They also found that building a 'homeland' was a seemingly difficult and at times impossible task, but that justice in the end prevailed; and that above all, as Rousseau said, a home is where the heart lies and the intellect is active.

I have had the privilege of appreciating the value of these propositions through my own life with Karma, my partner, companion, friend, accomplice, and intellectual guide. One day I know that the dream of a homeland for her people will become a reality. To this extraordinary and miraculous person, I dedicate this book, the product of so many of our common endeavours and affections.

Sudhir Hazareesingh
Balliol College, Oxford
31 March 2001

CONTENTS

LIST OF PHOTOGRAPHS

Introduction:
Revisiting the Intellectual
Transformation of
Nineteenth-Century France

B ETWEEN 1851 and 1857 a group of intellectuals met regularly at the
Parisian house of the Countess Marie d'Agoult. The *Maison Rose*, as it was
affectionately known to all those who frequented this *hôtel particulier*, was a
small house at the upper end of the Champs-Élysées where Daniel Stern—as
the Countess was known in literary and political circles—held her *salon*. The
political context of these gatherings was sombre: in December 1851 Louis
Napoleon's *coup d'état* had overthrown the Second Republic and launched a
fierce wave of repression against the republican party. Its political and intellectual leadership went underground, and attempted to keep alive the party's
hopes through these informal private gatherings. Daniel Stern's *salon* attracted
much of the elite of French intellectual life, both present and future: leading
figures such as Jules Michelet, Alexis de Tocqueville, Hippolyte Carnot, and
Jules Grévy discussed the prospects for a republican Europe with younger
luminaries such as Ernest Renan, Jules Simon, Émile Ollivier, and Lucien
Prévost-Paradol. So intense and passionate were these discussions that the
Maison Rose became known in republican circles as 'the abbey in the Woods of
Democracy'.[1]

Five intellectuals who took an active part in these gatherings were Jules
Barni, Charles Dupont-White, Eugène Pelletan, Emile Littré, and Étienne
Vacherot. They came from different intellectual camps within the republican
party, but their concerns were broadly similar: they spoke of the mistakes
made by their fellow-republicans in the recent past, the possibilities of reviv-
ing the fortunes of the movement in the present, and above all their hopes for
a return to a republican government in France in the near future. None of
them was especially well known in the early 1850s, but this would soon
change. By the end of the 1860s, all would be recognized as eminent political
and intellectual figures in the French and European republican movement.

---

[1] 'L'abbeye au Bois de la Démocratie', in Stern, Daniel, *Mémoires, souvenirs et journaux de la
Comtesse d'Agoult*, Vol. 2 (Paris: Mercure de France, 1990), 38.

This book will focus on their public lives and political thought, and especially on their defining roles in the struggle for the republicanization of the French polity between the early 1830s and the late 1870s. This was a period of great uncertainty; and as the political community lurched among republics, empires, and monarchies these figures fought to secure a permanent constitutional solution, which would durably unite the people of France under a republican regime. In the end, their aspirations were fulfilled. The founding laws of 1875 and the legislative elections of 1877 confirmed the establishment of the Third Republic and dashed the hopes of a Bonapartist or monarchical restoration. Underpinning this settlement was a distinct brand of republican ideology, notably different from the formulations which had buttressed earlier republican regimes.

Our five intellectuals were direct witnesses and participants in this narrative. As writers, political activists, and members of the republican elite they occupied leading positions in French public life from the 1850s up to the 1880s. In these various capacities they experienced and decisively helped to shape the final republican victory; their thoughts about the future republican order fundamentally coloured the internal ideological *aggiornamento* which made it possible. The pivotal position they enjoyed, both as observers and as primary agents of change, will thus provide us with a privileged access to this critical moment in modern French political and intellectual history. By focusing on this small group of thinkers, and examining not only their public utterances but also—where possible—their more intimate thoughts and even their private voices, we shall be able to follow the peregrinations of the republican idea from 'the inside' in more senses than one.

This book thus combines three types of narrative. At an immediate level, it provides intellectual biographies of five key figures in the nineteenth-century French republican movement, and assesses their theoretical contributions to the development of republicanism; in the context of the history of political thought, it re-examines the ideological origins of the Third Republic, and locates the French republican intellectual experiences in comparative European settings; from a historical perspective, finally, it is a study of the transformation of French republican political culture from the 'revolutionary' model inherited from the 1789 Revolution to the modern version which had crystallized by the late nineteenth century.[2]

Revisiting the Origins of Modern French Republicanism

But before we consider the *dramatis personae* in greater detail, it might be asked from the outset what might be the justification for another book on the intellectual origins of the Third Republic. Surely this is a story which has been

[2] See Furet, François, *La Révolution*, 2 vols (Paris: Hachette, 1988); and Faure, Alain (ed.), *Le XIXe siècle et la Révolution Française* (Paris: Editions Creaphis, 1992).

comprehensively narrated. What could the voices of five intellectuals add except minor glosses on the sum of our knowledge in this area?

It is true that there has long been an orthodoxy about this process—or rather a series of convergent orthodoxies among different historical sub-disciplines. The common ground is an emphasis on the political experiences of republican elites during the Franco-Prussian war, the Paris Commune, and the early Third Republic itself. In most accounts of the ideological transformation of French republicanism, this emphasis on 'experience' and elite consensus-building lies at the heart of the explanation. For political historians, it was the 'opportunist' approach of the republican leadership in the 1870s which transformed republican thinking, most notably by forging a harmonious synthesis between liberalism and democracy;[3] for historians of political thought—to put the same point differently—it was the cultural revolution brought about by positivism which proved one of the decisive factors, and in particular its preference for science and reason over sentiment and concrete knowledge over ideological utopia;[4] and for social and cultural historians, more broadly, it was the republican state itself which created a new social and political culture after its accession to power and then imposed it on the country, largely through its control of the education system.[5]

Several features of this transformation of republican ideology typically stand out in these orthodox accounts. This change was seen to be facilitated by the growing intellectual hegemony of rationalist doctrines which were seen to supplant the 'romantic' and often utopian undertones of early and mid-nineteenth century republican ideology. It was also a process which was presented as operating largely 'from above'. Having captured state power after 1877 these republicans—often described as 'Jacobin'[6] in memory of their centralizing forebears of the 1790s—deployed its resources to the full in order to promote their conception of the good life. Its product was a well-rounded synthesis, which provided the basis for the republicans' political hegemony in the decades which followed.[7] Finally, for many historians—and not only those influenced by the Marxist problematic—this ideology was at its core a tactical assemblage, in which the language of universality concealed a particularist defence of bourgeois interests.[8]

---

[3] See for example Lévêque, Pierre, *Histoire des forces politiques en France 1789–1880* (Paris: Armand Colin, 1992), 340; Berstein, Serge, 'Le modèle républicain', in Serge Berstein (ed.), *Les cultures politiques en France* (Paris: Seuil, 1999), 121.

[4] Barral, Pierre, *Les fondateurs de la République* (Paris: Armand Colin, 1968); Nicolet, Claude, *L'Idée républicaine en France* (Paris: Gallimard, 1983).

[5] Weber, Eugen, *Peasants into Frenchmen* (London: Chatto, 1977); Déloye, Yves, *École et citoyenneté: l'individualisme républicain de Jules Ferry à Vichy* (Paris: Presses de la Fondation Nationale des Sciences Politiques, 1994).

[6] For a study of the Jacobinism of the Revolutionary era, see Higonnet, Patrice, *Goodness Before Virtue* (Cambridge, MA: Harvard University Press, 1998).

[7] Berstein, 'Le modèle républicain', 123.

[8] See Elwitt, Sanford, *The Making of the Third Republic: Class and Politics in France 1868–1884* (Baton Rouge: Louisiana State University Press, 1975).

Positivistic, centralist, intellectually coherent, and socially instrumental: such were the dominant characteristics of the ideology which underpinned the emergence of the Third Republic in the eyes of this historical orthodoxy. Despite their interest, I will argue that these explanations oversimplify. Rationalism and especially positivism operated alongside and through other doctrines, which on some issues offered more cogent and influential solutions to the intellectual and practical problems faced by republicans. Furthermore, the centralist ideology of Jacobinism was challenged, subverted, and eventually creatively redefined by republican conceptions of the good life which stressed the significance of territorial politics and local forms of civic engagement. More broadly it will become apparent that despite the presence of powerful elements of cohesion the republican doctrine which underpinned the Third Republic was riven with tensions and contradictions; and that even though republican intellectuals often spoke positively about the 'bourgeoisie' the promotion of its particularistic interests was by no means their political priority. Our overall approach will seek to move away from the notion that ideology merely served an instrumental function in the political objectives of French republicans.

New Thinking About Nineteenth-Century France

This book draws much sustenance from recent scholarship, especially from political and intellectual historians as well as from political scientists, all of whose findings have steadily eroded many of the central tenets of orthodox interpretations of the intellectual origins of the Third Republic. Despite its variegated methodology and aims, this body of scholarship represents a powerful challenge to the narrow and somewhat complacent accounts which have long dominated the field.

To begin with, republican ideological transformation took place within a much broader chronological framework than the 1870s.[9] As the classic works of Iouda Tchernoff and Georges Weill have shown, the generation of republicans who assumed power in the 1870s and 1880s were politically and intellectually socialized in the three decades preceding the Franco-Prussian war.[10] Grudglingly recognized by French historians for its economic dynamism and its robust roots in the peasantry, the Second Empire era (1852–70) is now increasingly acknowledged for its contribution to the transformation of French politics, notably through its cultivation of mass voting.[11] New research

[9] A point made by René Rémond recently: 'we must indeed place this decade [the 1870s] in a wider historical perspective, that of the 1850s and 1860s', in *La France des années 1870: naissance de la IIIe République*. Actes du Colloque de la Fondation Singer-Polignac, 27 April 2000 (Paris, 2000), 9.

[10] Tchernoff, Iouda, *Le parti républicain au coup d'état et sous le Second Empire* (Paris: Pedone, 1906); Weill, Georges, *Histoire du parti républicain en France de 1814 à 1870* (Paris: Alcan, 1900).

[11] Furet, *La Révolution*; Huard, Raymond, *La naissance du parti politique en France* (Paris: Presses de la Fondation Nationale des Sciences Politiques, 1996).

is beginning to restore the two decades of the Second Empire for what they were: a period of institutional experimentation and political development, marked by significant advances in a range of intellectual and economic fields.[12] Louis Napoleon effectively developed modern forms of ritual and political festivity to buttress his power, thus helping to found 'the new politics of a democratic age'.[13] For republican political culture, too, this was a remarkably creative period.[14]

Interestingly, the connection between these Napoleonic forms of political ritual and the republican festive tradition, which begins in earnest in the early 1880s, has yet to be made—evidence of a continuing reluctance among the French historical confraternity to regard the Second Empire as a legitimate object of study.[15] But there is no doubt that a great deal of the political thinking which went into the transformation of republicanism occurred in the 1850s and 1860s—and even earlier. This will become apparent in the output of our five thinkers, who were politically and intellectually active during this period at both the national and the local levels.

Also essential to our account are the currents and subcultures which operated alongside and below republicanism. It has always been regarded as axiomatic that the republicans were intellectually divided before the establishment of the Third Republic, and these internal ideological and generational lines of demarcation have been perceptively drawn. Yet republican thinkers did not live in a cocoon. As individuals they often frequented and enjoyed good relations with intellectuals of different ideological persuasions from their own; the salon of Daniel Stern, for example, included republicans but also socialists as well as liberal and conservative monarchists. In any event the republicans were surrounded at all times by parallel and rival systems of thought with which they needed to engage and through which they often defined and modulated their own political positions: legitimism, Bonapartism, Orleanism, pacifism, and anti-militarism. Republicanism lived in a dialectical relationship with these systems of thought and subcultures; in the case of freethinking, we shall appreciate how this approach helped republican intellectuals develop their own ideological positions, especially on such issues as secularism and education.[16]

Equally central to our concerns is the relationship between liberalism and republicanism. The intellectual history of nineteenth century republicanism, especially between the 1830s and the 1880s, needs to engage more directly

---

[12] For a study of the regime's innovations in the field of communal property and environmental conservation, see Vivier, Nadine, *Propriété collective et identité communale: les biens communaux en France 1750–1914* (Paris: Publications de la Sorbonne, 1998), esp. 253–82.

[13] Truesdell, Matthew, *Spectacular Politics: Louis-Napoleon Bonaparte and the Fête Impériale, 1849–1870* (New York: Oxford University Press, 1997), 191.

[14] Nord, Philip, *The Republican Moment: Struggles for Democracy in Nineteenth-Century France* (Cambridge, MA: Harvard University Press, 1995).

[15] A point underlined by Alain Corbin; see his chapter 'La Fête de souveraineté', in Corbin, Alain, Gérome, Noelle, and Tartakowski, Danielle (eds), *Les usages politiques des Fêtes aux XIXe–XXe siècles* (Paris: Publications de la Sorbonne, 1994), 37.

[16] See Lalouette, Jacqueline, *La libre pensée en France 1848–1940* (Paris: Albin Michel, 1997).

with the liberal problematic, particularly in light of recent scholarship which has underlined the richness and ideological sophistication of nineteenth-century liberal ideology.[17] The Third Republic, as we have always known, was the product of an ideological synthesis between liberalism and republicanism. The political thinking of our five intellectuals will, in varying degrees, reflect this external influence. But in overall terms the precise impact of liberal ideas and norms on republican ideology and practice remains largely uncharted.[18] We have many parallel accounts of republicanism and liberalism, but very few works which have attempted explicitly to identify the connections between the two structures of thought. This book will initiate this enterprise by examining the republican narrative not only from the inside outwards, as has been conventionally done, but also from the outside in. In their different ways the figures of Dupont-White and Vacherot will underline the critical importance of considering this process of liberal ideological 'grafting' on the republican system of thought.

Our study will also take considerable account of the vertical relationship among different levels of republican—and state—organizations in the nineteenth century. One piece of conventional wisdom about modern France is that it remained a 'Jacobin' state, committed to the principles of unity and indivisibility and allowing, despite the decentralization of the 1980s and 1990s, relatively little substantive autonomy to territorial localities. In nineteenth-century France, however, this state of affairs was not taken for granted. Local politics—especially the territorial conditions of political citizenship—were at the heart of public debate, and it is difficult to see how it could fail to be so given the relatively small number of large cities and the overwhelming concentration of the majority rural population in small and medium-sized communes.[19] And despite Eugen Weber's celebrated affirmations to the contrary, the works of Maurice Agulhon and others have shown that well before the end of the nineteenth century this local sphere was the theatre of substantive civic endeavour, evidence of a growing forms of political socialization 'from below'.[20]

---

[17] Jaume, Lucien, *L'individu éffacé ou le paradoxe du libéralisme français* (Paris: Fayard, 1997).

[18] A recent exception is Jean Garrigues' study of the penetration of republican elites by business groups and interests in the early decades of the Third Republic: *La République des hommes d'affaires (1870–1900)* (Paris: Aubier, 1997).

[19] See Gerson, Stéphane, 'Town, Nation, or Humanity? Festive Delineations of Place and Past in Northern France, ca 1825–1865', *Journal of Modern History*, 72 (2000), 628–82.

[20] Agulhon, Maurice, *La République au village* (Paris: Plon, 1970); *1848 et l'apprentissage de la République* (Paris: Seuil, 1973). On the late eighteenth and early to mid-nineteenth century see Dupuy, Roger (ed.), *Pouvoir local et Révolution* (Rennes: Presses Universitaires de Rennes, 1995). On the July Monarchy see Guionnet, Christiane, *L'apprentissage de la politique moderne: les élections municipales sous la monarchie de Juillet* (Paris: l'Harmattan, 1997). For a regional case study highlighting the importance of the 1860s, see George, Jocelyne, 'Mémoire révolutionnaire et tradition municipale républicaine. Le cas du Var au XIXème siècle', in Michel Vovelle (ed.), *Révolution et République: l'exception française* (Paris: Kimé, 1994), 534–45; and for a comparative study of Bordeaux, Lyon, Marseille, Saint-Étienne, and Toulouse, see Cohen, William B., *Urban Government and the Rise of the French City; Five Municipalities in the Nineteenth Century* (London: Macmillan, 1998).

Our account of the origins of the ideological transformation of republicanism in the 1870s therefore has to be fully sensitive to the evolution of these republican territorial doctrines and practices. In this context my own study of French territorial philosophies under the Second Empire suggests that, after a long and often arduous debate, republicans came to a broad agreement over a 'municipalist' conception of citizenship. Municipalism represented an ideological compromise between the classical centralizing doctrine of Jacobinism and what was generally perceived as the excessive devolution of power advocated by republican federalists.[21] The involvement of several of our thinkers in political activity at the communal level in the 1840s, 1860s, and 1870s will highlight the essential importance of these local political networks for the political and ideological transformation of the republican party.[22]

Another fruitful way of thinking about intellectual and cultural activities in the local sphere is through the concept of 'sociability', which has been creatively applied in recent times to a variety of nineteenth-century French contexts—most notably in bourgeois and urban,[23] peasant and rural,[24] and sacred and religious settings.[25] Furthermore, the study of commemorations and festivities has done much to draw attention to the complex forms of politicization which occurred at the local level in France after 1848. By the late nineteenth century the organization of local ceremonials had underscored the creation and consolidation of a new republican intimacy centred around communal institutions, a key moment when the parish finally gave way to the secular collectivity as the organizing framework for collective civic existence in France.[26] A similar set of conclusions about the critical importance of the local sphere emerge from our study, with the late Vincent Wright, of the provincial Freemasonry. Until the advent of the Third Republic the Grand Orient de France remained a pluralistic organization both politically and ideology, and arguably the most important factor in determining the ideological composition of a lodge was the local political and institutional environment in which it operated.[27] Through the practical involvement of our five intellectuals in a variety of professional and associational endeavours—editorship of journals and newspapers and membership of the Freemasonry and of educational and anti-militarist leagues—we shall draw out the dynamism of this local sphere

---

[21] On this theme see chapter 4 in Hazareesingh, Sudhir, *From Subject to Citizen: The Second Empire and the Emergence of Modern French Democracy* (Princeton: Princeton University Press, 1998).

[22] For a recent local study of republicanism see Ardaillou, Pierre, *Les républicains du Havre au XIXe siècle (1815–1889)* (Rouen: Publications de l'Université de Rouen, 1999).

[23] See Harrison, Carol, *The Bourgeois Citizen in Nineteenth-Century France: Gender, Sociability and the Use of Emulation* (New York: Oxford University Press, 1999).

[24] Baker, Alan R. H., *Fraternity among the French Peasantry: Sociability and Voluntary Associations in the Loire Valley, 1815–1914* (Cambridge: Cambridge University Press 1999).

[25] On this theme see Harris, Ruth, *Lourdes: Body and Spirit in the Secular Age* (London: Penguin, 1999).

[26] Ihl, Olivier, *La fête républicaine* (Paris: Gallimard, 1996).

[27] Hazareesingh, Sudhir and Wright, Vincent, *Francs-Maçons sous le Second Empire. Les loges provinciales du Grand-Orient à la veille de la Troisième République* (Rennes: Presses Universitaires de Rennes, 2001).

in the nineteenth century and highlight its essential contributions to the reshaping of republican ideology.

Finally—and in a sense most importantly of all—there lies the essential questions of state formation and patriotism in the transformation of nineteenth-century French republican ideology. These issues, which also raise the all-important question of the justification of political violence, have been illuminated by Karma Nabulsi's *Traditions of War*. In this defining work we witness the emergence of a republican tradition of war in eighteenth and nineteenth-century Europe, drawing from the writings of Rousseau and Kosciuszko and centring around the practices of collective civic resistance to military invasion and occupation.[28] The nineteenth century European states system was a Hobbesian arena in which force was the supreme currency and inter-state violence the norm. But states which invaded and occupied their neighbours often encountered spirited resistance from the local citizenry—a resistance cloaked in a variety of political and ideological garbs but whose essential character was republican. Russians, Germans, and Spaniards resisting the occupation of French troops, Poles challenging their domination by Russians, and Italians striving for national liberation from the Austrian Empire: all were expressing the common—republican—precept that when state institutions collapsed in times of war and occupation it was legitimate for the armed citizenry to become the bearers of the nation's political sovereignty. War, in short, was not an interruption of the republican political process but a resolute affirmation of it—indeed it often proved a central instrument in the construction of nineteenth-century European republics.[29]

The history of republican thought between the 1830s and the 1880s has largely ignored this fundamental international context, with its burning issues of nationalism, patriotism, peace, war, and the justification of force. European conflicts in the 1850s and 1860s and the Franco-Prussian war of 1870–1 had a dramatic impact on our five thinkers, and played a critical role in shaping their republican thinking, in ways which even went against the grain of orthodoxy. For example, French republican antimilitarism before 1870 was entirely consistent with a strong support for the use of force against unjust and despotic rule, both in France and in the rest of Europe. And in this sense, although it drew on the political mythology of 1792, Gambetta's rhetoric and policy of war to the death (*guerre à outrance*) in 1870–1 was an expression of mainstream republican thinking about war, not a sudden about-turn dictated by the calamitous course of the war. Republican patriotism, finally, was not incompatible with the principles of fraternity and cosmopolitanism—again a useful corrective to the common view that French republicanism took an unrelenting 'nationalist' turn after 1871. All of this will also indirectly serve to underscore the conclusions of recent scholarship on the Franco-Prussian war, which sees the conflict as one of the defining

---

[28] Nabulsi, Karma, *Traditions of War* (Oxford: Oxford University Press, 1999).   [29] Ibid.

moments in the making of modern French conceptions of collective identity and citizenship.[30]

Some Remarks about Method: Intellectual History and Political Theory

Republican ideology will be treated in this book as it was understood by its intellectual bearers and agents in nineteenth century France: as a broad and open system of thought and values, whose precepts constantly invited question and challenge—in all these senses the very opposite of a fixed system of thought.

In order to capture the full flavour of this comprehensive ideology, we shall draw upon a range of disciplines and approaches. The first point we wish to stress here is the broadness of our definition of the internal components of republican thought. Like most modern political ideologies, republicanism was constituted by a wide range of concepts. Specifying their meanings and range as well as their internal relationships to each other will enable us to highlight the sophistication and sheer inventiveness of nineteenth-century French republican thinking. Our conceptual analysis will also serve an important comparative purpose. Through the precise identification of the internal components of their republican ideology, and mapping out the interrelationships among them, we shall uncover the similarities but also the significant differences in the republican thinking of our five intellectuals. Particularly important here will be the presence of central or 'core' components in their political thought, serving as firm anchors for their moral and political values.[31]

An equally essential inspiration to our approach has been the 'contextual' emphasis through which Quentin Skinner and the 'new historians' of the Cambridge school have successfully redefined the field of the history of political thought. Rather than looking at 'seminal' texts and seeking to frame our understanding of them in terms of contemporary philosophical and political problematics, Skinner invites us instead to search for ideological meaning in the immediate discursive environment in which such texts are produced. In his words:

Intellectual historians will do well to focus not merely or even mainly on a canon of so-called classic texts, but rather on the place occupied by such texts in broader traditions and frameworks of thought.[32]

---

[30] See Audoin-Rouzeau, Stéphane, *1870: la France dans la guerre* (Paris: Armand Colin, 1989); Roth, François *La guerre de 1870* (Paris: Fayard, 1990); and Taithe, Bertrand, *Defeated Flesh: Welfare, Warfare and the Making of Modern France* (Manchester: Manchester University Press, 1999).

[31] For further discussion of this framework see Michael Freeden, *Ideologies and Political Theory* (Oxford: Oxford University Press, 1996).

[32] Skinner, Quentin, *Liberty before Liberalism* (Cambridge: Cambridge University Press, 1998), 101.

Our selection of this book's five thinkers was largely inspired by this injunction. There is a canon of nineteenth-century French republican thought, which typically includes 'liberal' figures such as Jules Michelet, Edgar Quinet, Alphonse de Lamartine, Léon Gambetta, and Jules Ferry; 'socialist' republicans such as Alexandre Ledru-Rollin, Louis Blanc, and Pierre Joseph Proudhon; and utopians and revolutionaries such as the Saint-Simonians, Charles Fourier, Étienne Cabet, and Auguste Blanqui.[33] Many of these figures have been the object of considerable scholarly attention.[34] The purpose of writing this book was to go beyond these archetypal figures and the undercurrents they are traditionally associated with so as to draw a more complex picture of the republican intellectual community in the decades preceding the advent of the Third Republic. Many important figures here remain to be rediscovered by modern scholarship, most notably Lamennais and Pierre Leroux, described by George Sand as 'two of the greatest intellects of our century'.[35]

The value of drawing this wider picture can be appreciated with reference to two pieces of writing from the 1860s and early 1870s, both of which are conventionally cited as exemplifying intellectual attitudes of the time. The first is Edgar Quinet's La Révolution, first published in 1865.[36] With its forthright denunciation of Jacobin terrorism and criticism of the religious failure of the Revolutionary project, this controversial re-assessment of the 1790s created a stir among the republican community in the late years of the Second Empire. The debate it triggered is generally seen as an important landmark in the ideological transformation of republicanism, enabling the emergence of more moderate and democratic voices which eschewed violence as a means of effecting institutional change.[37] The other canonical work is Renan's La réforme intellectuelle et morale, published in 1871 immediately after the Franco-Prussian war.[38] Following Tocqueville and Prévost-Paradol, Renan expressed his concern about the atomizing consequences of mass democracy for individuals, and warned against the continuing crushing of provincial political and intellectual life by Paris.

Undoubtedly both of these works were hugely influential at the time, and their essentially pessimistic conclusions about the Revolution, the excesses of administrative centralization, and the illiberal elements in republican political culture gained wide approval. But an examination of the writings of our five intellectuals will shed a very different light on works such as these. We will see that Quinet and Renan drew heavily from the works of their contemporaries; more importantly, it will also emerge that their pessimism was

[33] See Pilbeam, Pamela, Republicanism in Nineteenth-Century France 1814–1871 (London: Macmillan, 1995).

[34] See for example Crossley, Ceri, French Historians and Romanticism. Thierry, Guizot, the Saint-Simonists, Quinet, Michelet (London: Routledge, 1993); on Michelet specifically see Viallaneix, Paul, Michelet, les travaux et les jours (Paris: Gallimard, 1998).

[35] Sand, George, Histoire de ma vie (Paris: Stock, 1993), 316.

[36] Quinet, Edgar, La Révolution, 2 Vols (Paris: Lacroix, 1865).

[37] See Furet, François, La gauche et la révolution au milieu du XIXe siècle. Edgar Quinet et la question du Jacobinisme 1865–1870 (Paris: Hachette, 1986).

[38] Renan, Ernest, La réforme intellectuelle et morale (Brussels: Editions Complexe, 1990).

not necessarily shared across even the liberal republican intellectual spectrum in the 1860s and 1870s. If we take the two major issues of the Revolution and the excesses of centralization, we will see that liberal republican intellectuals were much more optimistic about the first, and creative about the second, than either Quinet or Renan. This is not to say that there is nothing of value in the writings of these two intellectuals; on the contrary. But a close examination of the literary and intellectual contexts in which they evolved suggests we should think more carefully about the status we typically accord to their works.

We can generalize from these two examples. In the course of our intellectual excavations we shall observe the significant rewards to be reaped from 'contextual' intellectual history. It will emerge, for example, that some of the views credited to a particular individual or intellectual undercurrent were in fact more widely shared, sometimes across the republican ideological spectrum. This will become evident when the positivist republicanism of Littré is compared with the neo-Kantian republicanism of Barni. It will also become clear that in many respects the greater intellectual originality and creativity was to be found outside the 'canonical' figures rather than among them. Finally our study will show that the conventional lines of demarcation among different republican undercurrents—utopians and realists, liberals and socialists, *quarante-huitards* and opportunists—were often much more blurred than previously thought.

Our approach here will also prove fruitful for the analysis of the complex ideological output of our five intellectuals. Several aspects of their writings highlight the importance of taking 'context'—broadly defined—seriously. First, a common stylistic device in nineteenth century French political thought, and not just among republicans, was the absence of citations and general acknowledgement of sources. Absence of evidence is not evidence of absence, however: by identifying key conceptual overlaps and substantive patterns of repetition we shall uncover effective traces of historical and contemporary texts in the writings of these five thinkers, manifestations of abiding ideological influences which were not explicitly acknowledged.

Furthermore, during certain periods—most notably the early 1840s, the 1850s and 1860s, and the early parts of the 1870s—these republican writers had to express themselves cautiously in order to avert legal and administrative persecution; as we shall see, several of them failed to avoid it. These subterranean characteristics of their discourse require that we pay special attention to 'hidden' layers of meaning inserted in their texts by way of analogies, historical allusions, and Aesopian references. We shall also repeatedly encounter strong connections between biographical events and textual output, most emphatically in the moral philosophy of these republicans, which was almost invariably grounded in personal experiences in both the public and the private domains. Context, in these senses, will not only at times help to elicit textual significance; we shall see that on many occasions it will fully constitute meaning.

Context, however, should not be given an unduly narrow interpretation, whether in space or in time. To be a republican intellectual in France between 1830 and 1880 was an act of allegiance to a community with a strong sense of identity and collective purpose, and a well-defined set of core values and rituals. Through the concept of 'political tradition'[39] we shall thus attempt to make sense of our thinkers' ideological output in these broader social and cultural contexts. Tradition was in this sense both a constraint and an opportunity. In its affective dimension it was a largely passive phenomenon, associated with sentimental attachments—notably to such republican symbols as the *Marseillaise* and the tricolour flag—symbolic practices—attendance of meetings and commemorative events[40]—and the political mythology of the great Revolution of 1789.

But 'tradition' was also an enabling instrument. As the key bearers of their political tradition, our republican intellectuals not only re-enacted and transmitted the political heritage of earlier generations to their own contemporaries but also creatively reinvented it. By occupying central positions in the republican community, our five intellectuals were able to exercise a supreme form of discursive power: that of providing their fellow-republicans with the concepts, references, and symbols which defined their collective identity as a group. Although Littré was the only one of the five who compiled a dictionary, there was a sense in which all of our intellectuals can be seen as the grammarians of modern French republican thought.

In broader terms, finally, looking at the specific intellectual and cultural terrain on which nineteenth century republican intellectuals evolved will enable us to resist teleological interpretations of the republican epic which have become especially fashionable in French liberal circles, most notably in the writings of Furet and his disciples. With the intellectual decline of Marxism, the collapse of communism in the Soviet Union, and the conversion of the French Left to capitalism with a human face, there is now a tendency in France among the liberal intelligentsia to look askance at the Revolutionary heritage and its 'Rousseauist' progenitors, and to restrict their achievements to the few years of constitutional monarchy which followed 1789. The democratic and egalitarian dimensions of Jacobinism have especially come under sustained attack, partly for their allegedly nefarious consequences in France in the late eighteenth and nineteenth centuries—most notably through the Terror and the Paris Commune—and partly for their alleged intellectual contributions to the Bolshevik nightmare which descended upon the international system after 1917.[41]

[39] On this theme see Hazareesingh, Sudhir, *Political Traditions in Modern France* (Oxford: Oxford University Press, 1994).

[40] On the importance of funerals during this period see Ben-Amos, Avner, *Funerals, Politics, and Memory in Modern France 1789–1996* (Oxford: Oxford University Press, 2000).

[41] This thesis was most trenchantly developed in Furet's *Le passé d'une illusion. Essai sur l'idée communiste au XXe siècle* (Paris: Robert Laffont, 1995).

Whether there is a straight line running from Rousseau to Pol Pot is an extremely broad question which cannot be pursued further here; indeed, it is doubtful whether such a question even makes sense. But a contextual reading of the utterances of nineteenth-century republican intellectuals shows that the relationship between the Revolution, democracy, and the justification of political violence was much more complex than linear French liberal accounts appear to suggest. It is a historical fact— which Furet's historical work itself has splendidly drawn out—that the founding elites of the Third Republic worshipped the Revolution and drew inspiration from its narratives to construct their own project for social emancipation. At the same time, however, nineteenth-century republicans were capable of recognizing that the circumstances of the 1860s and 1870s required different solutions to the ones imagined by their forefathers. There was thus no sterile fetishism of the Revolution, but instead a creative adaptation and harnessing of its liberating impulses. In this sense tradition and conceptual innovation were not antithetical but complementary activities.

Political and Social History

Alongside their political thought, our aim is to provide an account of the personal characteristics and narratives of these thinkers in order to bring back to life five eminent figures who have been buried by the passage of time.

Our *démarche* in this biographical endeavour is, thankfully, by no means isolated. The emphasis on the restitution of these complex lives will complement the patient work carried out in recent decades by historians of nineteenth-century France. Its scholarly endeavours have yielded a collective study of many of the key figures of the opportunist republic in the 1870s and 1880s,[42] portraits of such individual republican and liberal luminaries as Jules Simon,[43] Charles de Rémusat,[44] Albert de Broglie,[45] and Sadi Carnot,[46] and valuable analyses of a range of important figures in the intellectual and philosophical worlds.[47] Our contribution here will add to the emerging portraits of the remarkable individualities who shaped the political and intellectual life of the Second Empire and the early Third Republic: an area in which there is still much work to be carried out.

[42] Grévy, Jerôme, *La République des opportunistes 1870–1885* (Paris; Perrin, 1998).

[43] Bertocci, Philip, *Jules Simon: Republican Anticlericalism and Cultural Politics in France 1848–1886* (Columbia: University of Missouri Press, 1978).

[44] Roldan, Dario, *Charles de Rémusat: certitudes et impasses du libéralisme doctrinaire* (Paris: l'Harmattan, 1999).

[45] Grubb, Alan, *The Politics of Pessimism: Albert de Broglie and Conservative Politics in the Early Third Republic* (Newark: University of Delaware Press, 1996).

[46] Harismendy, Patrick, *Sadi Carnot, l'ingénieur de la République* (Paris: Perrin, 1995).

[47] See Logue, William, *Charles Renouvier, Philosopher of Liberty* (Baton Rouge: Louisiana State University Press, 1993); Brooks, John III, *The Eclectic Legacy: Academic Philosophy and the Human Sciences in Nineteenth-Century France* (Newark: University of Delaware Press, 1998); Whatmore, Richard, *Republicanism and the French Revolution: An Intellectual History of Jean-Baptiste Say's Political Economy* (Oxford: Oxford University Press, 2000).

Five Intellectual Founders: Biographical Presentation and Key Themes

Jules Barni, Charles Dupont-White, Émile Littré, Eugène Pelletan, and Étienne Vacherot: why choose these particular intellectuals to guide us through our study of the ideological transformation of nineteenth-century republicanism? Their most important common characteristic, as we noted from the outset, was that all five were central actors in the political and intellectual process which led to the establishment of the Third Republic. Indeed they literally founded the new regime, in that as members of the National Assembly in 1875 Barni, Littré, Pelletan, and Vacherot endorsed the constitutional laws which established the Republic, while from outside parliament Dupont-White's political writings also lent the new order his unstinting support. As lawgivers and public activists they all contributed directly to the institution of the republican regime in the crucial years between the early and the late 1870s.

This contribution was the culmination of decades of political endeavour on their part, on both the theoretical and the practical fronts. Their relative obscurity at the time of the meetings in Daniel Stern's house in the 1850s did not last long. By the time of the Third Republic our thinkers were among the best-known intellectuals of their time. Of the five, Littré was undeniably the greatest celebrity. His *Dictionaire de la langue française* had already become one of the cultural monuments of nineteenth century France; in the late Second Empire he also founded the review *La Philosophie Positive*, a highly influential publication which sought to forge a decisive synthesis between republicanism and positivism.[54]

Next in rank in terms of intellectual visibility was Étienne Vacherot, a highly respected republican philosopher during the 1860s and 1870s, whose work *La Démocratie* was probably the most widely read republican dissertation on political philosophy under the Second Empire and early Third Republic.[55] Dupont-White was a highly prolific neo-Jacobin pamphleteer whose fame also spread well beyond republican circles under the Second Empire. By the late 1860s his two main books *L'Individu et l'État* and *La Centralisation* had established his reputation as an eclectic and powerful thinker, whose ardent defence of the state reflected the continuing vibrancy of centralist Jacobinism within the liberal and republican traditions.[56]

---

[54] The standard biographies of Littré are by Aquarone, Stanislas, *The Life and Works of Émile Littré 1801–1881* (Leyden: Sythoff, 1958); and Rey, Alain, *Littré l'humaniste et les mots* (Paris: Gallimard, 1970).

[55] There is no full-scale biography of Vacherot. Useful information about his life may be found in Robert, Adolphe, Bourloton, Edgar, and Cougny, Gaston (eds), *Dictionnaire des parlementaires français* (Paris: Bourloton, 1891).

[56] The only available biography (incomplete) is by Villey, Daniel, *Charles Dupont-White, sa vie, son oeuvre, sa doctrine* (Paris: Alcan, 1936).

Eugène Pelletan established his republican credentials with his *Profession de foi du XIXe siècle*, a vigorous defence of the principle of progress; in the 1850s and 1860s he was also a productive republican journalist and pamphleteer.[57] Last, but by no means least, Jules Barni's treatises *La Morale dans la Démocratie* and the *Manuel Républicain* were celebrated in republican and liberal circles in the 1860s and 1870s, and in many senses provided the defining theoretical framework for the emerging republican regime.[58] These thinkers were thus known during their lives as creators of republican ideas, defining the principles of the good life and ensuring their dissemination through newspapers, journals, pamphlets, and public speeches. Another shared trait among them was a distinguished republican pedigree, often accompanied by strong and varied manifestations of political activism. Littré's and Pelletan's conversions dated to the early days of the July Monarchy, with the other three intellectuals embracing the republican faith around the time of the 1848 Revolution. All five men were politically active during the Second Republic: Littré and Dupont-White held public office—in the case of the latter, for the only time in his life—while Pelletan, Vacherot, and Barni attempted, without success, to get themselves elected to the National Assembly. They all subsequently shared the bitter disappointment of the Second Republic's failure, which was for them, as for all their fellow-republicans, a turning-point in their political lives.

After the advent of the Second Empire in 1852 their political views hardened, but this crystallization was expressed in a variety of forms of political engagement. Littré and Dupont-White generally avoided public political action and made their principal contributions through intellectual and discursive means. Dupont-White was thus a regular presence in the various republican salons of the Second Empire, an important, and still understudied, focus of republican political and intellectual life during these years.[59] Littré appears in the public life of the late Second Empire, for example in 1869 as a member of the electoral committee for Jules Ferry's candidature in the Seine.[60] The most active public militants were Vacherot, Barni, and Pelletan, who collaborated in the short-lived republican newspaper *L'Avenir* in 1855. Rising to public prominence as a protégé of George Sand and Lamartine in the 1830s and 1840s, Eugène Pelletan became one of the most popular republican national leaders during the Second Empire, where he championed the republican cause in the imperial Legislative Corps. At the

---

[57] His life is portrayed in Judith Stone's rich comparative biography of Eugène and Camille Pelletan, *Sons of the Revolution* (Baton Rouge: Louisiana State University Press, 1996). See also Baquiast, Paul, *Une dynastie de la bourgeoisie républicaine: les Pelletan* (Paris: l'Harmattan, 1996).

[58] Dide, Auguste, *Jules Barni, sa vie et ses oeuvres* (Paris: Alcan, 1892).

[59] On the nineteenth-century republican salons see Aprile, Sylvie, 'La République au salon: vie et mort d'une forme de sociabilité politique (1865–1885)', *Revue d'Histoire Moderne et Contemporaine*, 38 (1991), 473–87; and Joana, Jean, *Pratiques politiques des députés français au XIXe siècle: du dilettante au spécialiste* (Paris: L'Harmattan, 1999).

[60] Nicolet, Claude, 'Jules Ferry et la tradition positiviste', in François Furet (ed.), *Jules Ferry fondateur de la République* (Paris: EHESS, 1985), 27.

fall of the Bonapartist regime he became a member of the republican Government of National Defence, and ended his career as vice-president of the republican Senate.

These intellectuals, accordingly, were not merely thinkers in the narrow sense but militants who throughout their lives risked their freedom, and on occasion their very lives, for the republican cause. In July 1830 Littré enthusiastically participated in the Parisian insurrection which overthrew the Bourbon monarchy; Vacherot took up arms to defend the Second Republic against the working-class revolt of June 1848; and Pelletan took an active part in the 'popular' invasion of the Legislative Corps which ended the Second Empire in September 1870. Perhaps most remarkable of all was the activism of Jules Barni, who rose though the ranks of Kantian philosophy in the 1840s to become an exemplary republican intellectual. Barni was a victim of Bonapartist repression in 1851, an eminent republican exile in Geneva in the 1860s, where he directed the republican anti-militarist organization the Ligue de la Paix et de la Liberté. He also worked closely with Gambetta during the Franco-Prussian war and became a member of the Gambettist circles in the early 1870s. In the 1870s he was a member of local republican associations in his home town of Amiens, and he also became the leader of the influential republican propaganda organization the Société d'Instruction Républicaine.

These five thinkers shared a comprehensive conception of republicanism, constantly combining their abstract theorizing with an assortment of public interventions in politics. They all conceived of republican ideology as an overarching public philosophy which offered wide-ranging formulations about life in the *polis*: general questions such as the justification of public authority, the relationship between state and society, the principles of good citizenship, and republican patriotism; broad issues such as property, decentralization, religion, education, the place of women in society, and the principles of public and private morality; and individual concepts such as liberty, equality, fraternity, and popular sovereignty, as well, of course, as the inescapable issue of the interpretation of the 1789 Revolution.

At the same time, this comprehensive system of thought and values was not intended for external consumption alone. In their different ways, and in keeping with their varying views on some of these moral issues, these five thinkers sought to lead their own lives according to the public and private principles they professed. This aspiration to achieve a complete congruence between principles and personal life was a characteristic trait among nineteenth-century French republicans well before the advent of the Third Republic.[61] Our five thinkers sought to practice the republican virtues in public and in private through simple attitudes and gestures, such as Barni's humility and consistent avoidance of the limelight; Dupont-White's decision to offer shelter to

---

[61] On this theme see Nabulsi, *Traditions of War, passim.*

republican activists who were being pursued by Louis Napoleon's police in December 1851—an expression of the key principle of solidarity; or Littré's generous dispensing of free medical advice to poor peasants in his village of Ménil-le-Roi. At times, it was a matter of showing integrity by abiding by the consequences of one's actions, as when both Vacherot and Pelletan were goaled in the 1860s for political writings which were deemed seditious by the imperial courts of justice. In moments of crisis, this sense of republican virtue manifested itself in defiant public acts of opposition to established authority. Both Barni and Vacherot were dismissed from their academic posts after 1851 for refusing to swear the obligatory oath of allegiance to the new imperial regime, an oath which both men regarded as an unacceptable violation of their ethical principles. Republicanism, with these intellectuals, was not merely a system of thought or a collection of texts, but a scrupulously defined moral code.

French Republicanism in Historical and Comparative Contexts

This ethical aspect of their lives connects Barni, Dupont-White, Littré, Pelletan, and Vacherot to the wider republican epic which has been unfolding in Europe since before the Renaissance, and by the same token also draws their political thought and actions into our current moral and intellectual horizons.

The history of republican thought in Europe since the Renaissance has been admirably portrayed, most notably in the works of Pocock and Skinner;[62] and in contemporary political philosophy a 'republican' perspective is now vigorously being promoted by Philip Pettit in opposition and contradistinction to liberalism and communitarianism.[63] And yet the place of the theory and practice of modern French republicanism in both of these endeavours remains to be elaborated.[64] In the case of the broader conceptual history of republicanism, there is scope for a greater integration of post-eighteenth century French narratives into the English, continental European, and American experiences. This is not to deny the importance of the spirit of commerce and neo-Roman conceptions of liberty in these wider European republican traditions as they have come down to us since the early modern era.[65] At the same time, since at

---

[62] See most notably Pocock, J.G.A., *The Machiavellian Moment* (Princeton: Princeton University Press, 1975) and *Virtue, Commerce, and History* (Cambridge: Cambridge University Press, 1985); and Skinner, Quentin, *Liberty before Liberalism* (Cambridge: Cambridge University Press, 1998) and 'The Republican Ideal of Political Liberty', in Gisela Bock, Quentin Skinner, and Maurizio Viroli (eds), *Machiavelli and Republicanism* (Cambridge: Cambridge University Press, 1990).

[63] Pettit, Philip, *Republicanism: A Theory of Freedom and Government* (Oxford: Oxford University Press, 1997).

[64] For two recent attempts, see Kriegel, Blandine, *Philosophie de la République* (Paris: Plon, 1998) and Nicolet, Claude, *Histoire, Nation, République* (Paris: Odile Jacob, 2000).

[65] See in this respect Johnson Kent Wright's study, *A Classical Republican in Eighteenth-Century France: The Political Thought of Mably* (Stanford: Stanford University Press, 1997).

least the early nineteenth century modern republicanism has also been centrally concerned with such concepts as equality and fraternity, concepts which do not occupy a pivotal position in the 'classical' formulations of republicanism mentioned above. Such notions of equality and fraternity not only form an essential part of the French experience, as we shall see in this book, but also of continental European republicanism between the late eighteenth and early twentieth centuries.[66]

And there is more. The same two concepts are also integral to the communist experience in the twentieth century, and in this respect too there is an essential ideological filiation with republicanism which awaits further exploration. All of this makes the writings of our five intellectuals relevant not only to the French experience in the nineteenth century but also to a wider understanding of how a substantially different strand of republicanism from the Anglo-American came to emerge and exercise a powerful ideological appeal to the modern imagination. We only have to look at the history of the Latin American continent since the early nineteenth century to behold the extraordinary potency of French republican ideology and political mythology.

The same point, put differently, can be made with respect to contemporary analytical philosophical renderings of republicanism, whose premises are often anchored in an Anglo-American intellectual framework which does little justice to the ideological breadth and vigour of the republican tradition. Contemporary political philosophy, to put things bluntly, often presents republicanism as a close ideological relative to liberalism. It is arguable that the underlying purpose behind the elaboration of this 'republican' perspective is to offer a palatable alternative—or is it complement?—to the Rawlsian strand of political liberalism which has dominated Anglo-American political theory in recent times. But proceeding in this way runs the obvious risk of oversimplifying and distorting the conceptual relationship between republicanism and liberalism, and ignoring the range of wider influences which have historically shaped modern political doctrines.[67] This is where a detour into the French republican experience in the nineteenth century may prove enormously rewarding. Through the lives and political thought of Barni, Dupont-White, Littré, Pelletan, and Vacherot, we will encounter a much richer and complex formulation of republicanism, open to fruitful dialogue not only with liberalism but also with socialism, Saint-Simonism, and Bonapartism—and much else.

The lesson to be taken away here is a simple one. If nineteenth-century republicans did not feel condemned to frame their political thought in terms which responded exclusively to liberal preoccupations and anxieties, nor

---

[66] Nabulsi, *Traditions of War*.

[67] On this theme see the illuminating comments by Stears, Marc, 'Beyond the Logic of Liberalism', *Journal of Political Ideologies*, 6 (2001), 215–30.

should we. French republican ideology, in its richness and diversity as well as in its multiple contradictions, thus invites us to make Horace's injunction our own: *sapere aude*.

Émile Littré, by Pierre Petit
Bibliothèque Nationale, Paris

1

Between Positivism and Republicanism: Émile Littré and the Founding of the Third Republic

MAXIMILIEN-PAUL-ÉMILE Littré is in every respect the obvious choice for opening this study of nineteenth century republican political thought in the era of the founding of the Third Republic. Of the five intellectuals whose lives and political thought will be appraised in this book, Littré was in his time—and remains—by far the best known, both in elite circles and among the wider public. His intellectual stature as one of the *savants* of his age was established by his monumental *Dictionnaire de la Langue Française*, an epic enterprise which took 18 years to complete.[1] By the time the final volume appeared in November 1872, Littré's reputation as one of the eminent scientists of his age had already been confirmed by his election to the *Académie Française*. The Dictionary was seen by its contemporaries not merely as an extraordinary work of erudition but also as a cultural expression of the scientific capacities of the emerging order. In Philip Nord's felicitous words, it was one of the 'monuments of the republic':[2] not as a relic but as a living instrument for helping contemporaries to make sense of their world and understand their place within it. Littré was thus, in a literal sense, one of the intellectual founders of the new order.

As a member of the republican political elite after 1871, Littré was no less a prominent figure. He joined the National Assembly after February 1871 and participated directly in the process which led to the passage of the constitutional laws of the Third Republic in 1875. Later in that same year his colleagues elected him to serve as a life peer (*sénateur inamovible*) in the newly-established republican Senate, a position he occupied until his death in 1881. From these vantage points in the lower and upper legislatures of the early Third Republic Littré observed the unfolding republicanization of the political process, and took a direct part in all the epic battles between progressives and monarchists: the rise and fall of Adolphe Thiers, the struggle against the 'Moral Order' governments, the climactic elections of 1876 and 1877, and the defeat and resignation of President MacMahon. During these difficult

---

[1] The five volumes of the first edition were published by Hachette between 1863 and 1872.
[2] Nord, *The Republican Moment*, 191.

years Littré provided strong moral support to the republican political leadership, and was on excellent personal terms with Thiers, Gambetta, and Ferry. He was therefore not only a prominent intellectual but also one of those who helped to carry the new regime to its baptismal fonts.

At a personal level Littré's pre-eminence is also manifest in terms of age and political experience. He was born in Paris in February 1801, as Napoleon Bonaparte was scheming to convert the decaying republican Directorate into the First Empire. His childhood memories included an encounter with the Emperor in the Champ de Mars—a meeting which, however, did little to sway the virulent anti-Bonapartism of the young Émile, largely acquired from his Jacobin parents.[3] Littré's mother publicly opposed the Eighteenth Brumaire *coup d'état* of Bonaparte; and although he loyally served the imperial administration Littré's father remained a devout Jacobin throughout his life—it was his admiration for Robespierre which led him to give his young son the name Maximilien. Born of pure Revolutionary stock, Émile Littré bore witness to all the vicissitudes of the French political tradition in the nineteenth century. As a youth he saw his beloved country invaded and occupied at the end of the First Empire; he then actively witnessed the July Revolution of 1830; later welcomed the re-establishment of the Republic in 1848; lamented its demise in 1851 and the ensuing resurrection of the Bonapartist Empire; and finally watched with despair as France collapsed into the cruelties of war, invasion, and civil strife in 1870–1. Thus, the republican victory of the late 1870s was for him the climax of a long political pilgrimage through the century—a journey which profoundly marked him and decisively shaped his political thinking.

Littré was thus a remarkable figure as a scientific celebrity, as a law-maker, and as a witness of the political vicissitudes of his age. But perhaps his most distinctive claim to count among the founders of the Third Republic lay in his ideological contribution. Littré was the most eminent French disciple of Auguste Comte—despite his rupture with his philosophical master in 1851— and also a skilful popularizer of positivist doctrine. His *Auguste Comte et la philosophie positive* (1863) was hailed as one of the most accessible critical introductions to the new 'science'. And in his intellectual and journalistic writings Littré tirelessly celebrated the core virtues of the positivist faith: the values of order and scientific progress, the rejection of all forms of 'metaphysical' reasoning, and the forward march of humanity according to predetermined laws. His ambitious intellectual project was to effect a synthesis between these positivist principles and republican social and political thought, and in this manner to ground the emerging regime in an ideology which was all at once new, coherent, and pragmatic. This is where Littré's contribution has been hailed as decisive: both by his intellectual influence on leading republicans such as Gambetta and Ferry, and through his articulation of republican opportunism, the 'dominant ideology' of the 1870s and 1880s.

---

[3] Littré, Émile, *Conservation Révolution Positivisme*, 2nd edn (Paris: Bureaux de la Philosophie Positive, 1879), 317. All subsequent citations refer to this edition.

Littré has been presented by historians of republicanism such as Mona Ozouf and Claude Nicolet as one the 'founding fathers' of the Third Republic.[4] How far this accolade is merited will be one of the central underlying questions which this chapter will seek to answer.

In Littré's political thought and practice we shall thus encounter a number of critical conceptual and ideological sites for the exploration of nineteenth century republicanism. Through his eyes we shall see the difficult emergence of a moderate form of republicanism, struggling to define itself in opposition both to monarchist and religious authoritarianism on the one hand and to insurrectionary violence on the other. Littré also enables us to appreciate the centrality of the Revolution of 1789 in the political imagination of the nineteenth century. His own intellectual trajectory captures the momentous transition from the Revolutionary problematic of Jacobinism, which largely preoccupied republicans during the first half of the nineteenth century, to the concerns of a modern democratic and participatory polity, which became their central axis soon after 1848. Through him also we behold the dialectical relationship between extraneous systems of thought—in this case positivism—and the central tenets of mainstream republican doctrine. At an individual level, finally, Littré's political thought is illuminating for the tensions it constantly encounters and strives to overcome: between scholarly detachment and political commitment; between disciple and master; between cosmopolitanism and patriotism; between moral and religious belief and political affiliation; and between the orderly regularities of nineteenth-century 'science' and the untidy realities of practical politics.

Auguste Comte, the Infallible Master

At the relatively late age of 40, Littré converted to Comtian positivism.[5] Until that moment he had largely devoted his life to medical, historical, and philological studies, culminating in the publication of an edition of the works of Hippocrates. The Revolution of 1830 brought him into the republican camp, and under the July Monarchy Littré had also become a regular editor in the liberal republican newspaper, *Le National*, edited by Armand Carrel.[6]

Littré's encounter with Comte's *Cours de Philosophie Positive* radically and irreversibly transformed his intellectual and political life. By the mid-1830s Auguste Comte had established himself as one of the most celebrated disciples

---

[4] Ozouf, Mona, 'Entre l'esprit des lumières et la lettre positiviste: les républicains sous l'Empire', in François Furet and Mona Ozouf (eds), *Le siècle de l'avènement républicain* (Paris: Gallimard, 1993), 417. See also Nicolet, *L'idée républicaine en France*, esp.187–217.

[5] Comte's voluminous writings are matched by an equally massive critical literature. For a judicious sample of the first and overview of the second, see Jones, Stuart (ed.), *Comte. Early Political Writings* (Cambridge: Cambridge University Press, 1998). On Comte and the Comtian contributions to the emergence of sociology, see Lepenies, Wolf, *Between Literature And Science: The Rise of Sociology* (Cambridge: Cambridge University Press, 1988).

[6] Littré later produced an edition of Carrel's political writings: *Oeuvres politiques et littéraires d'Armand Carrel* (Paris: Chamerot, 1857).

ideational teleology, which defined progress as 'the tendency to make general ideas more and more prevalent'.[17] All societies were influenced by this trend towards greater progress. However, this historical movement did not manifest itself evenly, because not all societies were at the same phase in their development. These temporal distinctions between the different stages in the historical evolution of the human species were still spatially visible in the world of the mid-nineteenth century. On the basis of the positive theory of progress, Comte and Littré established a clear hierarchy of nations, led by Italy, Spain, Britain, France, and 'Germany', here taken to include the German States as well as Holland, Denmark, and Sweden. The second level consisted of the Slavic peoples, headed by the unfortunate but gallant Poles; the third comprised the 'moslem nations'; the polytheist nations of the Asian continent made up the fourth level; and resting on the bottom rung of the civilizational ladder were the 'fetichist' nations of Africa.[18]

Comte's system was teleological, but, he claimed, not determinist. Human agency was desirable—necessary even—to enable and facilitate the transformation of societies in a progressive direction. However, these transformations could not alter the fundamental laws of social development. Even with the best will in the world a fetichist community could not transform itself immediately into an advanced industrial society; and despite their best efforts 'retrograde' politicians could not push France back into the 'Catholico-feudal' era.[19] In sum, any attempt to swim against the tide of progress was counterproductive and ultimately futile: 'in our societies any attempt to resist or deflect the force which directs them is useless and even dangerous.'[20] The role for positivist politics and political activity was thus clearly marked out: theoretically, to identify the direction of historical change, and to specify the place of any particular society within this general trend; and practically, to assist the 'natural forces' which were working towards positive change.[21]

The issue of how, when, and under what circumstances such a change could come about was a central question—*the* central question—in Comte's philosophy of history, which Littré also dwelled upon considerably in his writings. Since 1789, it was obvious that France had constantly but fruitlessly been in search of political and social stability. Between the Revolution and the mid-nineteenth century French politics had oscillated between 'negative' phases of revolutionary upheaval and 'positive' phases marked by attempts to 'close' the era of destruction.[22] For both Comte and Littré the positive sciences had been one of the main instruments in the ideological breakdown of the old order, and the doctrine aspired to nothing less than to provide the intellectual structure around which the new one would finally crystallize.[23] In Littré's formulation: 'a transitional phase to pass through, a definitive state to attain, these

[17] Littré, *De la Philosophie Positive*, 51.
[18] Littré, 'République Occidentale', in *Application de la philosophie positive*, 113–15.
[19] Littré, 'Des bases scientifiques du nouvel ordre social', in *Application de la philosophie positive*, 17.
[20] Littré, *De la Philosophie Positive*, 53.   [21] Ibid., 54.
[22] Littré, 'Des progrès du socialisme', in *Conservation Révolution Positivisme*, 161.
[23] Littré, 'Des bases scientifiques du nouvel ordre social', in *Application de la philosophie positive*, 27.

are the two correlative notions which positive philosophy, *alone*, can bring to light.'[24] Why was positivism ideally suited to perform this pivotal role? For two interconnected reasons: it readily embraced 'positive' change and innovation, while at the same time providing the material stability for which the peoples of Europe had been longing. Only the positivist slogan of 'order and progress' could thus offer the solution to the revolutionary crisis which had destabilized Europe since the late eighteenth century: 'to ask that necessary changes be carried out without disorder, or that the conservation of order should not be subverted by the accomplishment of necessary changes, is, by two equivalent expressions, to pose the problem of politics in its totality.'[25]

It is against this intellectual backdrop that the positivists' enthusiastic response to the Revolution of 1848 has to be appreciated. As early as 1842 Comte had predicted the end of Orleanist rule in France, and Littré regarded the occurrence of this event as evidence of the prophetic qualities of his master, whom he congratulated for successfully identifying the 'anarchy' which underlay the apparent order of the July Monarchy.[26] Far from being the work of a small group of conspirators or of chance, however, the 1848 Revolution was the product of deeper movements in the social and intellectual fabric of Europe. Littré's evidence for this claim lay in the fact that the revolution did not manifest itself only in Paris: the earthquake of 1848 had been experienced in Berlin, Vienna, Milan, Venice, and Florence; the Pope had been chased out of Rome; and minor tremors had been felt even in Madrid and London.[27] This seemed to suggest that a powerful underlying force was at work here, a force which was destined to work itself out and could not be stopped by human intervention.[28] It was the sheer breadth and scale of this political movement across western Europe which undoubtedly helped to convince Comte that the moment of the great 'transition' had finally arrived, and that European societies, with France at the vanguard, were on the verge of moving into the 'positive' era of science and industry. The significance of this analysis, which Littré enthusiastically endorsed, for the political programme and ideological orientation of positivism cannot be overestimated. It coloured not only Comte's and Littré's overall appreciation of political events but also their strategic positioning in the complex politics of the Second Republic between 1848 and 1851.

This overall stance was summarized by Littré in four points. First, positivists condemned all the forces working against the process of change: this included not only the 'retrograde' political groups which were hostile to the Republic but also the 'stationary' movements which failed to recognize the momentous nature of the present situation.[29] Second, positivists rejected with equal vehemence the revolutionary groups' attempts, often through violence, to

[24] Littré, 'Antagonisme du pouvoir parlementaire et du pouvoir éxécutif', in *Conservation Révolution Positivisme*, 131; emphasis added.
[25] Littré, *De la Philosophie Positive*, 43–4.
[26] Littré, 'Prévisions', in *Application de la philosophie positive*, 2.
[27] Littré, 'L'événement de Février est-il fortuit?', in *Conservation Révolution Positivisme*, 111.
[28] Ibid., 113.   [29] Littré, 'Des bases scientifiques', 16–18.

across the continent, states had not resorted to force in their dealings with each other. This welcome absence of international conflict was, however, an essentially 'negative' peace, which could be damaged by political incompetence or the atavism of such semi-barbaric nations as Russia.[42] In order to actualize this potential for peace, therefore, specific political measures needed to be introduced, the most important of which was the reduction of the size of the army. 'Peace is secured', announced Littré grandly in an article published in October 1849: European governments were too busy with their domestic problems to consider declaring war against the French Republic.[43] But the emasculation of the army was not merely desirable due to the elimination of the external threat to France; it was also necessary from the point of view of the construction of the new positivist order. A smaller army would release manpower which could be deployed more productively in industry and agriculture.[44] The reduction of the military budget would also allow for a massive programme of public works, which would enable the building of roads and canals and the clearing of insalubrious areas.[45] This was the completion of a virtuous circle: the reduction of the army would strengthen the spirit of industry, which would in turn reinforce the movement towards peace.

An important political measure needed to promote pacific attitudes among French—and European—peoples was the elimination of all monuments celebrating past military triumphs. Littré and Comte were aware of the continuing popularity of the Napoleonic legend among the French masses, and for this reason the removal of such commemorative emblems as the Arc de Triomphe and the Colonne Vendôme was a matter of considerable urgency: 'We shall eliminate, in our midst, all signs of the victories of the Empire, and in other countries we shall eliminate all signs of the victories over the Empire, until at last a common banner will bring together under its fold the whole European family, without abolishing the national flags.'[46]

Humanity as the Emblem of Spiritual Reform

Comte and Littré constantly stressed that positivism was not merely a matter of effecting political change and social engineering 'from above' but of orchestrating a radical transformation in collective thought, attitudes, and values. This 'spiritual' renovation—the term appears frequently in Comte and Littré—was the prerequisite for the achievement of all the pan-European political transformations desired by the positivists.

What made possible—necessary even—the search for this new ethical foundation of society was the disintegration of the exclusive control once enjoyed by the Church over all matters spiritual. Since the collapse of the 'Catholico-feudal' regime of the Middle Ages, writers, philosophers, and scientists had

---

[42] Littré, 'Organisation Temporelle', 78.
[43] Littré, 'Mesures à prendre les plus prochaines', in *Application de la philosophie positive*, 144.
[44] Ibid., 146.   [45] Ibid., 147.   [46] Littré, 'République Occidentale', 124.

begun to make significant contributions to the elaboration of new forms of spirituality. The task of positivism was to accompany and help complete this revolution in human understanding by integrating all forms of knowledge, including moral knowledge, into one 'science'. In so doing the positivist method would also help define the range of questions about which moral and intellectual enquiry could be usefully conducted. Metaphysical matters such as the existence of God and the properties of the human spirit, which were incapable of being given firm and demonstrable answers, were to be excluded from consideration.[47] This did not mean, however, that there could be no significant intellectual advances in the domain of spirituality. From a tactical point of view, moreover, it was imperative that this terrain be occupied by republicans. During the 1840s and early 1850s republican and socialist sceptics were repeatedly told by Comte and Littré that if all spiritual questions were simply left unattended morality would remain in the hands of 'retrograde' and reactionary forces.[48] But more fundamentally both men believed that political and economic changes which were not accompanied by radical transformations in the moral sphere were doomed.

So what did positivist spirituality consist of? As ever the initial definition given by Comte and Littré was negative: positivist ethics rejected both the deistic discourses of established religions and the equally groundless metaphysical propositions of atheism.[49] Atheism was misleading not only because its account of the world rested on unprovable 'essences', such as atoms, but because it promoted 'anarchy' and posited a fundamentally individualistic form of morality.[50] Positivism presented alternative moral foundations of republicanism which were spiritual but not deist, and scientific but not atheistic.[51] Religion, for the positivists, was an essential source of public and private order; unlike the atheists and materialists they believed that as man developed his moral and intellectual faculties religion would come to play an ever larger part in his existence. The core of positivist spirituality was the placing of 'humanity'—in Littré's terms 'humanity conceived in an ideal sense'[52]—at the heart of man's religious expression. The positivist religion of humanity was intended to cover all aspects of man's social existence, providing a beacon which would guide and shape his destinies in all wakes of life:

Humanity is a real ideal which must be known (science and education), loved (religion), embellished (fine arts), enriched (industry), and which in this manner holds all our existence—individual, domestic, and social—under its supreme direction.[53]

The religion of humanity brought with it all the trappings of traditional religious forms: man experienced 'revelation' through the discoveries of science, and ultimately arrived at 'felicity' through the full development of his moral

---

[47] Littré, *De la Philosophie Positive*, 60–4.
[48] Littré, 'Socialisme indéterminé', in *Conservation Révolution Positivisme*, 192–3.
[49] Littré, Émile, *Paroles de philosophie positive* (Paris: Delahays, 1859), 31.   [50] Ibid.
[51] Littré, 'Distinction de la religion d'avec la théologie', in *Conservation Révolution Positivisme*, 380.
[52] Ibid., 386.
[53] Littré, 'Idée religieuse de l'humanité', in *Conservation Révolution Positivisme*, 409.

and intellectual faculties; the teachings of the new religion were likened to a 'catechism'.[54] Littré offered the following summary of the positivist religious creed: 'to love, know, serve, and as we advance in life, to cultivate the memory of those we have lost, such is the foundation of our moral existence and of our permanent felicity.'[55] Devotion to the public good was another key facet of the positivist conception of felicity: 'the more man lives outside of his own selfishness, the more he feels improved and happy. It is an ineffable happiness to have sentiments which are ideal and disinterested.'[56] In this context Littré also saw the development of republicanism across Europe—and specifically the willingness of Germans, Italians, and many others to fight and even die for their political beliefs—as evidence of the ever wider dissemination of the positivist ideals of humanity.[57]

Institutional and collective public action could also help to accelerate the 'reorganization of opinions and values'[58] to which positivists aspired. In their writings between 1848 and 1851 Littré and his fellow-positivists campaigned tirelessly for the generation of optimal institutional conditions for the flourishing of positivist spirituality, for instance through the promotion of public festivals and commemorations, which would bring people together under the positivist banner and help create a sense of public identification with the collectivity.[59] On an immediate level their battle-cry was (negative) freedom: the removal of all barriers which might prevent human spirituality from expressing itself to its fullest degree. In the 1848 report produced by the Société Positiviste on the reorganization of public institutions Littré asserted that the state should adopt a policy of strict non-interference in all matters intellectual and spiritual. There should be no censorship of the press, and public subsidies to the university and the Catholic Church should be withdrawn. This would enable the establishment of a level playing field, upon which the various moral doctrines of religion, metaphysics, and positivism could compete under equal conditions.[60] In a positivist community, Littré noted, 'spiritual forces will be constantly left to their own devices'.[61] In this context he hoped that Comtian philosophy could be more widely disseminated through the establishment of positivist schools, in which the traditional curricular emphasis on literature would be replaced by scientific teaching. He stressed that education could become accessible to all, and most notably to workers and women, only if it was removed from the clutches of both state and Church.[62] At the same time education was viewed as a key instrument in elite recruitment and train-

---

[54] Littré, 'Loi sur l'enseignement', in *Conservation Révolution Positivisme*, 25.
[55] Littré, 'Théorie positive de la révélation et de la félicité', in *Conservation Révolution Positivisme*, 424.
[56] Littré, 'Idéal ou religion', 97.   [57] Ibid., 98.
[58] *République Occidentale. Ordre et Progrès. Rapport à la Société Positiviste, par la Commission chargée d'examiner la nature et le plan du nouveau gouvernement révolutionnaire* (Paris, 1848), 10–11.
[59] Littré, 'Mesures à prendre les plus prochaines', 148–9.
[60] *Rapport à la Société Positiviste*, 29.
[61] Littré, 'Révision de la Constitution', in *Application de la philosophie positive*, 141.
[62] Littré, 'Education et séparation du pouvoir spirituel d'avec le pouvoir temporel', in *Application de la philosophie positive*, 62–5.

ing: Littré sketched out the plans for a new École Positive which would be modelled on the existing École Polytechnique but would go much further in integrating the different sciences. The ultimate goal would be to provide France with an intellectual elite from which the nation's doctors, scientists, and judges could be recruited.[63]

What would humanity look like once enriched and galvanized with the principles of positivist spirituality? Littré here endorsed one of Comte's fundamental aspirations: to transcend the individualism which had been promoted by the Revolutionary tradition, notably through its emphasis on human rights. In the positivist Elysium—in which strong echoes of Rousseau could be heard—there would be a convergence of values around the notion of the public good: 'everything will combine to suppress the rebellions of individual interest and make prevalent the legitimacy of general interest.'[64] The benefits of positive education would spread to all classes: the people would become the true guardians of all the most elevated sentiments and noble virtues, most notably patriotism.[65] Women would become more enlightened and there would emerge a 'feminine public opinion' which, without abandoning the family, would exercise a significant role in directing public sentiments and values.[66] A different aesthetics would also help to cultivate a distinct sense of the beautiful: in the emerging positivist order a new type of artist would be created for a wider and more discerning public.[67]

Order and Progress in the Temporal Sphere: Positivist Politics

Bolstering and complementing the changes in the irenic and spiritual spheres were the specifically political transformations advocated by the positivists within France. As noted earlier, both Comte and Littré welcomed the 'negative' achievement of the Revolution of 1789 in overturning the decaying monarchical system. But France had still proved unable to transform this welcome change into a settled and permanent political order; all political experiments—republican, monarchist, and Bonapartist—had proved to be short-lived interregna.[68] The country had oscillated between 'negative' periods of revolutionary upheaval and 'positive' phases of intellectual ebullition, from which had progressively begun to emerge the key principles which would definitively 'close' the destructive era of violence and instability in France.[69] With the advent of the Second Republic in 1848 Comte and Littré had come to believe that the moment of final transition had arrived, and that the implementation of positivist proposals for constitutional and political

---

[63] Littré, 'Mesures à prendre les plus prochaines', 154–5.
[64] Littré, 'Culture morale', in *Application de la philosophie positive*, 101. [65] Ibid..
[66] Ibid., 103. [67] Littré, 'Loi sur l'enseignement', 25.
[68] Littré, 'Révision de la Constitution', 133.
[69] Littré, 'Des progrès du socialisme', in *Conservation Révolution Positivisme*, 161.

change would lead France into a 'definitive' era of stability.[70] Revolutionary agitation was in this sense a good omen, a sign of the birth-pangs of the new order. Littré warmly embraced the political fermentation of the late 1840s and early 1850s through an organic metaphor: 'I consider the revolutionary condition as a state of medical disorder, comparable to dentition or puberty, an inevitable, tempestuous, but salutary task, because it has to carry humanity, as the individual, to a higher point in its evolution.'[71]

The political solution offered by the positivists to France's endemic constitutional instability was highly original, and needs to be appreciated first in the wider context of their critique of the paradigms set out by their main political rivals. The 'conservative' British model of a constitutional monarchy, which was regarded as the ideal solution by many monarchists and liberals, was seen as flawed because it did not correspond to social and political conditions in France.[72] It was a classic example of 'metaphysical' thinking in politics: the imposition of an a priori framework on a society whose historical traditions and current needs were fundamentally different. In any event, the historical evidence since 1789 had clearly demonstrated the limits of such a political system when applied in France: the constitutional monarchy, in Littré's terms, was 'a useless clock which constantly breaks down and constantly needs to be wound'.[73] At the other end of the metaphysical spectrum were the socialists, whose ideas Littré had first encountered in 1840 during a commemorative ceremony for the republican leader Armand Carrel.[74] Like his fellow-positivists, Littré regarded socialism as a diverse and often contradictory ideology; and there appeared to be no rational basis for selecting any one of its many competing versions. Yet the very emergence of these doctrines was evidence of a strong collective aspiration for a better and more equitable political order. Littré particularly welcomed socialist political demands as an expression of working-class empowerment.[75] Similarly, he credited the socialist generosity of spirit with the abolition of the death penalty for political crimes, a measure taken by the Second Republic shortly after the 1848 Revolution.[76] But, however well-meant, sentiments of this kind could not provide a reliable guide for political action; furthermore many socialists were committed to a radical form of social equality which was dangerously utopian.[77]

What of the republicans? They were by nature more progressive than the monarchists and more orderly than the socialists, and to this extent they represented the closest potential allies of positivism. Littré and Comte warmly identified with the tradition of 1789, and in his 1848 report Littré specifically singled out the glorious achievements of the Montagnards after 1793, praising

---

[70] Littré, 'Fusion des républicains dans les socialistes', in *Conservation Révolution Positivisme*, 176.
[71] Littré, 'Hostilité contre la presse', in *Conservation Révolution Positivisme*, 39.
[72] Littré, 'Prévisions', in *Application de la philosophie positive*, 4–5.
[73] *Rapport à la Société Positiviste*, 13.
[74] Littré, 'Socialisme', in *Conservation Révolution Positivisme*, 153–4.
[75] Littré, 'Socialisme', in *Application de la philosophie positive*, 43–7.
[76] Littré, 'Du parti de l'ordre', in *Conservation Révolution Positivisme*, 446.
[77] Littré, 'Culture morale', in *Application de la philosophie positive*, 100.

them for successfully defending France from external invasion and internal peril.[78] But as it had developed during the first half of the nineteenth century Jacobin republicanism too was both sociologically and ideologically flawed. Its leadership—this was also true of the liberal party—was dominated by the chattering classes, 'lawyers, writers, rhetors, sophists',[79] many of whom attached more importance to eloquence and discursiveness than to substantive issues.

On a more philosophical level Littré rejected two of the cardinal precepts of the republican canon: popular sovereignty and the principles of *liberté-égalité-fraternité*. The popular will was of course an important element in the construction of a new political order, but this will could not yet be fully relied upon to provide intellectual and political direction to the rest of society, for, as Littré put it—using a celebrated Comtian formula—'capacity requires knowledge'.[80] The revolutionary trinity was dismissed as 'metaphysical'—because its principles were aspirational rather than real—and thus also incapable of offering a suitable foundation for a stable political order. In a stinging article published shortly before the collapse of the Second Republic in 1851 Littré launched a wide-ranging attack on the principles of liberty, equality, and fraternity. The historical record showed that since 1789 these precepts had been a source of division and controversy and had failed to provide France with constitutional stability. In proclaiming these principles, furthermore, the revolutionaries had been guilty of arrogance, denying that their political predecessors had made any significant contributions to social and political improvements in France. Of the three the most dangerous notion was equality, which was a valid precept when defined in civil terms but which represented a serious threat to political and social order if taken to signify equal distribution of wealth or equality between men and women.[81] The 1789 motto was thus a symbol of the historical failings and intellectual incoherences of the republican tradition.

'Society is governed by two equally powerful tendencies: order and progress.'[82] In intellectual terms, positivist politics was a synthesis which borrowed elements from all three of the broad political traditions with which it was in contention. From the conservative monarchist it stressed the essential importance of order and political stability, the continuities between past and present—and the respect for 'good' traditions—the value of decisive leadership, and the inexorable place of religiosity in individual existence; from the socialist the notion of moral generosity and working-class empowerment, and the belief in a society bound both by a sense of liberty and of collective purpose; and from the republican the essential values of reason and intellectual

---

[78] *Rapport à la Société Positiviste*, 9–10.

[79] Littré, 'Organisation Temporelle', 84. A later article extended the list to include 'professors, journalists, men of letters'. Ibid., 136.

[80] 'Pour pouvoir il faut savoir'. Littré, 'Du socialisme déterminé ou philosophie positive', in *Conservation Révolution Positivisme*, 208.

[81] Littré, 'De la devise révolutionnaire: Liberté Egalité Fraternité', in *Conservation Révolution Positivisme*, 334.

[82] Littré, 'Progrès parallèle de la société et de la science', in *Application de la philosophie positive*, 34.

freedom, the key functions of central government in the establishment of
political unity, and the legacy of political and economic rights established by
the Revolution of 1789. In the politics of the late Second Republic this cluster
of ideological views brought the positivists closer to the forces of 'progress'
than to the conservative groups which coalesced around President Louis
Napoleon. As mentioned earlier, Comte and Littré called for a 'fusion' of
republicans and socialists in the hope that the positivists could work alongside
both groups to further the objectives of the forces of 'progress'.[83]

It is against this ideological backdrop that the positivist political platform
has to be understood. Initially promulgated in the summer of 1848 and subsequently championed by Littré, it set out the constitutional and political
reforms deemed necessary to enable France to make the final transition to a
state of permanent stability. Several necessary conditions were identified for
the establishment of a just political order. To begin with, executive power had
to be concentrated in Paris. This neo-Jacobin centralism was justified for a
range of reasons, both intellectual and political:

> The capital is a centre where all the strengths and riches of the nation culminate; there
> are gathered all the most active intellects; there we find the most fruitful elaboration of
> sciences, letters, and arts; there also takes place the most rapid and constant exchange
> of ideas; there, finally, and precisely for all these reasons, lives the most revolutionary
> element.[84]

In case there was any doubt about the positivists' commitment to centralization and political unity, Littré later affirmed that the goal of politics should be
the elimination of 'all that is local and contingent'.[85] Furthermore, full executive powers would be granted to three principal administrative officers, to be
named 'governors'; they would be responsible respectively for external affairs,
the interior, and financial questions. These governors would be chosen among
the ranks of 'eminent proletarians'[86] and would be appointed in two stages.
The whole of the Parisian electorate would initially designate 85 great electors,
and the latter would then appoint the three office-holders.[87] Littré welcomed
the fact that the effect of such a nominating system would be to hand power
to the working class, the most numerous social group in the city. This was not
merely a matter of democratic political arithmetic. Since workers were
excluded from the exercise of state power and largely uneducated, their views
were likely to be disinterested and uncontaminated by 'metaphysics'. The
presence of workers at the helm of the state would also guarantee that the revolutionary process begun by the events of 1789 would be fully and irreversibly
completed.[88]

---

[83] Littré, 'Fusion des républicains dans les socialistes', in *Conservation Révolution Positivisme*,
176–77.
[84] *Rapport à la Société Positiviste*, 15. See also Littré, 'Révision de la Constitution', 138.
[85] Littré, 'Des progrès du socialisme', in *Conservation Révolution Positivisme*, 166.
[86] Littré, 'Révision de la Constitution', 134–5.   [87] *Rapport à la Société Positiviste*, 23, 30.
[88] Littré, 'Révision de la Constitution', 140–1.

This executive would also be assisted by an assembly elected by male universal suffrage, in which the industrial and agricultural interests of the departments would be represented. Littré rejected the notion of a legislative assembly, arguing that the role of these local delegates should be strictly circumscribed to the vote and control of public income and expenditure.[89] This limitation was necessary because law-making assemblies tended to be weighed down by particular interests and were inclined to make decisions on the basis of compromise rather than an agreed notion of the general interest.[90] In Littré's words, 'in a large country like France progressive law-making is less rapid at the circumference than at the centre'.[91] In contrast with the sociological inclusiveness he advocated for the designation of the governors, Littré proposed that the office of elected representative should be exercised only by the 'well-off classes':[92] these were the social groups which had the greatest wealth and thus the strongest expertise in financial matters; for the former reason their members would not require any public remuneration.

In the absence of substantive powers being granted to the assembly, how would the actions of the executive be controlled? Here came into play the final element in the positivist political programme: the creation of counter-weights at the societal level. Two institutions were deemed essential here: first, a free press, which as noted earlier was regarded by positivists as a fundamental feature of a free society; and second, the establishment of 'clubs' which would discuss all government projects and thus subject state action to close and continuous scrutiny. Comte and Littré regarded such clubs—again modelled on the revolutionary era—as the indispensable complement to the operation of universal suffrage.[93] This expressed the strong belief on the part of positivists that the mass vote was not an institution to be fetishized but was valuable only to the extent that it served the collective interests of the political community. In Littré's words, voting was not a right but a function: 'a right belongs to everyone; but a function belongs to him who is able to perform it well.'[94]

The Comtian conception of the temporal sphere was thus a unique ideological blend. Its distinctiveness was in many ways encapsulated in its political symbolism. The positivist Republic would keep the tricolour as the French national flag, but would replace the revolutionary motto of *liberté-égalité-fraternité* with 'order and liberty'.[95] A Republic indeed, but with a difference. Its indebtedness to the Jacobin model was clear, notably in its insistence on founding a community in which no 'caste' enjoyed a preponderant position, thus resolutely turning its back on the *ancien régime*.[96] It asserted that society had to be bound together by a common doctrine, but also stressed that this system of ideas and values had to be 'freely discussed and accepted'.[97] But

---

[89] *Rapport à la Société Positiviste*, 16.

[90] Littré, 'Révision de la Constitution', 135–6.

[91] Ibid., 136. This was a polite way of saying that cities and towns were politically advanced whereas rural France was backward.

[92] 'classes aisées'. *Rapport à la Société Positiviste*, 18.   [93] Ibid., 25–6.

[94] Ibid., 22.   [95] Ibid., 30.   [96] Littré, *De la philosophie positive*, 50.

[97] Littré, 'Progrès parallèle de la société et de la science', in *Application de la philosophie positive*, 40.

although the positivist political order was open, progressive, and tolerant it did not equate democracy with social levelling; Littré explicitly underlined that democracy went hand in hand with 'the appropriate respect for all superiorities, whether temporal or spiritual'.[98] In its emphasis on working-class empowerment and scientific education of elites, positivist politics represented a decisive step in the bold march of humanity towards 'the reign of industry'.[99]

Littré's Break with Comtian Positivism

'To admit the premises, and through discussion challenge the consequences, where necessary, at my own risk and peril, is the work of a disciple who wishes both the good of the doctrine and the glory of its master.'[100] Following his break with his philosophical master in 1851 Littré carefully chose this dialectical formula to characterize his relations with Comte and the Comtian system. On the one hand he emphatically rejected—and openly criticized—certain aspects of Comte's philosophy and politics, most notably his political stances after 1851 and his 'subjective' philosophical turn in the 1850s. On the other hand, Littré continued to proclaim his adhesion to the basic tenets of positivism, and regarded his critical intellectual posture as a vindication of the spirit of Comtianism.

It is true that the rupture was initially deliberately qualified. Littré remained on relatively good terms with his *maître* after 1851, and continued to make financial contributions to the 'positivist subsidy' which provided for Comte in the final years of his life.[101] Despite his opposition to many elements of his system Littré also continued to regard Comte as a 'powerful initiator',[102] and still publicly proclaimed his allegiance to the positivist creed despite his official excommunication from the 'orthodox' school established by Laffitte, Robinet, and Audiffrent.[103] This profession of loyalty was not merely a matter of rhetoric. In the 1860s and 1870s Littré prepared and watched over the dissemination of further editions of Comte's works, founded the review *La Philosophie Positive* with his colleague Grégoire Wyrouboff to disseminate the teachings of positivism, and through his own intellectual notoriety arguably did more to promote the creed than the sectarians of 'orthodox' positivism. In his political writings, furthermore, Littré took great pains to demonstrate his

---

[98] Ibid., 38–9.   [99] Littré, 'Organisation Temporelle', 81.

[100] Littré, Émile, *Auguste Comte et la Philosophie Positive*, 3rd edn (Paris: Bureaux de la Philosophie Positive, 1877), v–vi.

[101] After Comte's death Littré also set up a subscription for his widow. The brochure containing his appeal is in the Bibliothèque Nationale, LN27—4656: *Circulaire de M. Émile Littré, faisant connaître aux disciples de feu M. Comte qu'il ouvre une souscription afin de continuer à Mme.Comte, sa veuve, la pension que lui faisait son mari* (Paris, 1857).

[102] Littré, *Conservation Révolution Positivisme*, v.

[103] On the different schools of positivism see Charlton, D. G., *Positivist Thought in France during the Second Empire 1852–1870* (Oxford: Clarendon Press, 1959) and *Secular Religions in France 1815–1870* (London: Oxford University Press, 1963).

continued inspiration from Comte. He even attempted, somewhat disingenuously, to turn his own heterodoxy into a general feature of the positivist doctrine itself. In his preface to the fourth edition of Comte's *Cours de Philosophie Positive*, for example, Littré stressed that one of the advantages of positivism was that it did not need to be accepted in its entirety but could be embraced in logically separate parts.[104]

One of the keys to understanding Littré's rupture with Comte is to appreciate that it was a process, the result of a critical re-evaluation which began several years before 1851 and continued well into the following decade. The break not only stretched over time, it also extended across a range of dimensions, political, philosophical, and personal—Littré objected to Comte's cavalier treatment of his estranged wife;[105] as in any rupture between master and disciple psychological and even psychoanalytical considerations must also have played an important role.[106] In ideological terms the break has to be seen in two complementary dimensions: Littré's overall re-assessment of Comte's late philosophical system and his growing unease with the tensions between the authoritarian elements in positivist politics and the liberal republicanism which he increasingly espoused. In this sense it was fitting that the single event around which the rupture was consummated was Louis Napoleon's *coup d'état* of December 1851. Comte welcomed the overthrow of the 'empty talkers of the assemblies and newspapers' of the Second Republic and believed that Louis Napoleon's rule foreshadowed the triumph of a 'sociocratic' regime—a dictatorship of the workers. Littré, on the other hand, took the republican view that the overthrow of the Second Republic was an unacceptable violation of public legality, and that Louis Napoleon was nothing but a self-serving tyrant.[107] Little wonder, given these contrasting assessments, that Littré soberly commented of the 1851 coup: 'this event loosened my links with Mr Comte.'[108]

But this single event was much more of a catalyst than a first cause. In *Auguste Comte et la philosophie positive*, written in 1863 both as a celebration of positivist doctrine and as a justification of his dissident stance, Littré began by suggesting that Comte's political and philosophical mistakes were expressions of a single attitude.[109] In as much as it appeared to suggest a synchronicity between Comte's philosophical and political stances, this was a somewhat misleading statement, perhaps intended as an a posteriori justification of

[104] Littré, Émile, *Étude sur les progrès du positivisme* (Paris: Germer Baillière, 1877), 10.

[105] Simon, Walter Michael, *European Positivism in the Nineteenth Century. An Essay in Intellectual History* (Ithaca: Cornell University Press, 1963), 15–17.

[106] At the time of the rupture Comte accused Littré of lacking 'docility', to which the latter responded that he had been *too* docile. Littré, *Auguste Comte et la Philosophie Positive*, 587.

[107] On Comte's political views in 1851–2 see Comte, Auguste, *Correspondance*, Vol. 6 (1851–2) (Paris: Vrin, 1973), 443–51.

[108] Littré, 'Révision de la Constitution', in *Conservation Révolution Positivisme*, 246. Littré added that Comte had refused to acknowledge his political error in 1852 even as it became obvious that Louis Napoleon was about to restore the Empire; he believed that the people of Paris would prevent the proclamation of an imperial regime. Ibid., 290.

[109] Littré, *Auguste Comte et la Philosophie Positive*, v.

Littré's unfaltering public loyalty to Comte before 1851. Later in the same work Littré recounted that his master's 'subjective' turn had begun to occur as early as 1845, the year of his 'philosophical crisis', when he started to move away from his earlier conclusions and especially from his 'scientific' method. Comte then became increasingly preoccupied with spiritual matters, and this religious reorientation culminated in his later works, the *Système de Politique Positive* (1851–4) and the *Synthèse Subjective* (1856).[110] The core of Littré's objection was that Comte had lapsed into a form of religious mysticism in these works, an outcome which inevitably followed his replacement of the experimental method with a subjective and a priori approach. In this context Littré explicitly rejected the new 'cult of humanity' proposed by Comte and adopted by his 'orthodox' followers after his death. The religious worship of humanity, he opined, failed to meet the stringent test of the positivist method. The 'moral homogeneity' which such a religion presupposed was not yet in place, and would become so, if at all, only after a long period of education and spiritual development.[111] For this reason, Littré remarked dryly, the positivist Churches founded by Comte's orthodox disciples had not had much success to date.[112] From the Second Empire onwards Littré's stance on religious matters was explicitly pluralist, and he noted disapprovingly that Comte had been hostile to civil burials—an issue over which individuals should be allowed a free choice, as had been exercised by Littré's own father.[113]

Part of the motivation for the break, therefore, was Littré's concern that Comte had abandoned his own philosophical method in his later life. But his critique also extended to the broader range of irenic, spiritual, and temporal issues which Littré himself had championed during his 'orthodox' Comtian phase. In an article written in 1870, shortly before the fall of the Second Empire, he lambasted the 'utopian' character of Comte's political philosophy in terms which went well beyond his limited and qualified objections to his later works. In a telling analogy Littré began by placing the socialism of Fourier and the 'Catholic-feudal' socialism of Comte on the same methodological footing: 'they have both this in common: they are the result of a subjective process in which, following the preferences expressed in each mode of thought, a solution is fixed to match what is desired.'[114] Comte's ideal arrangements in the spiritual and temporal spheres were then likened to a form of neo-medievalism:

On both sides we have a spiritual power, pope and clergy, which has the direction of public and private conscience; on both sides we have a temporal power, there barons, here capitalists, who hold in their hands all the possessions of the community; on both sides we have a people, there serfs and vassals, here proletarians, who in return for their

---

[110] Littré, *Auguste Comte et la Philosophie Positive*, 513.
[111] Littré, 'Idée religieuse de l'humanité', in *Conservation Révolution Positivisme*, 410, 414.
[112] Littré, 'Du socialisme déterminé ou philosophie positive', in *Conservation Révolution Positivisme*, 220.
[113] Littré, 'Expédition de Rome', in *Conservation Révolution Positivisme*, 15–16.
[114] Littré, Émile, 'Socialisme', *La Philosophie Positive* (May–June 1870), 418.

work receive government and sustenance from the temporal power, under the direction of a morality overseen, there by priests of Jesus Christ, here by priests of humanity.[115]

This absence of freedom, it should be noted, was not highlighted exclusively with reference to Comte's religious views in the 1850s: it also referred to his political philosophy more generally, and in this sense went to the very heart of the ideological values which Littré had so enthusiastically endorsed in the previous decade.

By the time he published the second edition of his 'little green book' *Conservation Révolution Positivisme* in 1879, with retrospective comments methodically inserted after each piece, Littré's political assessment of his years as an orthodox positivist had become scathing. In his preface he noted that Comte's core political views in the 1840s and early 1850s, which he had enthusiastically endorsed at the time, were wholly mistaken. In this sense the additional remarks inserted into the second edition amounted to an over-whelming recantation by Littré of his Comtian political past. The new spiritual power which he had hoped for had not materialized—and Littré was unsure that it would be desirable that it ever did. As for the new temporal power to be vested in the hands of the 'big industrialists', this was nothing but a utopia—and probably a dangerous one.[116] The parliamentary system which had been so savagely decried by Comte was now, in the 1870s, seen by Littré as the most reliable source of order and progress.[117]

At the level of immediate events the mistakes in the positivist political analysis of the 1848–51 period were almost embarrassing to recount in the light of subsequent events. But with typical honesty—and perhaps a touch of masochism—Littré enumerated them: believing that the Second Republic would endure, and would mark the beginning of a historical transition to a new positivist order; [118] allowing the Bonaparte family to return to France; adopting universal suffrage as the mode of election of the president of the Republic; [119] failing to appreciate that voting was not merely a function but also a fundamental political right;[120] entrusting the political future of the country to the workers and to the socialist movement, despite the fact that neither of them were yet ready to exercise power; [121] and above all repeatedly asserting that a new irenic age of peace was about to dawn and that Europe was about to unite in a pacific republican federation.[122] In the latter respect Comte's dream had turned into a horrible nightmare, with the Franco-Prussian war, the Paris Commune, and the Prussian annexation of Alsace-Lorraine highlighting the continuing salience of conflict both within and between political communities. Events within France had also brought home to Littré the destructive potential of political ideas. Comte's suggestion that monuments glorifying war should be destroyed had been adopted by the Communards in 1871. But the uprooting of the Colonne Vendôme at the

---

[115] Ibid., 419.   [116] Littré, *Conservation Révolution Positivisme*, 65.   [117] Ibid., vi.
[118] Ibid., 233.   [119] Ibid., 137.   [120] Ibid., 63.   [121] Ibid., 248.
[122] Ibid., 480–2.

height of the Franco-Prussian war had been an untimely act, which showed
how little the Communards really understood Comtian ideas.[123]

These mistakes and errors of judgement ultimately led Littré to reconsider
the heuristic value of Comtian positivism. The list of methodological shortcomings was not insignificant. In *Auguste Comte et la philosophie positive* Littré
spelled out three key areas in which Comte's positivist methodology was defi-
cient: political economy, cerebral theory, and the subjective theory of humanity.[124] Comte had neglected political economy because he believed it to be a
false science, but in Littré's view this had been a critical mistake;[125] cerebral
theory—the science of how the brain functioned—had also been insufficiently
examined by Comte, who had failed to assimilate the most recent discoveries
in the biological sciences;[126] as for the subjective theory of humanity, which
included the study of morality, aesthetics, and psychology, all of these
appeared to be absent from Comte's conception of positivism.[127] In addition
to these problems of scope, Littré identified a fundamental mistake in the original design of Comtian positivism. The scientific domain, he now conceded,
needed to be distinguished more clearly from the empirical. Scientific politics
was concerned with 'grand themes', such as the transition from one historical
era to another, while empirical politics was about everyday and short-term
occurrences. Predictions could be made only in the scientific domain; any
considerations about what might happen in the field of empirical politics were
mere 'conjectures'. This significant restriction of the range of political events
over which predictive propositions could be advanced represented a considerable watering down of the prophetic potential of positivist doctrine. Most crucially, Littré explicitly acknowledged that the outcome of political struggles
conducted within the normal framework of democratic politics was no longer
foreseeable: 'the future is too complex to enable us to see very far ahead.'[128]
Littré, again with commendable candour, freely acknowledged that most of
his 'conjectures' concerning the 1848–51 period had been entirely mistaken.[129]

Where did all of this leave Littré's relationship with positivism? On the negative side, what he abandoned in Comtian positivism was the predictive element in methodological terms and all the substantive conclusions in the
irenic, spiritual, and temporal spheres which he believed to be inconsistent
with the principles of political, economic, and social liberty. After 1851 Littré
stressed that one of Comte's greatest mistakes was his inability to recognize
the importance of free discussion and free thought and the value of representative institutions.[130] At the same time, turning to the positive side, Littré
consistently repeated after his rupture with Comte that although he had
departed from some aspects of the canon he still regarded himself as a fully-
fledged positivist. In his own words, his views 'on the very essence of things'
had remained unaltered; the changes and disagreements had manifested

---

[123] Ibid., 471–2. [124] Littré, *Auguste Comte et la Philosophie Positive*, 659.
[125] Ibid., 660. [126] Ibid., 661. [127] Ibid., 663. [128] Ibid., 250.
[129] Ibid., 484. [130] Littré, *Auguste Comte et la Philosophie Positive*, 588.

themselves only on 'applied points'.[131] Littré made this claim not only with reference to the 1840s and 1850s but also, and especially, to the later periods of his life. Thus, as France slowly edged its way towards the Republic in the 1870s he stressed that his own political and philosophical principles continued to be guided by the positivist beacon, and that the new political order was largely based on the positivist principles of order and progress.[132]

As noted earlier in this chapter, this equation has become doubly axiomatic. It has provided the basis both for Littré's celebration as one of the intellectual 'founders' of the Third Republic and for the dominant interpretation of the ideological origins of the new regime.[133] How far this 'positivism' did in fact influence Littré, and through him the founding of the Third Republic, is the question which will be pursued next through an analysis of his political writings in the 1860s and 1870s.

The Philosophical and Theoretical Bases of Littré's Republicanism: The Cult of 1789

Littré's rupture with Comte represented one side—the negative—of his ideological evolution between the late 1840s and early 1860s. What partly underlay this break was his increasing embrace of republican political philosophy: an ideological readjustment which began in the early 1850s and which was essentially complete by the end of the Second Empire. By this time, Littré was universally regarded as one of the leading intellectuals in the republican political community, a position which he enjoyed not only by virtue of his eminence as a scientist and philologist but also through his overt political stances and commentaries on contemporary politics. In the summer of 1867 Littré launched *La Philosophie Positive*, a journal which appeared every two months. He edited this publication until his death in 1881, and wrote in almost every issue across a broad range of fields.

The wider intellectual objectives of this publication largely mirrored Littré's own ideological goals during his later life: to work on some of the lacunae he had identified in positivist philosophy, most notably in the spheres of ethics and political economy; to expand the audience of positivism by underscoring its heuristic and ideological potential as a source of individual liberation; and, finally, to develop and clarify republican thought by purging its political doctrine of all 'metaphysical' notions. As Littré put it in the opening issue of *La Philosophie Positive*:

The real strength of the party of renovation lies in the positive elements which it contains; its real weaknesses are the theological and metaphysical elements which it has still failed to shake off.[134]

[131] Littré, *Conservation Révolution Positivisme*, 267.   [132] Ibid., 123, 339.
[133] Nicolet, *L'idée républicaine*; Furet and Ozouf, *Le siècle de l'avènement républicain*.
[134] Littré, 'Les trois philosophies', *La Philosophie Positive*, 1 (July–August 1867), 29–30.

Littré's ambitious intellectual agenda was thus to narrow down republicanism by expunging its ideological incoherences through exposure to the scientific tenets of positivism, and at the same time to expand positivist philosophy by opening it up to republican concerns about political liberty and moral autonomy. The following sections will examine how far he achieved this creative synthesis by exploring the philosophical and theoretical foundations of Littré's republican politics in the late Second Empire and early Third Republic. We begin with his conception of the Revolution of 1789, the founding myth of the republican generations of the 1860s and 1870s.

In his magnificent posthumous homage to his colleague in the Académie Française, Ernest Renan asserted that the cornerstone of Littré's mature republicanism had been his attachment to the Revolutionary tradition: 'son of the French Revolution he believed that it contained all justice. Others, more refined, made distinctions, concessions, and compromises. Littré, entire in his faith, did not accept any attenuation to what he held to be the truth.'[135] But the reality was somewhat more complex. Littré would not have subscribed to the proposition, later canonized by Georges Clemenceau, that the Revolution was a 'bloc' from which no single principle or series of events could be taken away. On the contrary, his later writings were littered with specific criticisms of the 1790s, notably the 'sanguinary fury' of the Convention, which he condemned without equivocation,[136] and the destruction of large numbers of archives pertaining to France's feudal age, a vandalization of historical relics which highlighted the revolutionaries' futile efforts to obliterate the past.[137] And there was more. As we have already seen, during his phase as an orthodox Comtian Littré had been highly critical of certain conceptual and symbolic elements in the Revolutionary tradition, most notably its motto of liberty-equality-fraternity. Far from retracting these views in the second edition of *Conservation Révolution Positivisme* in 1879, Littré expanded upon them by applying his earlier critique to the post-1870 period. The revolutionary motto had been adopted by the new republican government which had emerged after the revolution of 4 September 1870. However, the equality and fraternity which this Republic had aspired to promote had collapsed abjectly in the violence and bloodshed of the Paris Commune.[138] Thus in the final decade of his life Littré, even though a fully-fledged republican, continued to believe that at least two of the core precepts of the Revolutionary tradition could not provide a propitious symbolic basis for founding a moderate system of government in France. This was a far cry from Renan's assertion that Littré saw the Revolution as the source of all justice.

So on what basis did he continue to identify with the events of 1789 and the political order they aspired to found? For Littré the Revolution had to be seen both as a specific moment and as the beginning of a transformative

---

[135] Renan, Ernest, speech at the Académie Française, 27 April 1882, quoted in *La Philosophie Positive* (July–August 1882), 142.

[136] Littré, *Conservation Révolution Positivisme*, 315.   [137] Littré, 'Les trois philosophies', 29.

[138] Littré, *Conservation Révolution Positivisme*, 338.

process. Both had been beneficial to France, although both had failed to bring themselves to a successful close. The moment—in the 1790s—had witnessed the growth of moral and intellectual life in France, and in this sense was not without its merits. But the greatest contribution of the Revolutionary era was its long-term, and continuing, impact on both French political culture and society. After the 1790s, in Littré's view, the monarchy, the nobility, and the clergy had lost all legitimate claim to govern the country.[139] In the social and economic spheres the transformations had proved equally momentous. The post-1789 governments had emancipated the peasantry from social and religious domination, promoted industrial and scientific development, and begun the process which was inexorably leading to the emergence of a secular and modern society in France.[140]

What of the turbulences of the 1790s? Like most moderate republicans Littré was clearly embarrassed by the Terror. However, in his view this problem had to be understood in its specific context, one which justified an indulgent assessment of Jacobinism despite its manifest excesses:

I like neither Jacobinism nor the Terror; however, when we imagine the struggle between revolution and counter-revolution, the implacable threats of the emigration, the coalition of kings and the insurrections of Vendée, Lyon, and Toulon, we can, in this furnace, see Jacobinism in its proper perspective.[141]

Littré further relativized these events by noting that the religious persecutions of the absolutist monarchy, most notably the revocation of the Edict of Nantes by Louis XIV, had been much more murderous and destructive, in both numbers and duration, than the Terror.[142] He directly confronted the problem of Jacobinism in his review of Edgar Quinet's *La Révolution*, one of the best-sellers of the late 1860s in France and the source of much ideological controversy among French republicans.[143] Although he fully endorsed Quinet's criticisms of Robespierre and of the Terror, Littré pointedly refused to call the latter event a 'crime', for the somewhat strange reason that Napoleon continued to be regarded as a hero despite the carnage and pillage which had accompanied his European campaigns.[144] Littré then proceeded to challenge Quinet for his misinterpretation of specific events—notably the rise of Bonaparte; his excessive Protestantism, which led him to overrate the role of religion and undervalue that of science in modern society; his disdainful treatment of Comte, many of whose views he had pilfered without acknowledgement; and above all his pessimistic philosophy of history.[145] Littré's disagreement with

---

[139] Littré, Émile, 'Restauration de la légitimité et de ses alliés', in *De l'établissement de la Troisième République* (Paris: Bureaux de la Philosophie Positive, 1880), 250–3.

[140] Ibid., 239.

[141] Littré, Émile, review of E. Bourloton and E. Robert, 'La Commune et ses idées à travers l'histoire', *La Philosophie Positive* (July–August 1873), 145.

[142] Littré, 'Un triomphe clérical', in *La Philosophie Positive*, September–October 1875, in *De l'établissement de la Troisième République*, 272.

[143] See the remarks in the Introduction.

[144] Littré, 'La Révolution par M. Edgar Quinet', *La Philosophie Positive* (November–December 1868), 384.

[145] Ibid., 386–96.

regarded any monarchical restoration during this period as potentially disastrous, Littré again concentrated his fire on Bonapartism, which he saw as the most serious threat to French internal and external integrity. Indeed in the run-up to the decisive elections of 1877 he warned that he would prefer exile to facing up to a Bonapartist political victory, which would inevitably be the prelude to the ruin of France.[153] Part of Littré's distaste for Bonapartism stemmed from his profound aversion to Napoleon, the 'retrograde Charlemagne' who had devastated Europe in his time.[154] The *petit caporal*—and this had also been Comte's view—had never possessed a flair for politics or a moral sense; most fundamentally he lacked the capacity for self-analysis: 'that internal eye, which enables us to evaluate and make sense of ourselves . . . he never possessed it.'[155]

Littré took the opportunity of the Second Empire's celebrations of the hundredth anniversary of Napoleon's birth in 1869 to provide an overall assessment of the Emperor and his regime. The verdict was damning. The First Empire had ruled by despotism, and all its wars had been wars of conquest rather than civilization.[156] Furthermore Napoleon's military reputation was overplayed, and he had also made several critical diplomatic mistakes, the most egregious being his failure to reconstitute an independent Polish state.[157] Napoleon was thus an unworthy object of public celebration, an ineffective and immoral leader who had usurped the mantle of the 1789 Revolution.[158] As for the Second Empire, the proximate source of his rupture with Comte, Littré rounded on its founding act—the *coup d'état* of December 1851—as one of the most savage and inhuman events in recent French history.[159]

So much for the moral and political evaluation of Bonapartism. But Littré's 'sociological' appreciation of the phenomenon was considerably more nuanced, and in some senses ran counter to these categorical ideological conclusions. As an observer of French society, both past and present, Littré could not fail to notice that the Bonapartist legend remained extremely powerful in French public consciousness throughout the nineteenth century. Its success rested partly on the cult of Bonaparte but also on specific events which had become embedded in the collective memory of the nation, notably the flamboyance of Napoleon's return to France during the Hundred Days and the grandiose repatriation of his ashes in 1840.[160] The cult of Bonaparte was also one of the reasons why Louis Napoleon had triumphed in the 1848 presidential elections and why Bonapartism had retained such a powerful political base in the countryside under the Second Empire.[161]

---

[153] Littré, 'Les deux issues de la crise du 16 Mai', in *De l'établissement de la Troisième République*, 420.

[154] Littré, 'Politique', in *La Philosophie Positive* (July–August 1867), 136–7.

[155] Littré, 'Du génie militaire de l'Empereur Napoléon Ier', in *La Philosophie Positive* (May–June 1868), 325.

[156] Littré, 'Centième anniversaire de la naissance de Napoléon I', in *La Philosophie Positive* (September–October 1869), 193.

[157] Ibid., 198.   [158] Ibid., 199.   [159] Ibid., 207.

[160] Littré, 'Du suffrage universel en France considéré comme une expérience sociologique', in *La Philosophie Positive* (January–February 1869), 41.

[161] Ibid.

This led Littré to two important conclusions about the Bonapartist vote: first, it was in some significant sense a vote for the principles and values of 1789, particularly the notion of civil equality; and second, it was often an expression of rural defiance against the moral and social power of the clergy.[162] This appreciation of the progressive character of Bonapartism was also extended to the Second Empire. Despite his principled opposition to its foundation in violence and illegality, Littré made numerous positive references to the regime, especially during the 1860s. The Second Empire, he often remarked, was a great improvement on the First, notably in that its policies were influenced by public opinion.[163] Littré also credited Napoleon III with being the most liberal member of his government, and applauded his policy of transforming the authoritarian political system into a quasi-parliamentary regime despite the opposition of conservative forces within the Bonapartist camp.[164] After his overwhelming victory in the plebiscite of May 1870 Littré also acknowledged the political skill of Napoleon III in catching the republican opposition off guard.[165] Like most republicans Littré's anti-Bonapartism became retrospectively virulent after the events of 1870–1; in an article written in 1872 he thus savaged the 'corrupt' and 'decadent' reign of Napoleon III.[166] Yet he recognized in the final years of his life that the Second Empire had implicitly carried on the positivist heritage: it was not only an orderly regime but had had certain progressive aspects, notably its Haussmanian policies of urban modernization and its commitment to free trade.[167]

In short, there was a significant tension between Littré 'republican' evaluation of Bonapartism, which was based on moral and ideological considerations and was unrelentingly hostile, and his 'positivist' overview of the phenomenon, which recognized the progressive character of the Napoleonic tradition when seen from the perspective of the 1789 Revolution and credited Napoleon III's regime with specific and durable achievements in the social and economic realms.

The Moral Necessity of Socialism

In an article which appeared in *La Philosophie Positive* in late 1871, Littré confessed his mortification at having espoused Comte's belief in the imminent triumph of socialism during the Second Republic: 'today I feel embarrassed by the revolutionary utopias which I allowed myself to follow.'[168]

---

[162] Ibid., 42.
[163] Littré, 'Des élections prochaines', in *La Philosophie Positive* (May–June 1869), 461.
[164] Littré, 'Le plébiscite', in *La Philosophie Positive* (May–June 1870), 532.
[165] Littré, 'Le régime plébiscitaire', in *La Philosophie Positive* (July–August 1870), 154.
[166] Littré, 'De la situation de la France en 1872', in *La Philosophie Positive* (July–August 1872), 18.
[167] Littré, *Conservation Révolution Positivisme*, 338.
[168] Littré, 'Sur la situation que les derniers événements ont faite à l'Europe, au socialisme, et à la France', in *La Philosophie Positive* (November–December 1871), in *De l'établissement de la Troisième République*, 114, n. 2.

This emphasis on the present moment gave a particular flavour to this utterance. Written in the immediate aftermath of the Paris Commune, Littré's assessment of his earlier socialist sympathies was inescapably coloured by recent events. Unsurprisingly he recanted his earlier endorsement of a close political alliance between republicans and socialists. Reviewing the period between 1840 and 1851, Littré stressed the fundamental ideological discontinuities between republicans and socialists at the time. He highlighted the constant hostility shown by the latter towards the Second Republic, as evidenced by the June 1848 revolt, the support given by many socialists to Louis Napoleon in the presidential election of 1848, and their apparent refusal to mobilize mass resistance against the 1851 *coup d'état*.[169]

Comte, for his part, had made three fundamental mistakes in his assessment of socialism: he had thought that its dissemination could prevent war, and that workers were morally and intellectually prepared to exercise power; most fundamentally, he had believed that socialist doctrine had the capacity to articulate universal values and interests. For him socialism was not the ideology of a specific social group; it represented many of the ideals which positivists aspired to see fulfilled for the whole of humanity.[170] In 1871 the destructive fury of the Communards seemed to Littré to underscore how mistaken all these views had been. Although it had had certain Jacobin features, the Commune had been, for Littré, an essentially socialist insurrection, and as such offered an appropriate basis for re-evaluating both the doctrine and its political consequences.[171] Many of the core theoretical premises of revolutionary socialism now seemed fundamentally unsound to him: notably, its atheism and materialism; its rejection of property and espousal of 'collectivism'; its prioritization of the temporal over the spiritual and of equality over liberty; and above all its failure to recognize that order was the first condition of social existence.[172]

On the practical side, the Commune's record had been little short of catastrophic: it had used violence as a means of achieving its political ends, closed down religious schools and persecuted the clergy, and, most appallingly of all, had waged war against the legitimate French government at a time when the latter was attempting to deal with the Prussian invasion and its consequences.[173] The violence of the Commune had not been mere abstractions to Littré. In the final agony of the insurrection in May 1871 Communard troops had occupied his modest Parisian apartment in the Rue d'Assas for three days. When they were eventually dislodged by the advancing Versailles forces, they had set fire to the building. Littré's few worldly possessions and, more impor-

[169] Littré, *Conservation Révolution Positivisme*, 184–5.

[170] Littré, 'Sur la situation que les derniers événements ont faite', 114–15.

[171] This was something of a misunderstanding on Littré's part. The predominant intellectual influences over the Communards were Proudhonian rather than socialist. See Johnson, Martin Philip, *The Paradise of Association: Popular Culture and Popular Organizations in the Paris Commune of 1871* (Ann Arbor: University of Michigan Press, 1996).

[172] Littré, 'Remarques sur le socialisme', *La Philosophie Positive* (November–December 1871), 429.

[173] Ibid., 420.

tantly, his collection of books and papers had been saved only by the prompt intervention of the government forces.[174] Littré pointedly contrasted this physical attack against his property with the correctness of the Prussian army, which had not damaged his country house when it had marched through Ménil-le-Roi.[175] These events clearly intensified Littré's animosity towards revolutionary socialism, and further underlined the chasm which appeared to exist between his moderate republican politics and his earlier Comtian association with socialism.

Yet precisely at the moment when the political and historical case for a rupture between republicanism and socialism seemed almost overwhelming, Littré continued to argue for a constructive dialogue between the two camps. Between the late 1860s and the early 1880s he consistently defended the socialist idea when it came under attack from conservative and republican quarters: a stance, it is worth noting in passing, which runs counter to the traditional view of Littré's unequivocally 'conservative' political turn in the final years of his life.[176] This identification with socialism stemmed first from Littré's 'sociological' recognition that the doctrine was an ideological expression of worker interests:

The workers from towns, factories, collieries etc. who are all salaried form, in a society, a natural group. Socialism is the idea of the interests, the tendencies, and the aspirations of this group.[177]

But it was not merely a matter of dispassionate observation. Littré, as a republican, also believed that workers were entitled to defend themselves against their employers. From the late Second Empire onwards he thus championed the cause of a 'practical' socialism which resolutely rejected utopian communist schemes and the use of violence, and instead concentrated on specific everyday problems:

Socialism begins only when discussion begins. From the moment that workers discuss the social organization and the distribution of the common good, that they make their genuine grievances known, that they attempt to find solutions to them, and that they take the initiative in formulating theories, experiences, and facts, then public conscience and social science have to take note.[178]

Littré held up as a model of this 'practical' socialism the organization of labour unions in Britain and Germany. Trade unions could prevent the exploitation of workers by their employers and provide the collective mechanism through which disputes about wages and working conditions could be amicably settled.[179] However, if this resolution proved impossible and all avenues for

---

[174] Littré, Émile, *Comment j'ai fait mon dictionnaire de la langue française* (Paris: Delagrave, 1897), 35–6.

[175] Ibid., 38.

[176] See for example Aquarone, *The Life and Works of Émile Littré 1801–1881*, 114–16.

[177] Littré, *Conservation Révolution Positivisme*, 153.

[178] Littré, 'Socialisme', *La Philosophie Positive*, 6 (May–June 1870), 407.   [179] Ibid., 416.

conciliation had been fully explored, Littré fully defended the right of workers to go on strike.[180]

His recognition of the value of socialist doctrine and practice went even further. In the positivist scheme of things, it will be remembered, societies developed according to laws which were fixed and immutable. However, this 'plan'
still left room for human intervention to improve social and economic conditions: 'it is not in our power to change the fundamental lines of this plan; but
it is within our power to amend it, correct it, and improve upon it.'[181]
Throughout the 1870s Littré repeatedly stated that socialism deserved the
respect of all republicans for formulating the moral imperative of social
change. As he put it in 1878, it was largely thanks to the socialists that there
was at present a general agreement that 'all social resources should be devoted
to the material, intellectual, and moral improvement of all'.[182] In other words,
there was a fundamental ethical component in socialism which could not be
ignored by the Republican state. While Littré did not believe in government
intervention in labour disputes he urged the state to keep a close eye on the
conflict between labour and capital, 'one of the greatest events in modern evolution';[183] and in one of his very last articles he endorsed the notion of 'moral
socialism' and urged socialists and republicans alike to reflect hard about the
incidence of alcoholism and poverty among workers.[184] In his final years
Littré seemed to believe again in the possibility of an alliance between republicans and socialists. He noted with pleasure that the socialist leader Jules
Guesde had urged his comrades to support the Republic in its battle against
the monarchy in 1877.[185] Although the new Republic could not be socialist,
Littré concluded, socialists should always be listened to and respected under a
republican regime.[186]

After his rupture with Comte Littré was evidently ambivalent about his
political and intellectual relationship with socialism. In the early 1870s he
rejected the government's attempts to inhibit French workers from affiliating
to the International, and announced that he would vote against any such
measure in the National Assembly—even though he had utterly disapproved
of the International's encouragement of the Paris Commune.[187] His position
here seemed to be based on his strong distaste for repressive measures against
any forms of political belief, a stance which we shall encounter again in his
religious politics. However, throughout the 1870s Littré was also resolutely
hostile to granting any form of amnesty to the Communards, despite the
growing pleas of the republican left and the extreme left. The Commune, he

---

[180] Littré, 'Remarques sur le socialisme', 422–3.
[181] Littré, 'Préambule', in Aroux, Félix, *Ce que c'est que le socialisme. Projet de discours à un Congrès*
(Paris: Germer Baillière, 1870), 9.
[182] Littré, *Conservation Révolution Positivisme*, 189.
[183] Littré, 'Du programme de politique conservatrice', in *La Philosophie Positive*, July–August 1873,
in *De l'établissement de la Troisième République*, 226.
[184] Littré, 'Un cas de socialisme moral', *La Philosophie Positive* (September–October 1880), 309–11.
[185] Littré, *Conservation Révolution Positivisme*, 189.
[186] Ibid., 190.   [187] Littré, 'Remarques sur le socialisme', 421–2.

retorted, had not only acted with unqualified moral barbarism, it had also been inexcusably inept from a political standpoint.[188]

How is this *mélange* of generosity and inflexibility, not to say vindictiveness, to be explained? Littré's harshness towards revolutionary socialism stemmed partly from his sense of guilt at not having sufficiently distanced himself from hard-line socialists throughout the period between the late 1840s and the early 1870s. In the immediate aftermath of the Commune the conservative press in Paris asserted that some of Littré's earlier writings, notably certain blood-curdling passages in the first edition of *Conservation Révolution Positivisme*, had provided the ideological inspiration for the insurrection. Although he vehemently rejected such claims Littré was undoubtedly stung by them. In any event he did not need to be reminded that the Commune had damaged the republican cause and that its excesses had temporarily held up the struggle against monarchical and conservative forces. Yet these 'republican' qualms about socialism did not drown out Littré's 'sociological' voice. It is evident that Littré's 'sympathy'[189] for a peaceful, gradualist, and pragmatic form of socialism remained a powerful underpinning of his political thought throughout the 1860s and 1870s, and that he hoped that French workers would follow the lead given by their moderate counterparts in Britain and Germany.

This inescapable conclusion invites three general remarks about Littré's republicanism. To begin with, the imprint of his Comtian phase remained very deep, and effectively more so than he seemed willing to acknowledge. As we noted earlier, Littré claimed explicitly to have rejected Comte's view that socialism had a capacity to articulate universal values. Yet his own recognition that socialism had to be credited with creating an awareness of the need for greater justice in the material, intellectual, and moral spheres was essentially a restatement of the same position. Furthermore it is clear that socialism performed an important function in Littré's conception of positivism, providing a fruitful terrain for the development of social and economic investigations. It is worth remembering here that Littré had identified political economy as one of the disciplines which positivists ought to cultivate more assiduously. His embrace of socialism as an object of social enquiry partly enabled him to move in this direction. This explains why Littré seemed to regard the tentative and underdeveloped condition of his 'pragmatic' socialism in France as an opportunity rather than a constraint: 'it is through experience, which lends itself to everything, that we should begin, and not through systems, which lend themselves to nothing.'[190]

Yet—here we come to the final point—Littré's embrace of socialism, both for its substantive values and for the 'positive' knowledge it could help elicit about social and economic relations, raises some awkward questions about his

---

[188] Littré, 'Question de sociologie pratique: par quelle conduite la république française peut-elle consolider le succès qu'elle a obtenu?', in *La Philosophie Positive* (March–April 1879), 300.

[189] A term he used explicitly in the 1870s, in, for example, 'Remarques sur le socialisme', 428; 'Un cas de socialisme moral', 308.

[190] Littré, 'Socialisme', *La Philosophie Positive* (May–June 1870), 409.

republicanism. Why did the moral sympathy which Littré regarded as an essential component of our humanity not spring from republican sources? And why, similarly, was the study of the social and economic conditions of workers not an ongoing concern of the Republican state? The intellectual strengths of socialism with which Littré identified also represented an implicit acknowledgement on his part that there were significant deficiencies in these areas in republican doctrine—and practice. This recognition of republican failings will appear in manifest terms in Littré's reassessment of the political experience of the nineteenth century, as we shall see next.

The 'Just Preponderance of Time'

The superiority of the republican form of government over its monarchical, imperial, and revolutionary alternatives was one of the main objects of political argument in France during the 1870s. Littré's important contribution to this debate was to offer a complex and highly original philosophical justification of the emerging republican order—a justification which was largely grounded in his equation of the latter with the accomplishment of the historical laws of social development. The Republic, in his elegant and oft-quoted expression, was 'the regime which best allows time to keep its just preponderance'.[191] This formula captured the essence of Littré's republican philosophy, which integrated the principles championed by Gambetta and his allies into a positivist conception of history.[192] The 'just preponderance of time' could be interpreted in three dimensions: historically, it saw the Republic as the culmination of an inexorable process of social evolution, a process whose 'primary laws' concerning the successive stages of human development had been uncovered by positivist science;[193] politically, it was predicated upon the failure of all previous monarchical regimes to avoid war and despotism and to accommodate themselves to social and political change;[194] sociologically, *enfin*, it was the product of an understanding by republican elites of the need for ideological temperance and respect for present circumstances, which were not to be 'violated'.[195] Littré's formula was not only intricate but also astute in that it claimed to offer a justification of the Republic which was grounded neither in the vagaries of the Revolutionary era nor in the abstractions of a preconceived ideological blueprint. The notion of the 'just preponderance of time' was intended as a fundamental inversion of the 'Jacobin' model of republicanism, which since the 1790s had sought to promote a purely 'rationalist' politics on the basis of a prior—and comprehensive—conception of the

---

[191] Littré, 'Préface', *De l'établissement de la Troisième République*, x.
[192] On the political context of this period, see Grévy, *La République des opportunistes 1870–1885*.
[193] Littré, *Conservation Révolution Positivisme*, 217.
[194] Littré, 'De la durée de la République', *La Philosophie Positive*, November–December 1879, in *De l'établissement de la Troisième République*, 512–16.
[195] Littré, 'D'une influence de la philosophie positive en nos affaires', *La Philosophie Positive*, July–August 1878, in *De l'établissement de la Troisième République*, 439.

good life. Under the influence of positivism, the new republicanism advocated by Littré sought instead to mould itself into the immediate context: its motto was to 'comply with the situation by directing it'.[196] In Littré's summary: 'this means that the republic today, the Third Republic, the necessary republic[197] should originate not from some theoretical formula, but from a precise accommodation to men, facts, and things.'[198] This was in effect his definition of the 'opportunist' philosophy of the new republican elites in the 1870s:

> By opportunism I understand the care which those who guide our public destinies take in accommodating all moral and material interests for the sake of the common good, that is by preparing what is best adapted to circumstances.[199]

This sober and pragmatic politics was typically contrasted with the political programme of the Radicals, whose 'advanced' republican platform—amnesty to the Communards, anticlericalism, separation of Church and state, abolition of the Senate and of the presidency, and administrative political accountability—Littré rejected as entirely inappropriate for the volatile political context of the 1870s.[200]

Despite what some of its critics alleged, opportunism was not a purely empiricist method of politics. It was guided by the twin principles of order and progress. But the first was clearly a more valued commodity than the second. Order and conservation were prioritized as the supreme principles of the new Republic: 'order is the guarantee of our internal peace, of our work, of our wealth, of our reorganization, and of the consolidation of our republic. It is on this basis that it [the republic] must be profoundly conservative.'[201] This conservative Republic stood for 'peaceful legality',[202] which guaranteed the freedoms of all citizens irrespective of their religious or political beliefs; here Littré particularly emphasized the importance of freedom of thought and opinion and freedom of worship.[203]

A fundamental source of order in the republican state was the regular practice of universal suffrage. This was a complex problem for Littré, and his position on the matter was carefully nuanced. On one level he continued to assume his positivist heritage, which was essentially sceptical of the value of the mass vote. Popular suffrage, he thus wrote in 1880, was not a universal right but merely a function, conferred upon the individual who 'according to the circumstances is fit to fulfil it for the common good'.[204] He also continued

---

[196] Littré, 'La situation fait sentir sa force', *La Philosophie Positive* (July–August 1874), 145.

[197] A pun on Adolphe Thiers' formula of 'necessary liberties', which had been one of the decisive slogans of the liberal opposition to the Second Empire during the 1860s. As we shall soon note, Littré strongly identified with the conservative liberalism of Thiers.

[198] Littré, 'Le moment actuel', in *La Philosophie Positive*, May–June 1873, in *De l'établissement de la Troisième République*, 199.

[199] Littré, 'Question de sociologie pratique', 299.

[200] Ibid., 299–303.

[201] Littré, 'Politique du jour', in *La Philosophie Positive*, November–December 1872, in *De l'établissement de la Troisième République*, 177.

[202] Littré, *Conservation Révolution Positivisme*, 142.   [203] Littré, 'Politique du jour', 178.

[204] Littré, 'De l'établissement brusque et sans transition du suffrage universel en 1848', *La Philosophie Positive*, July–August 1880, in *De l'établissement de la Troisième République*, 149.

explicitly to reject any 'metaphysical' doctrine of popular sovereignty. When the radical and revolutionary republicans referred to *le peuple*, he stated somewhat acidly, they tended to denote a specific social group such as the working class or the inhabitants of cities such as Paris, Lyon, Marseille, and Bordeaux— or merely themselves. But these were mere sections of the community; the only *real* people whom republicans should recognize were the 'sociological' majorities produced by universal suffrage.[205] This was the other side of the coin. Littré saw that, on the whole, universal suffrage tended to vote for order and stability—provided its voters were educated.[206] In any event, regular elections provided a mechanism for change and re-evaluation. When, for example, the mass vote had returned a monarchist majority, as in 1871, it had very rapidly 'corrected' this mistake by returning republican majorities in 1876 and 1877.[207]

The popular vote thus occupied a considerable strategic position in Littré's notion of 'the just preponderance of time'. It also provided the institutional means of operating two key principles underpinning the new order: 'patience' and 'breadth'. The latter was needed so as to include as many converts as possible under its fold, and the former in order not to challenge existing interests by excessively brusque policy changes.[208] Social reform was thus not abandoned but effectively delayed by making it conditional upon the political appreciations of republican statesmen, wisely counselled by positivist principles: 'the legitimate Republic, if we understand by this a better arrangement of social forces, will come about only through experience, in other words through a gradual perfectioning of what exists with the help of the meditations of heads of state and the suggestions of sociology.'[209] These 'suggestions', which illustrated the influence of positivism on the emerging political order, were usefully summarized by Littré for the benefit of the republican leadership: policy should be made not in the abstract but after taking into account the historical experiences of the citizenry; public opinion could be won over to the Republic but only through a slow and gradual process of political socialization; problems should be resolved not through reliance upon general theories but by looking for short-term practical solutions.[210] The just preponderance of time, again—with the emphasis on this occasion on means and tactical considerations. The republican form of government, noted Littré, may not have been in existence for as long as the monarchy, but it was also beginning to acquire a 'tradition'—and its success would be based on the continuation of that tradition.[211]

[205] Littré, 'La Paix Probable', *La Philosophie Positive*, July–August 1878, in *De l'établissement de la Troisième République*, 455–6.

[206] Littré, 'De la méthode en sociologie', *La Philosophie Positive* (March–April 1870), 294.

[207] Littré, *Conservation Révolution Positivisme*, 121.

[208] Littré, 'Politique du jour', 183.   [209] Littré, *Conservation Révolution Positivisme*, 236.

[210] Littré, 'Éducation Politique', *La Philosophie Positive*, November–December 1876, in *De l'établissement de la Troisième République*, 388.

[211] Littré, 'De la forme républicaine en France', *La Philosophie Positive*, March–April 1872, in *De l'établissement de la Troisième République*, 156.

So much for Littré's positivist account of the emergence of the new republican order, which was essentially a teleological narrative of the accomplishment of historical laws. The superiority of the republican form of government, it suggested, almost spoke for itself: all the Republic needed to do was to continue to establish itself 'by the fact'.[212] Yet when Littré cast a retrospective historical eye over the republican tradition in nineteenth century France this ideological superiority appeared anything but self-evident. As we have already noted, he was highly ambivalent about the 1789 Revolution, the central myth of all French republican generations during the first half of the nineteenth century. His identification with this period was ultimately grounded more in family tradition and loyalty than in an explicit communion with the chronology and characters of the epoch.

As to the republican political legacy prior to 1871, Littré was nothing short of scathing. Between 1789 and 1848, he asserted, republicanism had been thoroughly perverted, notably by the 'anarchical inspirations' of Jean-Jacques Rousseau, whose decisive intellectual influence had turned the republican idea into a heterogenous and metaphysical political doctrine.[213] On the few occasions when he explicitly praised republican figures from those generations, such as the legendary editor of the *National* Armand Carrel, Littré focused more on his personal virtues and charismatic qualities than on his political thought, core elements of which he fundamentally disagreed with.[214] Furthermore—scarcely surprising given its precarious theoretical foundations—republican political practice during much of the nineteenth century had proved consistently ineffectual. The First and Second Republics had failed to sustain themselves over time and had collapsed into Bonapartist despotism.

In his late political writings Littré also frequently returned to the question of political violence and its justification. There were in his mind only three historical examples of legitimate rebellion against the state: the English and American revolutions and the French revolution of 1830.[215] Surprisingly, there was no mention of 1789—so much again for Renan's view of Littré as a child of the Revolution!; unsurprisingly, he roundly condemned the June 1848 revolt of workers, the 1851 Bonapartist *coup d'état*, and the 1871 Paris Commune, none of which in his view represented a valid resort to force. More interestingly, he also censured the February 1848 revolution, which he regarded as an illegal seizure of power.[216] And such illegal acts, he added, could not be retrospectively vindicated through universal suffrage: if it were accepted that the Second Republic was effectively legitimized in this way, then

---

[212] Littré, 'Le moment actuel', 198.   [213] Littré, 'Éducation Politique', 384.

[214] Carrel, he wrote, was fundamentally wrong in his appreciation that France should have gone to war in the early 1830s to defend Belgium and Poland. But Littré nonetheless paid a warm tribute to his integrity, identifying him as one of a race of men who possessed 'a happy spontaneity which admits neither perverse inspirations, nor shameful advice; their soul is a privileged terrain upon which deadly germs cannot alight.' Littré, 'Armand Carrel', in Littré, Émile and Paulin, J.-B. Alexandre (eds), *Oeuvres politiques et littéraires d'Armand Carrel*, Vol. 1 (Paris : Chamerot, 1857), lix.

[215] Littré, *Conservation Révolution Positivisme*, 127.

[216] Littré, 'Expérience rétrospective au sujet de notre plus récente histoire', *La Philosophie Positive* (July–December 1879), 144–7.

the same argument had to be allowed for the Second Empire.[217] Littré's point here was that for too much of the nineteenth century French politics had been dominated by a culture of violence, and the republicans had more than amply contributed to this sorry state of affairs.[218] Hence his melancholic conclusion: the republican political record for most of the nineteenth century was 'appalling' and the republicans' responsibility for many of the country's political failings could not be overlooked. [219] It might be convenient to blame Napoleon III for the political and military catastrophes of 1870–1, but this was not the entire story: 'let us not ignore our own culpability.'[220]

Littré therefore drew no ideological inspiration whatsoever from his diachronic account of the republican tradition in the nineteenth century. Even more intriguingly, a close inspection of his writings suggests that his praise for the temperate strategies pursued by the opportunists in the 1870s relied largely on his identification with the values and sense of leadership of figures who were not explicitly associated with republicanism. Particularly instructive here is his resolute support for Adolphe Thiers, the liberal monarchist statesman who emerged as the linchpin of the political process in the early 1870s.[221] Littré established a close personal and intellectual rapport with Thiers. He welcomed his energetic leadership in suppressing 'the anarchical pretensions of the big cities'[222] in 1871; and in the immediate aftermath of the 1871 elections, which saw Littré's election to the National Assembly, he supported his emphasis on the need for a period of political calm and internal reconstruction.[223] And when Thiers vented his frustration with the National Assembly in 1872 by threatening to resign Littré was one of the delegation of parliamentarians who visited the president to ask him to remain in office.[224] What was the basis of Littré's identification with Thiers? Above all he praised his 'wise political empiricism'[225] and his recognition that the Republic could be founded only if it was grounded in the positivist principles of order and progress: order based on social conservatism and progress on the provision of basic political and intellectual freedoms.[226] Political empiricism, it should be noted, had long been a hallmark of the French Orleanist liberal tradition, and, after vigorously denouncing it during his Comtian years, Littré was here explicitly attempting to bring this conception of politics into the republican fold. It was only on such a basis, he believed, that the new regime could hope to appeal to the peasantry, the majority of the French working population and the electoral key to political stability.[227] Thiers was effectively a symbol of cer-

---

[217] Littré, 'Expérience rétrospective au sujet de notre plus récente histoire', *La Philosophie Positive* (July–December 1879), 149.

[218] Ibid., 151.   [219] Ibid.

[220] Littré, 'Sur la situation que les derniers événements ont faite à l'Europe', 137.

[221] On his critical role during this period see Guiral, Pierre, *Prévost-Paradol 1829–1870. Pensée et action d'un libéral sous le Second Empire* (Paris: Presses Universitaires de France, 1955), 370–489.

[222] Littré, 'Préface', *De l'établissement de la Troisième République*, v.

[223] Littré, *Conservation Révolution Positivisme*, 77–8.

[224] Littré, 'De la forme républicaine en France', 152.

[225] Littré, 'D'une influence de la philosophie positive', 433.

[226] Littré, *Conservation Révolution Positivisme*, 2.

[227] Littré, 'D'une influence de la philosophie positive', 436.

tain key conservative liberal qualities which the republicans themselves did not yet fully possess, notably 'wisdom, prudence, and moderation'.[228] To highlight this ideological borrowing Littré recognized that the republican regime which he hoped to establish was a 'bastard' regime,[229] the product of an alliance between the republican left and the 'centre-left', former liberal monarchists who had rallied to the Republic.[230]

Littré's justification the superiority of the republican form over its ideological competitors thus produced some curious tensions. The positivist vindication of the new republican order as 'the just preponderance of time' was meant to rest on a vision of the accomplishment of historical laws and the rejection of abstract 'metaphysical' theorizing. However, on neither of these scores were his arguments entirely consistent. There was a strong diachronic tension between his *positivist* thought that the Republic was a product of social laws and his forceful *historical* realization that the republican political record for most of nineteenth century had been little short of disastrous. In the positivist scheme of things, events were meant to unfold gracefully and inexorably until the 'revelations' of the new scientific era of politics impressed themselves upon the entire community. Instead of this smooth operation of historical laws, Littré found history to be governed by brute force and prejudice: 'once the deed is done, everyone follows his instincts, his opinions, his judgement, his interests, and takes his place among political groups.'[231] On the face of it, his record as a scourge of the 'metaphysical' components of republican doctrine appeared more successful. There was little doubt that Littré dispensed with many of the cardinal political myths of the republican tradition, notably the holy trinity of liberty-equality-fraternity and the attachment to the principles of popular sovereignty. Most importantly, he succeeded in detaching the justification of the Republic from the turbulent and controversial events of the 1790s. But it is arguable that the vacuum created by this displacement of the Revolutionary myth was merely filled by a construct of a different ideological provenance, namely, liberalism. It was a commonplace among nineteenth-century French liberals that constitutions should be based not on ideological and historical blueprints but on the imperatives of the moment. The liberties which Littré promoted as most essential—freedom of opinion, religious practice and education, and property ownership—were also quintessentially liberal freedoms. And the moral and political qualities which republicans so lacked, and which were so typified by a statesman such as Thiers—order, incrementalism, moderation, consensus—were drawn in large measure from the value system of French liberalism. Littré's Republic, in short, was rooted in the central ideological myths of the liberal tradition: something of a paradox, it will be granted, both from a republican standpoint and from a neo-Comtian perspective.

---

[228] Littré, *Conservation Révolution Positivisme*, 235.   [229] Ibid., 235–6.
[230] Littré, 'D'une influence de la philosophie positive', 435.
[231] Littré, 'Expérience rétrospective', 149.

The Political Foundations of
Positivist Republican Citizenship

'It is in my capacity as a European, not as a French person, that I speak.'[232] The occasion for this 'cosmopolitan' statement was Littré's spirited protest against the Second Empire's lavish commemorations of the centenary of Napoleon Bonaparte's birth in 1869. But this careful formulation was revealing as to his open and inclusive conception of his territorial and political identity—a point which invites a closer examination of Littré's complex notion of citizenship.

In the same article Littré went on to note that all enlightened individuals were members of at least two *patries*, one being their native land, the other(s) representing universal moral, spiritual, and political ideals.[233] In his political writings in the 1860s and 1870s he constantly stressed that his special devotion to his French homeland went hand-in-hand with his love for the 'universal homeland' constituted by the European totality and, at a more abstract level, by humanity as a whole.[234] A throwback to his days as an orthodox Comtian, this concept of the 'universal homeland' illustrated the continuities in Littré's cosmopolitan thinking between the 1840s and early 1880s. The two levels of citizenship it denoted—the national and European—were complemented by a third sphere, about which he also expressed a strong commitment: the local. In the opening issue of *La Philosophie Positive* in the summer of 1867 Littré stressed that an essential precondition for a just political order was liberty, and he welcomed the emergence of 'self-government' across the European continent.

The peoples' management of their own affairs was one of the key demands of the liberal and republican opposition to the Second Empire, and it included both an advocacy of stronger representative institutions at the national level and an enhancement of local and territorial forms of democracy. In endorsing this notion of self-government Littré argued that it served three essential functions in the political system: providing better government through greater accountability, creating a more informed citizenry through wider political participation, and developing stronger civic bonds by opening public awareness to local and national issues.[235] In this section we shall dissect Littré's conceptions of overlapping citizenship at the European, national, and local levels. In doing so we shall proceed through three parallel sets of comparisons: first through observation of the interplay among its three different levels; second through an assessment of their respective evolution over time, especially after the 1870–1 events; and third through the ideological interaction among republicanism, liberalism, and positivism, each element of which appeared to pull Littré's notion of citizenship, especially its ideal of self-government, in somewhat conflicting directions.

---

[232] Littré, 'Centième anniversaire de la naissance de Napoléon I', 187.   [233] Ibid., 187.
[234] Littré, *Conservation Révolution Positivisme*, 398.   [235] Littré, 'Politique', 139.

Littré's warm identification with the peoples and civilizations of Europe and their historical traditions was very much in evidence in his late political thought. His interest in other European cultures was marked, and one of the many illustrations of this intellectual cosmopolitanism was his involvement in Dollfus's and Nefftzer's *Revue Germanique* (1858–68).[236] The opening issue of *La Philosophie Positive* hailed Europe as a 'vast and glorious' community, and boldly asserted that European issues would be given a prominent position in the journal: 'to the national interest we substitute the European interest.'[237] One of the central European interests of the late 1860s was the question of peace, and in the autumn of 1867 Littré prophetically denounced those around Napoleon III who pressed for a war against Prussia as a means of diverting public attention away from the regime's declining domestic support.[238] His endorsement of the republican peace programme took him to Geneva, where he attended the international conference convened by Jules Barni's Ligue Internationale pour la Paix et la Liberté, an event which symbolized in his mind the positive contributions made by European public opinion to the cause of liberty.[239] Liberty and peace seemed indissoluble to him at this point. As he wrote in his account of the 1867 Geneva congress:

To praise liberty is to praise peace; to praise peace is to praise liberty. This is the spirit which drives to the benevolent Congress of Geneva the renowned representatives of the ideas of progress and fraternity to symbolize the union of nations.[240]

Littré was not at all starry-eyed about the prospects for peace: he noted that there was still much sabre-rattling in Europe, and that public opinion was troubled but not necessarily revolted by the threat of war. He also identified the desire for military glory and expansion as one of the central underpinnings of German unification.[241] The republican goal of a pan-European federation was therefore a worthy idea, but only if it was accompanied by 'more knowledge' and 'more justice and humanity'.[242] In short, as Mazzini had correctly noted, moral autonomy and political liberty were essential preconditions of peace—and as long as despotic and autocratic regimes continued to reign the threat of war would remain.[243]

The Franco-Prussian war of 1870–1 shattered Littré's hopes for a peaceful evolution of Europe towards greater liberty. Like most republicans of his generation, the war also led him to reconsider his visceral opposition to standing armies. In the 1870s he thus strongly supported the nation's 'military

---

[236] Digeon, Claude, *La crise allemande de la pensée française (1870–1914)* (Paris: Presses Universitaires de France, 1959), 42.

[237] Ibid., 127.

[238] Littré editorial, *La Philosophie Positive* (September–October 1867), 324.

[239] Both Littré and Wyrouboff attended the Congress. For the full list of French republican grandees who came to Geneva in September 1867, see Scheurer-Kestner, Auguste, *Souvenirs de jeunesse* (Paris: Charpentier, 1905), 108–9.

[240] Ibid., 325.

[241] Littré, 'Pangermanisme et panslavisme', *La Philosophie Positive* (November–December 1867), 470.

[242] Ibid., 475.   [243] Ibid., 473.

The most powerful evidence for this semantic shift was his increasing emphasis on fear and anxiety as the grounding principles of French republican patriotism after 1871. During the Franco-Prussian war patriotic sentiment had been awakened and nurtured, in his view, because of the very threat posed to the French nation's survival.[256] In an article written in 1875 he explicitly linked France's occupation and defeat in 1870–1, the imperative of rearmament, and the generation of patriotic sentiment:

We must reorganize ourselves militarily with an inflexible determination, and retreat before no sacrifice, either material or moral, and nurture in our hearts a serious love of our homeland. In our reconstitution, let us never forget what it is to be defeated and invaded.[257]

Two years later he remarked that he had witnessed three invasions and occupations of France: in 1814, 1815, and 1870–1; he did not wish to live to see a fourth iteration.[258] His had now in effect become a Hobbesian republican patriotism, forged not so much out of love for his country's public institutions and a cosmopolitan communion with France's neighbours as out of fear: fear of internal political disintegration, fear of external attack, and fear of the people's bellicose instincts.

What of the third tier of Littré's conception of republican citizenship, the local sphere? Here, too, his discourse followed a somewhat sinuous course. During the Second Republic Littré gained first-hand experience of the appeals but also the vicissitudes of local politics, serving as a councillor for the Paris municipality for a short while in the aftermath of the February 1848 Revolution. However, he rapidly became disillusioned with the turn of events in Paris and tendered his resignation.[259] During the Second Empire, as we have already noted, Littré endorsed the concept of 'self-government', a notion which typically included the advocacy of greater local democracy. Shortly after the fall of the Second Empire and the end of the Franco-Prussian war he returned to local office, this time as a member of the Conseil Général of the Seine; in October 1871 this assembly of local notables elected him as their Vice-President.[260] Throughout the 1870s Littré was consistent in his support for some degree of decentralization. He thus voted for and publicly welcomed the local government laws voted by the National Assembly,[261] and explicitly commended the law on General Councils, even though it had been voted by a monarchist majority.[262]

In 1877 *La Philosophie Positive*, clearly with its editor's blessing, carried a series of articles by the republican pamphleteer Arthur Hubbard on 'commu-

---

[256] Littré, *Conservation Révolution Positivisme*, 398.

[257] Littré, 'La Prusse et la France devant l'histoire', *La Philosophie Positive*, January–February 1875, in *De l'établissement de la Troisième République*, 100.

[258] Littré, 'Les deux issues de la crise du 16 Mai', *Le Temps*, 4 October 1877, in *De l'établissement de la Troisième République*, 420.

[259] 'Émile Littré', in Robert, Bourloton, and Cougny (eds), *Dictionnaire des parlementaires français*, Vol. 4, 167.

[260] Ibid., 168.   [261] Littré, 'Politique du jour', 178.

[262] Littré, 'De la durée de la République', 520.

nal franchises', which offered a vibrant plea for greater municipal democracy. The articles were explicitly directed at those Jacobin republicans 'who believe that democracy consists in ruining the local spirit'.[263] Writing from an explicitly republican municipalist perspective, Hubbard pressed the government to extend the political and juridical powers of communal governments and to end the statutory constraints imposed by the administrative trusteeship (*tutelle administrative*), which placed these elected bodies under the surveillance of prefectoral authorities.[264] He ended by calling on all republicans to band together to form 'a league for the restitution of communal franchises'.[265] Littré explicitly endorsed this call for local political empowerment in 1877 when he urged fellow-republicans to make use of the Tréveneuc law in the event of an illegal conservative challenge to the Republic. This legislation had been passed by the National Assembly in the early 1870s so as to enable departmental councils to assume the constitutional powers of the state during any attempted *coup d'état* against the government in Paris. Littré's support for this law, which effectively endorsed the elected departmental assemblies as effective substitutes of the central republican state in times of emergency and national crisis, thus appeared as a further vindication of his commitment to the cause of local democracy.

Littré's late political thinking seemed to be fully supportive of the notion of greater local empowerment, a position which was fully consistent with his 'liberal republican' goal of cultivating a stronger civic sense in France through greater mass participation. But his permissive position on the issue of decentralization was rendered more complicated by his 'positivist' heritage, which in many ways pulled him in a radically opposite direction. In 1859 and 1862 Littré had written two comprehensive reviews of Charles Dupont-White's works, *L'Individu et l'État* and *La Centralisation*. His assessment of the first was glowing: he praised the author's vigorous style and agreed with his fundamental conclusion that the progressive development of society, and of the individuals who composed it, could occur only through the state. Littré specifically endorsed Dupont-White's rejection of Guizot's ideal of individual liberation through the emergence of a 'non-governed society'.[266]

As to the second book, while Littré disagreed with Dupont-White's emphasis on race as the critical underpinning of French centralization, he fully supported the liberal Jacobin pamphleteer's claim that the growth of state institutions, based on the development of scientific government, was the defining characteristic of the modern age. He also approved of Dupont-White

---

[263] Hubbard, Arthur, 'Les franchises communales', *La Philosophie Positive* (January–February 1877), 133.

[264] Hubbard, Arthur, 'Les franchises communales' (suite), *La Philosophie Positive* (March–April 1877), 228–44.

[265] Hubbard, Arthur, 'Les franchises communales' (suite et fin), *La Philosophie Positive* (May–June 1877), 425.

[266] 'une société non-gouvernée'. Littré, 'Du progrès dans les sociétés et l'État', *Revue des Deux Mondes* (15 April 1859).

The Conspiracies of Tolerance

The relative thinness of Littré's conception of citizenship from the perspective of individual political empowerment was not entirely surprising. For the republican positivists the key to redefining the civic order lay as much in political as in ethical change; and in this respect they were entirely representative of the republican ideological mainstream after 1851. The two decades of the Second Empire were seen as years of moral corruption and decadence by all republicans, and it was hoped that the advent of the new political order in the 1870s would trigger a much-needed process of moral regeneration in French society.

These ethical concerns were very much shared by Littré. As we noted earlier, the development of a positivist republican morality lay at the heart of his own ideological project after his rupture with Comte. His twin goals were to elaborate a specifically positivist ethics, which could incorporate republican concerns about the protection and promotion of individuals, and at the same time ideologically to sanitize republicanism, notably through divesting its value system of all morally noxious 'metaphysical' elements. In this final section we shall outline and evaluate Littré's philosophy and practice of secular moralism. In so doing we shall attempt to determine how far this 'secular saint', to use Pasteur's expression,[273] was able to enact his own civic ideals at a personal level, and more broadly how successfully his ethical vision compensated for the ambiguities in his political conception of citizenship.

The cornerstone of Littré's late moral philosophy, both theoretically and practically, was his affiliation to the Freemasonry in 1875. Claude Nicolet is right, in this context, to present Littré's two key Masonic texts of 1875 and 1876 as 'the outline of a moral testament'.[274] Littré's tryst with the Masonry was symbolic at multiple levels. For the Grand Orient de France, the main Masonic organization in the early Third Republic, the initiation of one of the country's most eminent men of science and letters—Littré had been elected to the Académie Française in December 1871—represented a milestone. For many contemporary observers Littré's affiliation to the lodge Clémente Amitié was the nineteenth century equivalent of the initiation of Voltaire almost a hundred years earlier.[275] It was no less an historic occasion for the 'opportunist' wing of the republican party, which celebrated Littré's embrace of Masonic principles as a portent of its own ideological ascendancy; it was in this sense highly significant that Jules Ferry was initiated at the same ceremony as Littré, in the presence of much of the republican political establish-

---

[273] Speech at the Académie Française, 27 April 1882, quoted in *La Philosophie Positive* (July–August 1882), 139.

[274] Nicolet, Claude, 'Littré et la République', in *Actes du Colloque Littré, 7–9 Octobre 1981* (Paris, 1983), 473.

[275] Caubet, Jean Marie Lazare, 'Réception d'Émile Littré dans la Franc-Maçonnerie', *La Philosophie Positive* (September–October 1875), 161.

ment.[276] In its immediate internal context, finally, Littré's initiation was a crucial moment in the fierce ideological battle between a religious, philanthropic and essentially apolitical vision of the Masonic ideal on the one hand and a secular, engaged, and republican conception on the other. Since the mid-1860s a growing number of free-thinking republican masons had campaigned for the removal of all references to the 'Great Architect of the Universe'—the consecrated expression for God—in the Masonic constitution. This battle was finally won in 1877, and there is little doubt that Littré's affiliation to the Grand Orient reinforced the hand of the secular republican camp. His speech at the 1875 ceremony on the duties of man towards God was a powerful reaffirmation both of his cult of science and of his philosophical agnosticism in all matters of religious belief. In this sense his embrace of the Masonry symbolized the growing hegemony of republican—and positivist—ideas within the institution: an ideological transformation which would be significantly accentuated in the following decades.[277]

Littré used the occasion of his Masonic initiation speech in 1875 to spell out the broad principles of his social and moral philosophy. Beginning with a pointed rebuke at those who decried the Grand Orient as an institution with machiavellian designs, he highlighted what he regarded as the defining characteristic of the Masonry in modern times:

The masonry has been accused of I know not what clandestine and sinister conspiracies. I know of only one for which I praise it unreservedly: it is, in the midst of all the bitterness and violence of fanaticism, the conspiracy of toleration.[278]

Toleration was not merely a passive sentiment, based on a negative acceptance of others, but an active feeling of empathy with all the forces of progress, both present and past: in short, the cultivation of a sense of open-mindedness and intellectual inclusivity.[279] In this ecumenical spirit he also welcomed the Masonry's celebration of the glorious scientific achievements of humanity across time, irrespective of religious or political beliefs: a celebration which was entirely consistent with the positivist morality of history.[280] Positivist ethics were grounded in the recognition of the existence of immutable laws but also of the transformative potential for human action. Finding an equilibrium between these two poles was the key to felicity: 'the right balance between activity and resignation is the attribute of the positivist conception of the world.'[281]

The boundaries between good and evil were determined by 'conscience', which Littré defined as the aggregate of agreed collective social norms: 'the sum of moral rules which any civilization, any epoch makes prevail in

[276] Among those present were Gambetta, Louis Blanc, Arago, Brisson, and Rouvier. Ibid., 161–2.
[277] On the growth of republicanism and secularism in the Grand Orient during the Second Empire and early Third Republic, see Hazareesingh and Wright, *Francs-Maçons sous le Second Empire*.
[278] Littré speech, 8 July 1875, in Caubet, 'Réception d'Émile Littré dans la Franc-Maçonnerie', 163.
[279] Ibid., 167.   [280] Ibid.   [281] Ibid.

society.'[282] Toleration, in short, was a recipe neither for absolute relativism nor for listless contemplation: it necessitated a continuous search by each individual for the principles and practices of the good life. This was where Littré thought the Masonry, along with other social and political institutions devoted to the public good, could make an invaluable contribution to the emergence of a more ethical and enlightened world.

Littré spelled out the main instrument of this moral quest for greater open-mindedness in a letter written to his fellow-members of the Clémente Amitié in 1876, on the occasion of the first anniversary of his admission to the Masonry.[283] Education was the key to the emergence of this tolerant and open social morality; and it represented a duty both for individuals and for the collectivity: 'the principal duty of man towards himself is education; the principal duty of man towards his fellow-men is to educate them.'[284] Education was linked to the progressive unfolding of scientific understanding, and was in this sense part of the immutable scheme of things. But it was also an imperative for individual and collective endeavour, because by developing a higher sense of morality education would provide the basis for more harmonious social relations: 'we are moving towards a growing dissemination, among men, of enlightenment procured by scientific work, and through this dissemination, a corresponding improvement in social relations.'[285] Beyond its appeal to the Masonry, this aspiration for widespread mass education was to underpin the social philosophy of the Third Republic.[286] It also represented the completion of a virtuous circle: collective conscience, abetted by positive and Masonic principles, would push humanity towards a greater level of self-understanding, which would create more toleration; and this, in turn, would raise the overall levels of public conscience. Toleration was thus a way of being open-minded but also a necessary tool for opening up the public mind to the principles of moral progress and modernity.

Through his explicit affiliation to the Freemasonry and its core principle of toleration Littré also situated himself intellectually within the wider community of freethinkers, to which he had a long-standing commitment.[287] 'Nothing can stand against the torrent of free thinking', he had declared enthusiastically in the first edition of *Conservation Revolution Positivisme*, a collection which contained numerous attacks against religious dogmatism and political intolerance.[288] Intellectual and political developments in the 1860s and early 1870s nonetheless led him to introduce some qualifications to his endorsement of the concept of *libre pensée*. In an article written in 1876 he

---

[282] Littré speech, 8 July 1875, in Caubet, 'Réception d'Émile Littré dans la Franc-Maçonnerie', 168.

[283] Littré was unwell and unable to attend this 1876 ceremony at the Grand Orient. His letter was read out by Charles Cousin, and the text published as a separate brochure.

[284] Littré, Émile, *Du devoir de l'homme envers lui-même et envers ses semblables* (Paris: Loge La Clémente Amitié, 1906), 4.

[285] Ibid., 24.   [286] On this theme see Nicolet, *L'idée républicaine*.

[287] See Lalouette, *La libre pensée en France 1848–1940*, 157.

[288] Littré, *Conservation Révolution Positivisme*, 8.

specifically distanced himself from some 'negative' manifestations of free-thinking:

Free thinking, as it very often manifests itself these days, contains a notable component of metaphysics; however we repudiate metaphysics for the same reason as we reject theology. Indeed let us be clear: science cannot include free thinking, as long we understand free thinking to signify a negative and indeterminate disposition.[289]

An unfortunate example of this contrary disposition was atheism, which Littré forcefully condemned as an anarchic and destructive doctrine—as the religious persecutions carried out by the Communards had demonstrated only too clearly.[290] Often accused, unjustly, by his opponents of being an atheist, Littré manifestly resented having his moral views assimilated to a doctrine of which he fundamentally disapproved.[291] Yet once this distinction between atheism and his own position was made clear, Littré was generally willing to include himself in the freethinking camp because he recognized its broad commitment to the ethical principles of toleration and intellectual freedom.[292] It was Littré's ultimate hope that the elements often lacking in freethinking—a constructive and creative intellectual disposition—could eventually be furnished by positivist moral doctrine.[293]

So strong was Littré's attachment to the principles of autonomy and toleration that it overrode his commitment to many other key republican and positivist precepts. This was especially true of his approach to the important issue of secularism. Like most republicans of the early Third Republic, Littré repeatedly affirmed his belief in the principle of a 'secular state',[294] and he expressed the hope that the triumph of the Republic would bring about a secularization of state institutions. As we have already noted, furthermore, his affiliation to the Masonry coincided with the final—and successful—phase of the internal battle for the secularization of the Grand Orient's constitution. In the blunt words of Littré's comrade-in-arms Wyrouboff, initiated at the Clémente Amitié on the same day as his friend: 'fraternity and toleration, here is our religion, we do not need any other.'[295]

But how was this secular principle to be applied in the sphere of education, where religious institutions continued to have a strong stake? Here Littré was much more cautious, generally prioritizing liberty whenever it came into conflict with other social and moral principles. For example, he asserted that the principle of freedom should be broadly applied to the sphere of higher

[289] Littré, 'École de la Philosophie Positive', La Philosophie Positive (May–June 1876), 323.

[290] Littré, review of E. Bourloton and E. Robert, 'La Commune et ses idées à travers l'histoire', 148.

[291] Littré, 'Des rapports de l'Assemblée Nationale avec le pays ou suffrage universel', La Philosophie Positive, January–February 1873, in De l'établissement de la Troisième République, 185.

[292] Ibid., 187.

[293] Littré, 'Le principe de la séparation de l'Eglise et de l'État', La Philosophie Positive, January–February 1877, in De l'établissement de la Troisième République, 399.

[294] See for example his article 'L'intérêt Européen dans notre dernière crise', La Philosophie Positive, January–February 1878, in De l'établissement de la Troisième République, 431.

[295] Speech at 1876 Convent (General Assembly) of the Grand Orient, quoted in Ligou, Daniel, Frédéric Desmons et la Franc-Maçonnerie sous la Troisième République (Paris: Gedalge, 1966), 84.

education. Such a pluralistic regime would enable the state, the Church, and the positivists to try out their respective educational schemes under conditions of open competition.[296] This concession of educational liberty to the Church was not especially welcomed in the republican camp. Littré had to defend his proposal against critics who claimed that this was an asymmetric freedom, which the Catholics would never consider devolving to the republicans if they were in power.[297] It was also, of course, a freedom which ran fundamentally counter to a comprehensive notion of the principle of secularism. But his commitment to this ideal seemed to falter when confronted with any external challenge. Thus Littré expressed clear views about the content of the educational curriculum, and in the 1870s he stood by Comte's view that the teaching of science should henceforth replace France's traditional educational emphasis on the humanities and particularly on literature. His stated preference was that the minimum common education given to all young people should consist exclusively of science.[298] But this positivist scheme was not pushed forward very forcefully. In his 1876 letter to his Masonic brethren Littré stated, somewhat surprisingly, that the ideological gap between the republicans and their opponents on the issue of education was not as great as it was sometimes made to appear: both sides were committed, for example, to the teaching of Greek and Latin.[299] The same ambivalence about the principle of laïcité could be found in Littré's approach to the controversial question of the separation of Church and state, a proposition which was strongly supported by anticlerical republicans, most notably the radicals and socialists. While recognizing that such a separation was in principle valid[300] Littré claimed in the late 1870s that it was not opportune.[301] In an article written in 1876 he went even further, seeming to suggest that such a separation was not fundamentally compatible with French custom and national character—'traditions and habits stand against such a measure':[302] a strange argument both from a positivist and republican standpoint.

Littré's extreme caution in his practical approach to the issue of secularism was in part a function of his turn towards political conservatism in the 1870s, which mirrored the prudence and incrementalism of the opportunist republican governments of the late 1870s and early 1880s. But his stance was not merely tactical. His reluctance to enforce the notion of secularism stemmed from his deep-seated commitment to the principle of toleration, which in his mind brooked no interference by the state in matters of opinion and belief. Already in the early 1870s Littré had severely condemned the monarchist

---

[296] The state, however had, in his view, to retain its monopoly over the award of grades. Littré, 'De la liberté de l'enseignement supérieur', La Philosophie Positive, January–February 1875, in De l'établissement de la Troisième République, 329.

[297] De l'établissement de la Troisième République, 324.

[298] Littré, 'Éducation et séparation du pouvoir spirituel d'avec le pouvoir temporel', 353–4.

[299] Littré, Du devoir de l'homme envers lui-même, 15.

[300] Littré, 'De la liberté de l'enseignement supérieur', 326–7.

[301] Littré, Conservation Révolution Positivisme, 28.   [302] Littré, 'Éducation Politique', 394.

'Moral Order' governments for attempting to suppress republican political and intellectual organizations.[303] His protest was not politically motivated but based on the principle that the modern state had no right to interfere in matters of political belief and philosophical doctrine. Any attempt to do so would be not only counterproductive but also fundamentally inconsistent with the liberal spirit of modern times.[304]

In 1878 he made his position even more explicit: 'it is dangerous to do battle against a spiritual force by means other than spiritual weapons.'[305] The real test of Littré's principles came when the Republic proposed controversial new legislation on higher education whose seventh article explicitly banned religious congregations from French schools. The measure, proposed by Littré's Masonic brother Jules Ferry, now Minister of Education, provoked a furore in the National Assembly and Senate as well as in the national and local press. Religious and conservative groups mobilized to defend the persecuted Jesuits and railed against the 'intolerance' of the new Republic. Despite the injunctions to remain loyal to his camp, Littré sided with the critics of the new legislation, and when the law came to the Senate for ratification in March 1880 he abstained, along with a small number of republican Senators.[306]

While it tested Littré's ethical principles and his support for the new republican regime, the controversy over Article VII also gave him the opportunity to strengthen his theory of political toleration. In 'Le Catholicisme selon le suffrage universel', published in La Philosophie Positive in 1879, he explained that although he believed that the Republic should be secular the principle of laïcité could not override the moral obligation to respect past agreements between Church and state, and this included the Concordat.[307] The problem posed by the Jesuits was not to be underestimated, but Littré distinguished two methods of dealing with it: the 'preventive', which consisted of prohibiting their organization from operating in France, and the 'repressive', which would tolerate them provided they did not break existing laws.[308] The Republic had intended to proceed down the preventive route, but this pre-emptive banning of religious congregations was likely to be counterproductive and, more importantly, would transgress the regime's commitment to intellectual and spiritual freedom.[309]

To those republicans who asked Littré whether this meant that liberty should be provided even for the enemies of freedom, his answer, unlike that of his Revolutionary forebears, was emphatically positive.[310] Only the passage of time could allow the scientific fallacies contained in traditional religious teachings to be dissipated; overt legislative measures could not do so. In a

---

[303] Littré, 'Sept ans de prorogation et de République', La Philosophie Positive, January–February 1875, in De l'établissement de la Troisième République, 294–5.
[304] Ibid., 296–7.
[305] Littré, Conservation Révolution Positivisme, 13.
[306] Robert, Bourloton, and Cougny (eds), Dictionnaire des parlementaires français, 168.
[307] Littré, 'Le Catholicisme selon le suffrage universel', La Philosophie Positive September–October 1879, in De l'établissement de la Troisième République, 494–5.
[308] Ibid., 498.   [309] Ibid., 499.   [310] Ibid., 500.

And what to say of Littré's conversion from the point of view of positivist philosophy? Taken at face value, it threatened the sanctity of one of the most important concepts in Littré's political thought: the passage of time. The more an individual was exposed to the sublimities of science, he repeated throughout his life, the more he would be able to see through the intellectual sham of 'metaphysics'. By providing this striking counter-example to the thesis of the 'just preponderance of time', the manner in which Littré's life ended threatened to bring down one of the key pillars of his positivist edifice.

Conclusion: The Paradoxes of Littré's Republican Positivism

'The temperament was absolutely calm. It was his spirit which was revolutionary.'[321] Renan's immaculate *sens de la formule* captured the essential contours of Littré's republican character and intellectual personality. Behind the calm and somewhat forbidding façade lurked a man of considerable personal qualities and public virtues. Here was a man endowed with a relentless commitment to the pursuit of truth, a strong sense of probity, a consistent inclination towards generosity both material and intellectual, an abiding sense of loyalty—which was demonstrated in Littré's public fidelity to Comte's legacy—and above all a remarkable disposition towards tolerance. His intellectual personality was rightly admired by the wider public for its scientific range and depth and by his colleagues for the creative and influential qualities of his political thought. He also took the republican principles of modesty and austerity to their extremes, perhaps as a reaction against Comte's opposite propensities. In 1863 Littré's friend and editor Hachette wanted to write an article on him to publicize his work on the Dictionary. A terse letter aborted the project: 'I don't care for any attention to be brought to my name.'[322]

If, as Furet rightly put it, science was the great idea which haunted the political imagination of nineteenth century France, Littré was incontestably the principal source of its dissemination in republican political thought.[323] For this reason, his influence on the first generation of republican political leaders was immense. To take but one classic example: it was many of his philosophical insights which underpinned Jules Ferry' education reforms in the 1880s.[324] More broadly Littré has been presented by his admirers as the critical intermediary between orthodox positivism and modern republicanism. In

[321] Renan, Ernest, Speech at the Académie Française, 27 April 1882, quoted in *La Philosophie Positive* (July-August 1882), 142.
[322] Littré, Émile, Letter dated 17 July 1863, Bibliothèque de l'Institut de France, Paris, Fonds Lovenjoul D.605 (Littré letters to Sainte-Beuve).
[323] Furet, François, *La Révolution*, Vol. 2 (Paris : Hachette, 1988), 367.
[324] On this theme see Legrand, Louis, *L'influence du positivisme dans l'oeuvre scolaire de Jules Ferry* (Paris : M. Rivière, 1961); Barral, Pierre, 'Ferry et Gambetta face au positivisme', *Romantisme*, 21–2 (1978), 149–59; and Nicolet, 'Jules Ferry et la tradition positiviste'.

the words of his modern biographer Alain Rey, 'between the closed, utopian, complex and rigid system of Comte and the bourgeois, secular, and satisfied progressivism of Jules Ferry, the social doctrine of Littré is positioned as an indispensable intermediary.'[325] Claude Nicolet takes the point further in his affirmation that Littré's late political thought after 1871 provided the decisive ideological synthesis which founded the Third Republic.[326] Positivism and republicanism were both doctrines which harked back to the Enlightenment's project of establishing a social and political order based on progress; both saw politics as a largely open and intelligible process which appealed to—and relied on—public reason; and both saw education as an indispensable instrument for the creation of a modern citizenry. In both doctrines there were also attempts to formulate new conceptions of spirituality which turned away from conventional religious forms.

All of this seems to suggest that Littré more than amply achieved his intellectual ambition of reconciling positivism and moderate republicanism. Already in the early 1880s this sense of successful closure was palpable, as evidenced by the decision by Charles Robin and Grégoire Wyrouboff to close down the review *La Philosophie Positive* in 1883 on the ostensible grounds that the positivist programme initially devised by Littré had been completed.[327] There can be little doubting the sheer intellectual force of Littré's synthesis of positivist republicanism. Synchronically, it constituted an ideological ensemble which gave a powerful philosophical resonance to the moderate political strategies pursued by Thiers, Gambetta, and Ferry in the 1870s, and thus accentuated in the public mind the distinction between 'republican opportunism' and the conservative and religious opposition to the Republic. The potency of Littré's thought is even more remarkable from a diachronical perspective. When seen across the entire period between 1830 and 1880, Littré's brand of positivist republicanism made a significant contribution to extricating the forces of 'movement' from the difficult and damaging problematic of the 1790s. Contrary to what Renan believed, there was no fetish in Littré's mind for the 1789 Revolution, merely a sentimental attachment grounded in family tradition. From the early 1850s Littré, with the assistance of other mainstream republicans such as Edgar Quinet, proceeded to liquidate the Jacobin legacy from republican social and political thought. He did this by bringing to fruition two parallel enterprises: the 'positivization' of republicanism and 'republicanization' of positivism. Littré eliminated the political authoritarianism which bedevilled the Comtian system and also sacrificed the eccentric spiritualism of the positivist 'cult of humanity'. In political terms he inspired positivists, and republicans more generally, to celebrate the rule of law, to defend representative institutions, and above all to cultivate a sense of toleration towards those with whom they disagreed. Positivism, in short,

---

[325] Rey, *Littré l'humaniste et les mots*, 271.   [326] Nicolet, *L'idée républicaine*.
[327] Robin, Charles and Wyrouboff, Grégoire, *La Philosophie Positive*, 31 (July–December 1883), 322.

Charles Dupont-White, Carnot collection, Chateau de Presles
Courtesy of Mr Thierry and Mrs Caroline Carnot

2

Centralist Defender of the State: The Eclectic Republicanism of Charles Dupont-White

C HARLES Dupont-White (1807–1878) was a French pamphleteer whose writings on political economy, history, philosophy, and politics achieved considerable recognition in French intellectual elite circles during his lifetime. His contemporaries regarded him as a 'famous publicist'.[1] One notable historian of the Second Empire counted him among 'the most distinguished men of the age'.[2] In his conceptual and historical study of the French state, Pierre Rosanvallon described Dupont-White as 'the most eloquent advocate of the principle of centralization in the 19th century'.[3] John Stuart Mill thought him 'an economist of the highest calibre; far superior . . . than most of these gentlemen in their own field'.[4] Juliette Adam, who welcomed him into her home on countless occasions between the early 1850s and the mid-1870s, described him as 'one of the greatest stimulator of ideas that I have known'.[5] Michelet saw him regularly in the 1860s and his *Journal* informs us that he wrote *Nos Fils* while reading Dupont-White.[6]

His views were often cited authoritatively in French philosophical writings on the state in the late nineteenth century;[7] and he came to be regarded in some quarters as the prophet of the emergence of welfare policies.[8] Fame, distinction, and eloquence were among the attributes recognized by many of his peers;[9] yet Dupont-White's writings also provoked adverse reactions and numerous misunderstandings. His celebration of the role of the state and his

[1] Freycinet, Charles de, *Souvenirs 1848–1878* (Paris: Delagrave, 1912), 94.
[2] Zeldin, Theodore, *Émile Ollivier and the liberal Empire of Napoleon III* (Oxford: Clarendon Press, 1963), 125.
[3] Rosanvallon, Pierre, *L'État en France* (Paris: Seuil, 1990), 331.
[4] Letter to Dupont-White, 10 October 1861, in F. Mineka and D. Lindley (eds), *The Collected Works of John Stuart Mill*, Vol. 15 (University of Toronto Press, Routledge Kegan and Paul, 1972), 745.
[5] Adam, Juliette, *Mes premières armes littéraires et politiques* (Paris: Lemerre, 1904), 86.
[6] Michelet, Jules, *Journal* (Paris: Gallimard, 1959).
[7] See for example Fouillée, Alfred, *La science sociale contemporaine* (Paris: Hachette, 1880), 372–4.
[8] See Leroy-Beaulieu, Paul, *L'État moderne et ses fonctions* (Paris: Guillaumin, 1890), 12–13; and Cauwès, Paul, *Cours d'Economie Politique*, Vol. 4 (Paris: Larose et Forcel, 1893), 603.
[9] On the stylistic qualities of his writings, see Augustin Cochin's review article in *Le Correspondant* (September 1858), 181–6.

fierce rejection of 'individualism' drove liberal and monarchist elites to dismiss him as a maverick whose paradoxical views vitiated the quality of his analysis. His belief that France's centralist instincts were the product of race rather than history[10] was at times derided, as for example by the legitimist pamphleteer who lambasted Dupont-White for reducing his countrymen to 'some sort of Hindoos who have to be led to the border'.[11] Others were even less charitable, accusing him of a quasi-Hobbesian penchant for political absolutism. Deriding his 'lamentable philosophy', one of his liberal detractors under the Second Empire thus accused Dupont-White of despising humanity and adoring the state.[12]

Such contrasting assessments were by no means atypical. Indeed, for the historian of nineteenth-century French political thought Dupont-White has always been something of an enigma. His precise location on the ideological spectrum was, and remains, a matter of considerable dispute. While most observers have recognized his intellectual originality,[13] his contemporaries and successors were often so confused by the synthetic range of his views that they identified him with every major *famille de pensée*. Thus one of his colleagues, the writer Maxime Du Camp, presented him in his memoirs as a liberal supporter of the Second Empire;[14] in his history of decentralization in France, in contrast, François Burdeau made him out as an authoritarian Bonapartist, whose language 'appealed to the diehards of imperial democracy'.[15] Critics of his views variously denounced his statist propensities as a worrying echo of 'revolutionary liberalism';[16] as a manifestation of 'degenerate monarchism';[17] or even—and it is not clear whether this is better or worse—as a French form of neo-Hegelianism.[18] For his part, however, his Belgian friend and necrologist Emile de Laveleye saw him as one of the forerunners of the doctrine of 'state socialism' in France.[19] The republican Larousse dictionary was thoroughly mystified by Dupont-White: its first edition depicted him as a 'liberal Catholic',[20] while the 1877 supplement deemed him a conservative Orleanist.[21] Dissatisfied with both labels, the successor *Larousse du XXe siècle* pronounced him to be a Christian socialist.[22] Finally, there were those who like Roger Soltau argued that Dupont-White was 'not so much a Liberal as a Radical Jacobin'.[23] While noting the influences of liberal-

[10] Dupont-White, Charles, 'L'administration locale en France et en Angleterre: De l'Esprit des Races', *Revue des Deux Mondes* (15 August 1862), 884–6.

[11] Raudot, Claude-Marie, *L'administration locale en France et en Angleterre* (Paris: Douniol, 1863), 4.

[12] Barrot, Odilon, *De la centralisation et de ses effets* (Paris: Didier, 1870), 72–3.

[13] For example, Morin, Frédéric, *Les idées du temps présent* (Paris: Michel Lévy, 1863), 273–4.

[14] Du Camp, Maxime, *Souvenirs Littéraires*, Vol. 2 (Paris: Hachette, 1883), 406.

[15] Burdeau, François, *Liberté, Libertés locales chéries* (Paris: Cujas, 1983), 165.

[16] de Ribbes, Charles, *La nouvelle école libérale et la décentralisation* (Marseille, 1859), 6–7.

[17] Faguet, Emile, *Le libéralisme* (Paris: Société Française, 1902), 30.

[18] Schatz, Albert, *L'individualisme économique et social* (Paris: Colin, 1907), 475.

[19] de Laveleye, Emile, *Un précurseur, Charles Dupont-White* (Paris: Imprimerie Nationale, 1878).

[20] *Grand Larousse Encyclopédique*, Vol. 4 (Paris: Larousse, 1961).

[21] *Grand Dictionnaire Universel, Supplement* (Geneva-Paris: Slatkine, 1982), 719.

[22] *Larousse du XXe siècle*, ed. Paul Augé (Paris: Larousse, 1929), 1002–3.

[23] Soltau, Roger, *French Political Thought in the 19th century* (New Haven: Yale University Press, 1931), 260–1.

ism and utilitarianism on his political thought, Claude Nicolet also hailed him as a republican whose doctrine of the state was in his view closely aligned with that of the opportunist republicans of the early Third Republic.[24]

If ever a nineteenth-century French thinker's position on the ideological spectrum was in urgent need of revisitation, therefore, it is Dupont-White's. In what follows we shall endeavour to make sense of the complex and often mercurial quality of his writings. Our overall conclusion, while underscoring the significance of his commitment to the republican cause, will dwell upon Dupont-White's ideological originality. Despite his unflinching commitment to the idea of a strong state, Dupont-White was fundamentally removed from the ideological universe of Bonapartism; equally, it will emerge that his 'socialist' thinking was of a very distinct kind. Furthermore, even though he was in key respects influenced by liberal and republican principles, and made a decisive intellectual contribution to the legitimization of the Third Republic in 1875, his theoretical synthesis was creative and distinctive from both mainstream liberal and republican positions. In a century when thinkers increasingly tended to define themselves by affiliation to specific political movements or ideologies, Dupont-White's independence of thought stands out remarkably.

This intellectual autonomy partly explains why his writings have been largely ignored by posterity. A number of elements conspired to conceal and even occult his writings from later generations. Although he was very well known during his life, he was also an unabashed intellectual elitist, making very little effort to publicize his writings beyond the relatively narrow circles of the Parisian political and intellectual elite within which he gravitated throughout his career.[25] In addition, most of Dupont-White's major political works were published during the Second Empire, a period whose political thought was long undervalued in France and which is only now beginning to receive notable scholarly and even public attention.[26] Furthermore, he was not a self-defined member of any political tendency or philosophical 'school' and left no recognizable disciples. Finally, in so far as his broad intellectual lineage could be identified at all, he was associated with a strand in French political thought which can be defined precisely by its lack of common substantive properties. Dupont-White belonged neither to the Revolutionary tradition, which unreservedly celebrated the heritage of 1789, nor to the anti-revolutionary lineage, which opposed it with equal vigour. He was instead part of a diffuse third group which sought to adapt, qualify, and moderate the legacy of the revolutionary era. This nineteenth-century French

[24] Nicolet, *L'idée républicaine en France*, 453–4.

[25] In the words of one of his associates: 'He had his works published at his own expense and did not even put them up for sale. It did not matter to him that they were bought; his personal fortune was sufficient to meet his needs, and it was for his personal satisfaction that he had his works published.' Bonnefont, Gaston, 'Dupont-White, un penseur contemporain', *Revue Britannique*, 6 (1889), 64.

[26] A recent example of this revival of French interest in the Second Empire is the June 1997 issue of the review *L'Histoire*, entirely devoted to answering the question: 'Should we rehabilitate Napoleon III?'.

version of the 'third way', which included liberals, liberal Catholics, Saint-Simonians, and Bonapartists, was not politically associated with the refounding of modern republicanism after 1871, and for this reason has received much less scholarly attention than the other two traditions.[27]

In the more specific context of the themes pursued in this book, Dupont-White is a crucial figure first and foremost because of this inherent eclecticism. The magnificent complexities of his thought will help to conjure up the richness of the political thinking which shaped the emerging republican order in the second half of the nineteenth century. Dupont-White's political thought also well serves to highlight the significance of cultural context on ideological output. For example, his 'English' background and upbringing constantly moulded his perspective on French politics, and his writings were littered with historical analogies, intellectual comparisons between England and France, and specific views borrowed from thinkers such as Hobbes and Burke. There are also powerful elements of overlap between Dupont-White's statism and the 'nationalist' republican tradition of the American founding fathers, especially James Madison and Alexander Hamilton.[28] His political thinking was also influenced by John Stuart Mill, whose two main political works *On Liberty* and *On Representative Government* he translated into French.[29] More broadly Dupont-White also has much to contribute to our understanding of the interface between republicanism and the French liberal traditions. Especially worthy of note will be the distinct quality of his liberalism, particularly in its complex relationship with the 'Doctrinaire' school typified by Guizot, of whom he is sometimes incorrectly presented as a disciple, and Dupont-White's intellectual justification of the Third Republic, which offers important insights into the reasoning which enabled many Orleanist liberals to rally to the new republican order after 1875.

Finally, Dupont-White's writings are no less revealing when set against the republican intellectual context of their time. In his clear and comprehensive defence of the role of the state this vigorous centralist thinker articulated what many republicans believed but did not explicitly spell out; in this sense his political views were far more representative than might at first glance be apparent. Most fundamentally, Dupont-White's political thought will also bring home the strong resistances to positivism which were mounted in republican and liberal intellectual circles between the 1850s and early 1880s. For although he was on good personal terms with Littré, and moved in the same intellectual coteries during the 1850s and 1860s, Dupont-White was strongly critical of many key aspects of the positivist political platform propounded by Comte's most eminent disciple.

[27] For the division of post-1789 French political culture into these three strands, see Thomson, David, *Democracy in France* (London: Oxford University Press, 1946), 10–35.

[28] I am grateful to Karma Nabulsi for making this point and spelling out its wider implications, and to Marc Stears for underlining the specific similarities between Dupont-White's thought and nineteenth-century English political thought and American nationalist republicanism.

[29] See Villey, Daniel, 'Sur la traduction par Dupont-White de "La Liberté" de Stuart Mill', *Revue d'Histoire Économique et Sociale*, 24 (1938), 193–231.

In short, our argument here is twofold. Dupont-White helped the ideological founding of the Third Republic by providing an intellectual justification for republicanism which appealed to many of the specific concerns of conservative liberals; in this sense his theory of politics opens a window on to the crucial process which broadened the social and political base of the new regime. If Adolphe Thiers provided the conservative liberals with the political guarantees they needed to support the Third Republic in the 1870s, it may be said without exaggeration that Dupont-White, who greatly admired the Orleanist leader,[30] performed the same function at the intellectual level. Furthermore, it will become clear that Dupont-White's political writings cannot be evaluated in the abstract. His political thought was embedded in a plurality of cultural and ideological contexts, and can be adequately understood only when set against these discursive backgrounds. It is generally the absence of such contextualization, or, even worse, the effort to force his thinking into an exclusive ideological straightjacket, which has been the source of most of the errors and misunderstandings concerning the classification of his political thought.

A Life of Detachment and Passion

Charles Dupont-White grew up in an affluent, albeit somewhat unconventional, bourgeois setting. His father Jean-Théodore Dupont was the natural son of the marquis Charles-Marie de Créqui, a wealthy nobleman who left his considerable fortune to the young man.[31] Dupont never accepted the 1789 Revolution, and remained throughout his life a devout and somewhat eccentric Catholic legitimist. He spent the last ten years of his life away from his wife and three children, occasionally breaking his silence with long epistles filled with religious and philosophical homilies.[32]

In June 1798 Jean-Théodore Dupont married Mary, the beautiful daughter of John White, the Lord Mayor of Glastonbury. Their second son, Charles-Brook, was born in 1807. After spending most of his childhood years in Normandy the young boy was sent to Paris for his secondary and higher education; between 1827 and 1829 he was a student at the law faculty. It was in Paris, 'dazzling, electrifying, and sensitive capital',[33] that the young Charles came under the influence of Jacobin republicanism for the first time. Although he was not present in the capital during the revolution which overthrew the Bourbon regime of Charles X, the young Dupont-White warmly welcomed the

---

[30] 'The best type of historian' is how Dupont-White refers to Thiers in one of his letters. See undated letter, probably written just before 1848 Revolution, Cécile Carnot Papers, Archives Carnot, Chateau de Presles.

[31] Villey, Daniel, *Charles Dupont-White, sa vie, son oeuvre, sa doctrine*, Vol. 1 (Paris: Alcan, 1936), 293. Unfortunately the second volume of this work was never published, although it appears to have been completed by the author.

[32] Ibid., 297.

[33] Dupont-White, Charles, *Le progrès politique en France* (Paris: Guillaumin, 1868), 52.

July 1830 Revolution—to the great distress of his father, who wrote him an indignant verse after the event.[34] Despite his later hostility to violent political change, Dupont-White never questioned the necessity and legitimacy of the 1830 Revolution.[35]

Dupont-White was initially destined to a career in the legal profession. In 1836 he purchased a position at the Appeal Court but sold it in 1843, deciding instead to devote himself fully to a life of research and intellectual activity.[36] From this moment onwards he spent his active life between his Parisian apartment and the chateau de la Boitardière in the Touraine region.[37] This idyllic existence was interrupted by the Revolution of 1848, which marked a brief period of active involvement in political life for Dupont-White.[38] Under the Second Republic he served as a member of Louis Blanc's short-lived Government Commission for Workers and also as secretary-general at the Ministry of Justice. He even stood as a republican candidate in parliamentary elections in February 1848 in the Oise and July 1848 in the Seine. Disillusioned by his severe defeat, and increasingly wary of the passionate, unstable, and polarized politics of the republican regime, he resigned from his administrative position in early July 1848.[39] He was then offered an appointment as prefect of the Aude, but declined to take up the post.[40] In a letter to one of his close friends he outlined his disillusionment with the politics of the new regime:

I categorically refused the prefecture of the Aude: it is too little. What an awful dream we are having! Has the fate of a people ever been gambled with in this way? I wanted the Republic, but in truth I am overwhelmed; I did not care for so much universal suffrage. It seems there is a competition between long-standing and recent republicans to see who can be the more impetuous, the more scatterbrained.[41]

This excerpt afford us an early glimpse of many of Dupont-White's key personal and intellectual traits: a boldness of expression, illustrated by the frequent use of categorical terms; a sense of haughtiness, often conveyed through expressions of contempt for the foibles of his fellow-countrymen; an identification with republican institutions, qualified by a feeling of exasperation at the congenital inability of different republican factions to work together; and a visceral hostility towards universal suffrage, which he believed would destabilize the political system. In the same letter Dupont-White advised against the use of universal suffrage for the appointment of the president of the

[34] Villey, *Charles Dupont-White, sa vie, son oeuvre, sa doctrine*, 318–19.

[35] A 'heroic act' is how the 1830 revolution is described in Dupont-White, Charles, *La liberté politique considérée dans ses rapports avec l'administration locale* (Paris: Guillaumin, 1864), 293.

[36] On the circumstances of this decision, see Bonnefont, 'Dupont-White: un penseur contemporain', 61.

[37] Harismendy, Patrick, *Sadi Carnot, l'ingénieur de la République* (Paris: Perrin, 1995), 92.

[38] On the 1848 revolution, see Agulhon, Maurice, *La République au village* (Paris: Plon, 1970), and *Les quarante-huitards* (Paris: Gallimard, 1992).

[39] Harismendy, *Sadi Carnot*, 93.

[40] Villey, *Charles Dupont-White, sa vie, son oeuvre, sa doctrine*, 548.

[41] Undated letter to Gustave de Thou (probably late July 1848), in Cécile Carnot Papers, Archives Carnot, Chateau de Presles, France.

Republic, and warned that the election of Louis Napoleon would provoke 'a real disturbance'.[42] Within a few years of his designation by the people, the Bonapartist prince overthrew the Republic and proclaimed the Second Empire; Dupont-White's worst fears had materialized. But although he was frustrated by the republicans, he did not abandon them in their moment of need: in Victor Hugo's narrative account of the events of December 1851 we find Dupont-White offering shelter in his house to the republican opponents of the Bonapartist *coup d'état*.[43]

This brief encounter with the vagaries of public life left an indelible imprint on Dupont-White. For one thing, it drove him away from any temptation to pursue a career in politics. After the fall of the Second Republic, and excepting his membership of the short-lived imperial Commission of Decentralization in 1870,[44] Dupont-White remained completely detached from active politics. By the early 1850s he had chosen his path: he would be a thinker, writer, and publicist, seeking to exercise influence by addressing himself directly to social elites and the practitioners of politics. Despite an unhappy and eventually unsuccessful marriage to Olympe de Corbie, he also led a full and vigorous social life. Already well-connected through his family with the upper reaches of society, Dupont-White contracted an important alliance with one of the formidable political dynasties of nineteenth-century France, the Carnot family.[45] Through the marriage of his daughter Cécile to Sadi, son of Hippolyte Carnot and grandson of the great Lazare Carnot, Dupont-White confirmed his position in the republican social elite and further established himself as a member of the—very small—circles of the progressive *haute bourgeoisie*.[46]

By the time this wedding occurred this 'charming conversationalist'[47] was a recognized member of the intellectual and cultural elite in France, moving in circles which included the likes of Michelet—as we have already seen—Lamartine, Sainte-Beuve, George Sand, and Renan.[48] One of his close friends later remembered

his wonderful brilliance . . . his Herculean stature, his rugged hands which seemed to be fashioned more for handling the hammer or the sword than the pen . . . his powerful and meditative head, his contempt for all vulgarity, his predilection for reaching the summits of all things 'as high' as he used to say 'as one can climb'.[49]

Because of his complete independence from partisan and ideological groups, Dupont-White rarely hesitated to speak his mind, even if the timing of his

---

[42] Ibid.   [43] Hugo, Victor, *Histoire d'un crime*, Vol. 2 (Paris: Hetzel, 1884), 110.
[44] On Dupont-White's contribution see Aucoc, Léon, 'Les controverses sur la décentralisation administrative', *Revue Politique et Parlementaire* (May 1895), 242; and Basdevant-Gaudemet, Brigitte, *La Commission de Décentralisation de 1870* (Paris: Presses Universitaires de France, 1873), 65.
[45] For further discussion of its political roles see the conference proceedings, *Une lignée républicaine: les Carnot sous la IIIe République*, Actes du Colloque de Limoges (Limoges: Lucien Souny, 1989).
[46] Harismendy, *Sadi Carnot*, 92.
[47] An expression used in the necrology of Dupont-White in *Le Figaro* (12 December 1878).
[48] For a portrait of Dupont-White's activities in these circles, see Levallois, Jules, *Milieu de siècle, Mémoires d'un critique* (Paris: Librairie Illustrée, n.d.), 276–7.
[49] Baron La Caze, 'Le Père de Mme. Carnot', *Le Figaro* (15 July 1894).

arguments was often found unsuitable by those who respected and admired his work. His independence of spirit also made it difficult for him to achieve the full institutional recognition many believed his work merited. He was not elected to the Académie des Sciences Morales et Politiques of the Institut de France, probably because his name could not be readily attached to any of the dominant intellectual undercurrents or philosophical systems of his time—except perhaps eclecticism, which, however, had become decidedly unfashionable by the 1860s.[50] Although there is evidence that it frustrated him,[51] this lack of recognition was never for Dupont-White a source of rancour or bitterness. Such feelings were beneath his dignity: the qualities which he admired most in men were detachment and forbearance.[52]

He himself, it should be said, was a consummate practitioner of the first but not of the second of these virtues. Dupont-White did not suffer fools gladly, and his relations with his peers were often marred by his strong character and somewhat abrupt manner. In the words of Sadi Carnot's biographer, relations between Sadi and his father-in-law were made increasingly difficult by the 'irresolute, whimsical, and somewhat tyrannical character of Dupont-White'.[53] Intellectual disagreement with our passionate publicist was a highly risky exercise for those unfortunate souls who attempted it. This is how Dupont-White triumphantly recounted to his daughter Cécile his mauling of Jules Simon, one of the principal moderate republican leaders of the Second Empire and early Third Republic:

Dined on Wednesday at your mother-in-law's: excellent and agreeable dinner, with much enjoyment and cordiality. However as Simon was annoying me I flattened him like a bug, which is a fate I had been sparing him for a long time.[54]

Dupont-White in the Context of Nineteenth-Century French Liberal Traditions

Dupont-White's problematic status as a liberal thinker can be summarized in the divergent conclusions reached by three recent historians of nineteenth century French liberalism. [55] In his *L'Individu effacé* Lucien Jaume depicts Dupont-White as a 'libéral autoritaire', whose defence of the inviolability of

[50] See Étienne Vacherot, 'La situation philosophique en France', *Revue des Deux Mondes* (15 June 1868), 951–5.

[51] In a letter to Laveleye in September 1864, Dupont-White expressed the hope that he might be decorated by the King of Belgium. See Villey, *Charles Dupont-White, sa vie, son oeuvre, sa doctrine*, 44.

[52] Ibid., 59.   [53] Harismendy, *Sadi Carnot*, 97.

[54] Undated letter, Cécile Carnot Papers, Archives Carnot, Chateau de Presles.

[55] On the early history of liberal institutions and ideas, see Thureau-Dangin, Paul, *Le parti libéral sous la Restauration* (Paris: Plon, 1876); Welch, Cheryl B., *Liberty and Utility: The French Idéologues and the Transformation of Liberalism* (New York: Columbia University Press, 1984); on Constant, see Holmes, Stephen, *Benjamin Constant and the Making of Modern Liberalism* (New Haven: Yale University Press, 1984); for a comparison with Tocqueville, see Kelly, George Armstrong, *The Humane Comedy: Constant, Tocqueville and French Liberalism* (Cambridge: Cambridge University Press, 1992).

the state was far removed from the intellectual preoccupations of mainstream individualist and Catholic liberals during the nineteenth century.[56] In contrast, Louis Girard's *Les libéraux français* asserts that despite his centralist and anti-individualist views Dupont-White was an 'authentic liberal'.[57] Neither of these two conclusions would have impressed André Jardin, whose *Histoire du libéralisme politique* passes over Dupont-White in silence, even though the book devotes an entire chapter to the development of French liberal doctrines under the Second Empire.[58]

Part of the problem here is the conceptualization of liberalism itself , a notoriously difficult exercise in the nineteenth-century French and European context. Some historians, bewildered by the 'chaotic mixture'[59] on offer, have tended to view liberalism merely as a temperament or cultural disposition, rather like romanticism, as opposed to a fully-fledged ideology with a distinct set of core principles and a clear internal ordering of its concepts. However, over the past two decades the historiography of nineteenth century French liberalism has been revolutionized by two key works: Pierre Rosanvallon's *Le Moment Guizot*, a powerful re-evaluation of Doctrinaire thought whose publication coincided with the beginnings of the ideological revival of liberalism in France in the 1980s;[60] and Lucien Jaume's *L'Individu effacé*, a comprehensive study of French liberal political thought across the nineteenth century.[61]

Jaume's critical insight is that French liberalism was not a unified system of thought whose essence can be defined according to some schematic formula. It was, rather, a diverse ideological phenomenon articulated through a variety of discourses which overlapped at times with other systems of thought while at the same time sharing a number of core concepts, values, and preoccupations.[62] Jaume distinguishes three strands of liberalism, each with its distinct problematics. First, an 'individualist' school, associated with Germaine de Staël and Benjamin Constant, and later Alexis de Tocqueville. One of its central concerns was expressed in Constant's distinction between the 'liberty of the ancients', which was the public participatory form of freedom championed by Rousseau, and 'modern' liberty, which was constituted by 'the peaceful enjoyment of private independence'.[63] Modern citizenship, for this liberal individualist school, lay in the definition of a broad range of individual rights which could not be encroached upon by the state. The goal of public institutions was merely to enable members of society to develop their individuality through the enjoyment of these liberties, most notably freedom of opinion and judgement.[64] Beyond this enabling function the state had relatively little positive role to play, except in the sphere of education, and certainly could not aspire to define the good life for the rest of society.

[56] Jaume, Lucien, *L'Individu effacé ou le paradoxe du libéralisme français* (Paris: Fayard, 1997), 366.
[57] Girard, Louis, *Les libéraux français* (Paris: Aubier, 1985), 193.
[58] Jardin, André, *Histoire du libéralisme politique* (Paris: Hachette, 1985).
[59] Ruggiero, Guido de, *The History of European Liberalism* (London: Oxford University Press, 1927), 203.
[60] Rosanvallon, Pierre, *Le moment Guizot* (Paris: Gallimard, 1985).
[61] Jaume, *L'Individu effacé.*   [62] Ibid., 17.   [63] Ibid., 82.   [64] Ibid., 93–8.

The second, ideologically hegemonic, strand was typified in the works of the Doctrinaire school, most notably in the writings of François Guizot. This 'statist' or 'elite' liberalism was in many respects the mirror image of the first tradition. Rather than identifying a distinct sphere of 'civil society' and seeking to define a wide realm of individual action which was not to be invaded by the state, the Doctrinaires presented state and society as completely interpenetrated.[65] A specific number of individual rights were recognized in the civil sphere but not in the political: in Guizot's conception only groups could be the bearers of political rights, not individuals.[66] Government was based not on consent or will but on the metaphysical formula of the 'sovereignty of reason'; the state was the embodiment of this reason and its purpose was to establish truth: the very opposite of the pluralism which the individualist liberals championed in this context.[67] Guizot's conception of power rested on his notion of 'capacity', which defined a restricted electoral franchise effectively vesting political authority in the hands of middle-class and aristocratic elites.[68] This was a highly authoritarian and oligarchical liberalism; at its heart was the notion that the state was the only legitimate guardian of the public interest, which it defended through the reconciliation of conflicting group interests.[69]

The third strand identified by Jaume, the liberal Catholic, sought to transcend this dichotomy between individualism and statism. It aspired to reconcile the promotion of fundamental civil and religious freedoms—of education, of worship, of association—with the notion of the spiritual sovereignty of the Church. In the writings of Lamennais in the 1830s, and later in those of Montalembert, this conception of liberalism also championed the cause of decentralization and stressed the importance of press freedom. In sociological terms liberal Catholicism was strongly anti-statist, hoping for the emergence of a new aristocracy, open to all talents, which could be independent of the state and could thus act as a buffer against its excesses.[70] In the 1850s and early 1860s Montalembert's efforts were especially directed at reconciling Catholicism with parliamentary democracy, to which end he underlined the importance of freedom of conscience and political participation.[71] At the same time, there was a strong tension within this strand between on the one hand its emphasis on individual freedom and empowerment, and on the other its continued reliance on the irreducible spiritual authority of the Catholic religion—and the pope.[72]

This analytical framework provides an ideal starting-point for evaluating the relationship between Dupont-White's political thought and the multiple problematics of nineteenth-century liberalism. The first point to note in this context is a feature of Dupont-White's writing—and thinking—which was largely shared by his fellow-liberals across all three strands: an admiration for the British Constitution. Like many French and European liberals[73] Dupont-

---

[65] Jaume, *L'Individu effacé*122.   [66] Ibid., 123.   [67] Ibid., 142.   [68] Ibid., 153.
[69] Ibid., 166.   [70] Ibid., 218.   [71] Ibid., 228–31.   [72] Ibid., 208.
[73] See for example de Laveleye, Émile, *Du progrès des peuples anglo-saxons* (Bruxelles: Guyot, 1859).

White looked up to Britain as the homeland of political liberty and stable government: 'after God freedom comes from England.'[74] Dupont-White was steeped in English history, politics, and political culture, and this was well reflected, both stylistically and substantively, in his writings. In fact there was a real sense in which his own perspective on French politics was that of an anthropological observer looking in from the outside on a familiar but somewhat eccentric culture.

In his very last piece of writing he began by noting that one of the best observations on the 1789 Revolution had been authored by the English writer Arthur Young, and that it would have been interesting to know what he would have made of France in the late 1870s.[75] At the same time, he rejected the ideological universalism of many liberals, who believed that France's salvation lay in its uninhibited adoption of the British political system. For Dupont-White the 'English example' could not be transposed to France: historical and cultural conditions were too different.[76] That said, Dupont-White's 'Englishness' will emerge at several critical junctures in the course of this chapter, most notably in his scepticism of abstract systems of thought and preference for 'experience', his belief in instinct and spontaneity, his scepticism of human nature, his belief in the prevalence of force in international affairs, and above all in his aristocratic manner and his fiercely anti-plebeian demeanour.

As to his substantive affinities with liberalism, the most immediate ideological approximation to Dupont-White's thinking seems to be the 'statist' ideology of the Doctrinaires. Some analysts have gone so far as to portray Dupont-White as 'a disciple of Mr Guizot'.[77] It is true that several indicators might at first glance seem to point in this direction. He was on excellent personal terms with all the various shades of the liberal intelligentsia, entertaining close links with progressive liberals such as Nefftzer[78] and Renan.[79] As for the Doctrinaires specifically, Dupont-White's correspondence suggests that he not only was in close contact socially with many members of the Orleanist intellectual community—Decazes, Schérer, Cornélis de Witt, Pontalis—but also regularly exchanged political views with them, and specifically with Guizot[80] and Charles de Rémusat.[81]

---

[74] Dupont-White, *Le progrès politique en France*, 229.

[75] See Dupont-White, Charles, 'Perspectives Politiques I', *Revue de France*, 32 (December 1878), 685.

[76] Dupont-White, Charles, 'Impuissance politique de la philosophie', *Revue de France*, 17 (February 1876), 350.

[77] Martin, Maurice, 'Essai sur les doctrines sociales et économiques de Dupont-White', Ph.D thesis (University of Grenoble, 1899), 4. Bibliothèque Nationale 8.F.11656.

[78] As for example is shown in his letter of 10 June 1868 to Auguste Nefftzer, the editor of the influential liberal newspaper *Le Temps*, in Arch.Nat.113 AP 3, Papiers Auguste Nefftzer.

[79] The Bibliothèque Nationale's collection of Renan's books contains a carefully-marked copy of *L'Individu et l'État* in the 1857 edition, with a dedication from Dupont-White. See Bib.Nat. Z-Renan 3318.

[80] In an undated letter to Cécile Carnot (probably from the late 1860s or early 1870s), Dupont-White notes: 'I have received from Mr Guizot lately an excellent and curious letter, as if written 20 years ago'. Cécile Carnot Papers, Château de Presles.

[81] In the same letter Dupont-White mentions that he was reading the works of Bagehot. He then complains about the current state of French intellectual life before promising to take up the matter

centralization had been primarily responsible for the creation of a sense of national identity in France. Devolving power from central government would not only threaten this sense of collective identity but also give a free rein to the arbitrariness and despotism of local communities. In stark contrast with individualist and Catholic liberal opinion at the time, Dupont-White thus asserted that decentralization was inherently incapable of nurturing the values of good citizenship and enlightened statesmanship.[97] Dupont-White retained this firm belief in the virtues of centralization throughout the 1870s, and his ideological commitment appears its full splendour in his final pieces of political writing, 'Perspectives Politiques', published posthumously by the *Revue de France* in late 1878 and early 1879. Casting his mind back to the Second Empire era, he ridiculed liberal efforts in the 1860s to promote greater local political freedom—an aspiration which he summed up in this scornful formula: 'a yearning to give freedom to the butcher's, the pharmacy, the bakery, and even, it would appear, the communes.'[98]

There was a further reason to uphold centralization in the political context of the 1870s: the even greater prominence accorded to universal suffrage in the republican political system. In the face of the enormous uncertainty created by the mass vote, it was essential that the state should rely upon the continuity afforded by centralization, whose crucial significance was underlined by Dupont-White: 'if it did not exist it would have to be invented in the presence of universal suffrage.'[99] But the key purpose of centralization, which was as much needed now as in earlier decades, remained the protection of the public good and the defence of the interests of minorities. In Dupont-White's words:

Nothing is threatened if a mayor cannot, of his own initiative, move the cemetery right next to your castle, or the school half an hour away from your cottage; or if you can appeal to the prefect against the mayor, and to the Minister of the Interior against the prefect. Governments come and go but centralization remains, and with it everything necessary for the suppression of local tyrannies and for the protection of minorities.[100]

This conception of the state upholding the public interest in the face of the 'fantasies' and 'outbursts'[101] of local potentates seemed far removed from the vision of the good life championed by French liberal individualists such as Tocqueville, with their emphasis on the 'private' character of freedom, the necessity of upholding a wide range of individual rights, and containing the state within strict limits. Dupont-White emphatically rejected the 'negative' conception of freedom which was generally upheld in individualist liberal circles. Liberty, as he repeated consistently, was not to be measured in terms of the absence of state intervention in society but consisted in the possession of a number of moral and intellectual capacities nurtured through the state.[102] This conception of liberty was strongly rejected by Mill, who regarded it as one

---

[97] Dupont-White, *La liberté politique considérée dans ses rapports avec l'administration locale*, 158–61.
[98] Dupont-White, Charles, 'Perspectives Politiques' II, *Revue de France*, 33 (January 1879), 59.
[99] Ibid.   [100] Ibid.   [101] Ibid.   [102] Dupont-White, *L'Individu et l'État*, 3.

of the most contentious elements in Dupont-White's system of thought.[103] Mill believed that liberty was generally enhanced through the absence of state intervention, whereas for Dupont-White freedom was achieved through the actions of public authorities, and against the wishes and instincts of individuals and local groups.

Dupont-White's territorial views were also diametrically opposed to the liberal Catholic vision of the future. His attack on 'local tyranny' represented a frontal challenge to the political power and social authority wielded by aristocratic and religious forces in small villages and towns across France—and these were precisely the groups which the liberal Catholics hoped to empower in their proposals for greater decentralization. In this sense Dupont-White's upholding of the 'sovereignty' of the state and of its capacity for rationality, combined with his defence of the public-interest functions of state institutions, all seemed to place Dupont-White's liberalism squarely in the Doctrinaire camp. This consistent hostility to decentralization earned him numerous admonitions from individualist and Catholic liberal quarters.[104]

But matters were not so simple. Although he seemed to identify much more immediately with Guizot and his colleagues than with either the individualists or the liberal Catholics, a close inspection of Dupont-White's writings also shows that he had a number of important intellectual and political reservations about the Doctrinaire platform. His most serious criticism was directed at Guizot's ideal of a 'non-governed society'. Although the Doctrinaires believed in the necessity of a strong state, they also thought that as civilization advanced society would become increasingly able to govern itself without public intervention: hence their ideal of a future society subsisting through 'the free development of human intelligence and will'.[105]

For Dupont-White such a view rested on a double fallacy. Looking back at French social and political history since the Middle Ages, he saw no evidence to correlate progress with spontaneous 'societal' activity. On the contrary, all the major advances in human civilization had been consolidated through greater state action.[106] One of his favourite examples in this respect was the abolition of slavery, which would not in his view have occurred without the decisive intervention of the state, which on grounds of justice and humanity had overridden the particular interests of the colonial settlers—and the relative indifference of the rest of society to the plight of the slaves.[107] As society reached a higher plane of civilization, it needed more laws and therefore more government—because progress was necessarily accompanied by 'an increase in criminality'.[108] This was a far cry from the complacent Doctrinaire ideal of a society whose members harmoniously pursued their self-interests with little requirement of public intervention.

---

[103] Mill, John Stuart, 'Centralisation', *The Edinburgh Review*, April 1862, in Mineka and Lindley (eds), *The Collected Works of John Stuart Mill*, Vol. 19, 610.
[104] See for example the review of *La République Conservatrice* by L. Derome in *Revue de France* (October 1872), 273; and his review of *Politique Actuelle* in the issue of January 1875, 308–9.
[105] Dupont-White, *L'Individu et l'État*, 204.   [106] Ibid., 212.
[107] Ibid., 27–30, 52–3, 75, and 184.   [108] Ibid., 214.

return to—and on the value of constitutional government;[123] furthermore he underlined the necessity of ideological compromise;[124] the positive influence of enlightened opinion;[125] the wealth-creating attributes of private property;[126] and especially the political and moral value of a free press.[127] The latter area was one in which Dupont-White's liberal credentials were entirely immaculate: much more so, in fact, than those of some individualist and especially Catholic liberals. Throughout his active life he rejected the proposition that the state had any right to regulate individual thought, on the grounds that 'man and thought are one and the same'.[128] While the state had every right to maintain its own organs of expression and opinion, it also in his view had a duty to be 'tolerant' and to allow individuals and groups unrestricted freedom of expression.[129]

Entirely liberal in inspiration, also, was Dupont-White's constitutional agnosticism, which was typically expressed in his scepticism of grand constitutional designs: 'a disproportionate weight tends to be attached to the form of a government.'[130] In the early 1870s, at a time when the question was provoking heated disputes among republicans, monarchists, and Bonapartists, Dupont-White argued for the formalization of the status quo. A new constitutional settlement did not therefore need to be reached and solemnly 'proclaimed': it already existed.[131] This empiricism—again, very 'English'—was accompanied by a real commitment on his part to the principle of intellectual pluralism, one of the cornerstones of the liberal ideal in the individualist tradition. Let us again hear Dupont-White explain himself here:

The plurality of principles is necessary for the conduct and treatment of societies; they have always lived on mixture and accommodation . . . there is no reason to take exception to the alarming extremities of a principle, because this principle is not alone in the world, because it will not carry to its full extent, because it will be intercepted by other principles.[132]

So where does this leave our evaluation of Dupont-White's relationship with the French liberal traditions of the nineteenth century? At an immediate level there can be no denying that he was philosophically inspired by the Doctrinaires and conversely rejected many of the core tenets of individualist and Catholic liberalism, such as the sanctity of individual rights, of associational activity, and of decentralization. In these—important—respects he was

---

[123] La centralisation, suite à L'Individu et l'État, 139–140.
[124] Dupont-White, La liberté politique considérée dans ses rapports avec l'administration locale, 194.
[125] Ibid., 284, 292.
[126] Dupont-White, L'Individu et l'État, 116. On his preference for small-scale industrial organization, see Weill, Georges, Histoire du mouvement social en France (Paris: Alcan, 1924), 32.
[127] Dupont-White, Charles, La liberté de presse et le suffrage universel (Paris: Douniol, 1866), 15.
[128] Dupont-White, L'Individu et l'État, 222.   [129] Ibid., 233.
[130] Dupont-White, Charles, La République Conservatrice (Paris: Guillaumin, 1872), 3.
[131] Dupont-White, Charles, Ce qui pourrait tenir lieu d'une Constitution (Paris: Revue Britannique, 1872), 3–4. On the prevalence of this approach among liberals, see Guiral, Pierre, Prévost-Paradol 1829–1870. Pensée et action d'un libéral sous le Second Empire (Paris: Presses Universitaires de France, 1955), 756.
[132] Dupont-White, Le progrès politique en France, 219.

out of step with the writings of leading liberals such as Tocqueville and Mill, whose views tended to be cited favourably in liberal and even legitimist circles during the Second Empire and early Third Republic.[133] Dupont-White was also instinctively irritated by the intellectual contortions of liberal Catholicism, which offended his own Gallican spirit. After reading one of Lacordaire's books he wrote exasperatedly to one of his friends: 'where we were expecting a Christian philosopher, we only found a sectarian—and from what a sect!'[134]

But a closer inspection reveals greater subtlety on Dupont-White's part. He flatly rejected many of the authoritarian features of Guizot's thought and practice—most notably his restrictions on freedom of expression—and, through his espousal of law-based government, the impartial administration of justice, and the importance of ideological pluralism, he exhibited a shared concern with many of the central tenets of individualist liberalism. Not for the first time, therefore, we have to deduce that Dupont-White's thought defies simple classification. *Pace* the conclusion reached by Jardin, he was a liberal—but neither quite the 'authentic' liberal depicted by Girard, if 'authenticity' is taken to signify correspondence with all the core tenets of individualist liberalism, nor merely the 'authoritarian' liberal dismissed by Lucien Jaume. In fact, the strength of Dupont-White's anti-authoritarian credentials will be confirmed through our evaluation of his intellectual relationship with Bonapartism.

An Improbable Bonapartist

It is not altogether surprising that Dupont-White should have been characterized by some as a Bonapartist. His repeated assertion of the beneficial and transcendental power of the state mirrored the traditional imperialist emphasis on the virtues of centralization. In a speech given shortly after his *coup d'état* of December 1851, Louis Napoleon noted that 'in our country, monarchical since 800 years, central power has always been on the increase'.[135] In 1858, a year after the publication of Dupont-White's *L'Individu et l'État*, Napoleon III reaffirmed his belief in a strong state:

The Empire requires a strong power, capable of overcoming all the obstacles which might impede its advance, for, let us not forget, the advance of every new order is always a struggle.[136]

Throughout the 1850s and 1860s, it was in authoritarian Bonapartist circles that the principle of centralization was most consistently and vehemently

---

[133] See for example Béchard, Ferdinand, *Du projet de décentralisation administrative annoncé par l'Empereur* (Paris: Gazette de France, 1864), 51.

[134] Undated letter, shortly before the 1848 Revolution, Cécile Carnot Papers, Archives Carnot, Château de Presles.

[135] Speech of 14 January 1852, in *Discours, messages, et proclamations de l'Empereur* (Paris: Plon, 1860), 208.

[136] Speech of 19 January 1858. Ibid., 373.

The state, no matter its difficulties, has nonetheless to respect humanity and morality, that is to say beings that it has not created, a law which it has not made. Such are the limits of a dictatorship even most justified by circumstances. The state, on grounds of public safety, can kill or despoil neither a caste, nor a party, nor a race, nor a sect, nor even an individual. This would be to destroy rights which it has only the power to put to use.[154]

In this critical passage, Dupont-White began by justifying the recourse to dictatorship, as defined in the classical sense of a temporary suspension of democratic rule for the purpose of restoring public order. But in so doing his liberalism drew clear limits upon the extent to which the state could resort to force: limits which the Bonapartist government had clearly exceeded in the early 1850s, most notably in its confiscation of the possessions of the Orléans family,[155] its savage and at times indiscriminate repression against the individual opponents of the *coup d'état*, its destruction of the republican party's political organization, and its suppression of independent associations such as the Freemasonry. [156] Beyond these specific events, Dupont-White was also making a fundamental point here about the pre-existence of certain individual and group rights which the state was not entitled to destroy under any circumstances: the classical liberal rights to life, political liberty, and property. In all these respects, therefore, Dupont-White expressly signalled to his readers his reservations and disagreements both with Bonapartist political theory and with its state practice.

In addition to its founding actions and its personalization of power, Dupont-White took exception to several aspects of the imperial political system. At the hands of the Second Empire, universal suffrage was in his view merely an instrument of 'despotism'.[157] This was not merely a circumstantial judgement: he consistently held the view that the recourse to mass suffrage under a monarchical regime could lead only to dictatorial government.[158] Dupont-White was also uncomfortable with the oppressive role of the police and the excessive formalism of the administration under the Second Empire.[159] Like the liberal, legitimist, and republican opposition to the regime, furthermore, he deplored the repeated intervention of local administrative agents in elections. Unlike the constitutional opposition, however, his objection was consequentialist rather than principled: public functionaries were not in his view reliable translators of the public mood.[160] His disillusionment with the Second Empire appears very strongly in his letters of the mid-late 1860s, where he noted with dismay the growing physical decrepitude

---

[154] Dupont-White, *L'Individu et l'État*, 186.

[155] On this affair see Wright, Vincent, 'Le Conseil d'État et l'affaire de la confiscation des biens d'Orléans en 1852', *Études et Documents*, No. 21 (1968), 231–49.

[156] On the post-1851 violence against opponents of the coup, see Wright, Vincent, 'The coup d'état of December 1851: Repression and the Limits to Repression', in Roger Price (ed.), *Revolution and Reaction: 1848 and the Second French Republic* (London: Croom Helm, 1975).

[157] Dupont-White, *Le progrès politique en France*, 3.

[158] Dupont-White, *Politique Actuelle*, xxxii.   [159] Dupont-White, *La liberté politique*, 157.

[160] Dupont-White, Charles, *Des candidatures officielles* (Paris: Guillaumin, 1868), 23.

of Napoleon III[161] and the incapacity of the political system to operate effectively: 'France which is poorly governed is hardly represented any better; it could be said, it is true, that this is the fault of the government which has spoiled the last elections.'[162]

Even if allowances are made for the ideological diversity of Second Empire imperialism—notably the classical distinction between its 'liberal' and 'authoritarian' subcultures[163]—the claim that Dupont-White was in any way politically and intellectually indebted to Bonapartism cannot survive serious scrutiny. He was strongly critical of the Second Empire's attempts to control opinion and especially the press. As we noted earlier, Dupont-White firmly believed that tolerance was a mark of civilization and progress and that freedom of thought and expression should be guaranteed by the state: 'all intelligences have an equal right to expression.'[164] The press was not only a means of controlling the government but also an essential instrument for the education of public opinion; he went so far as to argue that press freedom was more important than mass education.[165]

Even Dupont-White's commitment to centralization, which superficially seemed to converge with the Bonapartist conception of the state, was founded on fundamentally different principles. The Bonapartist doctrine was Napoleonic; it traced most of the benefits of centralization to the era of the Consulate and First Empire. In contrast, there is little trace of sympathy for the Napoleonic epic in Dupont-White's writings. His notion of centralization was cultural and transhistorical: it was a natural and immemorial phenomenon, whose roots reached deep into the early modern history of France.[166]

The ostensible purpose of centralization was also defined in rather different terms. For Bonapartists, centralization was a means of ensuring political order through dynastic stability; it was in this sense closely associated with the personal rule of Napoleon III. For Dupont-White, however, centralization was essentially about the rule of law and civil equality: 'the necessary organ of law'.[167] Again in contrast with the Bonapartist and Jacobin republican approaches, Dupont-White did not regard centralism as a useful—or even necessary—instrument of nation-building: 'what constitutes a nation is the quality of its government, it is the prevalence of law in society, it is not the unity of race, language, and religion.'[168] His ideological pluralism was matched by a

---

[161] One of the letters notes: 'decline of France, lost prestige . . . Marshal MacMahon says that it will take two and a half years to renew the armament of our infantry. The most curious experiments have been made at the Châlon camp on new weapons: the Emperor was so unwell that he was unable to attend. I was given details of all of this, as well as an audience which had to be granted but which the Emperor had to refuse, because of the moral and physical prostration in which the grand master of ceremonies found him.' Undated Dupont-White letter, probably late 1860s: Cécile Carnot Papers, Archives Carnot, Chateau de Presles.

[162] He was referring to the elections of 1869. Undated Dupont-White letter, late Second Empire: Cécile Carnot Papers, Archives Carnot, Chateau de Presles.

[163] Rémond, René, *Les droites en France* (Paris: Aubier, 1982), 108.

[164] Dupont-White, *L'Individu et l'État*, 220–4.

[165] Dupont-White, *La liberté de presse et le suffrage universel*, 35.

[166] Dupont-White, *La centralisation, suite à L'Individu et l'État*, 188.

[167] Ibid., xi.   [168] Ibid., 10.

cultural eclecticism: he was a passionate advocate of the 'blending' of races, which for him was the root of civilizational progress. As he put it: 'the more men mix and mingle with one another the more civilization improves.'[169] This, as noted earlier, was an explicit rebuttal of the views of Gobineau, whose beliefs were exactly the opposite.

Above all Dupont-White was strongly critical of universal suffrage and personal rule, two political institutions which lay at the heart of Bonapartist ideology.[170] In a late Second Republic letter, written shortly after the election of Louis Napoleon to the presidency, Dupont-White mocked the voters, the electoral process, and the unfortunate victor, his disdain revealing his true personal sentiments about the latest embodiment of the Bonapartist dynasty:

as for the masses they no sooner get given their say that they vote for a cretin, or at the very least, as Thiers says, for a clod.[171]

Dupont-White as a Social Reformer: State Socialism or Aristocratic Paternalism?

So far we have seen attempts by both liberals and Bonapartists, with equally uncertain results, to claim Dupont-White as an exclusive member of their tribe. We can now consider the submissions of a third group seeking to assimilate Dupont-White's political thought, this time by defining its essence in terms of 'state socialism'. It was in Henry Michel's *L'Idée de l'État,* published towards the end of the nineteenth century, that Dupont-White was most emphatically presented as one of the forerunners of this doctrine.[172] In his analysis of Dupont-White's writings, Michel detailed a range of features which in his view anticipated the development of statist and collectivist forms of socialist thought in Germany during the second half of the nineteenth century.[173] For Maurice Martin, too, there was little doubt: Dupont-White was 'the inspirer of most of the socialist and authoritarian legislation which governs modern states'.[174] This conclusion was also forcefully advanced by Henri Spriet:

A conception of the state as an entity superior to men in morality and intelligence; a belief in the idea that there are strong and weak elements in society, and that the state

[169] Dupont-White, *L'Individu et l'État,* 330.

[170] In a letter to Laveleye in May 1869, he attacked the Bonapartist recourse to the plebiscite, 'a machine which I see as the aggravation and the perversion of democracy'. Quoted in Villey, *Charles Dupont-White, sa vie, son oeuvre, sa doctrine,* 44.

[171] Undated Dupont-White letter, late Second Republic: Cécile Carnot Papers, Archives Carnot, Chateau de Presles. At the time of his election to the presidency of the Second Republic, Louis Napoleon was commonly regarded, by both conservatives and republicans, as a political and intellectual mediocrity.

[172] Michel, Henry, *L'Idée de l'État* (Paris: Hachette, 1898), 572–8.

[173] On German 'state socialism' see Andler, Charles, *Les origines du socialisme d'État en Allemagne* (Paris: Alcan, 1897).

[174] Martin, 'Essai sur les doctrines sociales et économiques de Dupont-White', 46.

owes protection to the weak; hostility to freedom and especially to economic freedom; intervention of the state in the distribution of wealth . . . these are the principles of state socialism; these principles we have found them in Dupont-White.[175]

The strongest period of socialist impregnation in Dupont-White's social philosophy can be witnessed in the 1840s and early 1850s; after the collapse of the Second Republic his intellectual interests perceptibly shifted away from political economy to political philosophy.[176] Throughout the 1840s he was highly critical of the complacent attitude of the Orleanist and republican ruling elites to the 'social question'. In a letter written in late 1849 Dupont-White expressed his frustration in typically forthright terms: 'it is rather bizarre: our future perhaps depends on a number of social reforms, and yet there is not a single man in office who up to now has even hinted that he has the taste or the intelligence for them.'[177]

Before examining these social reforms, let us begin by considering the range of intellectual influences which shaped his social thinking. Dupont-White was extremely well-versed in the classics of political economy and also acquired an intimate familiarity with French writings on the subject, most notably the works of Buret, Villermé, Pecqueur, Vidal, and Villeneuve-Bargemont.[178] Through the works of these thinkers he began to develop his own views on the limitations of the classical conception of *homo economicus*, especially the proposition that the capitalist market was self-regulating and therefore required very little by way of state intervention. Several thinkers were especially influential in structuring Dupont-White's views here. In Dupont-White's own estimation probably the most important was the republican socialist Pierre Leroux, with whom he engaged in active correspondence in the 1840s and whose *Revue Sociale* he enthusiastically subscribed to. In *L'Individu et l'État* he sang the praises of this 'original and creative mind', describing Leroux as 'one of the writers who, granted some eclecticism, one could plunder with the greatest effect and impunity'.[179]

For his part Henri Spriet believed that the two greatest intellectual influences on Dupont-White's social thought were Pierre Buchez and Charles Sismondi. In his *Introduction à la science de l'histoire* (1833) Buchez had described the state as an 'essential agent of civilisation'; this view corresponded exactly with Dupont-White's conception of public authority, so much so that he frequently used the expression himself.[180] Sismondi inspired Dupont-White to think of political economy as an essentially moral doctrine whose purpose was the creation of happiness for the whole of society and not just for some sections of it; as an instrument for appreciating the historical specificities of societies rather than relying on the universal socio-economic

---

[175] Spriet, Henri, *Dupont-White: étude sur les origines du socialisme d'État en France* (Paris: Giard et Brière, 1901).
[176] Villey, *Charles Dupont-White, sa vie, son oeuvre, sa doctrine*, 253–4.
[177] Letter to Gustave de Thou, Cécile Carnot Papers, Archives Carnot, Chateau de Presles.
[178] Spriet, *Dupont-White: étude sur les origines du socialisme d'État en France*, 21.
[179] Dupont-White, *L'Individu et l'État*, 122.
[180] Spriet, *Dupont-White: étude sur les origines du socialisme d'État en France*, 19.

categories privileged by classical political economists; and above all as a means of alleviating the social distortions of market capitalism.[181]

Although Dupont-White did not use the term consistently, and was often critical of the egalitarian and revolutionary impulses of 'socialist' political groups during the Second Republic, he also frequently spoke of the 'necessity' of a particular type of socialism: 'a special and direct application of politics to the good of the masses.'[182] A key passage in *L'Individu et l'État* explains the extent and the distinct contours of Dupont-White's conception of socialism. Doctrinaire liberals, in his view, had accurately pinpointed the insufficiencies of economic and political liberalism in the first half of the nineteenth century but had failed to lay down a clear defining framework for the 'duties' of the state. Socialists and Saint-Simonians, on the other hand, had a strong appreciation of the necessity of public intervention in the economy and in society but conversely lacked a conception of the proper boundaries of state action.[183] In his social philosophy Dupont-White aspired to negotiate a median position between these two poles, highlighting the spheres where state action was required but also attempting to circumscribe this intervention within firm moral and political limits. His 'socialism' was at least as much an ethical doctrine as a social and economic philosophy. As he made clear in a letter in the late 1840s, citizens should not expect everything from the state, and socialist ideas and values could also penetrate the public mind by other means:

Socialism as a purely critical theory can be of great consequence, for society can transform itself by customs as much as by laws. If the religious precept which holds men to be brothers, if the political principle which treats them as equal, if the article of the constitution which treats them as sovereign were to govern our attitudes you would soon see the fate of the worker improve in all respects, without any state interference. As far as improvements are concerned, there are not only those which are decreed.[184]

Having said this, it was undeniable that all the key social issues which Dupont-White believed had be addressed by the state offered loud echoes of early socialist thinking. Among the most important—and difficult—was the incidence of class conflict, which was intimately linked to the question of property, a constant poison in French politics since the 1789 Revolution. In the 1840s Dupont-White urged the state to come to terms with the existence of a large social class—the workers—which was entirely dispossessed. He was not sure how far the state could go in turning these workers into *propriétaires*, but he clearly believed that such a social conversion would be desirable; he also prophetically warned that failure by the Republic to address the issue of property ownership would lead to another '1793'.[185] In his early study of relations

---

[181] For a comparison of Dupont-White and Sismondi, see Hartmann, Max, *Sismondi und Dupont-White als Begrunder des sozialen Interventionismus in Frankreich* (Zurich, 1943). On Sismondi's political and economic thought more generally, see the chapters by Francesca Sofia and Jean-Jacques Gislain in Jaume, Lucien (ed.), *Coppet, creuset de l'esprit libéral* (Paris: Economica, 2000), 55–98.

[182] Dupont-White, *Le progrès politique en France*, 223.

[183] Dupont-White, *L'Individu et l'État*, 96, 294.

[184] Letter to Gustave de Thou, undated: Cécile Carnot Papers, Archives Carnot, Chateau de Presles.

[185] Letter to Gustave de Thou, undated: Cécile Carnot Papers, Archives Carnot, Chateau de Presles.

between labour and capital Dupont-White deplored the fact that modern governments tended to ignore the conditions of weaker sections of society more generally. While this disregard was sometimes the result of incapacity or weakness of will, it was more often a necessary consequence of the state's penetration by aristocratic and bourgeois interests. Dupont-White here anticipates the Marxist conception of the state as the institutional expression of dominant social power:

The interest of the lower classes is never so well ignored as in a free government, whether defined as a weak government, for it will prove incapable of defending this interest, or defined as a strong government in the hands of certain classes, for it will make the interest of these classes prevail over all else.[186]

Individuals, as Dupont-White constantly repeated, did not exist outside society: man was essentially constituted by his social relations.[187] But in the context of the relationship between labour and capital these relations were characterized by a relentless struggle;[188] this general phenomenon was exacerbated in France by the particular intensity of class conflict: 'we are a country where individuals hate each other like everywhere but where classes detest each other like nowhere else.'[189]

The state's response, in Dupont-White's eyes, needed to be twofold. The conflict between labour and capital had to be arbitrated by public authority. His notion of state 'regulation'[190] was not neutral: labour had a collective right to be protected against the depredations of the capitalist, for example through legislation on conditions of work: a form of social security which he termed 'socialism of Governments'.[191] Dupont-White berated the classical political economists for failing to recognize the need for safeguards for workers: 'Of the three instruments of production, land, labour, and capital, you protect the first two and abandon the third, forgetting that labour, according to your own theory, is the very source of wealth.'[192] Furthermore, the state had a humanitarian duty, albeit an imperfect one, to assist those sections of the community which were too weak to help themselves: for example, to set up pensions, to build hospitals, and to undertake charitable work.[193] In his introduction to the French edition of Mill's *Representative Government*, Dupont-White went so far as to declare: '*Every* law should be an alleviation of the situation of the most numerous and least fortunate classes.'[194] This notion that the laws of political economy could be moralized and humanized lay at the heart of Dupont-White's redemptive conception of political action, demonstrating a clear

---

[186] Dupont-White, Charles, *Essai sur les relations du travail avec le capital* (Paris: Guillaumin, 1846), 123.

[187] Dupont-White, 'Le Positivisme: A Propos d'Un Livre de M.Littré', *Revue des Deux Mondes* (1 February 1865), 569.

[188] Ibid., 57.

[189] Dupont-White, *Ce qui pourrait tenir lieu d'une Constitution*, 17.

[190] Dupont-White, *L'Individu et l'État*, 238.   [191] Ibid., 95.

[192] Dupont-White, *Essai sur les relations du travail avec le capital*, 348.   [193] Ibid., 85.

[194] Dupont-White, 'Introduction', John Stuart Mill, *Le Gouvernement Représentatif*, xliv; emphasis added.

affinity between his thinking and that of early French socialists and Saint-Simonians.

But how far could the state proceed in intervening in the economy without jeopardy? As we noted earlier Dupont-White explicitly rejected the recipes proffered by socialists and Saint-Simonians, both of whom, in his estimation, recognized no effective limitations on the regulatory and providential mandates of public authority. In Dupont-White's mind the state had to maintain public utilities, such as roads and railways, and organize charitable assistance to the poor, but this did not mean, as Montesquieu had suggested, that the state had a duty to clothe and feed all its citizens.[195] In 1848 he also firmly rejected the notion of 'right to work' which was put forward in socialist and revolutionary republican circles: for Dupont-White the state had no obligation to provide work for its citizens.[196] These lines of demarcation highlighted the strictly circumscribed nature of his 'socialism'.

On the ideological front his reservations were more substantial. Even though early socialist thought in France was notoriously diverse, it generally possessed at least two elements which were absent from Dupont-White's approach even at the height of his interest in questions of political economy: a concern for political and social equality, and a desire to increase the associational and representative rights of workers.[197] On the issue of equality he was extremely cautious, if not timorous. If socialist equality is considered as a comprehensive notion which includes civil, political, and social elements,[198] Dupont-White's notion of equality never went beyond the first: equal treatment of all citizens by the law and universal right of access to public offices. Political equality was a notion he found difficult to stomach: this was reflected in his fear of universal suffrage and his consistent yearning for the enlightened government of the upper classes: 'the right and duty of the upper classes is to govern.'[199]

As for the associative rights of workers, he was, to say the least, hostile. He did not regard freedom of association as a 'necessary' freedom in a liberal society;[200] in any event, even if he had done so, it is very unlikely that he would have welcomed its use by a social class he regarded as 'dangerous'.[201] Furthermore, there was no sense in Dupont-White's writings that workers could help themselves: progress, if it were to occur, could be imposed only by enlightened political elites on what he termed 'the backward and dissident crowd'.[202] This rugged paternalism was ultimately justified by his philosophical anthropology. The theme of human egoism was ever-present in Dupont-

---

[195] Dupont-White, *L'Individu et l'État*, 86.

[196] Martin, 'Essai sur les doctrines sociales et économiques de Dupont-White', 82.

[197] This was not true of all socialists, of course; Fourier, for example, was virulently anti-democratic and anti-egalitarian. For a succint discussion, see Armelle Le Bras-Chopard, 'Les premiers socialistes', in Pascal Ory (ed.), *Nouvelle histoire des idées politiques* (Paris: Hachette, 1987).

[198] For a discussion of socialist equality, see Freeden, *Ideologies and Political Theory*, 430–3.

[199] Dupont-White, *Politique Actuelle*, xxx.   [200] Dupont-White, *L'Individu et l'État*, 224.

[201] Dupont-White, *Le progrès politique en France*, 81.

[202] Dupont-White, *L'Individu et l'État*, 192.

White's writings, and although he claimed to reject the notion that 'men are purely sharks'[203] his view of human nature was deeply coloured by Hobbesian assumptions. 'Men cannot touch each other without clashing, and cannot clash without hating':[204] statements of this nature, which are littered throughout Dupont-White's works, were fundamentally at variance with the positive and optimistic view of human nature commonly entertained in nineteenth-century socialist writings, from the 'utopians' to the Marxists. Only when he encountered it in the state could Dupont-White wax lyrical about humanity, because in this exalted sphere mankind had been purged of all the defects he associated with the lower orders: 'humanity is better in the state than among individuals. It purifies itself, because it elevates itself in this collective being.'[205]

Set alongside his preference for elite rule, his instinctive contempt for the working class, and his ambivalent view of human nature, Dupont-White's social philosophy seemed at least as much an expression of paternalism as of socialism; in a comparative English perspective again there are powerful echoes here of the nineteenth-century Tory tradition, especially Disraeli and Salisbury. Dupont-White felt a moral concern for poverty and exploitation, and remained convinced that the state should correct the most grievous injustices of capitalism.[206] He never departed from the basic view that capitalist society was responsible for 'the misery of the masses'[207] and that the state had a duty to defend weaker sections of society. He reaffirmed his belief in this progressive notion in 1873, at a time, it should be noted, when he is often regarded as lurching towards more conservative views.[208] In his later writings, Dupont-White even acknowledged, in contrast with the opportunist republican elites of the 1870s, that 'the social question' had become the dominant and most pressing issue in French politics.[209] But by the end of his life he did not believe that the solution to this problem could come from the political and intellectual recipe offered by socialists. The failure of the Commune, in his view, had irremediably destroyed all hopes for communism, Fourierism, and Saint-Simonism. All that remained was the age-old conflict between labour and capital.[210]

---

[203] Dupont-White, *Le progrès politique en France*, 132.

[204] 'Les hommes ne peuvent se toucher sans se heurter, se heurter sans se haïr.' Dupont-White, *La centralisation, suite à L'Individu et l'État*, 14.

[205] Dupont-White, *L'Individu et l'État*, 305.

[206] For other instances of such thinking, see Weill, Georges, 'Les Saint-Simoniens sous Napoléon III', *Revue des Études Napoléoniennes*, 3 (1913), 391–406.

[207] Letter to Laveleye, 1862; quoted in Villey, *Charles Dupont-White, sa vie, son oeuvre, sa doctrine*, 44.

[208] Dupont-White, 'Réflexions d'un optimiste' (1873), in *Politique Actuelle*, 306.

[209] Dupont-White, Charles, *Le suffrage universel* (Paris: Douniol, 1872), 9.

[210] Dupont-White, 'Perspectives Politiques' II, 65.

A Resolute but Unorthodox Republican

As with each of the systems of thought from which he drew inspiration, there is as little agreement on the precise nature of Dupont-White's republican credentials. The public record shows that he clearly endorsed the Republic in the 1870s and argued until the end of his life that the ideological alternatives to republicanism were both ineffective and dangerous.[211] But how far was he ideologically committed to the core principles of republicanism? Was he too, like Littré, nothing more than a formal republican? Writing in the late nineteenth century the radical republican Emile Leverdays had little doubt: Dupont-White's centralist state had 'nothing in common with what a republican people should be'. He added: 'we will never make citizens with subservient people believing in state providence.'[212] Nearly a century later, the opposite case was made most forcefully by Claude Nicolet, who argued that Dupont-White's theory of the state rested on positivist republican premises and that his doctrine of public authority was 'exactly that of the founders of the Third Republic, Gambetta and Ferry, they too directly inspired by positivism'.[213]

As mentioned earlier, Dupont-White moved in republican political and intellectual circles under the Second Republic and Second Empire. During the late 1840s and early 1850s he was a strong supporter of Eugène Cavaignac, the brother of the legendary Godefroy Cavaignac, regularly visiting the republican leader at his house and celebrating his 'vigorous but humane' crushing of the June 1848 insurrection.[214] After 1851 Dupont-White was a lively presence at republican intellectual gatherings in Paris. He was often seen at the conferences organized at Hippolyte Carnot's house, where he mingled with the likes of Goudchaux, Jules Simon—who, as we recall, annoyed him—and Garnier-Pagès.[215] He also frequently attended the salons of Juliette Adam and Marie d'Agoult; in both places his exchanges with republican and neo-republican intellectuals were passionate and often heated.[216]

That there were strong affinities between Dupont-White and the classical republican tradition is also undeniable: both recognized the transformative role of the state, the necessity of political and administrative centralization, and the foundational nature of civic equality.[217] The overall conclusion, however, again calls for nuance; it should by now be clear that Dupont-White's

---

[211] Dupont-White, *La République Conservatrice*, esp. 50–1.

[212] Leverdays, Emile, 'La centralisation', in *Œuvres posthumes*, Vol. 3 (Paris: G. Carré, 1893), 214.

[213] Nicolet, *L'Idée Républicaine en France*, 454.

[214] Letters to Gustave de Thou, undated, late 1840s, Cécile Carnot Papers, Archives Carnot, Chateau de Presles.

[215] Texier, Edmond, 'Dupont-White', *Le Siècle* (16 December 1878). It was at this juncture that his daughter Cécile met her future husband Sadi Carnot.

[216] For a flavour of these discussions see Adam, *Mes premières armes littéraires et politiques*, 93, 111–17.

[217] On the Jacobin tradition in the nineteenth century, see Furet, François, 'Révolution Française et Tradition Jacobine', in Colin Lucas (ed.), *The French Revolution and the Creation of Modern Political Culture*, Vol. 2 (Oxford: Pergamon, 1988), 335–7.

thought was not 'exactly' similar to any of his peers. A number of central elements of post-1848 republican thought were missing from Dupont-White's approach, suggesting that, like his approach to other political doctrines, his embrace of republicanism was singular and original. As for positivism, it will be shown that far from upholding its conception of knowledge Dupont-White was highly sceptical of the heuristic value of an exclusively 'scientific' understanding of the world.

The republican influence on Dupont-White is first apparent in his identification with the 1789 Revolution, which was presented as an inherently civilizing event which brought positive—and irreversible—transformations to political and social relations in France.[218] Since 1789, in his estimation, France had begun its journey towards 'perfectibility'.[219] Particularly in line with Jacobin republicanism was his hostility to the 'Girondist' tradition which *quarante-huitard* intellectuals such as Lamartine, and later Jules Ferry, attempted to rehabilitate. Dupont-White was a fervent admirer of Robespierre, and especially warmed to his notion of 'charity in the laws'. As he explained in a letter:

I cannot view [Robespierre] as a vulgar man. Perhaps revolutions, like battles, need blood; however, has the warrior who carries out this law of his function ever been accused of cruelty?[220]

Unlike Littré, furthermore, Dupont-White welcomed all three elements of the republican trinity of liberty, equality, and fraternity, although he stressed that their supreme manifestation was in the legal system.[221] The French Revolution had created a nation of free and equal citizens, and the completion of its ambitious programme would rid France of the endemic political instability it had experienced in the nineteenth century.[222] Largely republican, in this sense, was his contrast between public reason and individual passion in order to justify the pre-eminence of the state: 'the essence of the state is to be the power of reason expressed through law, and not that of man perverted by fantasy.'[223] The importance of a rationalist form of politics appeared further in Dupont-White's constant references to progress. Here he often quoted the definition offered by Pierre Leroux and echoed by Eugène Pelletan: for both men progress was 'an enhancement of life'.[224] Against those who maintained the exclusive rights of tradition, Dupont-White asserted humanity's privilege to fashion the world anew:

The generality of a fact does not prove that it is right, but only offers the presumption that it is necessary; this relative necessity gives its excuse to the past but takes nothing away from the Empire of conscience, and the rights of Progress.[225]

[218] Dupont-White, 'Introduction', in John Stuart Mill, *Le Gouvernement Représentatif*, xx–xxi.
[219] Dupont-White, *L'Individu et l'État*, 342.
[220] Letter to Gustave de Thou, undated, late 1840s, Cécile Carnot Papers, Archives Carnot, Chateau de Presles.
[221] Dupont-White, *L'Individu et l'État*, 40–3.
[222] Dupont-White, *La liberté de presse et le suffrage universel*, 71.
[223] Dupont-White, *L'Individu et l'État*, viii.
[224] See for example Dupont-White, *L'Individu et l'État*, 65; *Mélanges philosophiques*, 9, 62.
[225] Dupont-White, *L'Individu et l'État*, 123.

A characteristically republican centralist conception of rationalism also informed Dupont-White's notion of territoriality. It was this aspect of Dupont-White's thinking which drew the loudest applause from centralist republicans such as Etienne Vacherot during the Second Empire.[226] Three interlocked features are particularly worthy of mention here: his exalted attachment to Paris; his praise of urban living; and his rejection of local politics. Paris was for Dupont-White the uncontested symbol of French intellectual power: 'France only attains its collective thoughts through its capital, and its force through its government.'[227] It was this symbiotic relationship between the 'lettered classes' and high politics which gave French public life its distinctly intellectual flavour.[228] Like many republicans who shared his admiration of the capital city, Dupont-White deduced that 'agglomerated'[229] urban living was inherently more rewarding than life in the countryside. Hence a typically cutting formula, which mirrored Marx's sarcasm about pastoral life: 'land of mountains, land of idiots.'[230] In his private correspondence his contempt for everything which was not Parisian was almost offensive in tone; a letter to his daughter, written from a resort in the countryside, gave a typical flavour of his snobbery, which seemed all at once social and intellectual:

I cannot speak of those from the provinces, and I especially don't speak to them; we are too far off the mark with them.[231]

It was this same belief in this political superiority of the Parisian centre over the peripheries of France which animated Dupont-White's virulent hostility towards any substantive measure of local political autonomy. Communes, he repeated argued, were incapable of 'political' sentiments because political knowledge presupposed an appreciation of a world beyond the narrow confines of the village hall.[232] Decentralization could only lead to government by interest instead of government by principle; this would constitute the negation of a just polity: '36,000 small republics replete with omissions and injustices towards minorities, towards progress, towards reason, and national force.'[233] Local power, in short, was incapable of producing a society of citizens, a society capable of imparting justice and experiencing collective happiness.[234]

There were also conspicuous centralist republican undertones in Dupont-White's characterization of the relationship between the state and the individual. Individuals were in his view incapable of defining the public good; this was a matter only for the state. The concept of the general interest was distinct from the norms of private social and commercial relations, and could not in

---

[226] Vacherot, Etienne, *La Démocratie* (Paris: Chamerot, 1860), xxii n.1.
[227] Dupont-White, *La centralisation, suite à L'Individu et l'État*, 347.   [228] Ibid., 349.
[229] 'Man reaches his full value only when he is agglomerated.' Ibid., 269.   [230] Ibid., 270.
[231] Letter to Cécile Carnot, undated, Cécile Carnot Papers, Archives Carnot, Chateau de Presles.
[232] Dupont-White, *La liberté politique considérée dans ses rapports avec l'administration locale*, 216–17.
[233] Ibid., 227.   [234] Dupont-White, *La centralisation, suite à L'Individu et l'État*, 10.

any way be derived from such norms: 'the public interest is not the sum of private interests.'[235] Dupont-White robustly denied that there was a necessary conflict between economic efficiency and the public interest, citing Colbert's policies as an example of their judicious reconciliation.[236] The cornerstone of his conception of the public good here was his belief that financial considerations were entirely accessory in determining the economic intervention of the state: what mattered was whether any given service was essential and, if so, whether it could be reliably provided by commercial groups. Dupont-White thus concluded that the state should continue to provide postal services, even if they could be offered more cheaply by private means, because the reliable delivery of the post was a matter of public interest.[237]

In addition to guarding the public good, the state was also responsible for the moral education of the citizenry. Dupont-White was careful here to distance himself from the excesses of revolutionary Jacobinism, repudiating, on classic liberal individualist grounds, any doctrine which imposed a particular notion of the good life on society by terroristic means.[238] But his intellectual debt to the republican tradition was clear in his rejection of Mill's liberal equation of freedom with the diversity of human endeavours. Not all human desires and aspirations were equally worthy of pursuit;[239] and the state was entitled to make clear which of these goals were consistent with the good life. But this strong perfectionist claim was qualified by the assertion that this was a matter of moral persuasion rather than legal compulsion; in this sense doing good was for the state a conditional imperative, not a categorical one. Speaking of the state in *L'Individu et l'État,* he stressed: 'it is not for it to compel men, by the terror of punishment, to do good and to practise the duties of virtue.'[240] Finally, Dupont-White's centralist republicanism appeared in his appreciation that the republican state was the best guarantor of public order in France. When individuals and groups challenged this order, it was the republicans rather than the Bonapartists, Orleanists, or legitimists who were the most reliable instruments of its restoration.[241]

Seen in the above light, the republican credentials of Dupont-White appear unimpeachable; and it was invariably these statist aspects of his political thought which were underlined by those commentators who stressed his republicanism.[242] Yet, in a manner which was characteristic of his attitude to existing political doctrines, he consciously held back from a comprehensive espousal of republican values. It is true that French republicanism was an extremely diverse and heterogenous community between 1848 and 1875. But, irrespective of these differences, republicans tended to share a commitment to a number of core principles: universal suffrage, representative government, mass participation in public life, and secularism, especially in education. By

[235] Dupont-White, *L'Individu et l'État,* 259.   [236] Ibid., 105–9.
[237] Ibid., 314.   [238] Ibid, 188.
[239] Dupont-White, 'Préface', in John Stuart Mill, *La liberté* (Paris: Guillaumin, 1864), 4–5.
[240] Dupont-White, *L'Individu et l'État,* 77.
[241] Dupont-White, *La République Conservatrice,* 5–8.
[242] See for example Louis Joly, 'M. Dupont-White', *Le Moniteur Universel* (12 December 1878).

the late 1860s it was difficult to find any mainstream republican undercurrent which did not uphold these values.[243] Dupont-White did not merely pass over them in silence: he adopted diametrically opposite positions on each of these questions. Secularism, for example, was not a principle which appealed to his spiritual sensibilities; it lacked elevation and ambition because it was 'limited to well-being, too close to the ground';[244] he also rejected the religious individualism associated with Protestantism.[245] The state, for Dupont-White, was among other things the necessary agent of 'eternal laws'[246]—hardly a formulation which would have found favour in secular and anti-clerical republican circles in the second half of the nineteenth century.

The strength of his opposition to universal suffrage has been recently acknowledged with the suggestion that his views were broadly representative of conservative opinion in the 1860s and 1870s.[247] What is interesting in Dupont-White's critique of universal suffrage, however, is his rejection of both republican and conservative approaches. In response to the republicans' optimistic faith in the mass vote, Dupont-White argued that universal suffrage could only exacerbate class conflict: 'political elections are an inevitable terrain for class struggles.'[248] He also disputed the republican claim that elections would make for a more transparent political system, arguing instead that the mass vote would lead to false promises and electoral bribery, disillusionment with the political system, and eventually pave the way for dictatorial government.[249]

But he also consistently rejected many conservative arguments against universal suffrage. He did not accept, for example, that the mass vote was necessarily a source of political instability, and contemptuously dismissed the assertion that it was the prelude to mob rule.[250] The most common conservative elitist argument against universal suffrage was the lack of discernment of those upon whom it was bestowed.[251] This, too, Dupont-White rejected: simple moral and political notions were sufficient to exercise the vote, and these instincts were in ample supply among the people.[252] The problem with universal suffrage, in his view, was that its outcomes were both too uncertain and too categorical: too uncertain because the same electorate could vote for freedom at one moment and despotism at another, as had happened in 1848 and 1852;[253] too categorical because political majorities were inherently despotic: like many of his liberal predecessors and contemporaries, Dupont-White was constantly haunted by the fear of a tyrannical majority.[254] He thus suggested

[243] See Pilbeam, *Republicanism in nineteenth-century France*, 243–63.

[244] Dupont-White, *Politique actuelle*, 243.

[245] Dupont-White, *Mélanges philosophiques*, 124. His support for the public funding of religion was outlined in 'Du Budget des Cultes', *La Politique Nouvelle* (6 April 1851), 378–92.

[246] Dupont-White, *L'Individu et l'État*, 174–5.

[247] See Rosanvallon, Pierre, *Le sacre du citoyen* (Paris: Gallimard, 1992), 310, 312.

[248] Dupont-White, *Le suffrage universel*, 5.   [249] Ibid., 21–2.   [250] Ibid., 18.

[251] For a typical example, see Renan, *La réforme intellectuelle et morale*, 44–6.   [252] Ibid., 17.

[253] Dupont-White, *Le progrès politique en France*, 3.

[254] The theme of 'democratic despotism' appeared constantly in French liberal thought after Tocqueville. It was central to the first book of Prévost-Paradol, Lucien-Anatole, *La France Nouvelle*

the creation of institutions which would mitigate and deflect the effects of the mass vote: for example, an indirectly-elected senate or a strong and independent executive.[255] Although he did not advocate the suppression of universal suffrage, and recognized its ineluctable presence,[256] he also believed that a functional political system could operate without it:[257] a view which was alien to all mainstream republican groups in the 1860s or 1870s.

A further feature of Dupont-White's political thought which was distinct from traditional republicanism was his elitist conception of government. Control of the state, in his view, had to be vested in the 'upper classes'[258] because this was the only group which was enlightened enough to govern in the public interest.[259] In his *Mélanges Philosophiques* he stated bluntly: 'government does not belong to all without distinction, but to the most capable'[260]—a deliberately provocative reference to a Doctrinaire concept—*capacité*—which republicans categorically rejected. Even though Dupont-White's definition of aristocracy was somewhat elastic—it included men of culture and elevated spirit as well as the aristocracy of birth[261]—this belief in a 'natural' ruling elite was strongly at odds with the core republican postulate that social class should not be a relevant consideration in determining participation in government and public affairs. Dupont-White went even further, however, arguing that the main object of democracy was to reinforce the rule of the upper classes:

Democracy is made, not for governing, but to form those who govern, to support and renew the upper classes, to allow natural superiorities to rise to the summit of the political system. In short democracy is good for making aristocracies.[262]

Again, the originality of Dupont-White's position is manifest here. His vision of aristocratic rule was markedly distinct from the monarchist position, for unlike the legitimists he did not believe in the inherent virtues of natural order or the necessity of social hierarchy;[263] in fact he was often scathing about the influence of 'castes' on local communities.[264] It was only because of its experience and intellectual abilities that the aristocracy was entitled to govern.[265] At the same time, his view was also at variance with the Jacobin republican notion of the state, which abhorred the notion that the ruling class could be drawn from the privileged aristocracy. It was also contrary to the 'liberal'

(Paris: Calmann-Lévy, 1868). Dupont-White's notion of democratic despotism was somewhat different in that he welcomed the extension of bureaucratic and welfare state functions which Tocqueville and Paradol regarded as threatening civic freedom. His fears were exclusively directed at the political actions of majorities.

[255] Dupont-White, *La République Conservatrice*, 41.
[256] See his article in *Le Temps* (16 February 1870).
[257] Dupont-White, *Le progrès politique en France*, 46–7.
[258] Dupont-White, *L'Individu et l'État*, 60–1.   [259] Dupont-White, *Politique actuelle*, vi.
[260] Dupont-White, *Mélanges philosophiques*, 27.
[261] Dupont-White, 'Préface', in John Stuart Mill, *La liberté*, 57–8.
[262] Dupont-White, *La liberté politique considérée dans ses rapports avec l'administration locale*, 243.
[263] Dupont-White, *L'Individu et l'État*, x.
[264] See for example 'Centralisation et Liberté', *Revue des Deux Mondes* (1 February 1863), 581–3.
[265] Dupont-White, *Politique actuelle*, xxxvii.

a different—and contrary—set of principles. In many areas, such as the definition of the political rights of citizens, Dupont-White did not even believe that
general principles were of much use. In the following passage he underlined
his continuing commitment to the Doctrinaire idea of 'capacity', and in so
doing highlighted the similarities between Guizot's political thought and that
of the first generation of republican opportunists:

> Political rights raise the issue of capacity, a thorny and uncomfortable question among
> all. Here there exists no more evidence, no more clear rules, not even for the age of
> majority, not even for the conditions of access to office. We evaluate, we proceed ten-
> tatively, we observe, and we arrive at a solution as best we can. Pure doctrines of rights,
> moral theories, here offer no guidance. We must take apart, analyze government and
> society in order to establish what can be offered and adapted from government for each
> class of society.[289]

Dupont-White's eclectic method guaranteed a measure of compromise among
competing ideological tenets, and such intellectual 'transactions' were for him
the stuff of political philosophy. This intellectual approach was one of the
most remarkable features of his political thought. He was willing not only to
draw from an extraordinary range of families of thought but also to play off
different sets of principles against each other, relying on this creative friction
to construct a fluid and highly original system of thought. This method
allowed him, for example, to identify the moral and intellectual limitations of
liberal political economy and liberal individualism; it also enabled him to pinpoint precisely the fault lines in different systems of thought.

This was perhaps the sense in which his political thought anticipated republicanism after 1880: not any of its particular doctrinal forms but rather the
general theory of politics which informed the development of the French state
under the Third Republic. In terms of ideological taxonomy, it might in this
sense be concluded that his political liberalism was qualified—or, more appro-
priately, enhanced—by republican and 'socialist' convictions concerning the
nature of the state and the object of law-making; these republican and 'socialist' aspirations were in turn bounded by a strongly liberal emphasis on pater-
nalistic government, the rule of law, and private property; and his centralist
doctrine, finally, was restrained by his core liberal beliefs in civil and political
freedoms. On the negative side, Dupont-White also shared much of the early
Third Republic's implicit sense of the superiority of European culture and civilization, and a tacit belief in the existence of higher and lower races, even
though he rejected Gobineau's narrow racialism and did not explicitly endorse
the positivist classification of racial groups. The influence of Herbert Spencer
on his political thought was profound and significantly coloured his views
about human perfectibility and its limits, although here too one could sense a
titanic dialogue between his 'liberal' and 'republican' voices on the one hand
and his quasi-Hobbesian instincts on the other.

---

[289] Dupont-White, 'Impuissance politique de la philosophie', 344.

Of all these different ideological categories, the centralist label is the one which in the final analysis fits Dupont-White most comfortably. This conclusion may be justified not only on the grounds that his defence of the state was at the heart of his political philosophy but also because his attachment to centralization did not waver significantly after 1848.[290] But it is important again to underline the specificity of Dupont-White's centralism. He was at one with all republican centralists, such as Louis Blanc,[291] in his attachment to the public interest, his celebration of Paris, his praise for urban living, and—not least—his contempt for local forms of power. But at the same time his was not the elite republican Jacobinism of the Second Empire and early Third Republic, with its defence of the Terror and emphasis on the unity of the republican tradition; or the 'Archimedean lever' perceived by Blanquists such as Tridon.[292]

Unlike the latter, Dupont-White's state respected civil and political liberties; and unlike the former, it was not concerned with nationalism and offered neither a comprehensive moral code nor a broad notion of the good life, even though Dupont-White's inflated prose at times seemed to suggest otherwise. The calmness with which he enunciated his principles was in stark contrast with the agitated style of republican Jacobinism; his synthetic and inclusive political method was far removed from the Jacobins' inveterate suspicion of any views which were not their own; and his sober willingness to recognize the value and even superiority of different political systems and ways of thinking was fundamentally at odds with the cultural parochialism of most Jacobin centralists.[293] In all these respects, Dupont-White staked out a distinctive position, giving his republican centralism a particular and highly original formulation.

Dupont-White's conception of the role of the state has been criticized for its lack of precision. Mill, who greatly admired his work, nonetheless regretted his absence of rigour and the 'confusion'[294] which marred his writings. It is true that he did not offer a precise mechanism for determining the extent of state intervention, and many of his critics saw him as a statist who recognized no natural or prudential limits to the extension of the public sphere. Some of Dupont-White's less careful statements were consistent with such an interpretation. However, a different reading may be offered. The reason he did not offer a comprehensive theory of state intervention was not that he thought the state could operate anywhere it wished but, on the contrary, that the precise bounds of state activity should be a matter of intuitive agreement among all enlightened men. It was the state's duty to guarantee civil and political liberties;

---

[290] Pécaut, Félix, 'Dupont-White', *La Critique Philosophique* (January 1879), 580.

[291] See for example Blanc, Louis, *La République une et indivisible* (Paris: Naud, 1851).

[292] Tridon, Gustave, 'Gironde et Girondins', in *Oeuvres diverses de Gustave Tridon* (Paris: Allemane, 1891), 130–1.

[293] Most uncharacteristically for a French thinker, he recognized the superiority of British intellectual life: 'England is today the first country in the world to dare all in philosophical matters', *Mélanges philosophiques*, 122.

[294] John Stuart Mill, 'Centralisation', 588.

uphold the rule of law and the rights of property; defend the nation against external threats; ensure that primary education was universally available; build roads, railways, and canals; tend to the basic health needs of the poor; and regulate the relationship between labour and capital. This was a defence of a liberal centralized polity, an adaptation to the later nineteenth century of the principles of public philosophy initially defined by Enlightenment thinkers and first implemented, very imperfectly, by the republican generation of 1789.

Said differently, Dupont-White's theory of the state was perhaps less an anticipation on the future than a gentle warning against the dilapidation of the existing intellectual heritage of the late eighteenth and early nineteenth centuries. This warning was especially addressed to liberals. One of the keys to understanding Dupont-White's political thought, in our view, is to imagine him as a centralist pamphleteer seeking to allay the concerns of liberals about the emerging republican order. When seen from this perspective, Dupont-White played a pivotal role in legitimizing the new republican regime in the eyes of the liberal intelligentsia. He did so in several crucial ways. He gave credibility to the Third Republic by his own public endorsement of its institutions in the 1870s and his severe criticism of the ideological alternatives which were on offer. Dupont-White's writings also forced French liberals to reconsider their visceral opposition to the state and their identification of the good life with its absence. In his view, the atomistic conception of society favoured by political and economic liberals was fundamentally incoherent if it was not accompanied by efforts to create favourable social and political conditions for individual growth. The principles of good citizenship could not be left to be determined by local oligarchies: Dupont-White helped through his polemical writings to convey the truth of this fundamental republican principle to the liberal intellectual community.

Furthermore, Dupont-White constantly sought to reassure liberals about the limited social and political consequences of mass democracy, a source of much anxiety to conservative liberals throughout the period between 1830 and 1875. In one of his late articles he argued that all these fears, so eloquently articulated by the likes of Royer-Collard, Guizot, and Tocqueville, had been misplaced. There had been significant advances in democracy in France throughout the nineteenth century, but these changes had in Dupont-White's view done little to alter the country's mores, opinions, and even laws.[295] The message was clear: the Republic was coming, but it would do little to affect the entrenched interests of the middle class groups which constituted the backbone of French liberalism. The Republic would help France back to an era of political stability: 'perhaps we can be allowed to think that we have finished with revolutions.'[296]

Dupont-White's strong sense of philosophical optimism effectively countered the theme of 'decline' which was commonplace in French liberal and conservative circles, especially in the aftermath of the Franco-Prussian war and

---

[295] Dupont-White, 'Perspectives Politiques' II, 76–7.   [296] Ibid., 81.

the Paris Commune. He vigorously denied that France was in 'decadence',[297] even though he accepted that the public spirit was at a low ebb: a fact he partly attributed to the growing political influence of the masses. But—and this is a point he directed specifically at the liberal intelligentsia—there was no need to be fearful about France's future; in this sense his Hobbesianism was clearly limited in scope. Despite the events of 1870–1, all of France's social, intellectual, and institutional forces were still intact and were growing in strength. The country may have experienced a temporary setback in recent years, but Dupont-White had every confidence in France's capacity for renewal.[298] Translated in political and institutional terms, this denial of French 'decline' represented an invitation to all liberals to rally to the new Republic and give the regime their full support.

Finally, Dupont-White's writings appealed to liberals not to allow the appropriation of the state by self-interested and exclusive social groups. The intensity of class conflict was such in France that it threatened to turn the state into an arena for the struggle among competing social forces, and this transformation would in his mind negate the essential purpose of public authority. The subversion of the general interest by particularist social concerns was for Dupont-White equally reprehensible whether undertaken by legitimists in the name of aristocratic interests, socialists for working-class interests, or republicans for bourgeois interests. In this respect, Dupont-White's correspondence with Mill in the early 1870s reveals that both men were deeply concerned with the political exclusion of the working class from French public life.[299]

Such was Dupont-White's political thought: original, moderate, and—paradoxically given his anti-individualism—deeply humane. In the words of one of his necrologists: 'a truly philosophical spirit, with a rare, natural and powerful eclecticism, it can be said of Dupont-White that never did a theorist hold on more passionately to his personal independence and, at the same time, more scrupulously respect the liberty of others.'[300] His message was as much directed at the republicans who were assuming the reins of power in France as at the liberals and monarchists who were fighting to retain control of them. For him the search for the truth was never to be subordinated to political expediency, nor the defence of the public interest to partisan considerations. As one of his liberal critics noted with some admiration: 'he prefers to satisfy his reason rather than the public'.[301] By providing many conservatives and liberals with the ideological justifications they needed to endorse the emerging institutions of the Third Republic, Dupont-White performed an invaluable service to the republican cause, and despite his intellectual heterodoxies fully deserves to be remembered as one of the founders of the new order.

---

[297] Dupont-White, 'Réflexions d'un optimiste', 186.
[298] Dupont-White, 'Perspectives Politiques' I, 698–9.
[299] Mill to Dupont-White, 6 December 1871, in Mineka and Lindley (eds), *The Collected Works of John Stuart Mill*, 1863–5.
[300] Texier, 'Dupont-White'.
[301] de Rémusat, Charles, 'De la Centralisation en France', in *Revue des Deux Mondes* (15 October 1860), 799.

circles of the *opposition avançée*. During the 1857 legislative elections he joined the Parisian Committee which coordinated the republican efforts,[6] and played a prominent role in subsequent campaigns in the capital.[7]

During the 1860s he collaborated with a number of vanguard republican publications such as *La réforme littéraire* and *Rive Gauche*,[8] and his prestige and influence were commended by leading members of the republican party such as Gambetta.[9] His belief in the principles of freethinking also earned him the same enemies as the republicans: his election to the Académie des Sciences Morales et Politiques of the Institut in 1868 provoked consternation in Catholic circles, and throughout his life his moral philosophy was denounced by ecclesiastical and clericalist writers.[10] During the short-lived liberal Empire (January–August 1870) Vacherot's republicanism remained uncompromising: he refused an appointment to the newly formed Commission on Higher Education, and in an open letter reaffirmed his hostility to the Bonapartist regime.[11] Both in his words and in his deeds, therefore, Vacherot appeared as a thoroughly committed republican; and it was in this spirit that one of his necrologists described him in 1897 as 'one of the men who has most honoured French philosophy during the second half of this century'.[12] In a similar vein, it is no doubt with these epic years in mind that Vacherot has been described as one of the 'founding fathers'[13] of modern republican ideology.

What is generally much less known—or at least commented upon—is that after 1871 this eminent thinker gradually drifted away from the republican regime which he had helped to found. Appointed as Mayor of the Vth arrondissement after the fall of the Second Empire, Vacherot condemned the proclamation of the Commune in March 1871 and welcomed the Versailles-led restoration of order by Adolphe Thiers.[14] Elected to the National Assembly in the same year, he remained aligned with the conservative neo-republican-ism of Thiers, serving on the parliamentary Commission which drafted the republican constitutional laws of 1875. After the turning point of 1877, which witnessed the political triumph of the republican Assembly, led by Gambetta, over the MacMahon presidency, he became increasingly estranged from his colleagues. Vacherot was irritated by what he regarded as the partisan and

[6] Weill, *Histoire du parti républicain*, 416.

[7] In one of his letters to Gambetta (15–20 April 1869), Jules Ferry briefly, and somewhat unflatteringly, described the chairman of one of his electoral meetings: 'Vacherot was presiding, you know how—such tedium and such unintelligibility.' See *Revue de Paris* (1 May 1914), 78.

[8] Dabot, *Souvenirs et impressions*, 156; see also Scheurer-Kestner, Auguste, *Souvenirs de jeunesse* (Paris: Fasquelle, 1905), 63–4.

[9] See for example Gambetta's commendation of Vacherot to Lavertujon, in a letter dated 30 August 1869, in Lavertujon, André (ed.), *Gambetta inconnu* (Bordeaux: Gounouilhou, 1905), 11.

[10] See for example Blanc, Abbé Élie, *Un spiritualisme sans Dieu. Examen de la philosophie de M. Vacherot* (Lyon: Librairie Générale Catholique et Classique, 1885); and Weill, Georges, *Histoire du catholicisme libéral en France* (Genève: Slatkine, 1979), 152–4.

[11] See Ollivier, Émile, *L'Empire Libéral*, Vol. 12 (Paris: Garnier, 1908), 539–40.

[12] Michel, Henry, 'Vacherot', *Le Temps* (30 July 1897).

[13] Ozouf, Mona, 'Entre l'esprit des Lumières et la lettre Positiviste: les républicains sous l'Empire', in François Furet and Mona Ozouf (eds), *Le siècle de l'avènement républicain* (Paris: Gallimard, 1993), 418.

[14] Ollé-Laprune, Léon, *Étienne Vacherot* (Paris: Perrin, 1898), 56–7.

sectarian behaviour of republican elites, especially on the increasingly divisive issue of *laïcité*.[15]

His critique of republican politics became progressively more trenchant, and in the 1881 and 1885 legislative elections he openly sided with the conservative critics of the Republic.[16] In 1892 his intellectual evolution came full circle with the publication of *La Démocratie Libérale*, which Vacherot described as both a sequel to his earlier work and his political testament.[17] In its substance as well as its tone, this work seemed to amount to a repudiation of his earlier republicanism. Indeed its most spectacular proposal was an explicit call for the replacement of the Republic by a hereditary monarchy, and its mediocre parliamentary rabble by a more refined and socially exclusive political elite.[18] To the dismay of many of his comrades, one of the intellectual founders of the Republic had joined the ranks of the enemy. Vacherot's ideological shifts in the 1870s and 1880s, culminating in his rejection of much of his Second Empire republicanism, have not received much critical discussion.[19] Yet this compelling story is worth examining for a number of reasons, not least because Vacherot's ethical and spiritualist form of republicanism has been granted much less attention than the positivist strand, which—as we have seen in the case of Littré—is often presented as dominant and even hegemonic after the 1860s.[20] More generally, there is a case for re-examining the ensemble of Vacherot's political thought rather than the truncated version which has hitherto been considered by historians of French political thought. Indeed, the conservative evolution of his political ideas under the Third Republic invites a closer scrutiny of his earlier republican beliefs. Precisely how much of his ideological baggage did he jettison in his subsequent years, and why? More intriguingly, perhaps, to what extent can intimations of these later fractures be sensed during his 'republican' years? In short, his later intellectual evolution invites a re-examination of the cohesiveness of Vacherot's philosophical republicanism during the Second Empire and of its precise intellectual foundations. Finally, his personal itinerary also connects with several broader themes already encountered in the lives and works of Littré and Dupont-White: the intellectual fragmentation of centralist republicanism after 1850, of which he offers a fascinating example; the tormented religious doubts of many freethinkers and secular republicans in their later years, which were mirrored in Vacherot's eschatological relationship with Catholicism; and

---

[15] See the series of articles on this subject by Dietz, Jean, 'Jules Ferry et les traditions républicaines', *Revue Politique et Parlementaire* (1934–35) esp. 3, 'La laïcité' (10 August 1934), 297–311, and 4, 'La bataille des congrégations' (10 September 1934), 495–513.

[16] See his letters in Target, P. F., *Élections du 21 Août 1881* (Paris, 1881) and *Élections du 4 Octobre 1885* (Paris, 1885); and the report on a conservative electoral meeting held in the Marais in *L'Univers* (2 October 1885).

[17] Vacherot, Étienne, *La Démocratie Libérale* (Paris: Calmann-Lévy, 1892), 1.

[18] Ibid., 11–12.

[19] Thuillier, Guy, 'Aux origines du radicalisme: "La Démocratie" d'Étienne Vacherot', *Revue Administrative* 254 (March-April 1990), 117–26, focuses on Vacherot's conception of the administration, and only very briefly discusses his political thought more generally.

[20] Nicolet, *L'idée républicaine en France*.

the difficult line of demarcation between republican ideology and conservative liberalism, an intellectual contradiction which, like a not inconsiderable
number of his colleagues in the late nineteenth century, Vacherot found
impossible to reconcile.

The Conversion of a Liberal

Unlike other philosophical eminences of nineteenth-century French republicanism such as Charles Renouvier, Émile Littré, and Jules Simon, Vacherot did
not incline naturally towards republicanism in his youth. His embrace of
republican values was partly the result of a personal philosophical evolution
towards rationalism and partly the product of the social and political turmoil
which engulfed France after the 1848 revolution. His early years were almost
exclusively devoted to the calmness of philosophical contemplation.

Born at Langres on 29 July 1809 in a humble peasant family, the young
Vacherot was soon noted for his prodigious intellectual talents at school, and
secured admission to the Ecole Normale Supérieure at the age of 18.[21] After
graduating he taught philosophy at Cahors, Angers, Versailles, Caen, and
Rouen. The teaching profession provided neither time nor inclination to think
about practical political activity; indeed Vacherot's living and working conditions were analogous to those which had inspired Sarcey's comment that
'nothing is more stultifying than teaching'.[22] As Vacherot later confessed,
although he greatly admired Michelet, his intellectual preferences at this time
generally went towards the liberalism of the Doctrinaires; he particularly
warmed to the works of Royer-Collard, de Broglie, Guizot, and Rémusat. He
later remembered the idealism of this period:

In these times of generous illusions, and also of grand schemes, we were not concerned
only with politics; we dreamt of poetry, of science, of philosophy, of religion, of a new
world in which all these beautiful and blessed things would re-emerge transfigured by
the light of an ideal not known to our fathers.[23]

This ethereal philosophical rationalism would initially be reinforced by his
return to Paris. After the award of his doctorate in 1836, he was recruited as
director of studies by the École Normale, and promoted in 1838 to the position of *maître de conférences*. The École was at this time presided by Victor
Cousin, a conservative liberal elitist who had founded the 'eclectic' school of
philosophy and who would serve as Minister of Public Instruction under the

---

[21] Two years before his death, Vacherot described the atmosphere of his student years in his contribution to the collective work *Le centenaire de l'École Normale 1795–1895* (Paris: Hachette, 1895),
260–1. Also richly evocative of this period is Simon, Jules, 'Un Normalien en 1832', in *Mémoires des
autres* (Paris: Testard, 1890), 217–89.

[22] 'Rien ne crétinise comme l'enseignement'; quoted in Gerbod, Paul, *La vie quotidienne dans les
lycées et collèges au XIXe siècle* (Paris: Hachette, 1968), 192.

[23] Vacherot, Étienne, *Notice sur Paul-François Dubois* (Paris: Picard, 1875), 12.

July Monarchy.[24] Cousin took Vacherot under his wing and in 1839 invited his young disciple to assist with his lectures at the Sorbonne.[25] Vacherot gradually began to find his own philosophical voice during the 1840s,[26] however, and by the time he published his three-volume *Histoire critique de l'école d'Alexandrie*[27] he had already formulated one of the principles to which he would long remain devoted: the need for a rigorous separation between theological speculation and philosophical enquiry. The third volume of the *Histoire critique*, which made this point explicitly,[28] provoked such a storm in orthodox Catholic circles that Vacherot was suspended from his post at the École Normale in June 1851.[29] The advocacy of freethinking was thus the source of his first direct encounter with political and administrative authoritarianism.

Another sign of Vacherot's intellectual development was his progressive embrace of 'democracy' during the 1840s. He formed part of a group of young republican academics among whom could be found Deschanel, Despois, Bersot, and Barni.[30] The overthrow of the July Monarchy in 1848 drew Vacherot into the electoral arena as a candidate in the Haute-Marne. Although he later claimed not to have approved of the 1848 revolution,[31] his manifesto seemed clearly to welcome the advent of the Second Republic which had come in good time, in his words, 'to destroy all privileges'.[32] Destruction within certain limits, however: during the June insurrection of 1848, Vacherot and the director of the École Normale Dubois, manned the barricades of the Pantheon with their students against the working-class insurgents.[33] Already regarded as something of a subversive by the university authorities, the free-thinking republican philosopher sealed his fate by refusing to take an oath of allegiance to the Second Empire in 1852. He described his difficult circumstances in a letter to his friend Jules Simon:

At last I have been asked to swear the oath. I am refusing to do so, despite the most pressing intercessions of my family. I am told that I am playing at very high stakes. But it is not a game, it is a duty of dignity and honour.[34]

Despite the injunctions of his relatives Vacherot could not bring himself to swear to be loyal to the regime of Napoleon III. He was dismissed along with

[24] For a sense of his political philosophy, see Cousin, Victor, *Oeuvres de M. Victor Cousin. Discours Politiques* (Paris: Didier, 1851).

[25] For these biographical details, see Larousse, Pierre, *Grand Dictionnaire Universel du XIXe Siècle* (Geneva-Paris: Slatkine, 1982), 717–18.

[26] He was a contributor to the six-volume *Dictionnaire des Sciences Philosophiques* (Paris: Hachette, 1844), 852.

[27] Paris: Librairie Philosophique de Ladrange, 1846–51.

[28] Especially the conclusion, pp. 450–521.

[29] Vacherot's views were challenged by Abbé A. Gratry, *Étude sur la sophistique contemporaine ou lettre à M. Vacherot* (Paris: Gaume, 1851).

[30] Dide, Auguste, *Jules Barni, sa vie et ses oeuvres* (Paris: Alcan, 1892), 12.

[31] Vacherot, *La Démocratie Libérale*, 2–3.

[32] Vacherot, Étienne, 'Concitoyens', Manifesto dated 14 March 1848. Bib.Nat.Le64.1113.

[33] *Le centenaire de l'École Normale*, 263.

[34] Vacherot to Simon, letter dated 14 June 1852, in Archives Nationales, Papiers Jules Simon, 87 AP 7.

a number of republicans academics who took a similar stance.[35] In order to survive, he was reduced to giving philosophical lectures at Sainte-Barbe and private lessons: a form of existence which he found deeply frustrating. In a letter thanking his friend Halévy for sending him a copy of his latest book, Vacherot gave a sense of the difficulties he faced: 'I am so often disturbed by my duties as instructor and pedagogue that I have only just finished the beautiful book you sent me.'[36]

His former student Hippolyte Taine was struck by his appearance during this period:

He is somewhat bent, sickly and thin; his features are drawn and tired by the habit of reflection, and his beautiful black eyes, full of penetration and passion, seem normally to see something other than what he looks at.[37]

He clearly paid little attention to his looks: 'his coat is not very well buttoned, his trousers flap a great deal around his feet, and it is not obvious that he has ever learnt how to knot his tie.'[38] But his public lectures were enthusiastically received, extending to an even wider circle the 'veneration without limits' with which he was regarded among young Parisian university students.[39] It was during these years, and particularly against this cultural and political context, that Vacherot would begin to produce his first proto-republican philosophical commentaries.

The republican party was prostrate in the early years of the reign of Napoleon III.[40] Persecuted in Paris and in the provinces, and politically defeated by the triumphant plebiscite which restored the Empire in 1852, the republican movement in effect fragmented into a 'mosaic of disparate organizations'.[41] Republicans generally kept their heads down and took refuge in private meetings—Vacherot was also a regular visitor at Daniel Stern's salon[42]—and in institutions and associations of various types, ranging from the teaching and legal professions to the Freemasonry. One of these havens was the Parisian literary and educational elite which gravitated around the university system.[43] Traumatized by the collapse of the Second Republic, this intellectual community slowly began to raise its political profile during the 1850s. While the dominant political inclination among faculty members

---

[35] There were 30 refusals, mostly from the secondary sector. For the full list, see Gerbod, Paul, *La condition universitaire en France au XIXe siècle* (Paris: Presses Universitaires de France, 1965), 300 n.73.

[36] Letter of 19 July 1854. In Bibliothèque de L'Institut de France, Halévy letters, Ms4490.

[37] Taine, Hippolyte, *Les philosophes français du XIXe siècle* (Paris: Hachette, 1857), 335.

[38] Ibid.

[39] Weill, *Histoire du parti républicain*, 406. Many of his former students became close friends, among them Pasteur, Challemel-Lacour, About, Sarcey, and Prévost-Paradol. See Loubeau, Pierre, 'Souvenirs sur Étienne Vacherot', *Le Figaro* (29 July 1897).

[40] For a vivid account of the weaknesses of the republicans in these years, see de La Gorce, Pierre, *Histoire du Second Empire*, Vol. 2 (Paris: Plon, 1894), 81–96.

[41] Huard, Raymond, *Le mouvement républicain en Bas-Languedoc* (Paris: Presses de la Fondation Nationale des Sciences Politiques, 1982), 86.

[42] Ollivier, *Journal 1846–1860*, 269.

[43] See Nord, *The republican moment*, 31–47.

remained prudently Orleanist, a growing number of young professors and especially students embraced republicanism with increasing fervour.[44]

One of the first signs of this ideological renewal was the journal *L'Avenir*, a philosophical and literary weekly launched in 1855 by a group of republican intellectuals; among its regular contributors were Frédéric Morin, Daniel Stern (Marie d'Agoult), and Henri Brisson. From the point of view of this book this journal was especially distinctive in that Jules Barni, Eugène Pelletan, and Vacherot himself were also among the collaborators.[45] Although it survived for less than a year—the imperial censors took offence easily in the 1850s—the journal succeeded in defining the moral and political priorities of the new republican generation.[46] The emphasis on youth was indeed pronounced; in the editorial of the first issue, Eugène Pelletan truculently announced that the time had come for the 'old men disillusioned with progress' to make way for the 'new literary generation'.[47]

Reacting against the effete sensualism of the times, these republicans also sternly propounded the virtues of puritanism. Vacherot thus fiercely denounced 'the distractions and pleasures of this soft and easy life in which characters are weakened, and hearts corrupted'[48]—a direct attack against the luxuriance and glitter of official life under the Second Empire. Above all, the spirit of the journal was defined by a passionate celebration of voluntarism and a rejection of any attitude which smacked of passivity or resignation. Vacherot again:

Do not come to us with the external concerns of opinion, the weariness of spirits, the thoughts which have lost favour. There are no social circumstances which can excuse laziness, discouragement, and impotence.[49]

The positive programme of *L'Avenir* was borrowed straight out of the Doctrinaire manual: 'we believe in the sovereignty of reason and in its omnipotence.'[50] This faith in free thought lay at the heart of the journal's conception of human morality, and was constantly counter-posed to the dogmatic assertions of theology. Throughout its brief existence, the journal vaunted the merits of rationalism and freethinking, and denounced the metaphysical absurdities of Catholicism. Because of its necessary reliance on dogma, Catholicism was also deemed to be incapable of internal reform.

In a spirited exchange of letters with the liberal Catholic François Huet, Vacherot thus asserted that Catholic theology was fundamentally incompatible

---

[44] Gerbod, *La condition universitaire en France*, 402.

[45] The solidarity of this group was reinforced by common adversity. Like Vacherot, Barni and Morin had lost their teaching positions in 1852 for refusing the oath of loyalty to the Second Empire.

[46] On the intellectual atmosphere of the 1850s and 1860s, see Lefevre, André, *La renaissance du matérialisme* (Paris: Octave Doin, 1881), 115–37.

[47] *L'Avenir*, No.1 (6 May 1855). 'Youth', it has to be said, was more a state of mind than a physiological property; Pelletan was already 42 at the time of the journal's publication; Vacherot himself was 46.

[48] *L'Avenir*, No. 2 (13 May 1855).   [49] *L'Avenir*, No. 4 (27 May 1855).

[50] *L'Avenir*, No. 1 (6 May 1855).

republicanism was almost certainly driven more by his passionate commitment to *la libre pensée* than an attachment to liberal and republican political institutions. In the words of his necrologist: 'in him it was not only the citizen, it was above all the apostle of free thought who refused the oath to the violator of law; and the event of December gave him an opportunity to reflect philosophically on the conditions of social and political life.'[66] Indeed, the relative cohesiveness of his moral philosophy during the years of the Second Empire contrasted with the heterodox and in many ways ambivalent nature of his political republicanism.

Vacherot as a Theorist of Republican Democracy

Vacherot's *La Démocratie* has generally been viewed by historians of French political thought as an emblematic statement of post-1848 republican political philosophy.[67] The very title of the book constituted as bold an admission of the author's political inclinations as the times would allow; if in 1859 it was scarcely possible to publish a work called 'The Republic', Vacherot found an alternative title which clearly conveyed the substance of his sympathies—so transparently, as we saw earlier, that it exposed him to the full rigours of imperial political justice.

The terseness of the work's prose also powerfully contributed to the impression of the author's intellectual coherence and political certainty. In contrast with the florid and somewhat rambling style favoured by liberal, monarchist, and classical republican pamphleteers, Vacherot set out his views in simple syntax and austere, and at times even forceful, language. The notable absence of literary allusions and stylistic embellishments was not merely a function of the author's personal distaste for aestheticism;[68] it was also the political statement of a rationalist philosopher aspiring to have his work judged purely on its intellectual merits. In all these respects, then, this appeared to be an archetypal piece of 'new' republican writing, light years away from the inflated rhetoric of Victor Hugo and the sentimental outpourings of Michelet and Quinet. Yet a closer scrutiny of the 1859 text reveals that Vacherot's political philosophy was by no means as unequivocally and comprehensively inspired by republicanism as might at first glance be thought. *La Démocratie* was certainly a celebration of its author's new political faith, but it was also an interrogation, both explicit and implicit, as to the validity of many of its core precepts.

The apparent strength of Vacherot's political commitment largely stemmed from the boldness with which he asserted those republican values and principles to which he was unequivocally attached. First on this list was a

---

[66] Boutroux, Émile, *Notice sur la vie et les oeuvres de M. Étienne Vacherot* (Paris: Firmin-Didot, 1904), 7.

[67] 'With M. Vacherot, the democratic school finds its true principle'; Michel, *L'idée de l'État*, 338.

[68] Taine, *Les philosophes français du XIXe siècle*, 336.

powerful hatred of the Bonapartists, which united all opponents of the Second Empire and was indeed the source of the republican renaissance after 1851.[69] Vacherot's barely contained anger suggested that he too had come to nurture a visceral hatred of the imperial tradition. Despite the obvious risks of committing such feelings to print, he indulged himself in a sarcastic tirade against the Napoleonic cult:

What to say of these scourges of their country and of their time who have been turned into glorious heroes or great statesmen, because they have succeeded in defeating their enemies or duping their fellow-citizens?[70]

If the great Bonaparte represented the plague, his nephew was nothing more than a sinister jester. After his denunciation of them in *L'Avenir*, the glittering spectacles of the *fête impériale* still found little favour with the puritanical philosopher: 'what to say of these crass parades, these insulting spectacles which flatter national vanity without respect for truth, for humanity, for justice?'[71] Also marked by the seal of republican orthodoxy was Vacherot's theory of public institutions, which was spelt out in the third section of *La Démocratie*. What was advocated here was largely derived from the constitution of the defunct Second Republic: a unicameral legislature, a president with considerable executive powers—but elected by the legislature rather than by universal suffrage—and an autonomous administration which served the public interest rather than the government.[72] The major reform to the structure of public institutions was the separation of Church and State, a position vigorously promoted by republicans during the Second Empire.[73] But Vacherot's republicanism was tempered by a strong endorsement of liberty, which was presented as the only philosophically valid principle of a democratic polity.[74] At the same time, this liberalism was fortified by a republican emphasis on the indissociability of freedom from justice: 'a society without laws, without public authority, without State, is abandoned to the empire of brute force. The most genuinely free country is the one in which authority has no mission other than justice.'[75] Individual freedom could thus not be achieved at the expense of justice:

Individual freedom is a blessed thing and an intrinsic good, but only when it has justice as its end. Otherwise the freedom of some will be the servitude of others.[76]

Vacherot's republican proclivities were displayed most graphically in his categorical conception of the role of the state. The political authoritarianism of the Second Empire and the atrophy of civil society during the 1850s had prompted Orleanist liberals, monarchists, and even a number of moderate republicans to reconsider the justificatory principles of public intervention in society; at the same time, rival schools also debated the proper limits of state

---

[69] Girard, Louis, *La Seconde République* (Paris: Calmann-Lévy, 1968), 309.
[70] Vacherot, Étienne, *La Démocratie* (Paris: Chamerot, 1860), 89–90.   [71] Ibid., 89.
[72] Ibid., esp. 337–67.   [73] Ibid., 269.   [74] Ibid., 11.   [75] Ibid., 239.
[76] Ibid., xxiv.

conflicting imperatives: deducing a broader notion of politics from a narrowly ethical conception of man; separating those elements of his Doctrinaire liberal past he wished to discard from the ones he saw fit to retain; and coming to terms with the diverse and sometimes contradictory nature of republican writings about the relationship between state and society. The effects of these tensions could not fail to appear in the text of *La Démocratie*.

Moral Certainties, Ideological Ambivalences

The ambivalence of Vacherot's republican politics first appeared in his evident discomfort with male universal suffrage. Despite its intelligent appropriation by Napoleon III, who made it the cornerstone of his political system, the mass vote tended to be regarded as a valid and necessary principle by most Second Empire republicans. Writing in 1863, for example, Jules Ferry described universal suffrage as 'the honour of the multitudes, the guarantee for the dispossessed, the reconciliation of classes, and a legal existence for all'.[102] Liberals and monarchists, in contrast, were inclined to highlight the shortcomings of such an electoral system in a country where voters lacked an established democratic culture and could thus be easily manipulated by the government. As Victor de Broglie opined in 1860:

When universal suffrage will cease blindly to take its instructions from the local administration, where will it take it from? Not from sensible people and enlightened men; drowned everywhere in the crowd, everywhere the object of envy and suspicion, such people will nowhere have their say. When universal suffrage deserts the flag of authority, it abandons it to the enemy.[103]

On this question, Vacherot remained much closer to the view of Broglie, one of the Doctrinaire heroes of his youth, than to the republican position. He disputed the contention that male universal suffrage was in itself a guarantee of political freedom;[104] indeed the opposite seemed true: 'ignorance, superstition, immorality, poverty can make the exercise of popular rights vain or even dangerous.'[105] Under such conditions, he proposed the adjournment of this electoral system until such time as the French people were fully equipped for it: 'as long as the political education of a people is not complete, universal suffrage is impracticable in its full and free exercise.'[106]

Vacherot's scepticism extended to a number of other core principles and myths of the republican tradition. His sober assessment of the Revolution, for instance, fell well short of the typical republican celebration of 1789 as the dawn of a new age for mankind. While recognizing the Revolution's portentous character, Vacherot chose rather to dwell on the brutal and despotic aftermath of the event and its signal failure to deliver the promises to which it had

---

[102] Ferry, Jules, *La lutte électorale en 1863* (Paris: Dentu, 1863), 105.
[103] de Broglie, Victor, *Vues sur le gouvernement de la France* (Paris: Michel Lévy, 1872), lxi.
[104] Vacherot, *La Démocratie*, 303.   [105] Ibid., vii.   [106] Ibid., 353.

given rise. In contrast with abrupt change, he preferred the temperate adjustments of incrementalism: in his terms, 'evolution' rather than 'revolution'.[107] Indeed in Vacherot's mind 1789 was almost a counter-model, an example of precisely what had to be avoided if France wished to found a truly democratic polity: 'evil cannot engender good . . . despotism is never the father of liberty.'[108] He reinforced this point by expressing strong reservations about the republican triad of liberty-equality-fraternity. The first concept was in his view the only one which could serve as a principle of public philosophy; equality was merely a derivation of liberty. As for fraternity, which he had celebrated in his 1848 election manifesto,[109] he now even denied it the status of a political principle:

Fraternity is but a sentiment. But any sentiment, however powerful, however profound, however general it is, is not a right; and it is impossible to make of it the foundation of justice.[110]

Following Littré in this respect,[111] Vacherot's objection to the concept was partly driven by his suspicion of revolutionary and socialist groups, which had subverted the emancipatory ideals of fraternity for their own self-interested purposes.[112] However, at a deeper level—and this is where he radically departed from the republican canon—he had few illusions about the benign character of man: 'although human nature is not radically flawed, evil comes to it more easily than good; experience teaches this only too well.'[113] It was this very sense of guarded pessimism which also prevented Vacherot from subscribing to another of the great pillars of Second Empire republicanism: antimilitarism. While he accepted that standing armies constituted a 'danger for any free society', he ultimately rejected the republican advocacy of a citizens' militia as even more perilous at a time when France was bordered by powerful and potentially aggressive states.[114] Far from entertaining the Comtian utopia of a world in which violence was for ever eliminated, Vacherot extolled the martial virtues of military service, 'a very useful discipline, necessary, indeed, to a virile education . . . a school of courage and abnegation'.[115]

In addition to the liberties it took with critical elements of the republican tradition, the text of *La Démocratie* was full of hesitations about the precise application even of those political principles which it endorsed. This uncertainty was further evidence of the limited extent to which Vacherot's political thought had congealed during the first decade of the Second Empire. Examples of such hesitations included his view of the importance of the martial spirit, whose virtues he applauded but whose beneficial consequences he himself seemed to doubt when he noted that 'the military spirit does not make citizens'.[116] Also symptomatic of this intellectual ambivalence was his

---

[107] Ibid., 356.
[108] Ibid., 14.
[109] Vacherot, 'Concitoyens'.
[110] Vacherot, *La Démocratie*, 9.
[111] See Littré, Émile, 'De la devise révolutionnaire: Liberté, Egalité, Fraternité', in *Conservation Révolution Positivisme*, 329–40.
[112] *La Démocratie*, 9–10.
[113] Ibid., xvi.
[114] Ibid., 215 and 261.
[115] Ibid., 313.
[116] Ibid., 38.

commune where it has been erected, is of national interest, and thus becomes a matter of state interest.[135]

In the end, it was hardly surprising that Vacherot seemed to endorse the alarmist view that decentralization represented a threat to the integrity of France:

Political unity is a condition of internal order. Unity of jurisdiction and unity of taxation are the conditions of civil equality. Indeed what is a nation without independence, without order, and without justice in equal terms for all? To give back to the communes these great institutions of public utility, under the pretext of decentralization and communal liberty, would be to return modern societies back to the middle ages.[136]

The verdict of history is that *La Démocratie* was one of the first signs of the intellectual renaissance of liberal republicanism after 1851. That this work was a source of moral and political inspiration to republicans of the Second Empire cannot of course be disputed; and indeed Vacherot's persecution by the imperial authorities provoked sympathy and consternation among progressive intellectuals across Europe. In a letter to his friend Dupont-White, the Belgian Emile de Laveleye could barely articulate his indignation:

To condemn a book! To suppress a book—just think about it! In the nineteenth century!!![137]

Yet what has been shown above suggests that 'democrats' who read Vacherot's text carefully must have been somewhat perplexed. Here was a republican philosopher who found little solace in the events of 1789 and thought its revolutionary motto incoherent; a political activist who favoured suspending universal suffrage until the civic education of the people had been completed; a 'democrat' who believed that human nature was fundamentally flawed; and a moralist who maintained that military service was an appropriate means of encouraging public virtue.

Even more confusing to his republican readers would have been Vacherot's theory of the state, which under a liberal and decentralist veneer seemed in fact to offer a powerful restatement of republican centralist orthodoxy. These elements of tension in Vacherot's discourse in the late 1850s underscored the comparative frailty of his philosophical republicanism. Of course, republicans were not an ideologically homogenous community in the 1850s and early 1860s: Proudhon and Blanqui questioned the validity of universal suffrage, Quinet the Jacobin heritage of 1789, and Littré the relevance of the motto liberty-equality-fraternity. But none of the above seemed as unsure about as many core elements of the republican canon as Vacherot. This intellectual uncertainty was no accident. Rather, it was the logical result of an ongoing process of sifting through an accumulated body of political beliefs and values, many of which dated back to the early 1830s. As for Vacherot's apparently

---

[135] Vacherot, *La Démocratie*, 250; emphasis in original.   [136] Ibid., 260.
[137] Letter to Dupont-White, 27 October 1860, in Laveleye letters to Dupont-White 1860–77, Académie Royale de Belgique, Brussels.

contradictory views on decentralization, these were a reflection of the profound dissensions within the republican camp over the question of local liberty. In 1865 he himself recognized the ambivalence of his position when he wrote a somewhat defensive letter of endorsement to the authors of the *Projet de Décentralisation*, confessing that his views had changed in relation to his 1859 text: 'I have become very liberal.'[138]

A number of overall conclusions emerge from this analysis of Vacherot's political thought under the Second Empire. First, and most obviously, the inspiration for his ideas was not exclusively republican. There was evidence of a significant residue of Doctrinaire liberalism in many areas, notably in the prominence given to civil and political liberty, the considerable place accorded to 'social conservation', the economical interpretation of 1789, the suspicion of male universal suffrage and mass politics, the unitary view of the state and relative absence of a sociological vision of society, and the belief in the virtues of rationalism in politics. Indeed *La Démocratie* can in many senses be seen as a late answer to the question which obsessed the first generation of nineteenth-century French political thinkers: the reconciliation of liberalism and democracy.[139] Furthermore, Vacherot's theory of public institutions was also profoundly influenced by the Doctrinaire tradition: his emphasis on the general interest, his reluctance to discuss the limits of public intervention in society, his positive appreciation of the role of the administration, the notable absence of reference to intermediate groups, and his suspicion of local self-government were all largely borrowed from the intellectual armoury of the Doctrinaire heroes of Vacherot's youth. At the same time, this philosophy was hesitant and even somewhat uncertain, as shown in his profoundly contradictory declarations on the question of decentralization.

This hesitation was compounded by an explicit subordination of politics to morality, the former being seen as the sphere of the contingent while the latter appeared as the domain of necessity. In *La Démocratie* Vacherot insisted that practical politics was not a matter of absolutes, and indeed that the application of logic to the political realm was not merely mistaken but also dangerous.[140] Morality, on the other hand, could be grounded in precise, categorical, and fixed principles. In other words, the intellectual certainty which came with the discovery of truth could not be attained in politics but only in the higher spheres of ethical—and religious—knowledge. Fully acknowledged by Vacherot in his later years,[141] this distinction between the experimental and 'artistic' nature of politics and the 'science' of ethics shed a revealing light on the character of his political thought under the Second Empire. What gave strength and cohesiveness to his cerebral republicanism was its underpinning in absolute moral precepts concerning the rationalist and spiritual essence of man. It was this moral vision which allowed for the stipulation of a range of key precepts: the inviolability of human rights and particularly individual freedom, the absolute necessity of education and civic

[138] *Un Projet de Décentralisation*, 222.
[139] Rosanvallon, *Le moment Guizot*, 13.
[140] Vacherot, *La Démocratie*, 64.
[141] Vacherot, *La Démocratie Libérale*, 2.

instruction, the respect for the principle of *laïcité*, and the scrupulous attachment to fairness and impartiality. In short, it was the intellectual certainty afforded by moral reasoning which nourished Vacherot's republican politics, rather than a commitment to a specific set of political institutions and processes.

The Constitution of the Republic: From Status Quo to Revisionism

A letter written by Vacherot to his friend Du Mazet in early 1870 gives a good sense of his frame of mind about republican politics in the dying days of the Second Empire. His correspondent—a future republican *préfet à poigne* and a man with a deep aversion to 'disorder'—had clearly expressed his appreciation for Vacherot's attempt to calm down a public meeting at which radical republicans had sought to inflame proceedings by their fiery rhetoric. The philosopher's reply was firm but also gave a hint of his growing frustration with the excesses of many in his own camp:

You are most kind to commend as you do my efforts to bring reason to a gathering of men always too ready to be carried away towards savage declamations and violent solutions. No one more than I has in his heart a contempt and hatred of the government which has weighed on our unfortunate country for the past 18 years. But this sentiment does not dispense us of the political sense which assesses our situation reasonably, nor of the social sense which establishes the reforms which are possible and necessary in our society, and excludes vague and useless utopias.

When I say utopias, I should really use another term. There are utopias which have become truths and practical institutions with the passage of time. Our demagogues from public and private meetings intoxicate themselves and the heads of their naive and ignorant audience with words and cries of passion which are more or less sincere. How and when our poor country will emerge from the blind alley in which it is cornered by the alternative struggle between despotism and anarchy, I cannot predict. But I hope and indeed pray for a rapprochement between all those who have a love of liberty and a sentiment of morality.[142]

Much about Vacherot's past, present, and future politics was encapsulated in this capital text: his commitment to the republican struggle against the Second Empire, to which he remained loyal; his irritation with the empty rhetoric of radical republicanism, which he would soon believe posed a threat to French political order; and his hope for the emergence of a cross-party alliance of like-minded moderates, about whose prospects he became increasingly pessimistic. Vacherot's alienation from republican politics after the fall of the Bonapartist regime would hinge on the interplay between these three factors and his increasing sense that the moderation and pragmatism he hoped for could not be delivered by the Republic.

[142] Vacherot letter to Du Mazet, 18 January 1870, Bibliothèque Nationale, NAF 22869.

In ideological terms Vacherot's disaffiliation from republicanism was not driven by a single factor or event. Among the principal sources of his intellectual evolution were a disenchantment with the constitutional practices of the new regime; a change of heart on the 'social question', inspired by an incipient fear of the political influence of the working classes; an ideological shift first from conservative republicanism to conservative liberalism and then towards conservative monarchism; and finally a vehement disagreement with the republicans' handling of the issue of *laïcité* after 1877, notably their closure of Congregationalist schools and deportation of members of unauthorized religious orders.[143] Discussing his reasons for abandoning the republican movement in the final years of his life, Vacherot drew a distinction between his public commitment to the Republic, which he withdrew, spectacularly, in the 1880s, and his intellectual identification with core republican values, which according to him had remained unchanged.[144] In Vacherot's own mind, he did not abandon the Republic; it was the republicans who left him. This is the language of all renegades, it is true; but as we shall see it was not in this case entirely devoid of substance.

The constitutional settlement which was reached in France in 1875 was largely determined by three key events between 1870 and 1873: the fall of the Second Empire, which permanently ended the rule of the Bonapartists; the suppression of the Paris Commune, which reinforced the moderate and constitutional strand of republicanism; and the failed attempt to restore the Bourbon monarchy, which crystallized the union of republicans, progressive liberals, and pragmatic conservatives around the republican form of government. Vacherot was a direct witness to these events. Elected to the National Assembly as a member for the Seine in February 1871, he voted for the end of the Bonapartist reign with undisguised enthusiasm. However, the defeat and occupation of France by Prussia was a traumatic occurrence, bringing back childhood memories of the Cossack incursions of 1814–15.[145] Between October 1870 and March 1871 he served loyally as Mayor of the Vth arrondissement in the besieged Paris, devoting himself almost entirely to the needs of the civilian population and the management of national guards stationed in his heavily shelled precinct.

His position as an elected municipal officer within Paris also gave him a first-hand view of the emerging conflict between the republican Government of National Defence and the Commune. In a letter to the moderate republican Henri Martin in early February 1871, Vacherot discussed the preparations for forthcoming elections; he lamented the absence of preparation within the moderate camp as well as the failure of the republican community to hold together in the face of the external enemy:

---

[143] On the religious conflict in the late 1870s and early 1880s, see Mayeur, Jean-Marie, *Les débuts de la Troisième République* (Paris: Seuil, 1973), 117–19.

[144] He thus noted in the preface of *La Démocratie Libérale*, ii, that his core political values had not changed since 1859.

[145] Ollé-Laprune, *Vacherot*, 5.

I have not yet given much thought to the electoral question in my own precinct, so pressing are the necessities which constrain us at the moment. There is no organized committee among moderate republicans. I do not know what is happening in the camp of the supporters of the Commune. But these people are always ready. It appears that the moderate lists, just as the red lists, are systematically excluding members of the Government [of National Defence]. It is more than regrettable, it is deplorable. What a mess![146]

Staunchly loyal to the Government of National Defence, Vacherot resigned when the Commune was proclaimed, thereafter refusing all transactions with an institution he regarded as illegal and seditious.[147] After the defeat of the Commune Vacherot testified to the Commission of Enquiry on the Government of National Defence, and spelled out his views and his conception of his role during the events of 1870–1. He went to great lengths to defend his record as mayor, but also stood by the republican government, whose 'patriotism' he commended.[148] He distinguished between the mass of the republican party, among whom could be found a 'horrifying tail', and its elites, who were honest and competent.[149]

Most interesting of all were Vacherot's comments on the functions of local government, especially when compared with the theoretical postulates of his earlier work *La Démocratie*. Between October 1870 and March 1871 the 20 precinct mayors of Paris held regular meetings with the mayor of Paris, Arago, to discuss municipal issues; a somewhat larger group of around 80 officials also met regularly in the Ministry of the Interior to talk about political matters, including the war effort.[150] Vacherot thoroughly disapproved of the latter meetings, and pointedly remarked that municipalities had no business getting involved in politics. His conception of the role of the mayor was equally restricted: in contrast with his view in *La Démocratie*, where he had argued that the authority of the first magistrate of the city needed no endorsement from the government, he now stated that the true responsibility of the mayor was to the government, not to his municipal council.[151] This was the negation of what all republicans had claimed during the Second Empire; Vacherot's republicanism was thus already beginning to fray in the summer of 1871.

Thus there is no doubt that the events of 1870–1 initiated the first reconsideration of Vacherot's political views. Explaining his more conservative orientation in a letter to a republican newspaper in 1875, he noted: 'I have witnessed the war, the siege of Paris and the Commune.'[152] His admiration for the conservative liberalism of Adolphe Thiers also dated from this period.[153]

---

[146] Vacherot letter to Henri Martin, 1 February 1871, Bibliothèque Nationale NAF 21597.

[147] 'Protestation des Maires', Paris 22 March 1871, in Andréoli, Émile, *Le Gouvernement du 4 Septembre et la Commune de Paris* (Paris: Bocquet, 1871), 200–1. After the fall of the Commune Vacherot was re-appointed mayor of the Vth arrondissement and served until 1873.

[148] *Enquête Parlementaire sur les Actes du Gouvernement de la Défense Nationale*, Vol. 6 (Paris, Assemblée Nationale, 1876), 456. Vacherot testified on August 29, 1871.

[149] Ibid., 457.   [150] Ibid., 457–8.   [151] Ibid., 458.

[152] Vacherot letter dated 19 January 1875, *La République Française* (21 January 1875).

[153] According to a police report Vacherot had told a friend that Thiers had promised him the Ministry of the Interior if he returned to power after 1873. Arch.Pref.Police BA–1289, report dated 9 October 1873.

After fervently supporting the Thiers presidency between 1871 and 1873, Vacherot aligned himself with the 'Moral Order' government of Albert de Broglie. This was already evidence of a re-alignment in his social and political philosophy; indeed many republicans were irritated by his support for a coalition led by an unabashed monarchist and backed by conservative, legitimist, and clerical groups. Speaking of Vacherot's subsequent failure to be elected to the Senate, Juliette Adam noted: 'Vacherot has not been elected. The republicans who have been able to vote for members of the right have refused to vote for one of theirs who has given too many pledges to the right.'[154]

It was with the blessing of these anti-republican forces that Vacherot was appointed to the committee which drafted the 1875 Constitution. In the end, however, he voted for the founding of the Republic in 1875. As he noted a year later, France had accepted the republican regime with 'resolution' rather than 'enthusiasm';[155] this was undoubtedly an accurate translation of his own position. The 1875 Constitution was acceptable because, in the expression of Thiers, it had created a regime which divided France the least.[156] But Vacherot also endorsed the Republic because it provided a potential framework for rallying all conservative forces; indeed he hoped for the formation of a coalition bringing together 'the sensible legitimists, the constitutional Orleanists, and the liberal republicans' as well as 'the patriots of all parties'.[157] In 1875 there appeared to be no contradiction between this ecumenical conservatism and the republican form of government.

In institutional terms, Vacherot's main preoccupation was to see the establishment of an effective system of counter-weights to the power of the National Assembly, which was elected by universal suffrage. Unlike many conservatives he refused to demonize the latter institution, 'fertile in good as well as bad results';[158] he was particularly grateful to universal suffrage for saving France from the ravages of the Paris Commune.[159] At the same time, he believed the effects of the mass vote needed to be mediated by alternative institutions, especially as voters were coming under the influence of increasingly powerful—republican—electoral committees.[160] For this reason he supported granting significant powers to the president[161] as well as establishing an indirectly elected second chamber, a body which he had dismissed as a 'useless cog'[162] in 1859.

Although a Senate was indeed created by the republicans, Vacherot became rapidly disillusioned with the functioning of public institutions after 1875. In

---

[154] Adam, Juliette, *Nos amitiés politiques avant l'abandon de la revanche* (Paris: Lemerre, 1908), 301.

[155] Vacherot, Étienne, 'Les difficultés de la situation politique', *Revue des Deux Mondes* (15 October 1876), 723.

[156] Vacherot, letter to P. F. Target, in Target, *Élections du 4 Octobre 1885*, 4.

[157] Vacherot, Étienne, 'La situation politique et les lois Constitutionnelles: II', *Revue des Deux Mondes* (15 December 1874), 783.

[158] Vacherot, Étienne, 'La situation politique et les lois Constitutionnelles: I', *Revue des Deux Mondes* (1 December 1874), 595.

[159] Vacherot, *La Démocratie Libérale*, 9.   [160] Ibid., 15.

[161] Vacherot, 'La situation politique et les lois Constitutionnelles: I', 604.

[162] Vacherot, 'La situation politique et les lois Constitutionnelles: II', 756.

his view the Third Republic consecrated 'the triumph of pure democracy':[163] instead of promoting a balance of power among the Assembly, the Senate, and Presidency, the republicans had completely eviscerated the latter two institutions. Far from playing an active role in the legislative process, the Senate was simply an echoing chamber of decisions taken by the lower house.[164] When President MacMahon challenged the authority of the Assembly in 1877, Vacherot sided with him, arguing that the President of the Republic was constitutionally entitled to circumscribe the actions of the Assembly.[165] After the defeat and resignation of MacMahon, his successor Jules Grévy had meekly accepted the subordination of the Presidency to the elected representatives, an attitude savagely attacked by Vacherot, who contrasted the panache of his predecessors with the apparent mediocrity of Grévy.[166]

But it was not merely a question of individual leadership, even though Vacherot had a singularly low opinion of all the leaders of the republican party, from opportunists such as Waddington, Ferry, and Gambetta—'this character who is aiming for a dictatorship'[167]—to the Radical Clemenceau, the author of the 'abominable' doctrine of the indivisibility of the Revolution.[168] He was clearly dismayed by what he saw as the illiberal political culture of the republican elites who came to power in France after 1877, offering a striking contrast with the values of the republican movement under the Second Empire. In place of a clear ideology and sense of moral purpose, the opportunists seemed to be motivated only by self-interest: 'no more tradition, no more direction, no more purpose, no more determination in a government where there are no principles, no ideas, no political passion, in the end, but only interests to be satisfied by constant concessions and transactions.'[169] The vague and general slogans, the absence of programme, the often random but always meaningless changes in government had all contributed to discrediting the republican system; indeed Vacherot suggested that parliamentary government had been better practised by the monarchy between 1815 and 1848 than under the present regime.[170]

Even worse, the republicans in office were behaving with greater sectarianism than the rulers of the Second Empire. Vacherot accused the government of instituting a 'reign of terror'[171] in the administration by proceeding to widespread purges in the ranks of the higher civil service in the late 1870s. The republicans' campaign against religious congregations was seen as particularly

---

[163] Vacherot, *La Démocratie Libérale*, 17.

[164] Vacherot, Étienne, 'La République constitutionnelle et parlementaire', *Revue des Deux Mondes* (15 November 1879), 244–5.

[165] Ibid., 246.

[166] Vacherot, Étienne, 'La révision des lois constitutionnelles', *Le Correspondant* (10 March 1883), 824–5.

[167] Letter to Jules Simon, undated; Archives Nationales, Papiers Jules Simon, 87 AP 7. Vacherot's scathing views on Gambetta were later reported by G. Mermeix, 'Le jugement d'un philosophe', *Le Clairon* (9 April 1881).

[168] Vacherot, *La Démocratie Libérale*, iv.   [169] Ibid., ix.

[170] Vacherot, 'La République constitutionnelle et parlementaire', 251–2.

[171] Vacherot, Étienne, 'La République libérale', *Revue des Deux Mondes* (1 March 1880), 9.

odious as it violated two of the sacred principles of Vacherot's politics: freedom and tolerance. 'If one deprives a class of citizens, let us go further, even a single citizen, of one of his basic freedoms, one no longer has the right to call oneself a liberal.'[172] The violence with which republicans manifested their anti-clerical sentiments deeply shocked him.[173] The struggle against Catholicism was for Vacherot a philosophical and not a political issue, a matter to be settled by intellectual rather than physical means;[174] his position on the matter was similar to that of Littré.

The motto of the new rulers thus seemed to be: 'he who is not for us is against us'[175]—a far cry from the open and inclusive conception of politics promised by the republicans when in opposition. This sectarianism could culminate only in the appropriation of all levers of power by the ruling elite. From this perspective, Vacherot energetically opposed republican efforts to revise the 1875 Constitution in the early 1880s. Defending the settlement he had helped to design, he argued in 1883 that a revision would give the French people the unfortunate impression that constitutions could be changed at will.[176] He was particularly alarmed by Radical proposals to suppress the Senate and Presidency; if carried these would surely institute a 'revolutionary republic'[177] in France. Ominously, he ended this article by suggesting that a royalist restoration might prove the only way of stopping France's slide towards revolutionary government.[178] In a letter to his friend Simon at around this time he confessed that he was seriously considering abandoning the republican camp: 'my scruples are abandoning me.'[179] Four years later he took this position to its logical conclusion by publicly endorsing the Comte de Paris and welcoming the prospects of a return of a hereditary monarchy.[180] Ironically, he too had now become a constitutional revisionist.

The Dangers of Socialism

In parallel with his disenchantment with the 1875 Constitution, Vacherot's ideological drift from republicanism was also influenced by a significant reappraisal of his views on social issues. Moving away from the progressive republicanism of *La Démocratie*, he emphasized in his later writings that his main political concern had become the question of 'social conservation'.[181] In the preface to *La Démocratie Libérale* he denounced the rise of 'state socialism'[182] and warned of the dire consequences of the rise of a 'workers' party which was united, organized, and disciplined for electoral battles'.[183] This was

---

[172] Ibid., 31.   [173] A point underlined in his letter in Target, *Élections du 21 Août 1881*, 8.
[174] Vacherot, 'La République constitutionnelle et parlementaire', 271.
[175] Vacherot, Étienne, 'Les nouveaux Jacobins', *Revue des Deux Mondes* (1 July 1880), 51.
[176] Vacherot, 'La révision des lois constitutionnelles', 809.   [177] Ibid., 804.
[178] Ibid., 825.
[179] Letter to Simon, undated, Archives Nationales, Papiers Jules Simon, 87 AP 7.
[180] Vacherot, Étienne, 'La Démocratie', *Le Correspondant* (10 April 1887), 3–22.
[181] Vacherot, *La Démocratie Libérale*, i.
[182] Ibid., ix.   [183] Ibid., xxi.

a reference to the rise of the Parti Ouvrier Français (POF), under the leadership of Jules Guesde and Paul Lafargue, which made significant electoral advances in France in the 1880s and early 1890s. Although his fears were somewhat exaggerated, the political and ideological threat posed by socialism clearly became a major source of preoccupation to Vacherot.[184]

This represented a marked shift from the positive spirit which had informed his writings on social issues under the Second Empire. The preface of *La Démocratie* had begun, symbolically enough, by ridiculing the fears of social conservatives and reactionaries who refused to countenance any form of political change.[185] Even as late as 1874 he was careful to distinguish himself from the 'panicked conservatives who cannot be reassured by anything';[186] a police report of 1876 also suggested that he was considering an electoral alliance with Louis Blanc.[187] While familiar with the works of the first generation of French socialists, notably the writings of Pierre Leroux, Vacherot was never intellectually seduced by socialism: he demarcated himself clearly from those who defined their republicanism primarily in terms of justice and equality. Only the principle of liberty could in his mind serve as the appropriate ideological foundation of the Republic.[188] At the same time, very much in the same spirit as Littré, his liberalism was largely open to the incorporation of certain 'socialist' ideas, notably on such questions as the regulation of work practices by the state and the promotion of the associative rights of workers. Indeed he almost seemed to wish to reclaim for liberal republicanism the ambition of alleviating the conditions of the poor: 'poverty is the worst of all servitudes. To seek to liberate the people from it is the most liberal enterprise which could be attempted.'[189] This noble aspiration was accompanied by a denunciation of the idle rich: liberty, he stressed, could not remain 'a privilege confined to the wealthy and lazy'.[190]

Vacherot's sympathy for socialist ideas under the Second Empire was essentially a function of three factors: an ethical concern for the well-being of workers, which he repeated on numerous occasions in *La Démocratie;*[191] a political understanding that social order was better preserved by intelligent and preemptive concessions to workers than by a dogmatic defence of the status quo;[192] and the influence of Radical and socialist republican thinkers such as Edgar Quinet and Louis Blanc, whose writings on social reform Vacherot greatly admired during the Second Empire.[193] Here it might be added parenthetically that in the golden years of opposition to Bonapartism the lines of demarcation between democratic socialism, republican socialism, and repub-

---

[184] The classic study of the POF is by Willard, Claude, *Les Guesdistes* (Paris: Editions Sociales, 1965). On Lafargue, see Leslie Derfler's two-volume biography, *Paul Lafargue and the Founding of French Marxism 1842–1882* (Cambridge, MA: Harvard University Press, 1991) and *Paul Lafargue and the Flowering of French socialism 1882–1911* (Cambridge, MA: Harvard University Press, 1998).
[185] Vacherot, *La Démocratie*, xv.
[186] Vacherot, 'La situation politique et les lois Constitutionnelles: I', 600.
[187] Arch.Pref.Police BA–1289, report dated 4 February 1876.   [188] *La Démocratie*, 5–9.
[189] Ibid., 13.   [190] Ibid., 14.   [191] Ibid., 230.   [192] Ibid., 173–5.
[193] Vacherot, *La Démocratie Libérale*, 5.

lican liberalism were sometimes difficult to distinguish. Vacherot, to repeat, was not a socialist, but like most republicans of the Second Empire he recognized at least the moral validity of socialist arguments against social inequality, and even accepted many socialist ideas about how it should be remedied. Finally, such solutions were also naturally congruent with Vacherot's republican centralism: since he generally believed in the beneficial nature of the state, he was all the more ready to accept the socialist contention that mass poverty could be resolved by public intervention.

After the collapse of the Second Empire, however, Vacherot's empathy with the poor and support for the rights of workers were rapidly dispelled by a number of factors, the most important of which was undoubtedly the Paris Commune. The events of 1870–1 in Paris left an indelible imprint in his mind, and under the Third Republic he consistently attacked the extreme left, 'the horde which has carried out and will again carry out the Commune'.[194] Denouncing the scourge of revolutionary republicanism at every occasion, Vacherot was of course dismayed by the republican government's amnesty of the Communards in July 1880, a measure which he saw as a political rehabilitation of the insurgency[195] as well as an acknowledgement of its moral justification.[196] However, in Vacherot's estimation the real threat to social order in the 1880s came not so much from the extreme left as from the Radicals, led by the flamboyant and intransigent Clemenceau. Well represented in the National Assembly, Radicalism represented a sinister alternative—in every sense of the term—to the emollient opportunism of Gambetta and Ferry. Vacherot drew an unfavourable contrast between the political values of the two groups: 'as much the liberal radical [moderate republican] is tolerant, sympathetic, generous, and confident in the relationships forged through public life, so much the Jacobin radical is exclusive, worried, touchy, and defiant.'[197] These were precisely the values of the extreme left, to which had to be added the Radicals' full agreement with socialist prescriptions concerning the social and political rights of workers. In its ideology as well as its political culture, Radicalism thus appeared as the antechamber of revolutionary republicanism.[198]

Alongside this political analysis, and no doubt driven by it to a very large extent, Vacherot also came to re-appraise his views about the beneficial nature of state intervention on social issues.[199] Indeed La Démocratie Libérale offered a strikingly minimalist reformulation of the proper bounds of state activity, which Vacherot had defined in extensive terms in the years of the Second Empire. The state, he now suggested, should not seek to accomplish those tasks which could be carried out through private initiative: included in this list

---

[194] Vacherot, 'La situation politique et les lois Constitutionnelles: II', 780.
[195] Vacherot, 'La République libérale', 10.   [196] Vacherot, 'Les nouveaux Jacobins', 59–60.
[197] Vacherot, 'La République constitutionnelle et parlementaire', 266; on this theme see also Hippolyte Taine, 'Psychologie du Jacobin', Revue des Deux Mondes (1 April 1881).
[198] Vacherot, 'Les nouveaux Jacobins', 62.
[199] His continuing interest in social issues was reflected in his membership of the Société d'Economie Sociale, of which he was the President in the early 1880s. Arch.Pref.Police BA–1289, report dated 23 May 1883.

were such areas as the arts and sciences and the provision of charity and public assistance.[200] Most significantly, whereas he had argued in 1859 that it was
the state's duty to regulate working conditions and generally provide assistance to the poor, he now suggested that such matters were best left to
employers and workers to settle among themselves.[201] Rather than seeking a
solution through 'state socialism', Vacherot tried to make the case for a form
of industrial paternalism, holding up the example of the construction of workers' homes and provision of schools by enlightened industrialists.[202]

However, even if such generosity of spirit was lacking among employers,
Vacherot refused to accept that the state had a duty to intervene: if living conditions of workers remained deplorable, the remedy could come only from
philanthropy and charity.[203] Even the associative rights of workers, which he
had endorsed in the 1850s, now found little favour in his eyes; although
Vacherot did not entirely condemn the 1884 Ferry law which granted legal
recognition to workers' unions, albeit in the private sector only, he noted that
such legislation gave unfair advantages to workers over their employers:[204] not
exactly a progressive conclusion. Vacherot still recognized the fundamental
vulnerability of the individual worker in relation to his employer: 'the worker
alone is weak, while the employer is strong.'[205]

He even accepted the concept of 'socialism', provided the adjective 'liberal'
was added to it, and he underlined his continuing sense of empathy with
workers: 'I still regard our workers as equals and brothers.'[206] But the solution
to their problems could not come from the state. Nor could it be pursued
through conflictual methods, but only through discussion and consensual
agreement between industrialists and workers and the progressive moral
improvement of the work-force through education.[207] Perhaps aware that the
measures he was contemplating could bear fruit only in the very long run,
Vacherot stressed the virtues of patience and incrementalism: only through a
slow and lengthy process of evolution would France achieve the 'reconciliation of classes'[208] which represented the true solution to its social problems.

Alongside his constitutional revisionism, the evolution of Vacherot's social
thought played an important role in undermining his republican allegiances
after 1871. By rejecting the contention that workers had a moral claim upon
the state, he threw out one of the key ethical underpinnings of progressive
republicanism. Furthermore, while he had earlier sought to avert the threat of
civil strife through social change, he later came to think that any substantive
state-led reforms would endanger social order: a classic conservative argument
for 'jeopardy'. This conclusion was not reached through abstract speculation,
of course, but largely as a result of the Commune, which inspired in Vacherot
a virulent hostility towards 'state' socialism. This sentiment was reinforced by
his growing conviction from the late 1870s that Radicalism was potentially as

[200] Vacherot, *La Démocratie Libérale*, 128.   [201] Ibid., 328.   [202] Ibid., 331.
[203] Ibid., 347.   [204] Ibid., 339.   [205] Ibid., 340.
[206] Vacherot, Étienne, 'La question sociale', *Le Soleil* (9 December 1893).
[207] Vacherot, *La Démocratie Libérale*, 355–6.   [208] Ibid., 360.

menacing to social order as the revolutionary republicanism of the Commune: hence his sombre warnings against the rise of the 'new Jacobins', a poor and unworthy imitation of the fanatical patriots of 1793.[209]

The Embrace of Monarchism

'Let us keep the Republic for which alas! you and I can only pray for. But if it is to be abandoned, we must resign ourselves to its loss.'[210] This weary letter to Jules Simon hinted that the evolution of Vacherot's political thought after 1875 was not characterized exclusively by negative considerations; he also found himself in increasing sympathy with another political philosophy.

His growing affinity with monarchism was undoubtedly the most distinctive feature of his intellectual transformation under the Third Republic. Despite a fear of socialism and a growing disillusionment with the constitutional practices of republican elites, most conservative republicans—notably the likes of Jules Simon, Jules Dufaure, and as we have just seen Émile Littré—remained firmly within the republican fold. After several years of flirtation, during which he seems to have been in active contact with the Comte de Paris,[211] Vacherot publicly crossed over to the monarchist camp in the late 1880s; he was regularly seen at royalist gatherings in Paris during this period.[212] His decision was partly inspired by a sense that only the hereditary monarchy could save France from anarchy, civil war, and bankruptcy;[213] but he also came to trust the monarchy to preserve what was necessary while reforming what needed to change—in other words, to promote the intelligent form of conservative liberalism which republicanism had failed to deliver.[214] More speculatively, perhaps, it is also tempting to see his conversion to monarchism as a moral response to the perceived ethical failures of the Republic: its inability to promote the values of honour, dignity, and moderation, and its celebration of mediocrity, corruption, materialism over the finer things of life. Three monarchist themes thus appeared with increasing prominence in his later political writings: the moral and political value of the monarchy; the social necessity of a 'new aristocracy'; and the administrative imperative of greater decentralization.

The monarchical solution was Vacherot's ultimate response to the Third Republic's failure, in his eyes, to provide a 'balanced' institutional system. Since the republican Constitution of 1875 had been perverted of its original meaning by the 'dictatorial' practices of the opportunists,[215] only an alternative framework could guarantee the combination of freedom and authority which France needed to face the future with confidence. Spelled out in *La*

---

[209] Vacherot, 'Les nouveaux Jacobins', 47–8.
[210] Vacherot to Jules Simon (undated), Archives Nationales, Papiers Jules Simon, 87 AP 7.
[211] Arch.Pref.Police BA–1289, report dated 13 November 1885.
[212] Arch.Pref.Police BA–1289, reports dated 24 August 1888 and 15 February 1889.
[213] Vacherot, *La Démocratie Libérale*, 114.   [214] Ibid., xxiii.
[215] Vacherot, 'La révision des lois constitutionnelles', 814.

Démocratie Libérale, this alternative consisted of a political system which combined elements of democracy, aristocracy, and monarchy. This 'composite democracy',[216] incidentally, was the very system which Vacherot had emphatically rejected in 1859, arguing that such a formula was neither morally nor politically acceptable.[217]

But the passing of time seemed to have worked wonders for Vacherot's appreciation of France's monarchical past. The regimes of 1815 and 1830, he admitted, were not as malevolent as had been made out: they had not only lasted but brought a considerable measure of economic prosperity.[218] This retrospective generosity was even extended to the Second Empire, whose despotism now seemed 'gentle and polite'[219] and under which at least 'public functionaries lived in peace'.[220] At the heart of Vacherot's new Constitution was the figure of the hereditary monarch, the Comte de Paris (Philip VII), to whom extensive powers were attributed: the appointment and dismissal of prime ministers and ministers, the supervision of the administration, the operation of diplomacy, and complete control over the army.[221] There would still be a democratically elected parliament, of course, but its attributes would be drastically curtailed: its actions would be confined to the discussion and control of government actions.[222] As for the senate, its role would be purely advisory.[223] This was a constitutional monarchy, but one in which the monarchical element was preponderant.[224]

It was not only because of the leadership it offered that Vacherot found the monarchy appealing. In the later years of his life his social philosophy was increasingly permeated with the notion of hierarchical order. This was most strongly manifested in his argument for a 'new aristocracy' to replace the existing parliamentary elites of the Republic, whose corruption, intolerance, and incompetence had in his view brought France to the brink of disaster.[225] His solution was threefold: to abolish all financial subventions to parliamentarians, so that only the principles of honour and public service would determine entry into politics;[226] to promote the candidatures of wealthy local notables, who would be respected by their electorate and would serve the nation with honour and distinction;[227] and finally to recruit the senatorial elite from a broad 'aristocracy' of elevated professions: industry, commerce, the arts and sciences, the clergy, and the administration.

Vacherot was particularly taken with the latter institution, whose elites— judges, magistrates, academics, military officers, and financial experts—represented an 'admirable mechanism' which the republicans had almost wrecked

---

[216] 'démocratie mixte'; Vacherot, *La Démocratie Libérale*, 25.
[217] Vacherot, *La Démocratie*, 17–18.   [218] Vacherot, *La Démocratie Libérale*, 29.
[219] Ibid., 71.   [220] Ibid., 94.   [221] Ibid., 90–5.   [222] Ibid., 103–6.
[223] Ibid., 110.
[224] Vacherot's scheme corresponded with the Comte de Paris' own view of France's constitutional future. See for example *Instructions de Mgr. le Comte de Paris aux représentants du parti monarchique en France* (Paris: Librairie Nationale, 1887), esp.7–10.
[225] Vacherot, *La Démocratie Libérale*, viii.
[226] Vacherot, 'La révision des lois constitutionnelles', 816.
[227] Vacherot, 'La situation politique et les lois Constitutionnelles: I', 598–9.

by their sectarian policies.[228] The appointment of this senatorial 'aristocracy' was to be entrusted to the monarch,[229] a method which was deemed preferable to indirect election because the sovereign offered a better guarantee of an impartial and scrupulous set of choices. Perhaps pricked by his former republicanism, Vacherot was at pains to distinguish his proposals from an advocacy of the restoration of *ancien régime* privileges. The old nobility, he noted, had been destroyed by the Revolution and could not be resurrected.[230] Yet in the next breath he asserted that the bourgeoisie had failed to govern France since 1789 and that the time had come to replace it with a different social elite.[231] If this elite was not bourgeois but at the same time was drawn from the upper echelons of French social and economic life, however, it was hard to escape the conclusion that what Vacherot was proposing was indeed a thinly disguised approximation of an aristocratic restoration.

The third central element in Vacherot's neo-monarchism was his limited conversion to decentralization, a strong royalist theme in the late nineteenth century.[232] There was, he now clearly recognized, too much centralization in France; the Republic had inherited the concentrated powers of all its predecessor regimes but also added to them significantly.[233] Echoing the words of the Comte de Paris,[234] Vacherot asserted that the monarchy would finally carry out the liberation of France's communes. The new sovereign would depoliticize local government and allow for the flourishing of greater local initiative in such fields as the arts and sciences, industry and commerce, education, and charity.[235] Yet, rather like his intellectual contortions on the matter in the 1850s and 1860s, this was something of a grudging conversion. The old Doctrinaire and republican centralist suspicion of localism still lurked in Vacherot's late writings. Thus he refused to concede any greater powers to local assemblies; the 1865 Nancy programme had been wrong to suggest that some of the attributions of central government should be handed over to departmental assemblies.[236] Even less desirable was the concession of greater autonomy to municipal councils. Vacherot warned that considerations of public order made it essential to preserve the 'rights of the state' in this area.[237] Even the restoration of provinces, a royalist theme par excellence, found little favour. Such a measure might tempt France into adopting federalism, a territorial system of government he rejected totally.[238] The division of France into departments was thus to be retained, for it was a guarantee of national unity.[239]

---

[228] Vacherot, *La Démocratie Libérale*, 47. No doubt his high praise for the administration was partly due to the fact that his son Arsène occupied a number of positions in the higher administration, notably in the Prefectorate and the Cour des Comptes.

[229] Vacherot, *La Démocratie Libérale*, 65–7.   [230] Ibid., 39–40.   [231] Ibid., 49.

[232] For an overview of the monarchist position see Maurras, Charles, *L'idée de décentralisation* (Paris: Revue Encyclopédique, 1898).

[233] Vacherot, *La Démocratie Libérale*, ii.

[234] See for example his 'Lettre-Manifeste aux maires sur le projet de réorganisation des communes de France', Sheen House (4 July 1888), Bib.Nat.Rés.Lb57–9615.

[235] Vacherot, *La Démocratie Libérale*, 134.   [236] Ibid., 241.

[237] Vacherot, 'Les difficultés de la situation politique', 745.

[238] Vacherot, *La Démocratie Libérale*, 134.   [239] Ibid., 231.

So in the final analysis what did Vacherot's decentralism really amount to? Its central message was that the republican tradition had developed in France at the expense of the rights of private groups and associations and that this imbalance needed to be remedied urgently, especially in the field of religious education, where the time had come to end the policy of 'secular intolerance'.[240] But even more importantly it was predicated upon a view of collective life which was radically apolitical. Decentralization, from this perspective, was not about encouraging greater public involvement in politics, as it was in the individualist liberal and republican perspectives. It was a means of encouraging precisely the opposite: the fulfilment of individual and collective aspirations outside the political realm.[241] This was perhaps the true measure of Vacherot's ideological shift: the philosopher who had celebrated the emancipatory potential of democracy ended his life believing that true freedom could be realized only outside politics.

Conclusion: From Republic to Monarchy . . . and Beyond

Writing for *L'Avenir* in his early 'republican' years Vacherot had emphatically voiced his preference for 'clear solutions and radical doctrines'.[242] In a paradoxical way he lived up to this profession throughout his life, siding with the Republic when the Second Empire seemed the only logical form of government possible and then switching to the monarchy when republicanism, in turn, became France's natural party of government. In this sense perhaps Vacherot embodied one of the characteristics which would later come to define the 'Sartrian' paradigm of the *intellectuel engagé*: a tendency to contest and resist all forms of established order.[243]

When considered in its totality, the most striking feature of Vacherot's political thought was the comparatively limited nature of its republican phase. Before his intellectual conversion to republicanism he was ideologically attached to the Doctrinaire school for nearly 20 years. Later in his life, he became a conservative critic of the opportunist Republic for another decade before committing the last ten years of his long existence—and his final book—to the service of the monarchy. A generous estimate would conclude that he spent as much of his life contesting republicanism as supporting it; more realistically, it has to be accepted that his republicanism was no more than an interlude between two long periods of devotion to the liberal monarchist cause. Supreme paradox, it will be granted, for a thinker who, rightly, came to be regarded as one of the intellectual founders of the Third Republic.

To reinforce this conclusion, we have shown that Vacherot's republican political philosophy during the Second Empire was more than mildly heterodox. *La Démocratie* was, among other things, sceptical of the role of universal

---

[240] Vacherot, *La Démocratie Libérale*, iv.   [241] Ibid., 375–6.   [242] See n. 57.
[243] For further discussion of this theme see our chapter 'The political roles of intellectuals', in Hazareesingh, *Political Traditions in Modern France*, 33–64.

suffrage, critical of the Revolutionary tradition, dismissive of the holy trinity of republican values, and essentially pessimistic and distrustful of human nature. Vacherot's dislike of mass politics was given its ultimate expression in his treatment of the question of decentralization, where he ended up, after considerable intellectual contortions, reaffirming the validity of the classical republican centralist notion of the state. What his evident discomfort highlighted above all was the weakness of his theory of citizenship and in particular the limited role he envisaged for any form of political action not directly sponsored by the state and its elites. The muscularity of his statism thus concealed elements of frailness in his republican politics. These latent tensions would later come back to haunt him, provoking an agonizing re-appraisal of Vacherot's political philosophy.

A strong sense of elitism never left Vacherot, even during his later monarchist phase; if anything, it came to be accentuated with his open rejection of mass politics and his repeated calls for the emergence of a new parliamentary elite. This 'aristocratic' obsession undoubtedly provides one of the keys to understanding his political philosophy. His elitism was not a product of his republican centralism but rather the reverse: it was his elitism which facilitated his drift towards republicanism during the 1840s. There were four powerful and mutually reinforcing strands to this elitism: the academic culture Vacherot acquired at the Ecole Normale, which celebrated the principle of intellectual superiority; the gilded halls of the Académie des Sciences Morales et Politiques, where elevation of taste and contempt for 'vulgarity' were de rigueur; the core principles of *libre pensée*, which created an explicit distinction between those who exercised their rational faculties and those who remained trapped in the absurdities of religion and metaphysics; and the ideology of Doctrinaire liberalism, with its cult of rational individualism, insistence on the necessity of social hierarchies, and belief that government should be exercised by 'superior' elements.[244]

In this context, numerous further traces of Doctrinaire thought could be gleaned from Vacherot's political philosophy during the Second Empire: the beliefs that liberty was more important than equality and that equality was merely a civil and legal matter, not a social or political one; the weight given to the conservation of social order; the hostility towards universal suffrage and mass politics, and the minimalist interpretation of 1789; and the attempt to reconstruct an aristocratic elite. More boldly, it might be suggested that these were the true foundations of his political thought, the elements which were never swept away by the relatively short-lived republican tide. Further evidence of the foundational character of his Doctrinaire period was his reversion to some of its core precepts when he came to reformulate his constitutional philosophy in the 1870s and 1880s. For instance, the notion of a 'mixed' constitution, combining monarchical, aristocratic, and democratic elements—in that order—came straight out of the Doctrinaire textbook. His advocacy of

244 Rosanvallon, *Le moment Guizot*, 109, 360–1.

such a formula in the late nineteenth century was a testament to the continuing intellectual fascination exercised upon him by Guizot, whose 'glorious
career'[245] he saluted in a letter written in 1865—at the height, it should be
noted, of Vacherot's 'republican' phase.

But it would be a mistake, by relativizing and contextualizing Vacherot's
republicanism, to undervalue it completely. Indeed, it should be remembered
that he claimed to have remained true to the spirit of republicanism even if
the force of circumstances had compelled him to abandon its letter. At first
glance such a claim might be rejected out of hand. The republican Vacherot
expressed a preference for a public and secular education system; his monarchist successor defended, and clearly preferred, the private education offered
by religious schools. The first celebrated the essentially egalitarian nature of
democracy, whereas the second posited an openly inegalitarian and hierarchical institutional alternative. The republican thinker also aspired to broaden
social access to public office, while the royalist ideologue in contrast sought to
facilitate a more aristocratic form of elite recruitment. There was also a considerable difference between the alleviation of the miseries of the poor
through state intervention, advocated under the Second Empire, and the later
exhortation that those in need should invest their hopes in private charity.
This list of Vacherot's intellectual repudiations could be pursued at length. But
their sheer scale should not occult the unmistakable elements of continuity in
his republican thinking. He never ceased to believe in the inalienable nature
of individual rights, and his judgement on his friend Dubois could be applied
with equal force to himself:

Every time a liberty was threatened by the political passions of his enemies or of his
friends, he would run to the battlefield to lay down the banner of principles.[246]

It was in the name of the banner of 1789 that Vacherot castigated both the
anti-clerical excesses of the Third Republic and the political authoritarianism
of the Second Empire. It was on similar grounds that he supported the principle of self-determination of peoples in Europe[247] and opposed Taine's suggestion, which would have been approved by the Doctrinaires, that political
rights should be withdrawn from those citizens who lacked the 'capacity' to
exercise them.[248] After his conversion to republicanism, he advocated the separation of Church and State and maintained this position in La Démocratie
Libérale,[249] even though it was scarcely in tune with the beliefs of most of his
new friends in the monarchist camp.

More tentatively, it might also be argued that his view of the state was
marked by an overall sense of continuity. Of course, there were changes both
within eras—his shift towards a slightly more decentralist position from 1859
to 1865—and between them—his support for a considerably less interven-

---

[245] Vacherot to Guizot, 31 January 1865: Ibid., 372.
[246] Vacherot, *Notice sur Paul-François Dubois*, 20–1.
[247] Vacherot, Étienne, *La politique extérieure de la République* (Paris: Germer Baillière, 1881), 45–8.
[248] Vacherot, *La Démocratie Libérale*, 237.   [249] Ibid., 293.

tionist state in the 1880s and 1890s. But underlying these nuances there remained the strong sense that public authority was the repository of the general interest and that a centralized administration was the only effective guardian of order and efficiency in France. It was the same statist logic which inspired Vacherot's opposition to the election of magistrates in *La Démocratie*[250] and his refusal to concede greater political rights to elected assemblies in his later writings: such forms of 'democratization' of the state would in his view only have compromised the general interest.[251] Finally, there was Vacherot's ethical and spiritualist philosophy, which was an integral part of his republicanism under the Second Empire and continued to sustain him in his later years. When he denounced the opportunism, cynicism, and corruption of the Republic in the 1870s and 1880s Vacherot appealed to essentially the same bedrock of puritanical principles he had defined in his articles in *L'Avenir*:[252] among its principal components were honesty, simplicity, sobriety, rigour, and integrity. This republican Jansenist expected these precepts to be fully upheld by the Republic, and when it appeared unwilling—or unable—to do so he naturally became disillusioned.

By far the most intriguing aspect of Vacherot's intellectual itinerary was his final leap into the monarchist camp. Even though our contextualization of his political thought has shown that he was in many senses reverting to an earlier cluster of political beliefs, there was still an element of mystery in his embrace of the royalist cause in the late 1880s. There were no shortage of de-alignments from republicanism during this period, which after all coincided with the tragicomedy of Boulangism.[253] But why did Vacherot alight upon the monarchy? Perhaps a key to resolving this mystery lay in the relationship between his personal religious views and his political and ideological affiliations. This is a complex and delicate question, for Vacherot himself never recognized any explicit connection between the two spheres. In fact he suggested that the two were fundamentally separate: religion and morality were areas where absolute principles could be found, whereas politics remained the domain of the contingent.[254] He also asserted in conversations with his colleagues that his philosophical and religious opinions had remained essentially unchanged throughout his life.[255] It is true that a number of themes appeared as a leitmotiv in his writings: the separation of theology from science, the incoherence of mysticism and metaphysics, the necessity of spiritualism, and the possibility of a philosophical synthesis bringing together idealism, empiricism, sensualism, and materialism.[256]

---

[250] Vacherot, *La Démocratie*, 291.

[251] An opinion strongly shared by his son. See Arsène Vacherot, 'Les rapports du pouvoir municipal avec l'État', *Revue des Deux Mondes* (1 July 1876), 197.

[252] See for example 'L'esprit philosophique' II, *L'Avenir* (24 June 1855).

[253] For a trenchant analysis of 'Boulangism' from a conservative republican perspective, see Simon, Jules, *Souviens-toi du Deux-Décembre* (Paris: Havard, 1889).

[254] Vacherot, *La Démocratie Libérale*, 1–2.

[255] Ollé-Laprune, *Vacherot*, 74; Boutroux, *Notice sur la vie et les oeuvres de M. Étienne Vacherot*, 25.

[256] See for example his article 'La situation philosophique en France', *Revue des Deux Mondes* (15 June 1868), esp. 965–77.

But on purely religious matters this continuity was, to say the least, much less apparent. The 1850s and 1860s represented the apogee of Vacherot's commitment to the principles of freethinking. Although he admired its metaphysical depth and moral beauty,[257] he clearly distanced himself from Catholicism, noting that he had once been a believer but that he had now 'ceased to believe'.[258] He saw no long-term future for the Catholic faith, whose 'immobility' he denounced repeatedly,[259] even allowing himself to envisage the time when all religious forms would wither away: 'I believe that science and philosophy should one day suffice for humanity.'[260] A statement of this type would not have been disowned by a philosophical materialist, and indeed in the 1860s he was viewed by 'advanced' freethinkers as a quasi-atheist.[261]

Entirely different were both the tone and the substance of his writings on religious matters after 1875. A turning point seems to have occurred with the anti-clerical policies of the opportunist governments after 1879. As noted earlier Vacherot was incensed by the republicans' policies on education under Jules Ferry; indeed such was his indignation that he embarked upon a late career in journalism in the early 1880s, denouncing the persecution of Congregationalists in *Le Courrier du Dimanche*, *Le Figaro*, and *Le Soleil*. In his mind, the problem posed by the religious policy of the republicans was of a much greater magnitude than the socialist threat.[262] Like Littré, what he condemned in the first instance were the violations of the individual rights of the Congregationalists, but there was no doubt that his expression of solidarity with these persecuted churchmen stirred something deeper in him. In the final page of his *Nouveau Spiritualisme* (1884), Vacherot admitted that in his old age he was becoming increasingly preoccupied with 'the thought of the Infinite'; he also attacked the rise of atheist forms of anti-clericalism.[263] And when in 1886 a group of conservative liberal and monarchist intellectuals founded the National League against Atheism, Vacherot had no hesitation in joining, along with such free-thinking deists as Jules Simon and Camille Flammarion.[264] The statutes of the association, it should be noted, enjoined its members to defend 'everywhere along with the existence of God the sacred principles of morality and religion'.[265] In *La Démocratie Libérale* Vacherot confessed that he was reading the Holy Scriptures with fresh eyes and that his moral and philosophical outlook was undergoing a momentous change: 'I feel myself becoming a Christian again.'[266] He confirmed this transition by informing his colleague Ollé-Laprune that Christ would have his 'final glance'[267]—a wonderfully ambiguous statement. He was given a religious

---

[257] Vacherot, *La Démocratie*, xxix.   [258] Ibid.

[259] For example, Vacherot, *La Démocratie*, 47; 'La crise religieuse au 19eme siècle', *Revue des Deux Mondes* (15 October 1868), 845.

[260] Vacherot, *La Démocratie*, xxviii.   [261] Lefevre, *La renaissance du matérialisme*, 276–7.

[262] A point he made in an article against the controversial 'Article 7' of Ferry's education reform, reproduced in *L'Univers* (19 November 1879).

[263] Vacherot, Étienne, *Le Nouveau Spiritualisme* (Paris: Hachette, 1884), 400.

[264] Lalouette, *La libre pensée en France*, 163.

[265] *Statuts de la Ligue Nationale contre l'Athéisme* (Paris, Rue de Richelieu, 1887), 1.

[266] Vacherot, *La Démocratie Libérale*, 309.   [267] 'dernier regard'. Ollé-Laprune, *Vacherot*, 91.

funeral in 1897. Having remarked in 1868 that 'the bottom of things is an unfathomable chasm',[268] he now seemed to have found a way out of the abyss.

It is thus tempting to conclude that it was the renewed affirmation of Vacherot's Catholic beliefs which finally tipped the ideological scales. Indeed, the symmetry is compelling: as we saw earlier it was his firm attachment to freethinking which had underpinned his republicanism in the 1850s and 1860s. Once he ceased to be a militant freethinker, and indeed began to resume his personal engagement with the Roman creed, he was not only pulled away from republicanism but also inexorably driven towards the only available ideology which combined elitism, strong centralized leadership, enlightened liberalism, and religious conviction: royalism. In an article written in 1880 Vacherot had criticized the positivist contention that the historical evolution of the human spirit had followed three successive stages: theology, metaphysics, and positivism. History, he retorted, was much more complex than such simplistic schemes seemed to allow.[269] Little did he know how truly he spoke. Starting with a quasi-positivist conception of knowledge, his own trajectory had then moved to a growing appreciation of the metaphysical beauty of religion, before culminating in the beatitude—and penitence—of a revived Christian faith.

[268] Vacherot, 'La situation philosophique en France', 950.
[269] Vacherot, Étienne, 'Les trois états de l'esprit humain', *Revue des Deux Mondes* (15 August 1880), 856–92.

Eugène Pelletan, by Perdriau and Leroy
Bibliothèque Nationale, Paris

4

A Republican Saint-Simonian: Eugène Pelletan and the Transformation of Nineteenth-Century Republicanism

THE republican politician and intellectual Eugène Pelletan (1813–1884) was one of the best-known publicists of the Second Empire and early Third Republic generations of French republicans, as well as one of its most compelling figures. Many who did not share the allegiances of the political thinker found it hard to conceal their affection for the man. The liberal pamphleteer Lucien Prévost-Paradol warmed to Pelletan's almost quixotic sense of integrity as well as his fierce sense of independence.[1] The imperialist writer Xavier Marmier, who crossed swords with him on many an occasion, thought him 'an ardent democrat but a decent man'.[2] When in 1861 the Bonapartist state auctioned Pelletan's books because of his inability to pay a fine of 2,000 francs, a public subscription was launched; among the contributors were Georges Clemenceau and the young Ernest Lavisse.[3] But it was the Orleanist duc d'Aumale who provided the major financial contribution which saved his library. Pelletan's personal magnetism was considerable: although they were characteristically disobliging about his writings the Goncourt brothers were transfixed by his physiognomy, commenting variously on his 'head resembling the sketch of an apostle' and his 'head of an ancient philosopher'.[4]

Even the police officials who kept a close watch over his movements were not insensitive to his charms. After listing his distinguished contributions to the promotion of public disorder, a report of the Préfecture de Police in October 1875 ended by describing him as a 'romantic republican'[5]—no doubt a homage to his literary talents, but also a reference to the glamorous affiliations which

---

[1] Letter dated 13 December 1863, in Prévost-Paradol, Lucien-Anatole, *Quelques pages d'histoire contemporaine*, Vol. 2 (Paris: Michel Lévy, 1864), 299.

[2] 'Democrat' in this context signified 'republican'. Marmier, Xavier, *Journal 1848–1890*, Vol. 1 (Geneva: Droz ed., 1968), 346.

[3] Lavisse, Ernest, *Souvenirs* (Paris: Calmann-Lévy, 1988), 249.

[4] de Goncourt, Edmond and Jules, *Journal* Vol. II (Paris: Fasquelle and Flammarion, 1956), 18, 643.

[5] Archives de la Préfecture de Police (Paris), dossier Eugène Pelletan, BA 1216, report dated 27 October 1875.

had launched his early career. During the late 1830s the young Pelletan had begun to make a name for himself in Paris as an imaginative and fiery journalist. But his notoriety in French artistic and political circles was established through his encounters with two politico-literary giants of the mid-nineteenth century republican generation, George Sand and Alphonse de Lamartine. Although he was dismissed after a mere three months, Pelletan's spell as the *précepteur* of young Maurice Sand in the spring of 1837 propelled the obscure provincial intellectual into instant fame—as much for his inclusion into the charmed circle of Sand intimates as for his creative, not to say extravagant, reconstruction of his short stay at Nohant.[6]

Pelletan's political thought took shape in the years of the July Monarchy through a powerful and eclectic range of intellectual influences, most notably the Saint-Simonian school, republican historians such as Jules Michelet and Edgar Quinet, and socialist thinkers Charles Fourier and Pierre Leroux. In the early 1840s one person in many ways personified this combination of deism, republicanism, and mystical identification with the 'people': Alphonse de Lamartine. Pelletan naturally gravitated towards his passionate brand of republicanism, and in the early 1840s he became one of the democratic poet's closest collaborators.[7] After the disappointing interlude of the Second Republic, during which he loyally supported Lamartine's short-lived career as a republican statesman, Pelletan established himself as an independent publicist and political thinker under the Second Empire. The years between 1852 and 1870 witnessed a spectacular production of pamphlets, articles, reviews, and commentaries on a wide range of moral, political, and literary issues. These years also saw the publication of his major philosophical works, beginning with his most acclaimed treatise, *Profession de foi du XIXe siècle* (1852), a highly individual celebration of the doctrine of progress.

It was during these years too that Pelletan made a name for himself as an implacable political opponent of the Bonapartist regime. He discharged this role with great effectiveness as an elected member of the Legislative Corps between 1863 and 1870; as a public speaker on social, political, and civic questions; and as the author of vigorously polemical pamphlets against Napoleon III's regime. At the time of the fall of the Second Empire in 1870 Pelletan was among the most popular republican leaders in Paris, and on this basis he was included in the Government of National Defence which was proclaimed at the Hôtel de Ville in the 'revolution of 4 September'. In the 'peace' elections of February 1871 he was again returned as a deputy, and alongside Gambetta he

---

[6] In his 'Lettres à une veuve', published in two instalments in *La Presse* (4 and 11 June 1837), Pelletan implied that he had had a sexual relationship with George Sand, a claim endorsed by subsequent generations of Pelletans including his main biographer, Edouard Petit. An angry letter from Sand to Pelletan suggests that the 'seduction' was entirely fanciful, and probably nothing more than a petulant act of revenge on Pelletan's part for having been dismissed from Nohant. See Sand, George, *Correspondance*, ed. Georges Lubin, esp.Vol. 3 (Paris: Garnier, 1967), 893; Vol. 4 (1968), 127–30.

[7] For a portrait of the young Pelletan by Lamartine's secretary, see Alexandre, Charles, *Souvenirs sur Lamartine* (Paris: Charpentier, 1884), 13–14.

continued to militate for the establishment of a Republic until 1876, when the local delegates of the Bouches-du-Rhône nominated him to the newly founded Senate. After bringing out a further set of philosophical and political writings in the 1870s and early 1880s, Pelletan ended his life as a respected republican patriarch. His colleagues in the upper house appointed him as one of their vice-presidents in 1879, and in 1884, a few months before his death, he was granted the ultimate privilege of being designated an *inamovible*—life peer—the last French senator to be granted this accolade under the Third Republic.

For all these public honours, and despite his prodigious intellectual, journalistic, and literary output, Pelletan was never taken entirely seriously as a political thinker, either by his contemporaries[8] or by subsequent historians of French political thought.[9] His friendships and affiliations with the republican generation of 1848 were treated with condescension by many younger republicans, who later came to equate the era of the Second Republic with 'utopian' thinking, political ineptitude, and institutional failure. His defence of the ideas of progress and cosmopolitanism appeared outmoded after France's defeat by Prussia in 1871, when many republicans began to turn to more robust and occasionally belligerent forms of patriotism. Such irenic ideas and values were normally welcome to the extreme left, but Pelletan exasperated revolutionary republicans with his fetish for constitutional propriety, his paradoxical combination of inflammatory rhetoric and moderate politics, and above all his enduring commitment to the principles of liberal Protestantism.

The anticlerical Jules Vallès nicknamed him 'the penitent' because his outstretched hands and imploring manner reminded him of a Lutheran pastor.[10] The Communard Gustave Flourens was equally unimpressed, deriding Pelletan as 'the terrifying ogre who disturbed the nights of Bonaparte, the executioner of 1793 in person, but nonetheless the scion of the best society, and the most incapable of men'.[11] In some ways his reputation never quite recovered from his three-month ordeal at Nohant in 1837, when George Sand indulged herself in her taste for practical jokes at the expense of her handsome 'Pelican';[12] typically, she later turned the tables on him and dismissed him as a 'joker'.[13] Pelletan's reputation was probably not strengthened either by his ministerial involvement in the much-maligned Government of National Defence which ruled France between September 1870 and February 1871: a government which presided over France's military defeat by Prussia. This

---

[8] Pelletan's political thought was described as 'absolutely useless from a social point of view' by the historian of the Commune, Georges Bourgin; quoted in Soltau, *French Political Thought in the Nineteenth Century*, 268 n.1.

[9] 'A minor writer' is how Pelletan is described in Charlton, D. G., *Secular Religions in France 1815–1870* (London: Oxford University Press, 1963), 119.

[10] Valles, Jules, *L'insurgé* (Paris: Gallimard, 1975), 140.

[11] Flourens, Gustave, *Paris Livré* (Paris, 1871), 59.

[12] The name given to Pelletan by Sand at Nohant; see for example her letter to the Comtesse d'Agoult, 3 April 1837, in Sand, *Correspondance*, Vol. 3, 764.

[13] Letter to Pierre Bocage, 7 May 1843, in Sand, George, *Correspondance*, Vol. 4 (Paris: Garnier, 1969), 410.

appearance of failure was compounded by the advent of the Paris Commune in the spring and early summer of 1871, which traumatized the republican community and severely shocked Pelletan, who later confessed: 'it seemed to us during these long months of a second siege that each detonation took away with every shred of the homeland a shred of our soul.'[14]

A good gauge of his image in positivist republican circles around this time was the rather caustic entry in the *Larousse*:

Mr Pelletan is a distinguished writer, although his style is rather too lyrical; a committed republican, attached to progress and freedom, but whose somewhat dreamy theories lend themselves to criticism.[15]

Yet Republican France's tribute to this 'dreamy' republican thinker was by no means ungenerous. In 1884 Pelletan was given a grand state funeral, attended by the Président du Conseil Jules Ferry and a string of republican eminences; his memory was saluted by the republican press, with the Gambettist Eugène Spuller recalling his implacable battle against the imperial regime and the example he set to his generation of Second Empire republicans;[16] Pelletan's wife was awarded an annual pension of 6,000 francs 'as a gesture of national reward';[17] the municipality of Royan, his home town, erected a statue in his honour in September 1892, and various republican municipalities in Paris and in the provinces renamed their streets after him. But the image of Pelletan remained essentially reified. He was seen as a dignified elder statesman whose republicanism, however, was nothing more than a throwback to the hazy decades of the 1830s and 1840s. As the reviewer of the *Critique Philosophique* put it politely, Pelletan's political ideas constituted a system of thought which was 'gentle and attractive', but his doctrine of progress was not attuned to the more sober and pessimistic *Zeitgeist* of the later nineteenth century.[18]

This has remained the predominant view of Pelletan's political thought in the historiography of modern French republicanism. Writing on the eve of the First World War, his main biographer Edouard Petit depicted Pelletan as a shining symbol of the values of *quarante-huitard* republicanism: 'devotion to principles, elevation and purity of sentiments, sincerity of convictions, enthusiasm for the popular cause, and passion for sacrifice.'[19] While stressing the significance of some of his ideas Judith Stone's recent study has similarly highlighted Pelletan's affiliation to the 'romantic' generation, whose values and principles were subsequently revised by the 'radicals' of the late nineteenth and early twentieth centuries.[20] There has also been a recent revival of interest in Pelletan from the perspective of political genealogy. For his descendant

[14] Pelletan, Eugène, *Première aux électeurs. Est-ce la République?* (Paris: Leroux, 1876), 15.
[15] Larousse, Pierre, *Grand Dictionnaire Universel du XIXe Siècle* (Geneva-Paris: Slatkine, 1982), 526.
[16] Spuller, Eugène, 'Eugène Pelletan', in *Figures disparues*, 2nd series (Paris: Alcan, 1891), 119–26.
[17] Archives de la Préfecture de Police (Paris), dossier Eugène Pelletan, BA 1216 (hereafter APP).
[18] Pillon, F., 'Eugène Pelletan', *Critique Philosophique*, No. 48 (27 December 1884), 346–7.
[19] Petit, Édouard, *Eugène Pelletan* (Paris: Quillet, 1913), 269.
[20] Stone, Judith, *Sons of the Revolution* (Baton Rouge: Louisiana State University Press, 1996), 17–59. This is mainly a study of Eugène Pelletan's son Camille.

Paul Baquiast, Eugène Pelletan was especially notable as the first member of a 'republican dynasty', carried through the Third Republic with his Radical son Camille Pelletan and the Ordinaire and Bonnet families, and maintained under the Fourth and Fifth Republics through the Debré clan.[21]

However, there was much more to Eugène Pelletan's political thought than a passive reflection of *quarante-huitard* republican idealism. His political trajectory in the 1840s and early 1850s enables a re-examination of many of the myths which have been constructed around the revolution of 1848. In the republican historiographical tradition, the Second Republic has always been regarded as something of an embarrassment, a frustrating failure which was eventually wiped out by the emphatic and lasting triumph of the Republic after 1875. A core element in this perception is the conventional distinction between the allegedly naive 'romanticism' of the 1848 generation and the rigorous 'positivism' of later nineteenth-century republicans.[22] But the political culture of 1848 contained elements which were much more hard-edged and potent than this simple dichotomy implies.

An excellent case in point is the representation of 1789. As we have already seen with Dupont-White and Littré, throughout the nineteenth century most French republicans identified with *la grande révolution* and saw themselves as the bearers of its essential values. This confrontation with the past, with all its attending contradictions and conflicting appeals to both sentiment and reason, was fully lived out in the writings of the republican 'generation of 1848', notably historians such as Michelet and Quinet. Pelletan, a disciple and friend of both men, saw the events of the 1790s not merely as historical occurrences but as an actuality, with their protagonists engaged in a constant dialogue with members of his own generation. At the same time Pelletan did not regard the revolution as sacrosanct, and the object of this intellectual engagement with the past was to ensure that the mistakes of the first generation of republicans were not repeated by their successors. Hence his elaboration of a trenchant critique of Jacobinism which focused particularly on the noxious effects of the Terror, the perversity of revolutionary violence, and the futility of extreme versions of social equality.

This redefinition of the principles of 1789 by publicists such as Pelletan was part of a re-examination of the revolutionary heritage which was significantly advanced in its conclusions by the late 1840s; 'opportunist' republicans such as Ferry and Gambetta later appropriated its main results and made them their own. This specific example—there are many others—shows how far the labels of 'idealism' and 'utopianism', which later republicans of the Third Republic wantonly attached to their colleagues of the 1830s and 1840s, were often nothing more than ideological constructs. Their purpose was to exaggerate the differences between the two generations, to belittle the political culture of the

---

[21] Baquiast, Paul, *Une dynastie de la bourgeoisie républicaine. Les Pelletan* (Paris: L'Harmattan, 1996). See also the shorter book by another Pelletan descendant, Touroude, Georges, *Deux républicains de progrès, Eugène et Camille Pelletan* (Paris: L'Harmattan, 1995).

[22] Agulhon, Maurice, *Les quarante-huitards* (Paris: Gallimard, 1992), 239.

quarante-huitards, and at the same time to appropriate many of its core elements: a strategically brilliant act of depredation not dissimilar to that perpetrated by Marx and Engels on their socialist precursors of the first half of the nineteenth century.

More broadly, this reappraisal of Pelletan's ideas will produce a more rigorous and nuanced evaluation of his political thought as a whole. Over and above his being identified—somewhat erroneously, as we shall see below—with the 'republicanism of 1848', a number of elements, both biographical and ideational, conspired to crystallize Pelletan's reputation as a dreamy idealist: his self-confessed exuberance as a young intellectual in Paris in the 1830s, his lifelong attachment to a 'progressive' philosophy of history, his quasi-pantheistic dreams of religious unity, his affiliations with the Freemasonry, and his irenic belief in the possibility and desirability of international peace. There were thus clear elements of idealism which underlay his life and political thought.

But Pelletan also played an essential practical role in disseminating republican ideas in France through his writings, and furthermore performed an invaluable function in bridging the gap between different ideological strands within the republican movement. In addition, his political critique of the Second Empire was buttressed by a coherent republican political ideology, which in essential respects anticipated—and influenced—the republican order which emerged in France after 1875. Among Pelletan's pragmatic and effective contributions to the political culture of the early Third Republic were his liberal interpretation of the revolutionary heritage and his rejection of the Terror and political violence, as mentioned above, but also his belief in the value of bourgeois rule and 'republican legality'; his defence of democratic institutions and political liberties, notably such 'intellectual' freedoms as freedom of the press; his sustained campaign for municipal liberties and a decentralized notion of republican citizenship; and his tempered secularism, emphasizing the need for both a separation of Church and State and a reinforcement of the place of religion and spirituality in the fabric of republican life.

Yet Pelletan had more to offer than an anticipation of the ideological principles of 'opportunist' republicanism. One of the most exciting features of his political thought was that into this highly orthodox republican fabric, soon to be emblazoned upon the official banners of the new order, he wove a dazzling array of creative patterns, many of which reflected continuing Saint-Simonian influences on his 'mature' thinking. Among the insightful and forward-looking conceptions developed by Pelletan were his emphasis on the need for a more equitable role for women in republican society; his celebration of the liberating and productive attributes of industry; and his sophisticated—and in many ways strikingly modern—conception of patriotism. When considered in the overall context of his political thought, these 'visionary' components were evidence not only of Pelletan's intellectual creativity but also of the extent to which his republican political culture—and by extension that of the early Third Republic—still bore the imprint of early socialist and Saint-Simonian notions.

Early Political Thought: Idealism and Realism

'When one has not been mad at the age of 20, something is missing from the brain.'[23] Pelletan himself acknowledged that one of the underlying elements of unity in his early political thought in the 1830s and 1840s was his predilection for speculative and 'utopian' forms of thinking. Much of his later reputation as a somewhat bohemian *quarante-huitard* was derived from his public image during these years as a prolific and fiery republican journalist and close companion of artistic and literary celebrities.

In the traditional view of Pelletan's intellectual development, this idealist era was ended by the Bonapartist *coup d'état* of 1851, which shattered the irenic dreams of the 1848 generation of republicans and drove men such as Pelletan towards a more hard-edged and pragmatic form of republicanism.[24] But while accurate in some respects this dichotomy contains a considerable degree of oversimplification. A closer analysis of Pelletan's political thought during these years reveals that something rather more complex was taking shape in the elaboration of his political philosophy well before 1851 and that the emergence of the Second Empire had a much less significant impact on his ideological value system than is commonly thought. There is no denying that during the 1830s and 1840s he was pulled towards certain idealist premises through a variety of mechanisms: the appeal of spiritualist concepts and categories; the inspiration of key republican and socialist political thinkers; and also a process—partly deliberate, partly unconscious—of intellectual sedimentation, whereby elements of ideological systems which he had once embraced continued to preoccupy and even influence his thinking at critical junctures.

Yet it is clear that these forms of idealism were constantly undermined by countervailing forces, even during the 1840s: the elaboration of a distinct liberal model of the 1789 Revolution, which forced Pelletan to confront the glib rhetoric of Jacobin republican discourse; his emphasis on the role of religion, and especially his own Protestant faith, which pulled him away from the abstract and often crusading rationalism of many of his fellow republicans; and above all the political realities of the late 1840s, notably the threat of radical republicanism, against which Pelletan launched a series of vigorous attacks; these polemics, in turn, also helped him define his own brand of constitutional democratic politics. In short, Pelletan's thought between the late 1830s and early 1850s should be characterized not as an unbroken 'idealist' phase but as a period during which his embrace of speculative forms of thinking was first loosened and then increasingly undermined by strong political and ideological cross-pressures.

Utopian ideas and idealist philosophical systems were in no short supply when Pelletan arrived in Paris in the autumn of 1833. The capital was still

---

[23] Pelletan, Eugène, *Élisée. Voyage d'un homme à la recherche de lui-même* (Paris: Germer Baillière, 1877), 51.
[24] Spuller, 'Eugène Pelletan', 125.

pulsating in the aftermath of the revolutionary upheavals which had swept away the restoration regime and established the July Monarchy in July 1830. The electrifying atmosphere of the times was well captured by the Comtesse d'Agoult (Daniel Stern):

We were tormented by the desire of an ideal life and we searched for divine meaning in all things. Barely emerging from these extraordinary struggles, where all the foundations of the ancient world had been shaken, we still quivered with an anxious expectation of the unknown, the extraordinary, the impossible.[25]

Throughout the 1830s and for much of the 1840s the Parisian cultural elite remained gripped by this sense of intellectual urgency and philosophical fervour, and this manic atmosphere undoubtedly exercised a profound influence on the young Eugène Pelletan's world view. An additional factor which encouraged his drift towards 'utopian' forms of thinking was the extreme porousness of the boundaries between the spheres of art, literature, and progressive politics during this period. Largely under the influence of romanticism, politics was elevated into a discourse which celebrated the transcendental quest for ideal categories and alternative worlds. Pelletan roamed widely across the variety of political, intellectual, and cultural circles which were active in these years. Thus in the early 1830s he was seen regularly at the literary salon of Alfred Tattet, where he mingled with the likes of Alfred de Musset, Victor Hugo, Emmanuel and Alfred Arago, Émile de Girardin, and Sainte-Beuve.[26] While immersing himself in the emerging cultural elite Pelletan was projected into the flamboyant world of the Saint-Simonians, and for a brief period he even became an ardent disciple of the new cult.[27]

By the mid-1830s this 'pure' phase of idealism had drawn to a close, and in 1836 he began his career as a journalist with a series of articles in La Nouvelle Minerve. These pieces were followed in 1838 by a spell with Girardin's La Presse, one of the leading liberal newspapers of its time. His articles, published under the pseudonym 'A Stranger', brought him a great deal of public attention, and by the early 1840s his name had appeared in the columns of such diverse publications as L'Artiste, La Revue de Paris, France-Littéraire, Le Siècle, and the Courrier de Paris. At the same time Pelletan retained strong links with the creative arts through the painter Adolphe Gourlier, with whom he travelled across Italy and whose sister Virginie he eventually married in 1843.[28]

By the mid-1840s Pelletan had thus become a familiar figure in the separate but overlapping worlds of art, literature, liberal journalism, and republican politics. His entrenchment in each of these spheres was underscored by close links with key intellectual figures: George Sand, with whom he maintained

[25] d'Agoult, Comtesse Marie (Daniel Stern), Mémoires 1833–1854 (Paris: Calmann-Lévy, 1927), 2.

[26] Martin-Fugier, Anne, La vie élégante ou la formation du Tout-Paris 1815–1848 (Paris: Seuil, 1990), 367.

[27] APP, report dated 18 September 1874.

[28] On this period of Pelletan's life see Du Camp, Maxime, Souvenirs Littéraires, Vol. 1 (Paris: Hachette, 1882), 277–8.

good relations despite his disastrous spell at Nohant in 1837;[29] Jules Michelet, whose disciple he became and at whose Parisian home he would be a regular guest in the 1840s;[30] Pierre Leroux, the former Saint-Simonian thinker whose writings on socialism inspired many republicans of the '1848 generation';[31] Victor Hugo, whose work he greatly admired and with whom he corresponded throughout his life;[32] and most importantly Alphonse de Lamartine, in whose newspaper *Démocratie Pacifique* Pelletan became a leading contributor in the early 1840s. As mentioned earlier he loyally supported the poet's political career during this decade, most notably by assuming the editorship of the pro-Lamartine newspaper *Le Bien Public* after the 1848 Revolution.

It is not difficult to isolate instances of philosophical idealism, not to say political naivety, in the writings of Pelletan during the years of the July Monarchy and Second Republic. The influence of romanticism pervaded his entire political thought, and was perhaps most apparent in his mystical references to the revolutions of 1789, 1830, and 1848. There were two particular manifestations of this revolutionary idealism. First, Pelletan often stressed that these transformations represented the triumph of ideas over brute force, and morality over power; indeed in a typically idealist hyperbole he went so far as to assert that Lamartine's *Histoire des Girondins* had laid down the first barricade of the February 1848 revolution.[33]

But his idealism went even deeper. What was striking about Pelletan's accounts of these momentous events was the absence of any conception of agency and the constant invocation of transcendental forces. Thus the 1830 revolution was not in his view primarily the product of individual or even collective action but an event which had sprung from 'the mysterious depths'.[34] In his eyewitness account of the 1848 revolution Pelletan again emphasized the mystical origins and character of the overthrow of the July Monarchy, a point he illustrated this time by a pious metaphor: 'there was everywhere something undefinably religious. God was bowing to the cradle of the Republic.'[35] As for the 1789 revolution, its ultimate character was so profound that it could be expressed only through an analogy with nature. As he noted in a review of Michelet's *Histoire de la Révolution*, the 'secret' of the great revolution could not be expressed in words: it was like a pantheistic force, whose cosmic beauty and tranquil power reminded him of a sunset he once observed on the west coast of France.[36]

---

[29] See for example Sand, George, *Correspondance*, Vol. 5 (Paris, 1969), 327–8, 338, 382, all of which show the close relations between Sand and Pelletan between 1840 and 1842. Pelletan was left in Sand's Paris home to act as her secretary and carry out a number of specific intellectual and administrative tasks.

[30] Michelet, Jules, *Journal*, Vol. 1 (1828–1848) (Paris: Gallimard, 1959), 369.

[31] In a letter to Pelletan in August 1841, Sand asked for news of Leroux, with whom Pelletan was in close and regular contact. Sand, *Correspondance*, Vol. 5, 411.

[32] Some of Pelletan's letters to Hugo are in the Bibliothèque Victor Hugo, Paris.

[33] Pelletan, Eugène, *Heures de Travail*, Vol. 1 (Paris: Pagnerre, 1857), 126.

[34] Pelletan, Eugène, 'Histoire de Dix Ans par M. Louis Blanc', *Revue Indépendante* (1 February 1842), 502.

[35] Pelletan, Eugène, *Histoire des trois journées de Février 1848* (Paris: Louis Colas, 1848), 170.

[36] Pelletan, Eugène, *Heures de Travail*, Vol. 2 (Paris: Pagnerre, 1854), 286.

This was the essence of Pelletan's idealist thinking: the repeated invocation of nature—and God; the emphasis on mysticism; and above all the celebration of feeling and instinct. 'An emotion is or is not, and when it is, it is always right.'[37] Even if he immediately qualified this statement by stressing that reason mattered too, Pelletan undoubtedly shared the romantic intuition that political action, and life more generally, was simply a matter of encouraging and liberating the potential for good which was present in man. This belief in the value of instinct and spontaneity—nature rather than nurture—thus led him to argue that there was no need to 'organize' the forces of democracy: republicans did not have to be regimented but simply allowed to exist without any interference.[38] Similarly the 'people' were seen by Pelletan before 1851 as an inherent force for the good: 'public opinion cannot err.'[39] Two factors particularly contributed towards this goodness: the existence of the bourgeoisie, which had an inherently civilizing effect on society—so much so that 'the people' could become virtuous merely by rising into the bourgeoisie[40]—and the capitalist economic system, which automatically corrected any social injustices it created.[41]

Pelletan's idealism was also manifested by the extent to which his political views contained echoes of the dominant myths and speculative philosophical undercurrents of the 1830s and 1840s. Thus before 1848 he fully subscribed—along, it is true, with a very large number of republicans of his generation—to the Napoleonic myth, expressing his uninhibited admiration for Bonaparte's 'prodigious military epic'.[42] In a comment on the tomb built at the Invalides in 1840 after the repatriation of Napoleon's ashes, Pelletan's invocation of the Emperor's stature was effusive in its lyricism:

Napoleon, indeed, has already transcended the limits of human nature in our minds: he belongs as much to poetry as to history; his life glides like a wonderful legend in the imagination of the people.[43]

This buoyant spirit was equally in evidence in Pelletan's research on world religions, where he offered sympathetic and benign thoughts on the teachings of Hinduism[44] and generally propounded views which bordered on pantheism. In his articles for Lamartine's newspaper *Démocratie Pacifique* Pelletan asserted that man's relationship with God had to be seen in a broader context which ultimately spanned 'the entire cosmogonical order'.[45] Seen from this elevated perspective, earthly divisions based on considerations of race, nationality, and religion appeared increasingly superfluous. In particular the solution to the religious divisions of modern times lay not in a reconciliation between

---

[37] Pelletan, *Heures de Travail*, Vol. 1, 253.
[38] Pelletan, *Heures de Travail*, Vol. 2, 62–4.
[39] *Le Bien Public*, No. 10 (2 June 1848).
[40] Pelletan, *Heures de Travail*, Vol. 1, 300.
[41] Ibid., 288.
[42] Pelletan, 'Histoire de Dix Ans', 497.
[43] Pelletan, Eugène, 'Le Tombeau de Napoléon', *Revue Indépendante* (1 December 1841), 511.
[44] Pelletan, Eugène, and Maury, Alfred, *Histoire universelle des religions*, Vol. 1 (Paris, 1844), 49–98.
[45] Pelletan, Eugène, 'Comment les dogmes se regénèrent. Le Catholicisme', in Eug. Pelletan, Aug. Colin, Hipp. Morvonnais, Victor Hennequin, *Les dogmes, le clergé et l'État. Études Religieuses* (Paris: Librairie Sociétaire, 1844), 19.

Catholicism and Protestantism, which were both irretrievably corrupted religious systems, but in a new creed which would transcend existing schisms and unite the whole of mankind:

Just as today there is only one great policy in harmony with the wishes of God, the policy which draws together the people, pacifies them, abolishes them as people, so in the same way there is only one true religion, that which draws together and pacifies religious systems and abolishes them as systems.[46]

This emphasis on the regeneration of the world through political and religious universalism could also be seen as expressions of lingering Saint-Simonian and early socialist influences on Pelletan's political thought during the 1830s and 1840s. His exposure to socialist thinking came mainly through his friendship with Pierre Leroux, who, like Pelletan himself, briefly flirted with Saint-Simonianism in the early 1830s before developing his own ideological system, focusing particularly on the organization of labour, the maintenance of private property, the emancipation of women, the collaboration of classes, and the necessity of religion.[47] Leroux remained an influential figure in French progressive circles in the 1830s and 1840s, and at republican social gatherings Pelletan often sang his praises.[48]

Even more durable were the effects of Pelletan's involvement with the Saint-Simonian saga. Upon his arrival in Paris he both observed and participated in the ideological upheavals which followed the founding of the Saint-Simonian church in 1829.[49] During these years Pelletan became closely acquainted with leading Saint-Simonians such as Enfantin, Bazard, and Michel Chevalier, and although his embrace of the Saint-Simonian cult itself proved ephemeral he retained close personal and intellectual affinities with the movement. These contacts were fostered firstly through his links with Enfantin, the 'Pope' of the Saint-Simonian church, a remarkable and attractive figure whom Pelletan did not hesitate to describe as his 'intellectual father'.[50] Furthermore in the late 1830s and early 1840s some of Pelletan's artistic and intellectual mentors, notably George Sand and the Comtesse d'Agoult, were still enthusiastic devotees of Saint-Simonianism, and the young man was clearly impressed by the resilience of their beliefs,[51]

In one of his first articles for *La Nouvelle Minerve* in 1836 Pelletan dwelled on his relationship with Saint-Simonianism. While his ironic detachment underlined his distance from the institutional eccentricities of the cult—the collar and inverted waistcoat, the financially ruinous operation based at

---

[46] Ibid., 25. [47] On Leroux's influence on Pelletan, see Petit, *Eugène Pelletan*, 54.

[48] Thus at a reception at Lamartine's house on 9 March 1843 Pelletan gave a complete exposition of Leroux's doctrine. See Alexandre, *Souvenirs sur Lamartine*, 14.

[49] On the history of Saint-Simonianism see Weill, Georges, *L'école Saint-Simonienne* (Paris: Alcan, 1896) and Charlety, Sébastien, *Histoire du Saint-Simonisme 1825–1864* (Paris: Hartmann, 1934).

[50] Letter of Pelletan to Enfantin (undated), Bibliothèque de l'Arsenal (Paris), Fonds Enfantin 7769/68.

[51] As the Comtesse d'Agoult wrote in her diary on 31 July 1837: 'among all our modern social systems the doctrine of Saint-Simon is the one which more completely appeals to my sympathies.' *Mémoires*, 102.

Ménilmontant, the search for a female goddess, and the calamitous expedition to the Near East—he nonetheless stressed his continuing admiration for the intellectual and spiritual project which underlay it. On balance, he concluded, the Saint-Simonians remained worthy of admiration despite their numerous failings:

> We must be fair to them: no doubt they rushed into their conclusions. But they shed much clear light on many obscure and painful questions which agitate our minds; they have stimulated the science of economics and put down their mark on the field of new interests.[52]

But Pelletan's admiration for the Saint-Simonians was not merely nostalgic and backward-looking. Strong evidence of lingering Saint-Simonian values could be found his journalistic and political writings throughout the 1840s. When in 1848 Amail and Arthur Enfantin founded the neo-Saint-Simonian weekly journal *La Politique Nouvelle*, Pelletan signed up as one of the collaborators.[53] His writings also bore the strong imprint of Saint-Simonian thinking. This was most evidently the case in his gushing evocations of the beneficial effects of 'industrialism', often presented in anthropomorphic terms. Thus a visit to London left Pelletan overwhelmed by the prodigious spectacle of human activity: 'it seems that matter itself has come alive, and that seized by an insane frenzy of movement, it has started to walk, to turn, to strike, to work, to whirl, and to spread in all directions.'[54] Pelletan's review of Tocqueville's *De la Démocratie en Amérique* turned into a celebration of the American conquest of nature through internal colonization: he was evidently much more taken with this pioneering aspect of American life than with its political system, about which he had comparatively little to say.[55]

To be precise, the Saint-Simonian aspect of Pelletan's thought here was not his admiration for economic modernization and technological development— this was, after all, common currency among most liberals and republicans—but his apparent belief in their absolute primacy. Economic and technological change, he often implied, was the real force which drove social and political transformations across the world: it was responsible among other things for the eradication of obscurantism and religious superstition,[56] the replacement of war by peaceful commercial interactions between states, and the extension of the concept of 'sovereignty' through great inventions such as the steam engine.[57] Most tellingly, he also suggested that industrial and technological development were the necessary and sufficient prerequisites for the advance of democracy itself. In an article on the spread of locomotion in France, written in the early months of the Second Republic, Pelletan described the railway system as 'the most energetic instrument of democracy which has

---

[52] Pelletan, Eugène, 'Des religions nouvelles', *La Nouvelle Minerve* (1836), 536.
[53] Weill, *L'école Saint-Simonienne*, 232.
[54] Pelletan, 'Comment les dogmes se regénèrent', 13.
[55] Pelletan, *Heures de Travail*, Vol. 1, 13–20.   [56] Ibid., 57.
[57] Pelletan, *Heures de Travail*, Vol. 1, 85–6.

ever existed'. He then broadened this proposition into a general claim which bore all the hallmarks of a 'republican' form of Saint-Simonian thinking:

Every political revolution finds, creates, accompanies or follows a similar revolution in the world of events, inventions, or industries. Each new idea has its representation in a new institution. The railway is in some way the inevitable institution of the Republic. It prepares its unity. What are we saying? It does not prepare it, it guarantees it.[58]

Taken together, all these features of Pelletan's value system seem to suggest the presence of deep layers of idealism in his political thinking during the 1830s and 1840s. A number of these characteristics—an idealized view of 'the people', a belief in the value of spontaneous action, an emphasis on political and religious universalism, and a faith in the beneficial political consequences of industrial progress—were commonly associated with the effusiveness of *quarante-huitard* republicanism. But, as we argued earlier, to view Pelletan in this 'utopian' light alone would be to ignore the hard-edged elements which were embedded in his political thinking and, in broader terms, in the republican political culture of the 1840s. Three interlinked aspects of this 'republican realism' are particularly worthy of note: his definition of the liberal tidings of the 1789 revolution and his accompanying denunciation of the dangers of Jacobin revolutionism; his defence of bourgeois rule and bourgeois values, which gave a firm social underpinning to his republican politics; and his elaboration of a sociology of political action, which highlighted the practical necessity of intellectual involvement in the life of the *polis*.

The meaning and relevance of 1789 remained a continuing source of controversy in French political culture throughout the nineteenth century. While republicans, legitimists, Bonapartists, and liberals frequently debated these questions with each other, the fiercest controversies often took place among republicans of conflicting ideological persuasions. During the 1830s and 1840s historians such as Michelet and Edgar Quinet developed an inclusive and synthetic approach to the Revolution which in important respects challenged prevailing liberal, Jacobin, and socialist assumptions and interpretations.[59] As a disciple of Michelet, Pelletan was very much embroiled in these battles, largely because he understood that their implications went considerably further than a historical dispute about the founding myths of republicanism. The events of 1789 provided an interpretive framework through which present and future events could be deciphered by all republicans; for Pelletan there was almost no temporal discontinuity between the late eighteenth century and the mid-nineteenth. He often suggested that the main actors of the great Revolution were still trapped in purgatory, and that only the advances and achievements of his republican generation could lead to their complete release.[60] This was an elegant and somewhat poignant way of expressing the point that 1789 was

---

[58] *Le Bien Public*, No. 48 (11 July 1848).
[59] On the historical debates of this period see Crossley, *French Historians and Romanticism*.
[60] Pelletan, *Heures de Travail*, Vol. 1, 226.

still a living force, bestowing authority and legitimacy upon those who were able to establish themselves as its rightful heirs.

In this sense the interpretation of 1789 was an eminently political act, and in the 1840s it became one of the main sites upon which liberal republican intellectuals such as Pelletan fought to influence, and assert control over, the destiny of the republican movement. A crucial element in this conflict was the interpretation of the Terror and, more broadly, the use of violence in republican politics. Pelletan followed Michelet and Quinet in condemning the doctrine of public safety as a permanent instrument of republican rule in the 1790s. The Terror had been completely inconsistent with the liberal and humane premises of the Revolution and had also served to discredit it; and because of its inability to maintain itself the Jacobin dictatorship had, perversely, facilitated the restoration of monarchical rule in France in the early nineteenth century. Evil governance was thus not just immoral and inconsistent, it was also highly ineffective. Pelletan's exhortation underlined the contemporaneous political ramifications of this conclusion:

Let us all enter the fray, such as we are, and from all the perspectives of democratic opinion, in order jointly to condemn this hideous doctrine which justifies the means by the end, and for a doubtful advantage commits a certain injustice.[61]

This was not to say that violence had no legitimate place in republican politics. In his writings in the aftermath of the 1848 revolution Pelletan drew a careful distinction between extraordinary and ordinary political circumstances. At critical historical junctures violence was effectively the only way in which the republican idea could advance:

[The revolutionary party] only has its *raison d'être* in those supreme and mysterious moments which spontaneously chime in the bells of nations; these moments when liberty has just been violently suppressed. The revolutionary party opposes force with force, the bayonet with the bayonet.[62]

But once victory had been decisively achieved over the enemies of the Republic, as after 1789 and February 1848, such internal violence had to cease. The very existence of a revolutionary party under normal democratic circumstances was a 'monstrous paradox'[63] given that republican politics stood for the rule of law, constitutional government, and the persuasion of majorities through public debate and rational argument. Pelletan's open, generous, and peaceful conception of republicanism was thus elaborated as the negation of revolutionary Jacobinism. It was personified by Lamartine's 'Republic of union, of attraction, of harmony, the Republic of the rights of the minority in the majority'.[64] Inspired by the Scriptures, and following the lead of 1789, the fraternal Republic of 1848 had abolished slavery and proclaimed the reign of universal fraternity.[65] But fraternity was not merely a metaphysical slogan; for

---

[61] Pelletan, *Heures de Travail*, Vol. 1, 280.   [62] *Le Bien Public*, No. 4 (27 May 1848).

[63] Pelletan, *Heures de Travail*, Vol. 2, 164.   [64] *Le Bien Public*, No. 1 (24 May 1848).

[65] Pelletan, *Heures de Travail*, Vol. 1, 344–5.

Pelletan it also had to be concretely applied to the sphere of domestic politics.[66] Fraternity thus made it necessary to practise 'social charity' in order to
alleviate the sufferings of the people;[67] it also meant rejecting the lead of those
sectarians who sought to divide groups of French people from one another:

No more bourgeoisie, no more working class, but citizens! This is the meaning of the
Republic. Reconciliation of all the old parties, fusion of all classes in democratic unity,
this is its goal![68]

So open was Pelletan's republicanism that it rejected any internal hierarchy
within the movement on the basis of past allegiances. All republicans were in
his view entitled to equal status, irrespective of the time at which they had
signed up to the principles of 1789.[69] This spirit of equality and fraternity was
not to be extended, however, to those who wished to threaten the liberty of
all the others. Pelletan warmly applauded the Second Republic's use of force
to suppress the workers' revolt of June 1848, for it not only put an end to the
utopian nightmare of a 'democratic and social republic'[70] but also demonstrated the martial vigour of the Republic and its capacity to maintain order,
even against dissidents from its own camp.[71] The strong message, in short, was
that republican violence was not just necessary but desirable and legitimate
against the republican enemies of freedom.

Pelletan's republicanism during the 1840s was thus firmly anchored in a
coherent set of beliefs and assumptions about political life: the validity of the
liberal principles of 1789 coupled with an emphatic rejection of revolutionary
violence as a systematic method of republican rule. This constitutionalism, in
turn, was circumscribed by a readiness to deploy public force against the enemies of the Republic, even if they happened to be republicans themselves. This
robustness, in terms of both the core republican values and the readiness to
defend them, was far removed from the 'idealist' colours in which Pelletan's
politics are typically represented during the 1830s and 1840s. This hard edge
to his republicanism was also both inspired and further reinforced by his
emphasis on bourgeois values, activities, and political rule, which constituted
another cohesive element in his political thinking.

Pelletan never ceased to wax lyrical about the bourgeoisie, 'this favourite
class of all classes, which is wealthy enough to be born to the life of the
soul through education, and sufficiently limited in its wealth to be held
to work'.[72] His conception of the bourgeois ideal was significantly influenced
by his Protestantism, which in many respects defined his vision of private
life:

---

[66] For a wider discussion of the concept of fraternity in French political thought during this period
see David, Marcel, *Le printemps de la fraternité: genèse et vicissitudes 1830–1851* (Paris: Aubier, 1992).
[67] *Le Bien Public*, No. 5 (28 May 1848).   [68] *Le Bien Public*, No. 6 (29 May 1848).
[69] In 1848 Pelletan attacked Jules Favre for distinguishing between 'long-standing' and 'recently-
converted' republicans. The Republic, he retorted, did not have to rely on 'an aristocracy of the cal-
endar'. *Le Bien Public*, No. 54 (17 July 1848).   [70] *Le Bien Public*, No. 31 (24 Juin 1848).
[71] *Le Bien Public*, No. 45 (7 July 1848).   [72] Pelletan, *Heures de Travail*, Vol. 2, 242.

There results from Protestantism a profoundly religious cult for internal life, and for industrial and commercial life. It develops the domestic virtues, order, cleanliness, economy, patience, and family traditions.[73]

Pelletan also upheld the centrality of the bourgeoisie's economic role in society against 'ruralist' thinkers who asserted the primacy of agriculture. In a response to Blanc de Saint-Bonnet, a fierce defender of monarchist traditionalism in all its forms, Pelletan stressed that without industrial activity there would be no agriculture:

Society is but a vast factory in which matter . . . is constantly elaborated and processed. The soil is the first step in this labour, nothing more; it is the preparatory ground for other labours. Far from being complete in itself, it is subordinated to industry. Without industry it is the desert.[74]

From this perspective the Revolution of 1789 had largely been a 'bourgeois' revolution in all its essential social, economic, and moral principles; Pelletan rejected claims from republican socialists such as Louis Blanc that the true 'popular' spirit of the Revolution had been perverted by the bourgeoisie.[75] The continuing strength of the bourgeoisie was a condition of republican success: 'the numerical strength of the bourgeoisie in the state is always the criterion of its prosperity . . . and even more so of its liberty, for freedom is bourgeois by origin.'[76] In this context the bourgeoisie's contribution to the good life through wealth creation, and particularly capital accumulation, was also invaluable:

Capital is thus the true redeemer, the true mediator, the true remunerator of our destinies on this earth. It is capital which has broken castes, slavery, serfdom, and which will break the proletariat. It is capital which, day by day, by its expansion, incessantly relieves the worker, like a sentinel, of the necessity of physical labour, in order to lead him towards his higher destiny, the life of comfort, the life of thought.[77]

Finally, Pelletan's republican political culture and his celebration of the virtues of the bourgeoisie came together to form a third key ingredient in his political thinking in the 1830s and 1840s: the definition of an ambitious philosophy of intellectual intervention in public life. 'He who thinks, believes, he who thinks, acts; the world belongs to action directed by thought.'[78] From his very first autobiographical work in 1838 Pelletan emphasized the value and practical necessity of political thought as a mediating influence between philosophy and politics. To the boorish 'men of action' who denied the utility of such a theoretically informed approach to politics, Pelletan was fond of quoting Royer-Collard: 'whoever shows contempt for theory displays the rather arrogant pretence of not knowing what he is saying when he speaks, nor what he does when he acts.'[79] The republicans, in contrast, offered the best exam-

---

[73] Pelletan, 'Comment les dogmes se regénèrent', 15.
[74] Pelletan, *Heures de Travail*, Vol. 2, 141.   [75] Pelletan, *Heures de Travail*, Vol. 1, 227.
[76] Ibid., 46.   [77] Ibid., 287.   [78] Pelletan, *Élisée*, 177.
[79] Pelletan, Eugène, *Les uns et les autres* (Paris: Pagnerre, 1873), 315.

ple of an ideologically-based political movement: 'the party of ideas is the democratic party.'[80]

Pelletan's development of this theme showed how far removed he was from the problematic of 'idealism' and speculative thought. Politics, he firmly indicated, could not be driven by the search for utopian goals and abstract categories. His French contemporaries' predilection for German transcendentalism was thus contemptuously dismissed: 'it is time and high time to put an end to the hot air of German metaphysics.'[81] It was essential to remember that societies were not at all like philosophical systems: 'while the idea is always one, as the absolute, society is always complex, ambiguous, mixed.'[82] It therefore followed that political action had to be guided by a sense of measured prudence and sobriety:

Philosophy and politics are thus essentially distinct: we should associate them but not confuse them. The one gives us the goal, the other the means; one abstracts itself from time, the other, on the contrary, specifically takes time into account and adapts its proposals to it; the one advances in tune with prophecy, the other with reality.[83]

The task of apprehending this reality and making it accessible to mass opinion was devolved to men of culture. It was they who had the intellectual capacity to make sense of the world around them and the elevation and refinement needed to empathize with the people. As Pelletan remarked a little later: 'the writer must put his life at the service of a truth.'[84] Recruited primarily from the bourgeoisie, republican intellectuals thus had an essential role to perform in the transformation of society. Pelletan underlined this point somewhat maliciously by pointing out that 'bourgeois' intellectuals were predominant not among moderate and constitutional republicans alone: all the great thinkers of modern republican socialism—Fourier, Considérant, Vidal, and Louis Blanc—had also emerged from the ranks of the bourgeoisie.[85]

These various republican elements in Pelletan's political thought had thus assumed a coherent shape by the late 1840s. Taken together they represented a conscious, and largely successful, effort on his part to move away from the speculative and utopian positions he had adopted upon his arrival in Paris in 1833. Perhaps more importantly, these robust republican components demonstrate the singular inappropriateness of the 'idealist' label when attached to *quarante-huitard* intellectuals such as Pelletan. In his definition of the liberal political culture of 1789, his unambiguous and lucid condemnation of the dangers of radical republicanism, in his celebration of the virtues of bourgeois rule and the necessity of intellectual intervention in public life, and above all in his emphasis on the need for political action to be based on social reality rather than metaphysical verbiage, Pelletan drew the contours of a robust and practical doctrine which would help to shape the ideological realignment of republicanism in subsequent decades.

---

[80] *Le Bien Public*, No. 4 (27 May 1848).   [81] Pelletan, *Élisée*, 308.
[82] *Le Bien Public*, No. 55 (18 July 1848).   [83] Ibid.
[84] A comment made at his trial in 1861; quoted in Petit, *Eugène Pelletan*, 277.
[85] Pelletan, *Heures de Travail*, Vol. 1, 231–2.

The Philosopher of Progress

'Last night I went to Mme. d'Agoult. Among those present were Freslon, Pelletan, Martin. The general character of these meetings is sadness and boredom with the present, fear rather than hope for the future.'[86]

Dated 12 February 1853, a little over a year after the Bonapartist *coup d'état*, and a few months after the triumphant proclamation of the Second Empire in December 1852, this gloomy entry in Emile Ollivier's diary underscored the plight of the French republican community after the failure of the Second Republic. Pelletan had particular reasons to appear morose at this juncture. Not only had the republican experiment he had so ardently welcomed in 1848 turned out to be an embarrassing failure, but his beloved leader Lamartine had been humiliatingly rejected by the French electorate in the presidential elections of 1849. Pelletan had also put himself forward for the constituent and legislative elections in 1848 and 1849, but had been rebuffed on both occasions.[87]

His theoretical response to this collapse of the world around him seemed almost obstinately defiant. In 1852 he published his *Profession de Foi du XIXe Siècle*, a lyrical history of human civilization which reaffirmed his belief in human progress and underlined his continuing commitment to an optimistic vision of republican society. Five years later Pelletan revisited the same theme with a vengeance in *Le Monde Marche*, a vigorous defence of the idea of progress against the criticisms of the now embittered and increasingly pessimistic Lamartine. Set against the backdrop of an assertively authoritarian Bonapartist regime and the almost complete political collapse of republican political activity in France, Pelletan's emphasis on progress throughout the 1850s seemed to provide further confirmation of his irreducible 'idealism'. To many of his contemporaries, and to subsequent historians, his defence of human perfectibility at this time was an illustration of his continuing devotion to speculative and utopian thinking, as well as a mark of his failure to appreciate the full political implications of the disaster of 1851.

Nothing could be further removed from the truth, however. Pelletan's writings on the theme of progress did not remain static but underwent significant changes between the early 1840s and the late 1850s. Furthermore, his concept of progress was complex and operated at many different levels of discourse simultaneously. Rather like his political thought as a whole during this period, his ideas about human perfectibility developed from an eclectic and speculative set of propositions to a more specific and concrete doctrine with explicitly political foundations. More broadly, his ideas about human progress performed several crucial functions in the development of his political thought. They enabled Pelletan to elaborate his distinct intellectual lineage as a republican Saint-Simonian, while at the same time offering an Aesopian

---

[86] Ollivier, Émile, *Journal 1846–1860*, Vol. 1 (Paris: Julliard, 1961), 144–5.
[87] Petit, *Eugène Pelletan*, 55–7.

critique of the Second Empire and defining a flexible and multi-layered conception of republican identity. 'Progress' was therefore no utopia but an overarching concept which could help to hold the republican community together at a difficult time in its history, and in this sense indirectly serve as a practical tool for waging the intellectual war against the evil rulers who had usurped power in France in December 1851. Pelletan was not, in short, reacting to adversity by merely asserting the desirability—and inevitability—of a better world in some distant future—the essence of pure idealist thinking. Rather, he was stressing the proximate reality of human progress as a means of working towards the overthrow of the Second Empire.

It is easy enough to conclude that Pelletan's doctrine of progress remained largely unaltered between the early 1840s and the late 1850s. He himself often asserted that his views on the subject had not changed significantly, and a superficial comparison of his writings seems to bear out this claim entirely. Thus in his early journalistic articles in *Démocratie Pacifique* he offered the following definition:

Progress, as considered from the point of view of humanity, is the enhancement of physical life by greater pleasures and accomplishments, of moral life by more love and charity, and of intellectual life by more science.[88]

In the late 1850s it was ostensibly the same conception of progress which informed his argument in *Le Monde Marche*, where progress was presented in terms of 'the enhancement of life' in all its dimensions.[89] Yet even this apparent consistency of definition was problematic for some. Many commentators, even those favourably disposed towards Pelletan, noted that given its extreme breadth such a conception of progress was neither edifying nor heuristically valuable.[90] Upon closer inspection, however, it becomes apparent that Pelletan significantly revised his formulations of progress during these years. In a sense this was inevitable given that he was committed to the view that human nature was not invariant but constantly evolving: 'man is an historical being always changing through progress.'[91]

Pelletan's personal circumstances changed dramatically between the early 1840s and the late 1850s, and it was therefore only natural that his philosophy of progress should have changed as well. A number of broad shifts may be noted, all of which represented attempts on his part to isolate the specific conditions and circumstances under which progress could be manifested. In the 1840s and early 1850s there was little evidence of any such discrimination; in the concluding pages of his *Profession de Foi* Pelletan explicitly stated that *any* positive change in the moral, physical, and intellectual conditions of mankind was sufficient evidence of the manifestation of progress.[92] By the late 1850s,

---

[88] Pelletan, 'Comment les dogmes se regénèrent', 19.
[89] Pelletan, Eugène, *Le Monde Marche. Lettres à Lamartine* (Paris: Pagnerre, 1857), vi.
[90] In the words of the republican critic Morin: 'M. Pelletan has just sung progress, it remains for him to define it'; quoted in Spuller, 'Eugène Pelletan', 125.
[91] Pelletan, *Heures de Travail*, Vol. 1, 81–2.
[92] Pelletan, Eugène, *Profession de Foi du xixeme Siècle* (Paris: Pagnerre, 1864), 386.

after nearly a decade of authoritarian Bonapartist rule, he had become much more prudent. Not only was it important to examine change carefully before determining its progressive character, but it was also essential to remember that progress could be temporarily delayed or even halted. The continuity of human perfectibility was thus not always apparent.[93]

A further evident shift in his conception of progress was the characterization of its ultimate object. In the 1840s, as we saw earlier, Pelletan's writings were often enmeshed in neo-religious and spiritualist problematics, and one of the manifestations of this approach was the belief in the ultimate emergence of a 'new humanity', a term often deployed in his writings at this juncture.[94] Progress, from this point of view, was almost a transcendental category, concerned more with spiritual redemption than material and intellectual advancement. Already in the *Profession de Foi* this providentialism had been significantly downplayed; and by the late 1850s the existence of God was merely one of a large battery of arguments deployed to demonstrate the reality of progress rather than its bedrock principle.[95] Even more striking was the shift in the spatial and temporal focus of the argument. In the 1840s and early 1850s Pelletan's writings on progress were concerned with the evolution of mankind from a very broad historical perspective; the *Profession de Foi* is an erudite but sweeping geographical account of the development of human civilization across the ages. During the 1850s, however, his concerns become much more specific and pressing. Through its vigorous polemic with Lamartine about the validity of the concept of progress, the real object of the argument in *Le Monde Marche* was the proximate future of France rather than the long-term prospects of 'humanity': a point noted by many observers at the time.[96]

These changes of emphasis on the nature and object of progress also enabled Pelletan to formulate a more ideologically precise philosophy of history during these years. In the late 1840s his political thought was sufficiently impregnated with socialist ideas for him to suggest that 'to believe in progress is to believe in socialism'.[97] After the collapse of the Second Republic statements of this nature completely disappeared from his discourse. Through this adjustment Pelletan was able subtly to redefine his intellectual relationship to the key political and ideological paradigms which had influenced him up to that point and particularly to clarify his position with respect to republican and Saint-Simonian thought. As we noted earlier, republicanism had become the most substantive component in his political thinking by late 1840s, and it was only natural that Pelletan's writings on progress should reflect this intellectual reorientation to an increasing extent. For example, his view on the vocation of humanity to cultivate its rationality while retaining a sense of the

---

[93] Pelletan, *Le Monde Marche*, 229.
[94] See for example *Heures de Travail*, Vol. 1, 20–1.
[95] Pelletan, *Le Monde Marche*, 137.
[96] See for example the entry of 29 June 1856 in Delacroix, Eugène, *Journal 1822–1863* (Paris: Plon, 1996), 587.
[97] *Le Bien Public*, No. 99 (31 August 1848).

divine was very much in line with the anthropological deism of *quarante-huitard* thinking:

Man, the reflection of divine spirit on earth, has a mission to accomplish the law of progress, not only through the increasing occupation of space, as the rest of creation, but also by greater participation in thought, the supreme essence of Divinity.[98]

This republican rationalism and spiritualism pushed Pelletan towards establishing a hierarchy in relation to the different spheres of progress he had previously identified in the 1840s. Thus while he still endorsed the view that the accentuation of 'physical' life through leisure was evidence of progress, his writings after 1848 clearly stipulated that education and learning were more important than the mere satisfaction of corporeal pleasures.[99] In the final pages of the *Profession de Foi* Pelletan appeared to settle for an exclusively rationalist definition of human advancement: 'progress thus consists in extracting constantly, from human matter, humanized by work, a greater amount of work.'[100]

But—again in keeping with his broader republican political and social philosophy—'thought' here was an ideological category as opposed to a merely descriptive one. In fact what was being celebrated was not abstract or speculative thought—'philosophy'—but rather a theoretically informed politics in which republican intellectuals were entrusted with the formulation of progressive ideas for the rest of society. The emphasis on this form of intellectual engagement was a notably republican political gesture in the context of the early 1850s. Because of his prominence as a republican political thinker Pelletan was very nearly arrested and deported in December 1851.[101] Far from deterring him, however, this experience of fear and uncertainty had reinforced his determination to continue his political struggle and publicly abide by his beliefs. It was through such a battle that Pelletan believed he could rise to the position of the virtuous intellectual:

I think, and when I write, I write like Pascal, and a chasm opens by my side. I know not, in these uncertain times, in what bed I shall sleep tomorrow. Well! In spite of this danger hanging over the head of the writer, but because of this danger which I do not defy but which I accept, I feel as though I have moved up a grade in my generation.[102]

This higher status accorded to ideological thinking and intellectual commitment was a crucial 'republican' element in Pelletan's doctrine of progress in the 1850s. It is worth noting that this republicanism had strong elitist undertones. Gone—or at least well hidden—was the *quarante-huitard* faith in the benign and positive attributes of the 'people'. Salvation and political progress, Pelletan seemed now to be saying, had to be entrusted to the literate classes; in the final analysis it was only they who could lead society forward towards

---

[98] Pelletan, *Profession de Foi*, 53–4.   [99] Pelletan, *Le Monde Marche*, 204.
[100] Pelletan, *Profession de Foi*, 390.
[101] His name was on a second list of proscribed activists, who, for some unknown reason, were never arrested.
[102] Pelletan, *Profession de Foi*, 392.

greater freedom. In *Le Monde Marche* Pelletan underscored this point by offering the example of the *idéologues* in early nineteenth century France. When they appeared on the political scene this small group of intellectuals had not been taken seriously, yet eventually the entire French bourgeoisie had come to embrace their conception of freedom.[103]

This was a respectable proposition as intellectual history, but even more importantly it was a highly revealing example. It confirmed that Pelletan was still strongly committed to the value of theoretically informed political action—and practically informed political theory—and this was very much a continuation of his republican political thinking of the late 1840s. At the same time the example of the *idéologues* showed that the resilience of Pelletan's belief in progress in the 1850s was not based on speculative or metaphysical considerations but on a concrete and realistic analysis of France's recent social and political history. Finally, and perhaps most intriguingly, the same example highlighted the relative fluidity of Pelletan's republicanism in the 1850s. The *idéologues* may have been a highly distinguished group of intellectuals, but many of them were republican only in a somewhat notional sense, if at all. That they should have been chosen as modern symbols of the positive effects of theoretically informed political action demonstrated how far removed Pelletan still remained from the orthodox mythology of republicanism at this time. But there was more to it than the mere use of heterodox political imagery. Pelletan's political philosophy continued to be nourished by significant non-republican ingredients throughout the 1850s. The most notable element in this respect was the continuing influence of Saint-Simonian thinking on his conception of progress. On the question of the role of women in society, for example, Pelletan was highly critical both of Western civilization in general and of the French republican tradition in particular. He pointedly remarked that the revolution of 1789 had done very little to liberate women from subjection and exploitation, and that it was only in the nineteenth century that positive changes in public attitudes towards feminine emancipation could be detected.[104] Even more strikingly, the underlying principles of Pelletan's economic philosophy were Saint-Simonian. In its treatment of the economic and social history of Europe since early modern times, the *Profession de Foi* was to all intents and purposes a Saint-Simonian tract, highlighting the civilizing influence of urban life;[105] the transformative effects of industrialization;[106] the revolutionary effects of the establishment of banking institutions for the development of international commerce;[107] and the pacific consequences of trade, which would eventually lead to a united, economically integrated, and cosmopolitan world.[108] Above all progress was manifested through the development of capitalism, 'the redeemer of our destiny'.[109]

In some passages of *Le Monde Marche* the accumulation of capital through human endeavour seemed to be described as the only real measure of progress:

[103] Pelletan, *Le Monde Marche*, 120–1.
[104] Pelletan, *Heures de Travail*, Vol. 2, 248–50.
[105] Pelletan, *Profession de Foi*, 261.
[106] Ibid., 268.   [107] Ibid., 305.
[108] Ibid., 346.
[109] Ibid., 352.

'labour, infinitely accumulated in this way over other labour, constitutes the social capital of humanity. This capital, always growing hour by hour by the simple fact of human activity, constitutes the historical phenomenon of progress.'[110] But this was something of a hyperbole, for there were clear limits to Pelletan's neo-Saint-Simonianism; one of the most interesting aspects of his writings on progress was his attempt to fortify the pure economism of Saint-Simonian thought with elements borrowed from republican political theory. Thus in a pamphlet on Condorcet written during the 1860s Pelletan defined the intellectual tradition which had inspired him as a blend of republicanism and Saint-Simonianism, and consciously presented himself as the inheritor of its values: 'the great intellects of our time descend in a direct filiation from the doctrines of Condorcet. Saint-Simon was indeed his most illustrious disciple, and through him all the flow of ideas, brought to our times by the Saint-Simonian school, can be traced back to the eighteenth century.'[111]

What this meant in practical terms was that positive changes in the economic and spiritual spheres were not sufficient to define a comprehensive sense of progress; substantive political transformation was required as well. Pelletan drove the point home in *Le Monde Marche* by stressing that industrial development and positive political change were not necessarily correlated. Industrial activity, after all, had taken off under the Second Empire, but this had promoted only a crude and materialistic conception of the human good, which had very little to do with the ideals of republicanism. His critique of this narrowly conceived 'industrialism' was particularly directed at Bonapartist Saint-Simonians such as his old acquaintance Michel Chevalier,[112] whose social and political philosophy was eloquently savaged in this passage:

For proper satisfaction, industrialism advises us to set aside all intellectual concerns. To allow the world to go where it wishes, according to the wisdom of the monk, always to speak with respect of the reigning priest, to slumber in peace on a carefree pillow, and to grab as much as possible for oneself, each for oneself, everyone at home, and after one's passing the end of the world, here is the morality of a society abandoned to the demons of industry. In such a society the mint suffices and the policeman to guard the mint, and the more the policeman interprets his orders rigorously, the more the public sphere is perfect.[113]

But taken in its broader and more political sense 'industrialism' could be a significant benefit to the republican cause, for several overlapping reasons. Industrial activity led to the development of human labour, which cultivated the intellectual and moral faculties of man; in this sense industrial endeavour was 'the first moralist of the world'.[114] Industrial activity was also an important factor in the growth of the bourgeoisie; Pelletan regarded it as its defining attribute, 'the bourgeoisie itself reduced to its true expression'.[115] Above all,

---

[110] Pelletan, *Le Monde Marche*, 24.
[111] Pelletan, Eugène, 'Condorcet', quoted in Petit, *Eugène Pelletan*, 127.
[112] See Thépot, André, 'Michel Chevalier', in Jean Tulard (ed.), *Dictionnaire du Second Empire* (Paris: Fayard, 1995), 284–5.
[113] Pelletan, *Le Monde Marche*, 114–15.   [114] Ibid., 116.   [115] Ibid.

industrialism was leading to the emergence of a new type of urban working class, which was already entrenched in such cities as Paris and Lyon and whose advanced political consciousness gave it a prominent position in the advancement of republican ideas. Pelletan underlined the centrality of this new class of workers by hailing it as 'the new intellectual army of liberty.'[116]

In terms of its internal components Pelletan's doctrine of progress was thus a complex and highly original synthesis in which the social and political values of republicanism were enriched by a distinctly Saint-Simonian underlying vision of economic progress. This Saint-Simonianism, in turn, was qualified by an emphasis on the beneficial political consequences of industrial development. A further layer of complexity in Pelletan's writings on progress during the 1850s was his deliberate use of the broad ideological framework it offered to confront the new Bonapartist order and remind republicans of the continuing truth and potency of their core values. As we have just seen in the case of Vacherot, it was difficult to attack the Second Empire directly in the 1850s and early 1860s, and Pelletan would later be fined and briefly imprisoned for one of his articles. But he made a number of transparent allusions to the wickedness of France's new rulers in *Le Monde Marche*. For example, while stressing the importance of education and learning in the development of the human spirit Pelletan made the point that all the violence in the world could not undermine this form of cultural progress: an obvious jibe at the French state's efforts to restrict freedom of thought and expression in the years of the authoritarian Empire.[117] The concept of progress was in this sense a metaphor for the idea of the republic itself; its function was to provide republicans with something which maintained their sense of identity and self-esteem in the face of adversity. It was from this angle that Pelletan stressed the importance of hope and confidence in the future, not out of a general teleological faith in the inevitability of progress but rather as an almost tactical weapon to lift the sagging morale of the republican community. This instrumentalization of the concept clearly underlay Pelletan's proposition that progress should not necessarily be equated with concrete and immediate change. The idea of progress also consisted of an intellectual identification with the values of intelligence and justice, espousing valid principles and remaining true to them: in short, progress was as much a matter of 'being' as of 'doing'.[118] *Le Monde Marche* was laced with invocations not to despair of the present:

The sky is heavy, time is still at the moment. Let us not worry unduly about this pause in history. It is the fifteen minutes of grace given to everything that is about to die. Something momentous is emerging from the depths of our hearts. Let us open our windows and deeply breathe the air of life into our lungs.[119]

The real point of such exhortations was to urge French republicans to remain faithful to their beliefs and values. The attitudes of those who, like Lamartine, had allowed themselves to succumb to feelings of despair and passivity were

---

[116] Pelletan, *Le Monde Marche*, 118.   [117] Ibid., 208–9.   [118] Ibid., 30–1.
[119] Ibid., 223.

sternly rebuked by the republican pamphleteer: 'resignation, that is to say immobilism, can be only the virtue of the lamb dragged to the slaughter-house.'[120] He added that, since man could change the future but not the past, turning one's gaze towards the future was not an expression of idealism but the only effective option available to those who wished to see progressive change in society.[121] In this context Pelletan also strongly condemned his former mentor's reactionary argument that the mere use of the term 'progress' was dangerous because it gave humanity illusory and false hopes; particularly dismaying was Lamartine's apparent belief that any popular attempt to resist political oppression was evidence of social and political regression. The opposite was true: 'it is not death which stirs, but life, and in the name of life let us pay homage to movement instead of making it an argument of decadence.'[122]

The true enemies of progress, from this perspective, were those who tried to hold society together by coercive means rather than through the cultivation of shared values. An exposition of the doctrine of progress in the 1850s in the republican journal *L'Avenir*, where he worked alongside Vacherot and Barni, allowed Pelletan to attack Napoleon III through a portrayal of the philosophy of Joseph de Maistre.[123] Speaking of the Roman world—another common republican metaphor for the Second Empire—Pelletan also offered a telling contrast between material and spiritual unity: 'the Roman world had known a unity which was purely external, mechanical, geographic, linguistic, and administrative; a unity of territories and roads; it was unable to attain the true unity, the unity of spirit.'[124] And just in case his readers were left in any doubt about what he really meant, Pelletan apologized for his former admiration for the Napoleonic myth; and his words were gradually transformed by the force of their own rhetoric into a tirade against Bonaparte, his nephew Napoleon III, and the entire imperialist political tradition:

Let him be admired! I too have yielded to the corruption of glory on the human spirit, and have colluded in this piece of historical debauchery; but I have lied to the God of justice, and I withdraw my words; I despise Caesar, I hate him as if he was my contemporary, I hate him for having made genius an excuse for crime, and for having taught the world the secret of trampling over legality and climbing to power over the corpse of liberty![125]

The most innovative aspect of Pelletan's doctrine of progress was his emphasis on its complexity, particularly in relation to its effects on the formation of social identity and political character. Complexity in modern society meant, first of all, that human beings could not be reduced to simple cultural or anthropological stereotypes. Human nature was highly differentiated and constantly evolving, and there were five, six, or seven persons present in each individual whose relationship often proved a source of tensions. But far from being destructive such internal conflicts were highly fruitful: 'the

---

[120] Ibid., 20.   [121] Ibid., 74.   [122] Ibid., 183.
[123] Eugène Pelletan, 'Théorie du Progrès', *L'Avenir* (3 June 1855).
[124] Pelletan, *Profession de Foi*, 238.   [125] Ibid., 232.

identity of natures exists only in fiction; but in life it is contradiction which is the truth.'[126]

Complexity was also manifested in humanity's capacity to forge new relationships between space and time. Pelletan often stressed the 'indivisible unity'[127] of these two concepts, which he illustrated in two complementary dimensions. On the one hand, the union of time and space was a consequence of the accelerated pace of modern life, reflecting a world in which 'time is abolished, space is shattered, and man henceforth endowed with the privilege of ubiquitousness lives everywhere and at such a pace that he jumbles the minutes and turns them into mere instants'.[128] On the other hand, the complexity of human character offered individuals the possibility of opting out of spatial constraints, even to the extent of seeing themselves as 'citizens of time' rather than members of particular institutional or cultural communities. This concept of a 'homeland in time'[129] played an important role in Pelletan's conception of social identity, in both analytical and normative terms. In the former sense it allowed him to differentiate societies from each other and within themselves in terms of their more or less advanced social components; hence his striking portrayal of Russia as a country which seemed to live in several historical epochs all at once:

The intellect looks there for something which resembles a society, and at best it finds a living museum of all societies, a jumble of all the advances of history; it sounds like a broken clock which in its folly chimes all the hours at once.[130]

But Pelletan also regarded his relationship with the progressive elements of his age in civic and quasi-contractual terms, providing a framework of rights and duties which were just as binding as those that could be generated by laws and public institutions. Thus it was the rationalist spirit of the times which provided the justificatory grounds for republican demands for greater civic and political rights; and conversely it was the moral truth and validity of these principles which made it incumbent upon Pelletan to fight for their advancement in France. Membership of the 'homeland in time' thus came with entitlements but also obligations, and at the same time provided a normative framework for stressing the continuing validity of republican ideals even when their implementation in France had been halted. Time, in this sense, could become an effective political substitute for space.

This flexible and multi-layered conception of social and political identity culminated in Pelletan's complex conception of territoriality. In societies untouched by the phenomenon of progress, life was conducted simply and entirely within the confines of particularistic communities. As modern societies became more sophisticated there was a natural tendency to move towards political centralization, which was manifested in the establishment of

---

[126] Pelletan, *Heures de Travail*, Vol. 1, 359.   [127] Pelletan, *Profession de Foi*, 20.
[128] Pelletan, *Heures de Travail*, Vol. 2, 264.
[129] 'Patrie du temps': a term used in *Les uns et les autres*, 106.
[130] Pelletan, *Heures de Travail*, Vol. 1, 38.

larger and more distant territorial structures such as cantons, departments, towns, cities, and ultimately nations. In the 1840s and 1850s most orthodox republicans—and Saint-Simonians—regarded this process not only as desirable but also as unidirectional and zero-sum: the more these larger territorial entities were created and reinforced, the less scope there remained for the continuing affirmation of local forms of identity.

Pelletan rejected this institutional and cultural centralism, and offered in its place a fluid conception of territoriality which allowed for the retention of diverse and multiple affiliations. In the Republic, he wrote in 1848, man could be 'a citizen of his commune, his city, his homeland';[131] there was no obligation to choose any one of these territorial frameworks at the expense of the other two. This is where Pelletan's personal narrative blended completely into his political thought: he had begun his life in a small provincial town but had eventually become rooted in France's capital city. In the words of his biographer Edouard Petit, Pelletan was 'a southerner who very quickly had become very Parisian'.[132] But this Parisianism was neither exclusive nor overbearing, like Dupont-White's; it remained entirely consistent with a continuing appreciation of the value of local habits, customs, and cultures. Pelletan thus praised George Sand's writings for their 'powerful scent of the soil';[133] and his own book on his home town of Royan stressed the wonderful achievements of progress in the locality since the Revolution but also underscored the imperative of maintaining a 'cult of tradition'.[134]

At the same time, Pelletan valued the positive changes brought about by the advent of national political institutions:

In the same way as the tribe associated with the tribe founded the city, the city founded with the city founded the nation. Man from then on had a homeland, that is to say a whole new type of relationships and sentiments . . . The homeland is the latest instrument of civilization.[135]

But national political institutions and the patriotism they engendered were only the most recent territorial symbols of political progress, not their ultimate or final manifestations. Beyond the locality, the city, and the nation loomed something even more momentous: humanity as a whole. As Pelletan declared portentously: 'progress still continues. Already the century is beginning to put the idea of humanity above the idea of homeland.'[136] This opened up one of the most controversial aspects of Pelletan's political thinking during the 1850s and 1860s: his 'cosmopolitanism' or, as it would be described in contemporary political discourse, his European internationalism. How this internationalism meshed with his conception of progress and his broader social and political philosophy will be examined in the following section.

---

[131] Pelletan, *Histoire des Trois Journées*, 184.   [132] Petit, *Eugène Pelletan*, 106.
[133] Petit, *Heures de Travail*, Vol. 1, 263.
[134] Pelletan, Eugène, *La naissance d'une ville* (Paris: Germer Baillière, 1876), 133.
[135] Pelletan, *Le Monde Marche*, 82.   [136] Ibid., 83.

Internationalism and Cosmopolitanism

'Universal fraternity knows no geography.'[137] Throughout his political career, and particularly during the 1850s and 1860s, Pelletan was strongly committed to the idea that the bonds of human civilization transcended narrowly conceived physical and institutional boundaries.

This universalism was closely connected to his doctrine of progress, and in many senses flowed directly from it. Thus in all his writings, and especially in *Le Monde Marche*, he held up the industrial, scientific, and moral achievements of modern Europe as evidence that civilization had not only survived over the ages but was still flourishing.[138] Europe was for Pelletan a cultural and civic totality, and few things irritated him more than attempts to divide the continent into distinct racial or ethnic groupings: 'when we will let go of this idea of race which is nothing but the brutishness of history? There are not two men or twenty in Europe, there is only one; by the same reasoning there is only one science and one morality.'[139] So far removed was he from the claims of ethnocentricity that he stressed the necessity of cultural intermingling for the survival of all peoples: 'each people needs to commune in the blood of several peoples in order not to die of languidity.'[140] France did not bear the imprint of one race but was the historical product of 'twenty thousand years of reflections and metamorphoses'.[141]

This attachment to the universality of human nature—all peoples were one, and each individual nation was constantly nourished by all others—was repeatedly emphasised by Pelletan, both as a core component of his own progressive philosophy of history[142] and as a rebuttal of the claims of theocratic particularists such as de Maistre.[143] But it was not merely a matter of restating the claims of the Enlightenment against its historical adversaries. In the political context of the 1850s and 1860s this conception of republican universalism was problematic for a wider set of reasons. Many believed that the embrace of 'humanity' threatened to pull its adherents away from their existing loyalties to their own political and cultural communities. Pelletan was vulnerable on this score because of his Protestantism, which was regarded in many, especially Catholic, circles as a seditious doctrine because of its anti-communitarian individualism as well as its tendency to cite Anglo-Saxon social and political practices as models. The subversive character of Pelletan's cosmopolitanism was further reinforced by his membership of the Freemasonry, a secretive proto-republican organization whose social and moral philosophy was explicitly steeped in the culture of Enlightenment universalism. Pelletan was an active mason in the 1860s and 1870s, and he played

[137] Pelletan, *Les uns et les autres*, 357.

[138] Pelletan, *Le Monde Marche*, 212.

[139] Pelletan, Eugène, *Le 31 Mai* (Paris: Pagnerre, 1863), 33.

[140] Pelletan, *Heures de Travail*, Vol. 2, 54.

[141] Pelletan, *Élisée*, 129.

[142] Pelletan, 'Comment les dogmes se regénèrent', 23.

[143] Pelletan, *Les uns et les autres*, 79.

a leading role in many of the internal debates of the Grand Orient during this period, especially on the burning issue of secularism.[144]

Above all the matter was controversial because this universalism, under the label of 'cosmopolitanism', provided the philosophical underpinning for anti-militarist and pacifist practices. Anti-militarism was a particularly divisive issue within the republican movement during the Second Empire, and later proved so embarrassing that many 'cosmopolitanists' entirely repudiated their beliefs after 1870–1. Even many of Pelletan's close friends were suspicious of this aspect of his philosophical universalism. In a piece which upheld the validity of Pelletan's doctrine of progress, his colleague Etienne Vacherot nonetheless remarked that there was something too irenic about his conception of universal felicity: 'the ceaseless chases of the warriors, in Odin's paradise, seem to us—however crude the image—a more faithful symbol of our future destinies than the listless intoxication of the saints of the Orient.'[145]

Such criticisms were again indicative of the extent to which Pelletan's political thought was open to misinterpretation. As with his general doctrine of progress, which could not be reduced to simple idealism, his universalism consisted of a rich and complex ideological assemblage which operated within a range of different discourses. The key to understanding Pelletan's cosmopolitanism was not to try to define its 'essence' but to appreciate the specific intellectual and political contexts of his utterances on the subject. At its most basic level Pelletan's internationalism was an expression of his fraternal sense of empathy with other peoples and cultures. Like Littré, his sense of identification with his fellow-Europeans was profound and allowed him to write sensitive and probing accounts of social, political, and cultural life in other European countries. But there were also political instrumentalities to this internationalism. Writing about the good civic and political practices of neighbouring states was often a means of highlighting the glaring failures of the imperial regime in France.

Thus in a polemic with a dignitary of the Second Empire in the early 1850s Pelletan invoked the British example to challenge the Bonapartist equation of political authority with brute force. The more societies were held together by voluntary civic and associational bonds, Pelletan retorted, the less need there was for the overt display of material force. Authority was respected everywhere in Britain despite the absence of a strong police presence on its streets.[146] Pelletan also highlighted Prussian good practices in the fields of education and intellectual liberties as a means of underlining the deplorable state of things in France in these areas under the Second Empire.[147] There was even a good word for Belgium, where a 'vigorous municipal tradition' had kept alive a

[144] On the political and ideological conflicts within the Freemasonry during this period, see Hazareesingh and Wright, *Francs-Maçons sous le Second Empire*.

[145] Vacherot, Étienne, 'La doctrine du progrès', *Revue de Paris* (15 September 1856), 559.

[146] Pelletan, *Heures de Travail*, Vol. 2, 172.

[147] Pelletan, Eugène, *Qui perd gagne* (Paris: Pagnerre, 1864), 11–12.

strong civic sense and thus helped to prevent the country's conquest by her predatory neighbours.[148]

Such exercises in comparative political culture frayed the nerves of the imperial authorities, and in 1861 a newspaper article unfavourably contrasting the revival of political liberties in Austria with their continued suppression in France led to Pelletan's prosecution by the imperial authorities; this particular expression of internationalism cost him a 2,000 franc fine and a three-month sojourn in the political prison of Sainte-Pelagie.[149] From his exile Victor Hugo sent him a letter as well as a copy of *Les Misérables*, which had just been published.[150] Pelletan replied in typical fashion by playing down his sufferings:

What are you saying about prison? It is a joke compared with deportation. I despise myself for having been so undeserving of the ranks of democracy. Sainte-Pelagie is in any case the most honest location and the most venerable palace in Paris. I am in communion with the spirit of Lamennais and Carrel, and now that I have your volume as well you can see that I am here in very good company indeed.[151]

His friend Vacherot was proved right: the world was still full of warriors. Undaunted, Pelletan extended his internationalist pronouncements to the cultural sphere. In the 1860s he often spoke warmly of the magnificent artistic and intellectual achievements of other European nations, and again was not unwilling to deploy high culture as a weapon in the ideological struggle against the Second Empire. Thus in April 1864 Pelletan enthusiastically signed up, along with artistic and literary eminences such as Berlioz, Alexandre Dumas, Lamartine, Victor Hugo, Michelet, and Guizot, to a project to set up a Shakespeare Committee in Paris. Such was the extent of the imperial authorities' alarm and paranoia—perhaps intermingled with a touch of cultural chauvinism—that they banned not only the launching banquet at the Grand-Hôtel but also all the planned performances of Shakespeare's plays.[152]

Pelletan's internationalism was also prominently displayed in his consistent criticisms of the foreign policies of the July Monarchy and the Second Empire. In the immediate aftermath of the 1848 Revolution he was scathing about the failures of Louis Philippe's regime in Europe. He blamed France not only for abandoning the cause of revolution in Poland, Italy, Switzerland, and Spain but also for going out of its way to suppress positive political change in Spain, Switzerland, and Portugal.[153] Under the Second Empire Pelletan's position on French foreign policy was even more critical. He did not share the Bonapartist regime's enthusiasm for Italian unity under monarchical rule, and like his fellow-republicans he was scathing about the numerous military expeditions

[148] Pelletan, Eugène, *Les fêtes de l'intelligence* (Paris: Pagnerre, 1863), 26.
[149] Petit, *Eugène Pelletan*, 156.
[150] Robb, Graham, *Victor Hugo: A Biography* (New York: Norton, 1997), 376–9.
[151] Pelletan letter to Victor Hugo, Sainte Pelagie, 16 April 1862. Bibliothèque Victor Hugo, Paris.
[152] The Committee membership is given by George Sand in a letter to Paul Meurice, 10 April 1864, in *Correspondance*, Vol. 18 (Paris: Garnier, 1984), 353.
[153] Pelletan, *Histoire des trois journées*, 8.

which dissipated France's energies across the world. As he put it in his electoral proclamation to the Seine voters in 1869: 'it is high time we ended these spurious wars which scatter in the winds the blood of France in all parts of the world, from Mexico to Cochinchina.'[154]

This emphasis on humanitarianism and anti-militarism had been one of the defining characteristics of Pelletan's conception of French foreign policy under the Second Republic. After its demise Pelletan staunchly defended the republican regime's record in these areas, particularly noting the abolition of slavery and the rejection of aggressive and expansionist war as a means of furthering French interests abroad.[155] The 1848 Revolution, Pelletan would later claim, had in this respect provided the ideological and practical bases for the foreign policy of the Third Republic, which would decisively reject, at least in Europe, the model of a 'restless and conquering republic like Rome'.[156] There appeared to be no room in Pelletan's internationalism for the forcible imposition of republican values on foreign peoples and cultures. Evoking the plunder and devastation wrought by the *Grande Armée* in Europe in the early nineteenth century, he mocked Bonaparte's singular conception of exporting the values of 1789:

It is clear, indeed, that the best way to teach a Thuringian peasant the rights of man must be to set fire to his shack and steal his hen or his pig.[157]

Pelletan was equally dismissive of those *quarante-huitard* republicans who believed in exporting revolutionary war: 'the revolutionary party has but one diplomatic policy: armed propaganda. It deals with other states only by force of arms. It believes that we need to set alight the four corners of Europe in order to dance around the universal fire of fraternity.'[158] This hostility to the unjust use of force in the international arena culminated in a philosophical tirade against all forms of militarism:

The art of war is merely the art of deceiving and killing the enemy. One could no more extract a philosopher, even less a philanthropist, from a military officer than one could compose a poem on the ammunition of a weapon. To kill is not to govern; to govern, on the contrary, is to put a stop to killing.[159]

It was statements of this nature which often created the impression that Pelletan's internationalism knew no bounds, and made him particularly vulnerable to the accusation of pacifism; after a heated discussion his friend Nefftzer thus described his anti-militarist tirades against the Second Empire as 'a blinding and senseless betrayal'.[160] Irenism was the orthodoxy in some republican and socialist circles during the 1850s and 1860s, and a superficial reading of Pelletan's discussions of international politics in Europe did seem

[154] Pelletan, Eugène, *Aux électeurs de la 9eme circonscription de la Seine* (Paris, 1869). Bib.Nat.Le 77–2483.
[155] Pelletan, Eugène, *Nouvelles Heures de Travail* (Paris: Pagnerre, 1870), 109.
[156] Pelletan, *Les uns et les autres*, 392.   [157] Pelletan, *Qui perd gagne*, 18.
[158] *Le Bien Public*, No. 4 (27 May 1848).   [159] Pelletan, *Nouvelles Heures de Travail*, 60.
[160] Quoted in Adam, Juliette, *Mes sentiments et nos idées avant 1870* (Paris: Lemerre, 1905), 444.

to suggest that pacifist considerations substantively influenced his political thought during these years. Unlike traditional 'realist' thinkers he asserted that progress was achievable in international relations; his evidence for this claim lay in the considerable reduction of violence in the conduct of inter-state relations since early modern times.[161] In some of his less careful state-ments Pelletan seemed to look forward to the irreversible abolition of war and standing armies[162] and the emergence of a 'perpetual peace' among European nations.[163]

However, such pronouncements had little to do with pacifism but were rather expressions of Pelletan's continuing fascination with Saint-Simonian thinking. The unification of Europe appeared in Pelletan's writings as a phe-nomenon largely driven by economic forces. Europe, as he argued in a pam-phlet in 1864, was essentially a 'house of commerce'.[164] The unification of the continent was an inevitable process against which the bellicose spirit was pow-erless: 'the spirit of war still seeks to maintain a wall of China around each state; but the locomotive passes and whistles . . . she knows that one day or another she will make Europe into one family.'[165] At a public conference in 1869 Pelletan spoke of the transcendence of traditional conflicts among nations; again the emphasis was placed on the harmonizing effects of techno-logical change: 'come now and speak to us of the past, come and tell us about the ancient quarrels of nations, come and tell us of the hatreds, of the rival-ries: the railway, the electric telegraph have overcome, have overturned all these old barriers.'[166] This Saint-Simonian faith in the beneficial political con-sequences of industrial development was sufficiently strong to provide an antidote to Pelletan's moments of self-doubt:

A day will come, no doubt, when the animosity in this world will be replaced every-where by solidarity. We hope for this, and indeed we are certain of it, even if we should thereby pass for autopian. If at times we renounce our belief in man and in his spirit of wisdom, we still rely for the direction of his destinies on the intelligence of railway and the telegraph.[167]

Pelletan's belief in the future emergence of 'the great confederation of the entire human race'[168] was thus almost an expression of technological deter-minism; in any event it had little in common with the philosophical premises of pacifism. Pelletan very rarely spoke of peace as being a valuable commodity in and of itself: his was rather the republican view that peace was desirable only in so far as it was accompanied by political freedom. He made the point explicitly in 1859: 'we love peace for more than one reason, no doubt, but above all because it gives liberty.'[169] Vacherot's fears concerning Pelletan's placid irenism were in this sense entirely misguided. In his youth Pelletan had

---

[161] Pelletan, *Le Monde Marche*, 143.   [162] 'A State needs no army'. Pelletan, *Qui perd gagne*, 28.
[163] *Le Bien Public*, No. 60 (23 July 1848).   [164] Pelletan, *Qui perd gagne*, 32.
[165] Pelletan, *Les fêtes de l'intelligence*, 12.
[166] Pelletan, Eugène, *Le travail au XIXe siècle* (Paris: Pagnerre, 1869), 30.
[167] Pelletan, Eugène, *Qu'allons-nous faire? Conférence de Zurich* (Paris: Librairie Nouvelle, 1859), 14.
[168] Pelletan, *Le travail au XIXe siècle*, 30–1.   [169] Pelletan, *Qu'allons-nous faire?*, 7.

learned the art of wrestling and throughout his life he retained a strong belief, rooted in classical republican philosophy, in the value of vigorous physical exercise. Hindu civilization, he asserted—perhaps with a touch of exaggeration—had failed to survive because of its insufficient martial qualities and its excessive consumption of vegetables:

Food acquired from plants loosens our muscular fibres; the empire of the world belongs to those who eat flesh and breathe oxygen with full lungs.[170]

In a more serious vein—and here he entirely parted company with republican irenists—Pelletan was committed to the use of military force in appropriate circumstances, both within and outside France. Internally he believed in the necessity of a strong defence and argued from the Second Republic onwards that France's security should be entrusted to a citizens' militia rather than to a standing army.[171] The model of the nation in arms had been affirmed not only by the French Revolution but also by the successful resistance of European peoples to attempted Napoleonic conquests in the early nineteenth century. As Pelletan affirmed: 'there is no human way of crushing by force a people who wish to retain their homeland. Let us remember Spain.'[172] In a striking anticipation of the events of 1870–1, Pelletan also stressed in a pamphlet written in 1863 that a Prussian invasion of Alsace would bring forth a patriotic resistance 'coalition' in France which would transcend existing partisan affiliations.[173] When the Prussians did invade in 1870, Pelletan, as a member of the French government, was unstinting in his political and practical support for the war effort; as his friend Juliette Adam noted with admiration: 'M. Pelletan is brave, passionate, he wants to tear into the Prussians.'[174]

But the real evidence of Pelletan's rejection of the pacifist problematic was that throughout this period he believed that just wars could be fought beyond France's borders. He enthusiastically supported Daniele Manin's revolutionary republican dictatorship in Venice in 1848 and praised his efforts to free the city from Austrian domination.[175] Although he was deeply suspicious of Italian unity under monarchical rule, which he feared would encourage Piedmontese militarism,[176] he strongly supported the cause of oppressed peoples throughout Europe, even to the extent of advocating the use of international force in pursuit of justice. Thus he did not hesitate to campaign for a French military intervention against Russia, which had drowned a patriotic insurrection in Poland in a sea of blood. In January 1864 his passionate plea in favour of the Poles in the Legislative Corps was frequently interrupted by angry Bonapartist supporters of Russia.[177] Pelletan did not welcome the recourse to war, which was to be pursued only after all diplomatic means had

---

[170] Pelletan, *Profession de Foi*, 149.   [171] *Le Bien Public*, No. 27 (20 June 1848).
[172] Pelletan, Eugène, *La tragédie italienne* (Paris: Pagnerre, 1862), 14.
[173] Pelletan, Eugène, *Le 31 Mai* (Paris: Pagnerre, 1863), 18.
[174] Adam, Juliette, *Mes illusions et nos souffrances pendant le siège de Paris* (Paris: Lemerre, 1906), 73.
[175] Pelletan, *Heures de Travail*, Vol. 1, 397–9.
[176] Pelletan, Eugène, *La comédie italienne* (Paris: Pagnerre, 1862), 27.
[177] Pelletan, Eugène, *Discours d'un député* (Paris: Pagnerre, 1864), 26–41.

proved fruitless. But in this case there was no realistic alternative. The fight against Russia on behalf of Poland was France's internationalist duty, and she could not afford to remain neutral: 'between the revolution and the executioner there is no middle way: we must choose.'[178] His internationalism shone through in this frustrated question:

Does France not know how to make war for the sake of an ideal? what am I saying? for humanity?[179]

Pelletan's conception of cosmopolitanism was thus highly complex and inventive. At its most basic level it was a celebration of the cultural and spiritual unity of Europe, an expression of enthusiasm for the principle of fraternity which had been proclaimed by the Revolution of 1789. But it was also a tactical political concept which was skilfully deployed as part of the ideological struggle against the Second Empire. Pelletan's celebration of European unity provided a means of highlighting the importance of technological progress and the growing irrelevance of political violence from a quasi-Saint-Simonian perspective; at the same time, however, this fraternal spirit was invoked to vindicate the use of force in the prosecution of just republican goals. Most importantly—and here the 'chauvinist' critics of Pelletan were entirely off the mark—his cosmopolitanism was entirely consistent with the defence of patriotic values.

As we have noted earlier, the strength of Pelletan's conception of political identity lay precisely in its open, fluid, and multi-dimensional character. While stressing the desirability and necessity of looking beyond the horizons of the nation-state, he also sounded an explicit warning against those who took their cosmopolitanism too far. In his review of Ernest Renan's *Vie de Jésus*, one of the cultural landmarks of the Second Empire era, Pelletan praised the author's humanization of Christ but criticized the portrayal of Jesus' love for humanity as excessively abstract and 'metaphysical':

The complete man must love his homeland and establish his credentials as a citizen, for he does not live in this world like a swallow; he lives in a fixed and precise corner of the earth; he is part of a political community; he receives protection from it and owes it his allegiance in return.[180]

Patriotism was not only an indispensable concept, it was also an inescapably political one: 'a homeland without liberty is not a homeland, it is merely mud and dust. If I am just a slave and not a citizen in the state, what is to me the name of my master and the language he speaks?'[181] In another pamphlet he equated the *patrie* with law-based government:

The homeland is characterized by law, this essential condition of thought. Soil makes the inhabitant. Law alone makes the citizen. I see a homeland, said Rousseau, where man is most himself, that is to say where he is most capable of developing his moral nature and contributing to the development of his fellow-man.[182]

---

[178] Pelletan, Eugène, *Le Crime* (Paris: Pagnerre, 1863), 48.   [179] Ibid., 39.
[180] Pelletan, *Nouvelles Heures de Travail*, 263.   [181] Pelletan, *Qui perd gagne*, 27.
[182] Pelletan, Eugène, *Une étoile filante* (Paris: Dentu, 1860), 31.

So strong was Pelletan's sense of patriotism that it sometimes appeared to slide into a representation of France as the universal nation. In this passage Pelletan ingeniously, and no doubt with a touch of amused irony, presented France's cultural complexity as the very justification of its claim to be the leading nation in Europe:

It is undoubtedly childish of a country to proclaim: I am the great people. France has no more right than England or Germany to claim the hegemony of Europe. We must love and admire the English genius, the German genius; we must give its due to the Italian tradition; but the supreme nation exists only in the kingdom of the mind; every country has its share of credit; however, the merit of France is to be cosmopolitan. Less original in the final analysis than the Saxon race or the German race, it perhaps has the advantage over them that it has a familial link with all nations, and can serve as a meeting point among them.[183]

This was the completion of the cosmopolitan circle. France was an element in a much larger political and cultural totality, yet because of her particular political and cultural characteristics she was the nation best placed to represent 'humanity'. Republican universalism was thus not only fully compatible with a robust form of French particularism, but the latter was in many senses the culminating point of the former.

Pelletan and the Founding of the Third Republic

'We shall see it, we shall see it, lady Juliette, our Republic, and it will be the great, the true, the noble, the strong, the triumphant, the third! The figure three is fateful, O my Grecian lady, and a beautiful social and political future will flow from the ugly task which we are carrying out at this time.'[184]

As this letter to his friend Juliette Adam indicated, Pelletan's mature political thought crystallized against the backdrop of his intense struggle against the Bonapartist regime in the 1860s. Pelletan's career as a roving journalist came to an end with his election as a deputy of the Seine in 1863, an event which immediately catapulted him into the republican political leadership in Paris. While he now expressed himself in public mainly orally, he nonetheless continued to write books and pamphlets during these years; and in 1868 he even founded a newspaper, *La Tribune*. If anything, his duties as a republican representative reinforced his determination to remain true to his vocation as a public intellectual.

Much of his political thought focused on laying the ideological foundations of the republican alternative to the Second Empire, and by the late 1860s Pelletan had established himself as one of the best-known republican pamphleteers in France. His prominence, both as a thinker and as an activist, was

---

[183] Pelletan, *Profession de Foi*, 276.
[184] Pelletan letter to Juliette Adam, 11 February 1868, quoted in Adam, *Mes sentiments et nos idées*, 202.

reflected in his inclusion in the Government of National Defence which ruled France between the fall of the Second Empire and the end of the Franco-Prussian war. In the post-armistice elections of February 1871 Pelletan was again returned to the National Assembly, and from the backbenches he loyally supported Gambetta's inclusive strategy to bring the republican party back to power. In 1876, as this approach began to yield its first significant fruits, Pelletan was elected to the newly-formed Senate. He spent the rest of his career as a dignified republican patriarch until his death in 1884, by which time he had been appointed to the vice-presidency of the Senate.

Despite his successful transition from political opposition under the Second Empire to the institutional apex of the new republican regime, however, Pelletan's contribution to the new political order which emerged in France during the 1870s and 1880s was not fully appreciated, either by his immediate contemporaries or by his later biographers or in some senses even by himself. There were several reasons for these oversights. From the perspective of posterity the intellectual history of the second half of the nineteenth century, as we have already noted, is conventionally seen as the era of the growing ascendancy of positivism in France, and the role of men with Pelletan's 'spiritualist' philosophical inclinations has been corresponding downplayed, if not ignored altogether.[185] From Pelletan's own perspective, too, things seemed to move on to a different plane after the end of the Second Empire. Although as from the early 1870s he continued to attend regular gatherings of republican political and intellectual leaders in Paris, such as the meetings of the Café du Pont de Fer,[186] Pelletan no longer occupied centre stage. He was not a member of Gambetta's inner circle—his personal relationship with the republican tribune was never easy[187]—and despite producing a number of pamphlets on republican policy in the 1870s he played no obvious role in the elaboration of the party's political strategy. Pelletan's sense of relative isolation was compounded by a heightened feeling of defensiveness after 1871, which was prompted by a number of specific factors: his participation in the 1870–1 government, which was the object of repeated attacks from conservative and anti-republican quarters in the early 1870s;[188] his experience of the Paris Commune of 1871, which severely wounded Pelletan's spirit;[189] and the perceived drift of the republican party towards materialism and even atheism, which alarmed his Protestant and spiritualist conscience and provoked an

---

[185] See our remarks in the Introduction.   [186] APP, report dated 5 November 1873.

[187] In early 1871 Pelletan was a member of the delegation sent to Bordeaux by the republican government to relieve Gambetta of his post of Minister of the Interior because of his refusal to accept the higher authority of his colleagues in Paris. He discussed this incident in his testimony to the Commission of Enquiry on the Government of National Defence. See *Enquête Parlementaire sur les Actes du Gouvernement de la Défense Nationale* Vol. 5 (Paris: Librairie des Publications Législatives, 1876), 471–2.

[188] Pelletan defended its record, and his own role in the government, in *Le 4 Septembre devant l'enquête* (Paris: Pagnerre, 1874).

[189] Referring to the events of 1870–1 and their aftermath, one of Pelletan's biographers thus noted: 'these disasters, these outrages seem to have poured into his soul—as from this period—an incurable sadness, a sort of stupor.' Gelineau, Pierre, *Pour l'Idée. Fêtes du centenaire d'Eugène Pelletan 1813–1913* (Saint-George de Didonne, 1913), 13.

anguished cry in his last published work, *Dieu est-il mort?*, where he complained about 'the wrong turning which democracy seems to want to take'.[190]

Yet even though his doubts and sense of grief were genuine, their overall political and ideological significance should not be overstated. There are many senses in which the image of Pelletan as an isolated, reactive and increasingly pessimistic former *quarante-huitard* is extremely misleading. Several interlinked aspects of his late republicanism particularly stand against this interpretation and underline the important and innovative role he played in French political life between the 1860s and the late 1870s: first, his further articulation of the necessity of intellectual involvement in public life, which he himself exemplified by the crucial 'federating' function he performed in the republican movement during the 1860s; second, his elaboration of a complex political and social theory of republicanism during the 1860s and 1870s, which departed in crucial respects from the canons of orthodox republicanism— in both its 1848 and its mainstream Second Empire versions—and offered a striking anticipation of the future political order of Third Republic. It will also emerge, finally, that Pelletan remained devoted in his later years to certain aspects of Saint-Simonian thinking, a continuing commitment which showed that his intellectual personality remained true to the progressive ideals he had cherished in his youth.

The Theorization of Republican Intellectualism

Pelletan's practical impact on the emergence of the new republican order in France has first to be appreciated in the broader context of the evolution of the French public sphere after 1848. From the mid-nineteenth century a revolution in the culture of politics began to take shape in the cities and towns of France, with the development of an increasingly wider range of published political products destined to an educated mass audience: books and newspapers, but also journals, almanacs, brochures, and pamphlets. With the acceleration of industrialization under the Second Empire, a sizeable literate political community had emerged by the end of the 1860s, constituting a body of 'informed opinion' within the wider political community. Directing and shaping the values of this informed opinion was a new breed of public intellectuals who acted as intermediaries between the political and cultural leaders in Paris and the literate citizenry across the country. Pelletan was one of the archetypes of this new generation of intellectuals and, as noted above, he had established himself as one of the best-known members of its republican component by the late 1860s.

It was in this capacity that his individual contribution to the dissemination of the republican idea was immense. Through his numerous books, articles, pamphlets, lectures, and speeches Pelletan's voice carried the tidings of

---

[190] Pelletan, Eugène, *Dieu est-il mort?* (Paris: Degorce-Cadot, 1883), 285.

'democracy' across the different corners of France;[191] and the effects of this political didacticism lasted well into the 1870s as this message was projected through quasi-republican professional and cultural associations such as the Freemasonry and education leagues. This growing network of civic institutions which blossomed in France during the 1860s and 1870s played a key role in the eventual political triumph of republicanism later in that decade.[192] Pelletan was one of the earliest and best-known members of the new republican politico-cultural elite, and by his actions and writings helped to define the moral and practical bases of its activities. In particular, he was one of the leading theoretical exponents of the role and responsibilities as the republican intellectual.

Pelletan's commitment to upholding the values of intellectual life was strongly manifested through his passionate defence of the freedom of the press during the 1860s and 1870s. His three-month stay at Sainte-Pelagie in the early 1860s did nothing but reinforce his determination to fight for the values of openness and tolerance, and he became widely known in republican and liberal circles as a champion of the cause of press freedom. In a pamphlet written in 1864 he urged the Bonapartist regime not to follow the nefarious example of the First Empire, which had banned all independent expression of opinion in France. Yet if Napoleon had retained a free press, he would almost certainly have been prevented from embarking upon some of his disastrous adventures abroad.[193] Pelletan ended by stressing the futility of attempting to censure free political thought in France: the experience of the nineteenth century had shown conclusively that if their public expression was banned, republican ideas would be carried across the country through oral communication.[194]

So strong was Pelletan's commitment to press freedom that he refused to contemplate the suppression of radical republican anti-government propaganda between September 1870 and February 1871, even though France was at war with Prussia. The free expression of opinion was a sacred principle; in any event it allowed the Government of National Defence to find out what the Communards were thinking.[195] This high priority accorded to political thinking and the free expression of ideas culminated in Pelletan's definition of the role of the writer in public life:

It is the writer who represents the genius of a people, it is he who constantly elevates its intelligence, it is he who morally directs society, who reforms it, transforms it, leads it from progress to progress, and extracts from century to century the idea of law which lies buried in our conscience, and carries this idea to power.[196]

---

[191] The Biblothèque de l'Institut in Paris (Ms.7330) has a large number of the letters sent by Pelletan to his editor Pagnerre; they reveal his concern to have his work effectively disseminated across all corners of France.
[192] See Nord, *The Republican Moment.*
[193] Pelletan, Eugène, *Le Termite* (Paris: Pagnerre, 1864), 11–12.
[194] Ibid., 24.   [195] Pelletan, *Le 4 Septembre devant l'enquête*, 74.
[196] Pelletan, Eugène, *Le droit de parler. Lettre à M. Imhaus* (Paris: Pagnerre, 1862), 10–11.

This was the essence of Pelletan's conception of the intellectual's function: to offer moral and spiritual leadership to the rest of society but also to act as a messenger for the cause of political justice. Intellectual activity was thus inexorably linked to republican proselytism; in his view this role had been consistently performed by writers in France since the Enlightenment.[197] There followed from this a clear republican code which had to be honoured by true intellectuals: it included celebrating the principles of reason and enlightened discussion, taking an active part in the public life of the community, and always seeking to establish the truth.[198] Above all this republican code made it incumbent upon all intellectuals to behave with complete integrity in both the public and the private domains, and to follow the dictates of their consciences rather than the self-serving requirements of expediency.

Pelletan drove this point home in a sweeping attack against the *chansonnier* Béranger, one of the cultural icons of the first half of the nineteenth century.[199] Despite his positive image in progressive circles, Pelletan argued that Béranger had never been a true friend of the liberal cause: he had not consistently supported republicanism after 1830, had often been harshly critical of republican principles and values in private, and, most unpardonably, had ended his life as a sympathiser of the new Bonapartist regime.[200] Pelletan's indignation at such duplicitous behaviour led him to draw a distinction between two types of intellectual: the 'lyrical' and the 'political'. The latter were men like Béranger, who took great care to stay attuned to prevailing orthodoxies and never risked their careers by taking up positions of principle. The former were the true men of integrity, who always listened to the edicts of their consciences, even to the extent of sacrificing their personal interests. Pelletan's description of the miseries and splendours of this demanding conception of intellectual activity no doubt contained a strong autobiographical element:

They often have deep falls, such people, weaknesses, setbacks, difficult pages in their biographies which are to be turned rather than read, for they forget to take account of the realities, etiquettes, manners, and hypocrisies of existence. No matter. They nonetheless constitute the superior family of the believers, apostles, martyrs, and the elect.[201]

Far from siding with the martyrs of the republican cause in 1851, Béranger had jeered at them. He could not therefore serve as a model for republican intellectuals: 'democracy for us is neither a song nor a matter for doubt; it is a truth and a virtue.'[202] Pelletan succeeded admirably in defining the contours of intellectual activity in republican terms, and by his actions he rapidly emerged as one of its paradigmatic representations. In the 1860s he became universally known as the scourge of the imperial regime, and his personal courage earned

---

[197] Ibid., 12.   [198] Ibid., 14–15.
[199] The classic study of his life and political thought is Touchard, Jean, *La gloire de Béranger* (Paris, Armand Colin, 1968).
[200] Pelletan, Eugène, *Une étoile filante* (Paris: Dentu, 1860), 12–17.   [201] Ibid., 17–18.
[202] Ibid., 32.

him the respect and admiration of liberals and republicans not only in France but also across Europe. Pelletan's moral and political authority over his peers was celebrated by his *maître* Michelet, who described him as 'irremediably aristocratic in appearance and in thought',[203] a natural leader and example to his fellow-intellectuals. From the depths of his Swiss exile his former mentor Edgar Quinet also commended Pelletan for his vanguardist ideological and political battle against the Second Empire, and represented his intellectual activity as the model for all republicans to emulate:

When I need to hope, my thoughts go towards you. You must have a hundred arms to strike thus at the enemy everywhere and incessantly. A nation sometimes is reduced to a few hundred men. The others are asleep and wait for the victory to awaken and take a stance.[204]

Just as important as this external role was the critical function Pelletan performed within the republican community during these years. The republican 'party' was an extremely broad church between the late 1840s and the 1880s, with divisions running across a variety of lines: social—workers and bourgeois; political—constitutionalists and revolutionaries; religious—theists, agnostics, and anticlericalists; generational—the 'men of 1848' and the group which emerged under the Second Empire and early Third Republic; and territorial— the split between Parisian and provincial groups, and between urban and rural forms of republicanism. In addition, these lines of fracture were periodically accentuated by violent conflicts such as occurred during the 'June days' of 1848 and especially during the Paris Commune of 1871. While a great deal of scholarly attention has been focused on these divisions, the institutional, affective, and ideological elements which cemented the republican coalition during these decades have until recently been considerably neglected.

Yet these elements were very strong, and among the most significant of them was the role played by key republican intellectuals such as Pelletan. It was they who held the republican community together by devising the common stock of myths, values, and principles which constituted the 'republican memory' in the nineteenth century. Pelletan performed two further crucial roles, which overlapped to some extent but were logically distinct: he served as a link between republican generations and also kept lines of communication open among the different ideological components of the republican party. These functions were mainly exercised through one of the important mainstays of republican intellectual sociability during these years: the salon. During the 1850s and 1860s Pelletan was an habitué of two leading republican salons in Paris, that of the Comtesse d'Agoult (Daniel Stern) and that of Madame Lamber (Juliette Adam). There, and in similar nocturnal gatherings across the city, he mingled with republican elites of different ideological per-

---

[203] Michelet, *Journal*, Vol. 1, 368.
[204] Quinet, Edgar, letter to Pelletan, 7 December 1862, in *Lettres d'exil*, Vol. 2 (Paris, Calmann-Lévy, 1885), 277.

suasions, often exchanging heated arguments over strategic and tactical issues facing the republican movement.

Despite the elegance and intimacy of the settings in which they were conducted, these private discussions—of which, sadly, few systematic records have survived[205]—performed an essential role for the republicans, helping to maintain an internal dialogue which enabled the continuing existence of their political community in times of adversity. It was no accident that Pelletan performed the role of intellectual 'federator' with such distinction: he was very well placed to bridge many of the salient divides within the republican camp. As a rural figure from the south-west who had eventually risen through the ranks to achieve fame in Paris, he spoke across the territorial gap between Paris and the provinces; as a discursively violent anti-Bonapartist he represented core elements of the common intellectual ground between the *républicains modérés* and the *démocrates éxaltés*; and as an older man who enjoyed the friendship and admiration of the likes of Michelet, Hugo, and Edgar Quinet but was not directly associated with the failures of the *quarante-huitards*, Pelletan was able to command respect across the different generations.

His fierce sense of independence also won him many admirers among republicans; in particular, his public split with Lamartine in the late 1850s reinforced his reputation as a man of principle who would not allow personal loyalties to interfere with moral and political judgement. Pelletan's authoritative and strategic position within the republican community in the 1860s was noted by his contemporaries. In his tribute to Pelletan, Eugène Spuller highlighted the magnetic effects of his words and deeds on both the republican community and the wider polity: 'Eugène Pelletan had the capacity suddenly to ignite sparks: we felt in him a vigilant conscience which would never let pass any opportunity to protest, and his firmness, his courage, his indignation, his enthusiasm would sustain, awaken, inspire our hearts.'[206] Juliette Adam underlined Pelletan's key role between republican generations even more forcefully:

There is only Eugène Pelletan who, through his passion on the one hand and his respect for tradition on the other, still serves as an intermediary between the young and those whom the latter still call the 'old fogeys'.[207]

Pelletan's Ideological Contributions to Republican Political Thought

Pelletan did not confine himself to writing about the role of thinkers and serving as a model for other republicans through his flamboyant parliamentary speeches and effective anti-Bonapartist agitation. He also made significant

---

[205] There are references to these gatherings in the memoir literature of the period; see for example Adam, *Mes sentiments et nos idées*, 27–9.

[206] Spuller, *Eugène Pelletan*, 120.   [207] Adam, *Mes sentiments et nos idées*, 66.

intellectual contributions to republican political thought in the 1860s and 1870s, and helped through these theoretical offerings to consolidate the variant of liberal republicanism which became the preponderant ideological force in France under the Third Republic.

At one level Pelletan's political theory displayed a remarkable sense of continuity between the late 1840s and the early 1880s. Throughout this period he defined the republican ideological project in terms of essentially the same set of core principles: constitutional government, the rule of law, civil and political equality, social fraternity, and religious toleration. Above all he repeatedly waved the banner of liberty at the Second Empire and was especially critical of the Bonapartist claim, eloquently articulated by Persigny, that political freedom was a variable commodity which had to be calibrated to suit the particular social structure and political circumstances of a nation. This was the typical Bonapartist justification of the fact that Britain enjoyed more political freedom than France. But such arguments did not pass muster with Pelletan: 'liberty does not wear Harlequin's coat; there are not many sorts, nor many colours of freedom; there is only one, always one and everywhere the same.'[208]

Again in contrast with authoritarian thinkers like Persigny, he shared the republican intuition that human nature was benign and sociable, and rejected the Bonapartists' Machiavellian contention that violence and immorality were the essence of life on earth.[209] In keeping with his rationalist conception of intellectual life, there was also no room in Pelletan's republic for sectarianism, and in the early 1870s he reaffirmed his commitment to an 'open' republican polity in unambiguous terms:

The Republic is not, and could not be, as some are suggesting, either a sect or the property of one party; it belongs to everyone, and demands neither a date nor a certificate of republicanism; whether one is a long-standing republican, a recent convert, by principle or through reflection, whether one has arrived first or last to the light of democracy, one belongs fully, and must be made welcome.[210]

This was very much an echo of the patient and inclusive republican strategy which would prove successful in the 1870s and 1880s. The only ones to whom Pelletan denied this republican 'communion'—he always retained his fondness for religious metaphors—were the 'factious groups' who refused to accept the peaceful electoral verdict of the people.[211] This was another consistent element in his political thought: a commitment to 'republican legality' and a corresponding hostility to all forms of revolutionary politics. In the same way as he had approved the suppression of the June 1848 workers' revolt, Pelletan remained implacably opposed to the republican groups which eventually formed the Paris Commune. After one such group invaded the Hôtel de Ville on 31 October 1871, he did not hesitate to support their prosecution.[212]

---

[208] Pelletan, Eugène, *L'Ombre de 89. Lettre à M. le duc de Persigny* (Paris: Pagnerre, 1863), 12.
[209] Pelletan, *Nouvelles heures de travail*, 158.   [210] Pelletan, *Les uns et les autres*, xxviii.
[211] Ibid., xxv.
[212] He defended this decision during his testimony at the Commission of Enquiry on the Government of National Defence. See *Enquête Parlementaire sur les Actes du Gouvernement de la Défense Nationale*, Vol. 5, 467.

Unlike a number of his republican colleagues, furthermore, he made no attempt to broker a settlement with the Communards after March 1871. He later maintained that the suppression of the Commune had not only been a good thing in itself but had constituted a successful test of the republic's capacity to maintain order.[213]

At the same time, however, these continuities in Pelletan's republican political thought should not be overplayed. As we have argued, there has been a tendency among both his critics and his sympathizers to regard his political writings exclusively through the prism of 'the republicanism of 1848', with the dual implication that he was an idealist republican whose thinking about domestic politics remained essentially static in the decades which followed the end of the Second Republic. As we have already seen, the label of 'idealism' is insufficient to do justice to the complexity of Pelletan's early political thought. A closer examination of his writings under the Second Empire and early Third Republic also comprehensively refutes the charge of intellectual immobilism.

One particular area where he substantively developed his ideas was the question of the social and institutional underpinnings of the future republican state. In the 1840s and early 1850s Pelletan's political sociology, like that of most of his fellow republicans, remained somewhat primitive. He believed that class divisions had ceased to matter, that the 'truth' of the republican idea would be self-evident to the people, and that the institution of universal suffrage would be sufficient in itself to draw together different sections of the political community. The emergence of a wide social base for the new republican state did not therefore require political calculation and human agency; it was merely a matter of allowing events to take their 'natural' course.

In the 1850s and 1860s these complacent views underwent significant change, largely under the influence of the Second Empire's intelligent manipulation of its plebiscitary form of democracy. Like many republicans Pelletan's experience of Bonapartist rule significantly influenced his thinking about the social preconditions and institutional properties of republicanism. For example, his emphasis after 1851 on the necessity of intellectual involvement in public life stemmed from his heightened awareness that the 'people' did not spontaneously identify with the cause of political justice and progress and that substantive political education was essential if the French people were to be won over to the republican cause. Pelletan was particularly dismayed by the continuing support given to the imperial regime by the countryside, and in this description of peasant life he vented his frustration with heavy sarcasm:

Up at dawn and asleep by sunset, the peasant lives alone, most of the time, in his hut or near his pastures. He makes conversation only with his dog or his herd . . . What does he know about politics? He is vaguely aware that he has a sovereign, because he sees his profile on his coins and banknotes. He has even heard it rumoured that there are high dignitaries who command the army and administer the country. But he has never been able to distinguish one from the other, and even less the living from the dead.[214]

---

[213] Ibid., iv–v.   [214] Pelletan, Eugène, *Aide-toi le ciel t'aidera* (Paris: Pagnerre, 1863), 7.

But frustration was never for Pelletan an excuse for despair. The strong social base of Bonapartism in provincial and especially rural France simply made it necessary to construct majority support for the republican cause by relying on the political allegiance of the cities and towns. As he noted in 1863, the 'capitals of commerce, of industry, of intelligence'[215] such as Lyon, Marseille, Nantes, and Bordeaux had moved into the republican orbit, and he correctly anticipated that this was the beginning of a trend which would eventually be replicated across the country. Pelletan also realized that this political coalition could be held together only if it appealed to the interests of different social strata. This required a considerable change of approach from his social philosophy in the 1840s and early 1850s in which, as we saw earlier, he had emphasised the privileged position of the bourgeoisie.

In his later writings under the Second Empire and early Third Republic this exclusivist approach was abandoned, as he recognized that many elements in the middle class had sided with the imperial regime through fear of social anarchy.[216] He continued to stress the importance of breaking down class divisions, but this emphasis now appeared from its proper perspective, namely, that of an ideologically driven argument:

There are no classes today, *there cannot be any*, universal suffrage has drowned them all, absorbed them all in the harmonious whole of the nation; he who speaks of classes today, who opposes the one to the other, sows discord and prepares the storm.[217]

The point was not to deny the sociological reality of class division but rather to work towards a political situation in which relationships between the working class and the bourgeoisie were cooperative rather than conflictual. To this end Pelletan stressed that there was no fundamental clash of interests between these two classes; in his view all workers aspired to nothing else except to become members of the bourgeoisie.[218] He thus offered a reformist and inclusive republicanism which was open to all social groups. While it sought to preserve 'order' this republicanism was distinct from conservatism, which in Pelletan's eyes was merely a recipe for continuing revolution: ' to conserve is not only to continue, it is also to improve.'[219]

Republicanism, in the final analysis, represented this necessary synthesis between tradition and progress. To the 'haves' it promised a regime which guaranteed political stability and prevented revolutions through the introduction of essential but gradual change;[220] to the 'have nots' it gave a solemn undertaking of betterment through 'social reform'.[221] This was essentially what remained of Pelletan's earlier commitment to 'socialism': a sense that the state had a moral obligation to alleviate the miseries of the people and a belief that the republic would stand by its promises in this respect. As evidence of

---

[215] Pelletan, *Le 31 Mai*, 14.   [216] Ibid., 24.
[217] Pelletan, *Le 4 Septembre devant l'enquête*, 169; emphasis added.
[218] Pelletan, *Le 31 Mai*, 27.   [219] Pelletan, *Les uns et les autres*, vi.
[220] Pelletan, *Le 4 Septembre devant l'enquête*, 167–8.
[221] Pelletan, *Aux électeurs de la IXe circonscription*.

the reliability of this pledge he noted that since the Revolution it had always been the republicans who had stood by the oppressed, notably through the abolition of slavery and the introduction of popular education.[222]

The Territorial Conditions of Citizenship

Another crucial contribution of Pelletan's later social and political thought lay in the fields of local democracy and republican citizenship. His thinking here was partly an extension of his earlier emphasis on the necessity of multiple territorial identities of individual citizens and partly a development of autobiographical experiences. He was introduced to the reality of municipal politics from a very tender age, as his father Achille twice held the position of mayor of Royan: first in 1808–9 and then again during the Hundred Days.[223] Although his poor relationship with his father, due in part to the latter's lifelong allegiance to Bonapartism, prevented him from mentioning the matter explicitly during his adult life, Eugène's early experience of communal institutions undoubtedly left a deep imprint on his conception of politics, so much so that in the final years of his life he closely monitored the ascendancy and eventual triumph of republicans in the municipal elections of Royan.[224] He also kept a close eye on the composition of the municipal council of Saint-George-de-Didonne, and after the republican victory in the 1877 legislative elections Pelletan lobbied successive ministers of the interior to promote republican interests in this town.[225]

His concern for communal politics was not purely sentimental. By the 1860s Pelletan, like many republicans of his generation, had come to appreciate that the consolidation of republican civic values in French society necessitated a greater degree of public involvement in political life; this, in turn, could not occur without breaking the centralized political and administrative order which had reigned supreme in France since the early nineteenth century. Unlike many of his republican colleagues, whose conversion to the cause of local liberty occurred under the Second Empire, Pelletan was already an enthusiast for decentralization by the late 1840s. His embrace of local democracy was significantly influenced by Lamennais, who blamed the French system of government for consistently producing 'an apoplexy of the brain and a paralysis of the parts'.[226]

But it was the advent of the Bonapartist regime after 1851 which fully confirmed Pelletan's belief in the republican virtues of decentralization. The

---

[222] Pelletan, *Le 31 Mai*, 28.   [223] Baquiast, *Une dynastie de la bourgeoisie républicaine*, 43.
[224] Petit, *Eugène Pelletan*, 252–3.
[225] This interest in local politics shines through some of Pelletan's correspondence. See for example the letter dated 6 May 1879, addressed to his neighbours M. et Mme. Pironneau, in which he complained about the government's failure to take a more active stance against the municipal council appointed by the Broglie government in 1877. Archives Nationales, Papiers George Coulon, 417 AP 2 (dossier 4).
[226] Pelletan, *Les uns et les autres*, 200.

Second Empire imposed a rigid system of centralized control on departmental and communal institutions, whose functions were strictly limited and regulated by the state. The inferiority of local institutions in the eyes of the Bonapartists was symbolized by their treatment of mayors, who were appointed by the state and treated as public functionaries rather than as elected representatives. Mayors were also used as electoral agents of the government during local and national elections, and any failure or insufficiency on their part could lead to their prompt dismissal. This was one significant illustration of a much wider problem: the absence of freedom of association in France, which Pelletan deplored in one of his most successful and trenchant works, *Droits de l'Homme* (1858).[227] In a speech at the Legislative Corps shortly after his election as a deputy, Pelletan took up the issue, attacking the Bonapartists' regulatory and intrusive approach to civic and associational life. For the Second Empire thought it proper to appoint not only mayors but also newspaper editors and even the heads of such diverse associations as the Freemasonry, the Saint-Vincent de Paul Society, the Institute of the Jardin des Plantes, and the School of Medicine. He warned the Second Empire that this hyper-centralized conception of the state was no way to construct a genuine civic order:

Be sure to hold back this devouring power of the State, for otherwise you will have accomplished some kind of social pantheism where the State would be all and the individual nothing.[228]

It is a measure of Pelletan's intellectual influence that this description of an anomic order in which the state was 'everything' and the individual 'nothing'—a contrast which was first made famous in Sieyès' description of the Third Estate—was repeated almost verbatim a year later by the Nancy notables who authored the *Projet de Décentralisation*, the pamphlet which became one of the most widely read statements of the liberal decentralist position in the 1860s.[229] Pelletan shared the liberal intuition that centralization offered the citizen no incentive to become involved in public life. France was a nation which was 'centralized and pulverized',[230] and this atomization needed to be overcome through greater political participation. From this point of view republican Jacobinism and authoritarian Bonapartism had equally calamitous social consequences. Distinguishing between the coercive 'unity' which existed in centralized states and the true republican idea of 'union', he concluded that 'union is active and unity passive; union makes the citizen, unity the subject'.[231] By performing an essential role in political and civic education, local representative institutions could become powerful instruments for promoting this republican sense of 'union'. Involving citizens in the management

[227] Pelletan, Eugène, *Droits de l'Homme* (Paris: Pagnerre, 1858), 255–76.

[228] Speech of 20 January 1864, in Pelletan, *Discours d'un député*, 24–5.

[229] *Un Projet de Décentralisation*. Pelletan was among the many republicans who publicly endorsed this manifesto.

[230] Pelletan, *Aide-toi le ciel t'aidera*, 26.   [231] Pelletan, *La tragédie italienne*, 12.

of their communal affairs was an excellent means of generating what Pelletan called a 'localized patriotism',[232] a sentiment which not only provided an intrinsically valuable source of civic pride but also offered the basis for an effective system of national defence.

More generally, this sense of public spiritedness was a vital underpinning of collective identification with the political institutions of the centre. The commune was from this angle 'an elementary school of patriotism'; as Pelletan noted: 'in three-quarters of France, the notion of homeland is understood only to the extent that it is seen through the commune and felt to live through the commune.'[233] Accordingly, Pelletan's solution to the problem of centralization lay in the 'emancipation of the commune' and—this was the distinctly republican position—the designation of the mayor by the municipal council rather than the state.[234] He not only rejected the Bonapartist conception of the mayor as a political functionary but also stressed that mayors had to be genuine members of their local communities, unlike for example those 'nomadic' Bonapartist first magistrates in the department of the Seine who lived in Paris and only episodically visited the localities they administered.[235] This emphasis on residency was part of a broader conception of territorial politics in which mayors performed a crucial function in the dissemination of republican values. This role was delineated clearly in Pelletan's description of the ideal republican mayor:

This man, whoever he is, and who is generally a doctor, a notary, a businessman, veterinary, cultivator, farmer, a man of independent means, liberal by character, having no ambition other than to cultivate his assets and bring up his family; he has no need to seek influence, influence comes to him naturally; he attracts it and holds on to it; whenever advice is needed, everyone turns to him; and when there is a quarrel to be settled, he is the one chosen to adjudicate it. The municipality can be entrusted to him in all confidence.[236]

Over and above the autobiographical references here—this was clearly a somewhat idealized portrait of his father Achille—Pelletan was broadly giving voice to the doctrine of republican 'municipalism', which had emerged as the dominant republican philosophy of territorial politics by the late Second Empire. Municipalism, as noted earlier, was a doctrine which rejected both the absolute centralization of the Jacobins and the absolute decentralism of federalism; it sought to establish a public-spirited and participant community by drawing the citizenry into the management of its local affairs, while at the same time clearly circumscribing the functional attributions of local institutions by the imperatives of the general interest.[237] This is where the republican mayor emerged as a crucial figure; his authority was a function of not only

[232] 'un patriotisme de clocher'. Ibid.   [233] Pelletan, Le 31 Mai, 40.
[234] Pelletan, Eugène, A Mm. les électeurs de la première circonscription des Bouches-du-Rhône (1863). Bibliothèque Nationale, Le77–724.
[235] Pelletan, Discours d'un député, 22.   [236] Pelletan, Droits de l'Homme, 282–3.
[237] See the Introduction.

his mode of designation—popular election—and his specific policies and practices—the promotion of education and social welfare, the settlement of local disputes—but also, most interestingly, of his social origins and professional qualifications. In the municipalist scheme, the ideal republican mayor was a man of the local bourgeoisie who already enjoyed a high status among the local population, and could use this privileged position to promote the cause of republicanism.

This was again an illustration of Pelletan's influential and far-sighted political vision, for what he was offering here was a highly intelligent formulation of the necessary republican strategy of consolidating its social and political base through local politics, a strategy which was largely, and successfully, followed in the 1870s. In this sense his portrayal of the ideal republican mayor provided a striking anticipation of what would become universally known under the Third Republic as the 'provincial republican notable'.

The Enduring Saint-Simonian legacy

'He never sought to be a personality, it was sufficient for him to be the servant of the idea.'[238] Pelletan's evocation of Lamennais could in many respects have served as an apposite characterization of his own persona. As an obsessive servant of the idea, as we have just seen, Pelletan made notable contributions to the successes of republicanism both through his vigorous intellectual opposition to the Second Empire and through his theoretical and practical elaboration of a republican political alternative. But, unlike Lamennais, Pelletan also became an official personality, ending his distinguished career as a parliamentarian in the gilded halls of the French Senate. All these public and intellectual achievements seemed to impart a smooth and almost linear republican character to his later life and political thought. Almost ironically in light of the ideological eclecticism and exuberance of his early years, Pelletan's thought seemed increasingly hemmed in by the canons of republican orthodoxy in the 1860s and 1870s. Indeed this is largely how his later political writings came to be portrayed in the classical republican historiography.

But this is again a misapprehension; even a cursory examination of Pelletan's output during these years demonstrates that he never became an entirely orthodox republican thinker under the Second Empire and early Third Republic. He did not embrace positivism or nationalism, for example, and despite his strong Protestant culture he did not celebrate the role of the individual or even regard the protection of individual rights as the primary object of republican government. At the same time he remained a committed deist, and in the 1870s and early 1880s went out of his way to stress the continuing relevance of spiritualism, notably by generously defending the memory and

---

[238] Pelletan, *Les uns et les autres*, 199.

ideological heritage of his former mentor Lamartine. None of these stances was consistent with the core values of the elites who came of age in the early Third Republic. Pelletan's tendency to lapse into mysticism also resurfaced periodically, as for example when he justified the revolution of 4 September 1870, which overthrew the Second Empire, as 'the explosion of a unanimous sentiment which no human hand could unleash and even less stop'.[239] Somewhat intriguingly, it appeared that behind the veil of his rationalist republican discourse Pelletan was still clinging to the idea of a supernatural pantheistic force guiding the destinies of humanity.

There was nothing fortuitous about such statements. The truth of the matter was that Pelletan's ideological value system in the 1860s and 1870s remained deeply marked by his earlier intellectual influences; put differently, his republican political and social values did not 'crowd out' the wider range of ideological principles to which he had earlier subscribed. Most interesting of all in this context was his continuing public commitment to certain idealist aspects of Saint-Simonian thought. After 1871 he became an active member of the Société d'Économie Politique, where he mingled with a number of figures, including a number of former Saint-Simonians, who shared his interests in the relationship between the two disciplines of politics and economics.[240] His political discourse during these years also betrayed his continuing fascination with the priorities and themes of the sect which he had briefly joined in the early 1830s. Thus he remained wedded to the Saint-Simonian distinction between 'idlers' and 'workers', and at a public conference given in February 1869 he did not hesitate to describe the idle man as 'a traitor to human destiny',[241] an expression which would have delighted his old mentor Enfantin. Pelletan's description of the building which hosted the Universal Exposition of 1867, in which his old acolyte Michel Chevalier played a prominent part, was also cast in the religious metaphorical language typically favoured by Saint-Simonians: 'this cathedral of iron and glass, elevated to the glory of labour, here is the true modern church, it is here that we have witnessed miracles which are well worth others.'[242] Even more striking was Pelletan's continued attachment to cosmopolitanism during the 1870s and early 1880s. After the Franco-Prussian war, when a large number of his friends and colleagues began to yield to the demons of nationalism and even bellicosity, Pelletan stressed the indissoluble unity of space and time, presenting Europe as one community welded together by industrial and technological progress:

Man has hired steam at his service, this day-worker who by herself does the work of 400 million arms . . . who draws together continents so close that they seem to be archipelagos, and mixes people in such a way through its incessant network of railways, that it seems that Europe is but one town and one has merely to cross the road to visit one's

---

[239] Pelletan, *Le 4 Septembre devant l'enquête*, 38.   [240] APP, report dated 18 September 1874.
[241] Pelletan, *Le travail au XIXeme siècle*, 22.
[242] Ibid., 25. The 'others' were the Lourdes miracles, which in typically republican fashion Pelletan could not even bring himself to refer to by name.

neighbour. What say you of the notions of time and space? Days are mere hours, and journeys have become excursions.[243]

Perhaps most extraordinary of all was his continuing Saint-Simonian view after 1871 that the development of industry within and commerce between nations constituted the driving force for international peace. In a discussion of future relations between France and Germany in 1873, Pelletan commented that the economic climate was highly conducive to closer political relations between states. He therefore clung on to the Saint-Simonian postulate of the progressive character of history:

In the current state of civilization, whichever side of the border one stands, there is not an industry, not a bank, not a railway, not a common bond created by import or export which does not preach peace and impose it upon all states.[244]

The most substantive issue which demonstrated both Pelletan's continuing republican heterodoxy and his enduring engagement with Saint-Simonianism was the redefinition of the role of women in society. With few exceptions, French republicans of the Second Empire and early Third Republic generations were silent about the question of feminine emancipation; and many of these exceptions were men like Proudhon, who were overtly and positively hostile to any equalization of gender roles.[245] In the 1860s and 1870s Pelletan was the lone voice among the republican political hierarchy to continue strongly to press the case for feminine liberation. He did so first and foremost by holding up the examples of women whose actions and writings had made decisive contributions to the public good: most notably his two friends Juliette Adam and the Comtesse d'Agoult—it should be remembered that his acquaintance with the latter dated back to Pelletan's Saint-Simonian years in the 1830s and 1840s.

In his work *La Mère* (1865) Pelletan dwelt at considerable length on the history of women since the origins of humanity, highlighting their suffering and exploitation but also underlining their positive contributions to the cause of democracy and progress in France, Europe, and the United States.[246] Because of their lack of education women were often on the side of political reaction and intellectual obscurantism, but Pelletan thought this in itself was an argument for their greater cultural and civic participation in the life of the community.[247] Exactly how far this involvement could go, however, was somewhat unclear. He believed that the Napoleonic *Code Civil*, which subjugated women to their husbands, should be abrogated and that women should be entitled to play an equitable role in managing the affairs of the family. Marriage, for him, was akin to constitutional government: 'the husband min-

---

[243] Pelletan, *Dieu est-il mort?*, 262–3.

[244] Pelletan, *Les uns et les autres*, xxx.

[245] For examples of Proudhon's anti-feminist views, see *La pornocratie ou la femme dans les temps modernes* (Paris: Lacroix, 1875).

[246] Pelletan, Eugène, *La Mère* (Paris: Lacroix, 1865), 329–33.   [247] Ibid., 339.

ister of foreign affairs, the wife minister of the interior, and all household matters decided at the council of ministers.'[248] But despite its quaint contractarianism this image implied that women's ideal place was really in the home, and Pelletan often made the point that child-rearing remained one of the essential missions of womankind.[249] The object of feminine education was not to establish equality between men and women, which Pelletan thought was 'a wrongly formulated question',[250] but rather to fortify the institution of marriage by enabling men and women to discuss wider political and moral issues, and to allow women to perform their educational duties with regard to their children in a responsible and productive manner.[251]

The most difficult problem remained the involvement of women in public life. Pelletan knew very well from the examples of his friends Juliette Adam and the Comtesse d'Agoult—and his memories of the formidable George Sand—that women had an equal capacity to think and act politically; he also accepted that if women were the objects of political action they had a right to influence it:[252] one of the chapters of *La Mère* was even titled 'the Woman as Citizen'. However, the content of this feminine citizenship was not clearly defined. Yet, although Pelletan could not quite bring himself to admit that women should be given full civic and political rights, he gave a strong signal in this direction in the appendix of the same work by quoting a long passage from John Stuart Mill's *Representative Government* supporting the principle of women's suffrage.[253] Another telling indication of Pelletan's strong commitment to the cause of feminine emancipation was his frequent championing of the issue at Masonic gatherings in the 1870s. At a meeting of the Lodge 'Les Trinisophes' at Bercy in March 1877, for example, he argued that women should take the lead on deciding certain familial issues; at another meeting a few months later he stressed the importance of philosophical education for women.[254] He took up the issue at the highest level of the Grand Orient de France, and in 1878 was one of the organizers of a 'Congress for the Rights of Women', which was held in the Masonic headquarters at the Rue Cadet in Paris.[255]

Pelletan's enduring engagement with the problematic of Saint-Simonianism in his later life assumes an even more compelling character when seen from a comparative biographical perspective. As his study of Condorcet showed, Pelletan continued throughout his life to identify with the 'tradition of progress' in eighteenth and nineteenth century French political thought, and he regarded Pierre Leroux, Saint-Simon, and the Saint-Simonians—notably Bazard and Enfantin—as among of the most distinguished exponents of this line of thought.[256] His intellectual identification with Saint-Simon himself appeared to strengthen towards the end of his life.

[248] Pelletan, Eugène, *La femme au XIXe siècle* (Paris: Pagnerre, 1869), 29.
[249] Pelletan, Eugène, *La charte du foyer* (Paris: Pagnerre, 1864), 18.   [250] Ibid., 16.
[251] Ibid., 18–24.   [252] Pelletan, *La femme au XIXe siècle*, 31.
[253] Pelletan, *La Mère*, 366–8.   [254] APP, reports dated 19 March 1877 and 29 February 1878.
[255] Ibid., report dated 30 July 1878.   [256] Petit, *Eugène Pelletan*, 127.

Pelletan's return to religion in his final work, *Dieu est-il mort?*, exactly mirrored Saint-Simon's commitment to the reinstatement of divinity as the legitimate horizon of collective experience in *Le Nouveau Christianisme*.[257] The similarity of themes between these two works was impressive: like Saint-Simon, Pelletan deplored the apparent collapse of morality in France and particularly the absence of moral and spiritual leadership offered by ruling political elites. The new Third Republic contained too many 'bigots disguised as Voltairians', and their cynicism could only set a bad example for the rest of society: 'when the top of society is incredulous, the bottom is already half-way towards incredulousness.'[258]

Also like Saint-Simon, Pelletan stressed the insufficiencies of philosophical rationalism. Man was not merely a reasoning animal but also a sentient being; and religion was one of the best ways of educating his sentiments, and in particular allowing him to experience the noblest and most elevated of all feelings: love.[259] Philosophical rationalism was also incapable of providing a sufficient basis for morality because positive knowledge tended to divide mankind into self-sufficient individual units. Only religion could bind humanity together and thus serve as the basis for a collective public morality.[260] But existing forms of Christianity could not provide the appropriate foundation for this revival of religiosity. In the same way as Saint-Simon had attacked Christianity for perverting the religious ideal and had called for the elaboration of a new religion to replace it, Pelletan devoted his final work to a full-scale assault on dogmatic Catholicism. While he did not follow the Saint-Simonians in explicitly calling for the establishment of a new religion, his emphasis on human regeneration through the transformation of all existing cults—as he put it, pouring 'new wine into old bottles'[261]—was tantamount to a call for a fundamental religious realignment and implicitly at least suggested that religious commitment should take precedence over political thought and action. But Pelletan stressed that this spiritual revolution did not need to rely on novelty; all that was required was a return to the primitive beauty and mystery of religion in its original form:

A temple, to be truly the sanctuary of a living God, must have a sense of the mysterious majesty of the past. Whether man knows it or not, by some instinctive logic what is contemporary does not well celebrate what is eternal. There is necessarily a disagreement between the two ideas. The soul can pray with faith only where prayers have been held for a long time.[262]

There was something poignant about Pelletan's late yearning, at the twilight of a life devoted to the transcendence of the present, for a better future through a return to the past. But what this emphasis on religiosity also highlighted was the strength of his spiritualism, which was clearly nourished

---

[257] de Saint-Simon, Henri, *Le Nouveau Christianisme et les écrits sur la religion*, ed. Henri Desroche (Paris: Seuil, 1969).
[258] Pelletan, *Dieu est-il mort?*, 268–9.   [259] Ibid., 283.   [260] Ibid., 273.
[261] Ibid., 294.   [262] Ibid., 293–4.

through his continuing commitment to Saint-Simonian ideals. What emerges from our overall analysis of Pelletan's political thought is that this Saint-Simonianism remained a constant feature of his ideological value system throughout his life. Pelletan was a member of the Church for only a very brief moment in the early 1830s; but, like many of his generation, the experience marked him so deeply that he never entirely discarded a number of its core concepts: the emphasis on the intrinsic value of work; the beneficial impact of industry; the progressive and pacific consequences of commerce; the inexorable unification of European peoples; the emancipation of women; and, as we have just seen, the absolute necessity of a spiritual dimension to public and private life.

Taken at face value these consistent Saint-Simonian themes suggest that at the very least Pelletan was a Saint-Simonian republican: in other words a thinker and political activist whose mature values remained republican in character but who at particular junctures, or over specific issues, allowed his republicanism to be overridden by Saint-Simonian ideals. Such an interpretation could make sense of Pelletan's lifelong commitment to the cause of feminine emancipation or his later emphasis on the necessity of religion. Neither of these stances appeared to subvert his theoretical and practical commitment to the republican cause; his plea for a more equal repartition of gender roles in the 1860s in no way undermined his intellectual and political battle against the Second Empire, and it is an incontrovertible fact that even as he criticized the moral failings of the Third Republic in the late 1870s and early 1880s he remained the Vice-President of its Senate.

This weak reading of Pelletan's Saint-Simonianism is one which would be favoured by the orthodox republican historiography; the use of the conditional is warranted here because many of Pelletan's historians and biographers appear altogether to have missed this dimension of his thought. But there is no disputing that a case along these lines could be made, especially if it is noted that there were also certain core Saint-Simonian notions which Pelletan emphatically rejected as from the 1840s, most notably the bizarre cultism—although arguably he found a decent substitute here in the Freemasonry—and the beliefs in authoritarian government, the abolition of private property, and the promotion of industrial 'association'. Pelletan was a Saint-Simonian, one might therefore conclude, but only in so far as its principles did not interfere with his republicanism.

There is, however, a somewhat stronger interpretation, and one which is potentially less comforting to the guardians of republican orthodoxy. In this view Pelletan was a republican Saint-Simonian, a thinker who retained his allegiances to the key principles of the Church, as we have seen above, but also allowed his republican values to be significantly influenced by his Saint-Simonian precepts, even to the point of allowing the latter to subvert the former. There were many ambivalent elements of his political thought which, although traditionally seen as republican, arguably belonged more clearly in the conceptual universe of Saint-Simonianism. This was true of Pelletan's emphasis on the city and his celebration of the urban way of living, which ultimately stemmed from the Saint-Simonian premise that industrial activity was incomparably superior to any other form of economic organization. The same was true of Pelletan's lifelong dislike of Jacobinism, which reflected an abhorrence of violence and ideological dogma which were also quintessentially Saint-Simonian. This would explain why Pelletan never hesitated to advocate and support the use of force against Jacobin revolutionaries: unlike many of his fellow-radical republicans, he felt absolutely no ideological or communitarian affinities with them. And it was also undeniable that the emphasis on the value of intellectual intervention in public life, which was one of the consistently strong themes in Pelletan's political thought from the late 1840s, partly stemmed from a sense that only elites could bring true enlightenment to the masses: again, a belief that Pelletan acquired in the course of his embrace of the Saint-Simonian faith.

This elitism could be underlined even more boldly. Most of Pelletan's republican contemporaries were committed, in some form or another, to the view that the political order was improved through greater public participation. For some nineteenth century French republicans consistent mass intervention in the collective life of the community was precisely what distinguished a republican political system from its monarchist or imperialist alternatives. As his views on decentralization and republican citizenship demonstrated, Pelletan shared this republican intuition to some extent, although he qualified its scope significantly by his emphasis on the 'notabilist' recruitment of mayors.

But it is also true that he spent much of his political life opposing, attempting to contain, or explaining away mass intervention in public life. And when he was forced to acknowledge its potency, most notably in 1848 and 1870, it was highly revealing that he attempted to justify mass action not as a valuable adjunct to republican politics but rather as an expression of mystical and transcendental forces. Even his belief in 'popular sovereignty' was highly circumscribed: Pelletan went out of his way to stress that universal suffrage was not the absolute test of the validity of a political principle but an institution which presupposed a higher-order principle:

The truth, in other words any key idea, any idea constitutive of a nation, such as thought, property, liberty exist outside, *above* universal suffrage. Universal suffrage has the floor in order to serve truth and not to enslave it; it judges, in one word, what appears right, but on condition that it is judged in turn.[263]

Certain principles were true a priori, and these truths could not be shaken or overturned by contingent popular beliefs: it is difficult not to feel that such a strongly teleological conception of politics was not instinctively republican and that behind the mask of the Vice-President of the republican Senate still lurked something of the Saint-Simonian high priest.

---

[263] Pelletan, *Droits de l'homme*, 120–1; emphasis added.

Conclusion: The Coherence of Pelletan's Republican Saint-Simonianism

'Do not be of any school, and do not imitate any model. Those who pretend to be such almost always envy the qualities of talent which they censure and suppress among their followers.'[264] George Sand would have been well pleased with the extent to which her promising young protégé acted on her advice throughout his political and intellectual life. Like her, he always remained fiercely independent—as the hapless Lamartine painfully came to appreciate—and his eclectic political thought could never be reduced to simple and uniform categories. His intellectual personality was composite in the true sense of the term: at any point between the early 1840s and early 1880s a careful observer could find in him some elements of the traditionalist, the liberal Protestant, the republican, the socialist, the Saint-Simonian, the cosmopolitanist European, and the irenist. He combined these different characteristics with an exuberance which reflected an uncontrollable appetite for everything that life had to offer and a willingness to accept the inevitable contradictions which this ideological eclecticism necessarily brought with it.

Pelletan was an austere moralist who loved pleasure; a Parisian who never ceased to hark back to his humble provincial roots; a rationalist who constantly acted on instinct, and himself admitted that he was often misled by his own passions; a lover of order and constitutional government who seized power by a revolutionary coup; a spiritualist who appeared to distrust all forms of institutionalized religion; an independent and creative thinker who was deeply loyal to his Protestant cultural tradition; a fatalist who believed in action; and an optimist who was plagued by inner doubts.

But one of the many attractive aspects of Pelletan's personality was his willingness to assume these contradictions candidly. In a world in which men around him increasingly spoke the languages of instrumentality and prudence, he did not hesitate publicly to stand up for what he believed and to take responsibility for his actions, even and perhaps especially when he had an intuition that he may not have been right. But making mistakes was part of his *déontologie* of the true intellectual, and while Pelletan was always happy to recognize his errors he never apologized for having put himself in a position to make them. In any event, since only dogmatic Catholics believed in human infallibility, Pelletan preferred the company of those who erred. As he remarked in a speech given at Geneva to commemorate the centenary of Rousseau's death: 'Rousseau is criticized for having been fallible, should he have been infallible?'[265]

---

[264] Sand letter to Pelletan, 28 February 1836, in Sand, *Correspondance*, Vol. 3, 292.
[265] APP, report dated 2 July 1878.

At the same time, there was a far greater degree of coherence and subtlety to Pelletan's political thought than he is conventionally given credit for. The analysis offered in these pages has demonstrated that the orthodox depiction of Pelletan as an idealist *quarante-huitard* republican is excessively reified, taking little account of the developing and changing nature of his political thought as well as its capacity to adapt to evolving circumstances. There were certainly idealist elements in his thinking during the 1830s and 1840s, but these were gradually undermined by a number of hard-edged principles which he internalized during the years of the Second Republic. Conversely, his later 'realist' phase as a crusading republican opponent of the Second Empire was complemented—some might even say overridden—by his reversal to spiritualist preoccupations in his later life. In sum, there was a complex symmetry to the structure of Pelletan's ideology: his early idealism was qualified by a growing understanding of the concrete realities of republican politics, and his later republicanism was in turn complemented by an appreciation that science and positive knowledge were not sufficient fully to furnish the moral and intellectual horizons of mankind.

In addition to its coherence, Pelletan's political thought also demonstrated a considerable degree of subtlety, the best example being his doctrine of progress. His writings on the question in the 1840s and 1850s had little to do with wishful thinking or naive optimism but rather offered a sophisticated doctrine which operated at different levels of discourse simultaneously. These conclusions concerning the overall coherence and complexity of Pelletan's thought have wider implications, particularly for the manner in which the ideological history of nineteenth century French republicanism is conventionally narrated. Most notably, Pelletan's political ideas show that the traditional dichotomy between the republicanism of 1848—idealist, simplistic, and doomed to fail—and post-1871 republicanism—positivistic, complex, and destined to triumph—is easily overplayed. The fluidity of his ideological thinking enabled Pelletan comfortably to transcend this duality and at the same time, through his particular position between republican generations, to help keep together his political community at a time when it faced great internal and external strains.

While Pelletan's thought was fluid, it has also been established that it was held together by strong elements of continuity. His passionate commitment to intellectual freedom never waned, earning him, in addition to a brief stay in the prison of Sainte-Pelagie in the early 1860s, the admiration of his contemporaries and the devotion of several generations of liberal and republican journalists. It was a testament to his belief in the intrinsic value of free thought that he refused to consider banning radical republican newspapers in 1870–1, even at a time when France was at war with Prussia. In terms of continuity our most remarkable finding is beyond doubt the scale and durability of Pelletan's intellectual commitment to Saint-Simonianism. While this discovery is significant in its own terms—whether through oversight or for ideological reasons none of Pelletan's biographers appears to have appreciated his Saint-

Simonianism to its proper extent—it is worth drawing out two broader points which follow from it.

First, the later nineteenth century variant of republicanism in France was a much more open and complex—or, put differently, a much less self-contained and polished—structure of thought than its orthodox historians often appear to suggest. As we have seen with Littré, Dupont-White, and Vacherot, the founders of the Third Republic drew on a wide variety of ideological sources and their republicanism was often a complex assemblage of different and sometimes openly contradictory principles and concepts, which included most notably Orleanist and Doctrinaire liberalism, early French socialism, liberal imperialism, Saint-Simonianism, and even certain aspects of conservatism. Pelletan's inner dialogue between republican and Saint-Simonian principles was in this sense not merely a personal eccentricity but a particular manifestation of a much wider phenomenon of ideological cross-fertilization which occurred in France in the 1860s, 1870s, and 1880s.

Second, the question of the broader lineage of Pelletan's individual synthesis between republicanism and Saint-Simonianism deserves to be raised. The conventional view of the history of Saint-Simonianism after the 1830s was that the movement divided into two strands: a 'technocratic' branch which flourished under the dynamic industrial capitalism of the Second Empire, and a 'socialist' wing—which strongly influenced the Marxist tradition—which stressed the elements of social justice contained in Saint-Simon's original message. Pelletan's synthesis points to the existence of a third variant. This 'republican' Saint-Simonianism was more political than the first and less overtly egalitarian than the second, but was nonetheless indubitably Saint-Simonian in its emphasis on the benefits of industrialism and entrepreneurship and the quality of the government provided by a 'scientific' elite. This strand of republicanism was perhaps at its most visible in the colonial expansion of the Third Republic in the late nineteenth century; in domestic politics its most successful exponent was the *Polytechnicien* Charles de Freycinet.[266] Closer to our times, the experience of the Fifth Republic has shown the continuing robustness of this technocratic republicanism, particularly in its capacity to influence elite culture in France.

This lineage moves Pelletan into the realms of modernity, and there is little doubt that his political practice and thought anticipated many important twists in French political culture in the century which followed. His writings on the necessity of intellectual intervention in public life prepared the way for the emergence of the Dreyfusard paradigm in the late nineteenth century; his principles of republican citizenship, particularly with regard to the role of communal institutions in the political education of the masses, were codified in the Third Republic's municipal legislation in the 1880s; similarly, his considerations on the necessity of women's personal and civic development

---

[266] On republican imperialism, see Conklin, Alice, *A Mission to Civilize: The Republican Idea of Empire in France and West Africa 1895–1930* (Stanford: Stanford University Press, 1997).

influenced the new regime's legislation on education and divorce. From a wider perspective Pelletan's belief in the unity of European culture can be seen as an expression of one of the powerful strands in French political thought which contributed to the crystallization of the idea of European political and economic unity in modern times. Specifically, his sense that patriotism and internationalism were not at all inconsistent, and that political and civic identities could overlap across a range of territorial levels—from the local to the supranational—offered an exciting foretaste of late twentieth century discussions of 'European citizenship' as well as a salutary reminder that 'Jacobin' centralism was not the only intellectual model which influenced the construction of the modern republican state in France.

Pelletan's 'modernism', however, should not be allowed to distort our appreciation of his overall intellectual personality, which in many respects belonged more comfortably to the eighteenth century world of Enlightenment politics than the turbulent and volatile century which followed it. In the way in which he voraciously accumulated knowledge and highlighted its fundamental unity of purpose, Pelletan was a true product of the encyclopaedist culture. He also identified with every fibre of his soul with the drama of 1789, and in his speeches and writings conducted a constant dialogue with the actors and principles of the great Revolution, as demonstrated in his very first speech at the imperial Legislative Corps, when he startled the assembled Bonapartist parliamentarians by inviting them to take heed of the 'principles of '89, these glorious absentees who have long had their seat here, and now knock at your door and demand to be let in again'.[267]

Furthermore, his idea of progress, although directly inspired by Saint-Simon, ultimately sprang from the late eighteenth century writings of Condorcet, the 'volcano under the snow' in d'Alembert's words, who was venerated by all the founding fathers of the Third Republic. Above all, Pelletan constantly drew inspiration during his own life from the example set in the eighteenth century by his maternal grandfather Jarousseau, the Protestant 'pastor of the desert', a profoundly saintly figure who was tormented by public authorities but never ceased to uphold the principles of justice, toleration, and humanism. How closely Pelletan identified with Jarousseau is suggested by the fact that these lines could just as well have served as a description of himself:

With this conviction that everything was planned and completed in advance, he walked straight ahead, without ever giving in to any consideration of human prudence or, let us say it clearly, of cowardice. He was cut out for danger. Danger was in the fabric of his mind. No one has better understood and practiced the beauty of persecution.[268]

---

[267] Speech of 13 November 1863, in Pelletan, *Discours d'un député*, 15.

[268] Pelletan, Eugène, *Jarousseau le pasteur du désert* (first published 1855) (Paris: Germer Baillière, 1877), 55.

So, father of republican modernity or late product of the Enlightenment? As ever, Pelletan would invite us to transcend this dichotomy, and ultimately his complex and synthetic political thought points to the fundamental unity of French political culture between the late eighteenth and the early twenty-first centuries.

Jules-Romain Barni
Private collection

5

Neo-Kantian Moralist and Activist: Jules Barni and the Establishment of the Municipalist Republic

THE republican philosopher Jules Barni (1818–1878) was among the most widely known and respected figures of the Second Empire and early Third Republic generation of French intellectuals. His professional reputation was established by his translation into French of the principal works of the German idealist philosopher Immanuel Kant, a labour of love which earned him the admiration of his peers and a prize of 3,000 francs from the Académie Française.[1] Barni remained throughout his life a devoted neo-Kantian, and his personal and public life as well as his philosophical writings were deeply coloured by his interpretation of his master's teachings. In the same way as Vacherot, it was a deontological sense of moralism which prevented Barni from swearing the statutory oath of allegiance to the Second Empire in 1852, provoking his resignation from his teaching post at Rouen and the effective end of a promising academic career in France.[2]

But this loss to the republic of letters proved a gain to the cause of political liberty. Indeed to French and European thinkers and politicians of the 1860s and 1870s the name of Barni became indissociable from the advocacy and dissemination of republicanism. From his Swiss exile at the Academy of Geneva Barni delivered a powerful series of lectures on republican moral philosophy and on eighteenth century French political thought. Published in France by the late 1860s, these works confirmed Barni's reputation as one of the most prominent secular moralists of his generation, alongside such men as Jules Simon, Etienne Vacherot, and Charles Renouvier.

In the last ten years of his life Barni complemented these philosophical endeavours by wide-ranging practical commitments to the republican cause.

---

[1] The works translated by Barni were *Critique du Jugement; Observations sur le beau et le sublime*, 2 Vols. (Paris: Ladrange, 1846); *Critique de la raison pratique; Fondements de la métaphysique des moeurs* (Paris: Ladrange, 1848); *Métaphysique des moeurs I; Essai sur la paix perpétuelle* (Paris: Ladrange, 1853); *Métaphysique des moeurs II; Traité de pédagogie* (Paris: Ladrange, 1855); and *Critique de la raison pure* (Paris: Germer Baillière, 1869). The manuscripts of two further translations, *Anthropologie considérée au point de vue pragmatique* and *Prolégomènes à toute métaphysique future* are kept at the Bibliothèque Municipale of Amiens, MS 931 B and MS 932 B.

[2] Verly, Hippolyte, *Essai de biographie lilloise contemporaine 1800–1869* (Lille: Leleu, 1869), 7.

to make three further points about French republican political thought during the second half of the nineteenth century.

In the first instance, it will reinforce the view conveyed throughout this book that this thought was fluid, complex, and cross-cutting in character, and not dominated by any single philosophical school or undercurrent. It will also show through Barni's life and writings that idealist forms of republicanism were not marginal but constituted a powerful intellectual force, which in many respects—most notably on moral issues—articulated the views of the republican mainstream. Lastly, Barni's years as an exile in Geneva, which were essential to his ideological development, will serve to highlight the importance of 'external' intellectual and cultural influences on French republican political thought in the era of the Second Empire and early Third Republic: an aspect which has often been noted but rarely examined closely.

Finally, focusing on Barni's political activities in the 1870s helps to provide a broader and less Paris-centred account of the making of republican citizenship and, in particular, to appreciate the crucial role of local political culture in the emerging political order. As Barni's practices—and his own political trajectory—would show, the republican civic project was not merely grounded in national practices, institutions, and myths. Its articulation took full account of local forms of political sociability, and indeed often made use of the latter in order to render the former intelligible. Barni's political and intellectual role in the 1870s thus underlines the fact that the idea of republican citizenship was not simply formulated by celebrating the myths of French nationality and the centralized state but also drew heavily on established notions of communal politics and territorial government.

Early Years: Barni's Conversion to Republicanism

Jules-Romain Barni was born in Lille in June 1818. His family originated from Milan and had settled in Amiens in the eighteenth century. The political sympathies of the French clan were somewhat divided. While one of his uncles had been an enthusiastic supporter of the French Revolution,[8] another became a devoted Bonapartist who scandalized the family by leaving nothing to his children, choosing instead to bequeath his entire fortune to the municipality of Amiens.[9] Barni's father was an optician who by a cruel twist of fate lost his sight in the later years of his life; his mother, to whom he remained devoted, enjoyed a comfortable private income. Despite later attempts to present himself as a man of 'modest' origins,[10] Barni was thus brought up in a comfortable bourgeois milieu.

[8] Dide, *Jules Barni, sa vie et ses oeuvres*, 2.

[9] Pietrzykowski, C., 'Jules-Romain Barni 1818–1878'. Mémoire de maîtrise (Université de Jules-Verne Picardie, 1995), 17. This thesis contains useful biographical information on Barni, and draws extensively from the archives of the Petit family.

[10] A claim made in the anonymous *Notice biographique sur M. Jules Barni, candidat républicain* (Amiens: Publications de l'Union Républicaine de la Somme No. 6, 1872), 33.

Indeed, notwithstanding the vagaries of his professional and political life he rarely suffered serious financial hardship. Soon after Jules's birth the Barni family moved back to Amiens, where the young man made his mark as one of the outstanding students of the Collège Royal. This promise was fully confirmed by the time he completed his studies in Paris at the Collège Rollin. In 1837 Barni entered the Ecole Normale Supérieure, from which he emerged three years later with the highest mark in the *agrégation* and a reputation for intellectual brilliance, energy, and tenacity. In 1841 these qualities were recognized by Victor Cousin, whose 'eclecticism' was at the time the predominant voice in French philosophy.[11] Cousin appointed Barni as his personal secretary, and for a year the two men worked closely together, Cousin relying heavily on his assistant's knowledge of German to prepare the publication of his lectures on Kant.[12] Although Barni was personally fond of his philosophical *maître*, there is little evidence to support the later contention that Cousin exercised a considerable intellectual influence on him;[13] indeed Barni soon left him to take up a number of teaching posts in Parisian and provincial secondary schools.

Two documents provide indications of Barni's philosophical personality in the early 1840s; the influence of Doctrinaire thinking appears markedly in both. In an unpublished piece written in 1843, he vehemently denounced all forms of scepticism and fatalism, and confidently proclaimed his optimism in the curative properties of philosophical reason.[14] Even more interesting was a speech given by Barni at the prize-giving ceremony of the Collège Charlemagne, in Paris, in August 1842. Here the young *agrégé* stressed the central position of God, 'supreme cause of the world and father of men';[15] there was little trace of the freethinking philosophy of which he would later become the ardent champion. Also running through his entire speech was a typically Doctrinaire sense of the distinctiveness and even superiority of philosophy: 'the soul of the philosopher reflects that of humanity; however, what was vague and obscure in the latter has become clear and precise in the former.'[16] There was even an element of smugness in his suggestion that philosophy had the task of elevating man's spirit 'above the vulgar';[17] again this was somewhat removed from Barni's later republican beliefs in the value, indeed the necessity, of bringing philosophical thought to the masses.

At what point and through what channels did this precious young idealist commence his journey towards the theory and practice of republicanism? As

---

[11] On Cousin's spiritualism, see Janet, Paul, *Victor Cousin et son oeuvre philosophique* (Paris: Calmann Lévy, 1885); for a more recent study, see Billard, Jacques, *De l'école à la République: Guizot et Victor Cousin* (Paris: Presses Universitaires de France, 1998), esp.105–91.

[12] These appeared, with no acknowledgement or even reference to Barni, as Cousin, Victor, *Cours d'histoire de la philosophie morale au XVIIIe siècle Vol. IV. Philosophie de Kant* (Paris: Ladrange, 1842).

[13] A claim made by Désiré Nolen, 'Jules Barni', in Barni, Jules, *La morale dans la démocratie*, 2nd edn (Paris: Alcan, 1885), ii.

[14] Quoted in Dide, *Jules Barni*, 10–11.

[15] Barni, Jules, *Discours prononcé à la distribution des prix du Collège Royal de Charlemagne par M. Barni, professeur agrégé de philosophie* (Paris, 1842), 5.

[16] Ibid., 3.   [17] Ibid., 7.

early as 1845 Barni's biographer Dide found evidence, in his personal correspondence, of a belief in the impending collapse of the July Monarchy and its
replacement by a Republic.[18] Rather than a specific date or event, it is likely
that a plurality of factors contributed to Barni's intellectual realignment. In
the first place, the political context of the 1840s was highly unfavourable to
any identification with the status quo. The final years of the July Monarchy
saw the complete degradation of the Doctrinaire conservative liberal project,
which appeared to offer little to French society except the crude satisfaction of
material interests.[19]

Philosophically this was also a period of fermentation in Barni's moral outlook, during which the loose principles of Cousinist eclecticism were gradually
making way for the stern and rigorous edicts of Kantianism. After 1843 Barni
became deeply immersed in translating the *Critique of Judgement* and the
Critique of Practical Reason, while preparing the submission of his doctoral dissertation 'De libertate apud Kantium'—he was awarded a doctorate with flying
colours in 1849.[20] Along with the failings of the July Monarchy, Kantianism
also greatly facilitated Barni's embrace of republicanism. It helped him definitively to abandon the pragmatism of Cousinist philosophy, with its careful,
not to say craven, cultivation of temporal and spiritual powers and its neo-
Hegelian 'morality of success'.[21]

The writings of Kant gave Barni an alternative intellectual framework which
set much more demanding ethical standards of public and private conduct,
against which the corrupt and decadent elites of the Louis Philippe regime
could hardly appear in a favourable light.[22] It was also through reading Kant
that Barni was brought into contact with the principles of freethinking, which
became the cornerstone of his moral and political philosophy thereafter. The
embrace of Kantianism and *libre pensée*, finally and most importantly, also
introduced Barni to a community of young Parisian academics who were committed to immediate political change. It was here that Barni first met Vacherot;
among the other leading members of the group were Deschanel, Amédée
Jacques, Eugène Despois, Bersot, and Anquez. All these men were, or were
soon to become, committed republicans.[23]

Through this group Barni came to collaborate with the journal *La liberté de
penser*, established in December 1847 as the standard-bearer of the principle of
'the absolute sovereignty of reason'.[24] In its language and style as well as the
professional affiliations of its main contributors this was the journal of 'the
aristocracy of the École Normale Supérieure'.[25] While its initial articles were
characterized by a somewhat vague and bland Doctrinaire liberalism, its con-

---

[18] Dide, *Jules Barni*, 12.   [19] Rosanvallon, *Le moment Guizot*, 305–12.
[20] He published his dissertation a year later: *Philosophie de Kant. Examen de la 'Critique du Jugement'
par Jules Barni* (Paris: Ladrange, 1850).
[21] Janet, *Victor Cousin et son oeuvre philosophique.*
[22] Tchernoff, *Le parti républicain au coup d'état et sous le Second Empire*, 186.
[23] Dide, *Jules Barni*, 12.
[24] Amédée, Jacques, 'Avant-propos', *La liberté de penser*, 1/1 (1848).
[25] Gerbod, *Paul-François Dubois*, 224 n. 89.

tents took a markedly republican colouring in the wake of the 1848 Revolution, triumphantly celebrated in an article by Jules Simon.[26] Barni would certainly have taken good note of another article by his friend and colleague Brisbarre calling for a more pronounced intervention of philosophers in the political realm:

Since philosophers have the science and the knowledge without up to now having had the dexterity and resolve necessary to put them into practice, and since political leaders have the instrument without knowing how to use it or without having a sufficiently worthy goal for it, it would be more than desirable that philosophical science should be involved in public policy . . . Without losing any of their elevation, their objectivity and especially their truth, theories must find a way of being put into practice; and practice must elevate itself, be enlightened and moralized through exposure to healthy theories.[27]

Intellectually and professionally, therefore, Barni was drifting inexorably towards republicanism by the mid-1840s. This ideological evolution was considerably accelerated by the 1848 Revolution, which irreversibly sealed his political loyalty to the republican cause. Like many intellectuals of his generation, his commitment was initially manifested by public involvement in new forms of republican political sociability. One of Barni's first gestures after February 1848 was his participation in the Société Démocratique des Libres Penseurs, a republican club formed by a group of Parisian freethinkers under the presidency of Jules Simon. The 30-year-old Barni was appointed as vice-president of the society.[28] Its most eloquent, if not exactly effective, act was the proclamation of a 'fraternal address' to the 'citizen soldiers' of the French army. The regime of Louis Philippe had fallen because at a crucial moment the National Guard had switched its allegiance to the republicans. The society's proclamation welcomed this 'patriotic' act, further expressing the hope that this political alliance between the people and the army would prove durable. This was to be the beginning of Barni's long-standing interest in military matters.

These dreams proved illusory, however. Within months the fraternal spirit of the Revolution was swept away by bitter class conflict, and in June 1848 a revolt of Parisian workers was brutally suppressed by the army. Although its influence on events proved negligible, the contents of the 1848 address indicated the extent of the young Barni's intellectual influence over his colleagues. The text was full of intimations of themes which he would develop in his later public life in Geneva and Paris: a commitment to national reconciliation and the universality of civic rights; a categorical rejection of political violence; a teleological faith in the ultimate triumph of 'true' principles; and a belief in the suasive moral power of public opinion.[29]

---

[26] Simon, Jules, 'Révolution de 1848', *La liberté de penser*, 1/4 (1848), 309–336.

[27] Brisbarre, J., 'La politique et les philosophes', *La liberté de penser*, 1/4 (1848), 473. The two men parted company after the 1851 *coup d'état*; by 1857, in his *Discours prononcé à la distribution des prix du Lycée Impérial d'Amiens* (Amiens, 1857), Brisbarre proudly proclaimed his *ralliement* to the Second Empire.

[28] Dide, *Jules Barni*, 13.

[29] For the full text of the proclamation, see Dide, *Jules Barni*, 13–14.

However, Barni's optimism in the benign nature of the 'people'—an axiomatic proposition in the ideological value system of *quarante-huitard* republicanism—was soon dented by his experiences in the electoral arena. Put forward as a republican candidate in the Somme for the April 1848 elections to the Constituent Assembly, Barni was soundly defeated; his long and somewhat rambling personal manifesto probably did little to help. To add insult to injury, he was also ridiculed as a 'verbose philosopher' in the conservative press.[30] He made another attempt in the legislative elections of May 1849, with equally inglorious results; out of a total of 33 candidates the voters of the Somme placed Barni in 30th position.[31] As in the rest of France, the people of the department had preferred familiar conservative notables to well-meaning but inexperienced young republicans, most of whom, like Barni, spoke a political language they did not really comprehend.

To compound his miseries Barni's electoral activities brought him to the attention of the conservative government in Paris; the Minister of Education de Parieu ordered his transfer from the city to a provincial *lycée* in Rouen. It was there that he learned of Louis Napoleon's 1851 coup and resigned from his teaching position in 1852 after refusing to swear the oath of allegiance to the new imperial regime.[32] The period of Barni's internal exile was about to begin.

The 1850s: Barni's Internal Exile

There is an unmistakable unity to Barni's life from the late 1840s through the 1850s. He lived in Paris for most of these years, earning his living mainly from private tuition.[33] It was during these turbulent years that he became fully committed to the republican cause; it was also through his contributions to such vanguard republican journals as *L'Avenir* that Barni established himself as a leading intellectual in Parisian circles. Furthermore, the political turmoil he experienced—the degradation and collapse of the Second Republic, the Bonapartist *coup d'état* of 1851, and the subsequent proclamation of the Second Empire—led him to an appreciation of the enormous difficulties France would face in giving its republican institutions a secure foundation. It was also during these years that he nurtured the intense and almost pathological sense of hostility towards all forms of Bonapartism which marked his entire political generation. In intellectual terms, finally and most notably, this 'French' period saw the development and crystallization of Barni's moral and political philosophy, with its particular ethical vision and distinct form of republican idealism.

Barni's first substantive piece of writing on political matters was an article on universal suffrage in the January 1849 issue of *La liberté de penser*. Although couched in entirely abstract and general terms it was nonetheless very clear,

---

[30] *Le Courrier de la Somme* (22 April 1848).   [31] *L'Impartial* (20 May 1849).
[32] Dide, *Jules Barni*, 42.   [33] Ibid., 43.

not for the last time, that the philosopher's personal experiences had strongly coloured his theoretical conclusions. In this case his somewhat pessimistic tone undoubtedly reflected his electoral misfortunes in the Somme in 1848—he would suffer another electoral humiliation there a few months after the publication of his article. There was much scepticism in France in the late 1840s about the value of (male) universal suffrage, and indeed in May 1850 the conservative majority in the National Assembly introduced restrictions to limit the number of voters on the electoral register.[34]

Despite his obvious misgivings about the mass vote, however, Barni's main purpose in the article was to respond to monarchist, conservative republican, and Bonapartist attempts to curtail the voting rights of the citizenry. Universal suffrage, he asserted, was an institution whose validity was not a matter of practical reasoning. It was the cardinal notion of republican politics and effectively provided the only means of determining the truly republican character of the state: 'only universal suffrage can give a republican character to legislative and executive power.'[35] Alongside this typically metaphysical view, Barni was careful to stress that universal suffrage was not a source of anarchy, as its opponents tended to claim; events since 1848 had shown that for every 'Jacobin revolutionary' elected in the National Assembly there were 'a hundred moderates'.[36]

The real cause of France's political instability was the absence of a robust civic culture. For this reason, universal suffrage needed to be strengthened by compulsory primary education: 'primary education is the necessary corollary of universal suffrage.'[37] Although he was confident about the long-term prospects for French democracy, Barni ended with a prophetic expression of concern about its immediate future. Until the whole of France had received its necessary civic education, he warned, 'the exercise of universal suffrage is not without inconvenience and without peril for the very cause for which we owe it . . . that is to say the cause of democracy'.[38] Perhaps intuitively Barni sensed that an uneducated electorate could be used not only to buttress conservative majorities but also to condone and legitimize an illegal seizure of power, as would prove the case under the plebiscitary democracy of the Second Empire. The time was not far off when he would bemoan the political passivity of the French people, 'profoundly asleep in the arms of its Ceasar'.[39]

The 1850s were not an easy period for a republican thinker openly to discuss political matters, even at a purely abstract and philosophical level. Like many republican and liberal intellectuals Barni found solace in the intimate gatherings of Parisian salons, such as that of Daniel Stern.[40] Intellectually he

---

[34] Rosanvallon, Pierre, *Le sacre du citoyen. Histoire du suffrage universel en France* (Paris: Gallimard, 1992), 305. The overall number of voters was reduced from 9 million to 6 million.
[35] Barni, Jules, 'Le suffrage universel et l'instruction primaire', in *La liberté de penser*, 14 (January 1849), 166.
[36] Ibid., 167.   [37] Ibid., 169.   [38] Ibid., 172.
[39] Barni letter to Edgar Quinet, 5 September 1861, Bibliothèque Nationale, Paris, NAF 20781 (hereafter BN–20781).
[40] Ollivier, Émile, *Journal 1846–1860.*

took refuge in the relative safety of the French Revolution. In an article on Kant's attitude towards the events of 1789 Barni spelled out his own commitment to the revolutionary legacy and particularly to its notions of political liberty and civil equality. Fraternity, on the other hand, was not in his view a legal concept but a moral one,[41] a view which would be echoed by Vacherot a few years later. Beyond its immediate exposition—and defence—of Kant's views the object of the article was twofold: to stress the continuing validity of the revolutionary heritage and to warn against its Bonapartist perversions. The Revolution had become a fundamental component of modern political French culture, and nothing the Bonapartists attempted could remove 1789 from its pedestal:

Some may well try, in its application, to restrict its range, to pervert its scope, to violate its spirit, it will still have to be taken into account; and those very ones who will show themselves most unfaithful to it will feel compelled to declare that they draw inspiration from it and will be forced to make some gestures towards it.[42]

That was as far as one could safely go in denouncing the ideological principles of the Second Empire in the 1850s, and Barni's writings concentrated on moral and social issues. Yet although he did not write about politics this decade marked a crucial phase in his intellectual development. It was in these early years of the authoritarian Empire that his neo-Kantian moral philosophy began to acquire its distinct shape, and indeed it was at this moment that he became convinced that his entire political philosophy should be anchored in his theory of ethics. At the core of his political thought was a vigorous plea for the principles of freethinking, which were presented as the necessary basis of human reasoning in all forms of public and private life. At a time when such declarations would have been regarded as highly provocative, Barni did not hesitate to affirm his commitment to free thought: 'rationalism is my only religion.'[43] His conception of freethinking was heavily influenced by Kant, whom he regarded as the most remarkable eighteenth century advocate of the secularization of morality.[44]

In a review of Jules Simon's *La Religion Naturelle*—one of the defining republican works on secular ethics under the Second Empire, along with *Le Devoir*—Barni carefully defined his own conception of *libre pensée*: a rejection of religious dogma—'theocracy'—but a sense of admiration for the beauty of religious sentiment;[45] a condemnation of institutionalized religion, coupled with an equally firm denial of atheism;[46] an affirmation of the principle of free discussion, alongside a condemnation of absolute scepticism;[47] and finally a rejection of the nineteenth century's temptation by 'materialism', tempered by an affirmation of the values of secular morality.[48] While these views placed

---

[41] Jules Barni, 'Kant et la Révolution Française', *Revue de Paris* (15 March 1856), 492.
[42] Ibid., 484.   [43] Quoted in Nolen, 'Jules Barni', iv.
[44] Barni, Jules, 'Idées de Kant sur l'éducation', *L'Avenir*, No. 12 (22 July 1855); No. 14 (5 August 1855); and No. 15 (12 August 1855).
[45] Barni, Jules, 'La Religion Naturelle par Jules Simon', *Revue de Paris* (1 August 1856), 28–9.
[46] Ibid., 26.   [47] Ibid., 33.   [48] Ibid., 37.

him squarely within the liberal republican fold, Barni was especially careful not to align himself with those strands of the republican movement which demonized religion. He had clearly moved on from the gushing deism he had manifested in the early 1840s, yet he did not become in the slightest degree anti-clerical. However misguided its practice—and indeed its theology—could prove from a philosophical point of view, Barni believed throughout his life that religion was an expression of feelings which were natural and indeed essential to the human condition; while its conclusions might be false, its essential concerns and optimistic vision of the future were worthy of intellectual respect.[49]

An essential corollary of this secular moralism was Barni's strong commitment to the cultivation of individual abilities, talents, and faculties. There were many groups in France in the 1840s and 1850s which were concerned with the treatment of the 'social question'; they included socialists and progressive republicans as well as liberal Catholics, Saint-Simonians, and also Bonapartists. Although their prescriptions were obviously different, they all appeared to Barni to share a number of misguided conceptions and approaches, notably a belief that the 'social question' was primarily a material issue rather than a moral one; a sense that an improvement in the social conditions of working people was a matter of targeting collective groups rather than individuals; and most importantly an assumption that the optimal design of political institutions was the most pressing task facing those working towards social and political change. The neo-Kantian philosopher's response was firm:

That every effort is made to identify the best arrangements for facilitating a better material life, well and good; that the reform of governments and political institutions be continued and that the freedoms and natural rights of man be cultivated, even better; but let us also demand the moral reform of the individual; *this is the principle and foundation of the rest.*[50]

This was the kernel of Barni's moral and political philosophy: not only were public life and ethics closely related but in many senses the entire edifice of republican politics rested on moral foundations. So what were the core principles of republican morality? Barni had a comprehensive conception of republican virtue, as we shall see later, but one of its striking characteristics was its Kantian sense of austerity. One of the overt manifestations of this puritanical spirit was a rejection of anything which smacked of artificiality or deceit. Arrogance and vanity were thus among the least attractive traits of the human character because they tried to make something appear different from its true essence.[51] In a similar vein eloquence was condemned for its tendency to 'debase things by adding ornaments and artifices which are unworthy of them'.[52] Closely following Kant,

[49] Barni, Jules, 'Terre et Ciel', *L'Avenir*, No. 2 (13 May 1855), 14.
[50] Barni, Jules, 'Du rôle de la morale dans la société', *L'Avenir*, No.9 (1 July 1855); emphasis added.
[51] Barni, 'La Religion Naturelle', 31–2.
[52] Barni, Jules, 'Des beaux-arts dans la philosophie de Kant', *La liberté de penser*, 9 (August 1848), 245.

Barni declared that lying was among the most despicable vices of all. In a transparent allusion to contemporary events he depicted human falsehood in these terms:

The liar is less a real man than the misleading appearance of a man. His face is covered by an impenetrable mask; never has this immobile face, never have these dull and evasive eyes revealed a true sentiment. If he opens his mouth it is to say the very opposite of what he thinks . . . The lie debases, degrades, perverts human nature, and renders it capable of all crimes.[53]

Most readers of *L'Avenir* recognized the portrait of Napoleon III in these lines; unfortunately so did the imperial judicial authorities, and the journal was promptly banned.[54]

Geneva: Republican Theory and Political Practice

Between 1860 and 1870 Barni went into quasi-exile in Geneva. He returned to France occasionally, in particular to visit his mother in Amiens, and remained in close contact with French intellectual life; he even narrowly failed to secure a place in the Académie des Sciences Morales et Politiques in 1865.[55] By this time, however, his expectations about French intellectual life were rather low: as he wrote in a letter to Jules Simon, 'I was neither surprised nor distressed by this result'.[56]

The locus of his intellectual and professional life shifted to Switzerland. The Academy of Geneva, which had just celebrated its 300th anniversary, appointed him to a chair in history;[57] and although he had turned down a similar offer in 1859 he decided to take up the invitation a year later.[58] The intervention of Edgar Quinet, the most eminent French republican exile in Switzerland, appears to have been decisive in securing the post for him; from that moment the two men developed a close social and intellectual relationship, although Quinet, as we shall see later, was not always the easiest of companions. Indeed in some ways he later came to resent Barni's intellectual and political accomplishments, and sought to play them down.[59]

A number of factors prompted the move to Geneva. On a personal level, Barni experienced his first serious health problems in the late 1850s, and was clearly encouraged by his doctors to spend time in the calmer surroundings of

[53] Barni, Jules, 'Le Mensonge', *L'Avenir*, No. 5 (3 June 1855).   [54] Dide, *Jules Barni*, 47–8.
[55] The final vote was 16 to 14 in favour of Ernest Naville, an obscure Swiss man of letters who was supported by the conservatives. Among the votes cast for Barni were those of Rémusat, Barthélémy Sainte-Hilaire, Jules Simon, Michelet, Mignet, and Michel Chevalier. See *Journal de Genève* (8 April 1865).
[56] Barni to Simon, Geneva, 4 April 1865, Archives Nationales, Papiers Jules Simon, 87 AP 7.
[57] The official letter of appointment was dated 8 December 1860; a copy is in the Geneva State Archives. See Instruction Publique, Cc3 (pp.115–16); Archives d'État, Geneva.
[58] Barni letter to Edgar Quinet, 31 October 1859, BN 20781.
[59] For further details see Marcel Du Pasquier, *Edgar Quinet en Suisse. Douze années d'exil (1858–1870)* (Neuchâtel: Editions de la Baconnière, 1959), 90–4.

the Swiss Alps.[60] He was also about to get married in 1860, and the prospect of living with his wife Louise as a titular professor in Geneva seemed to hold more attractions than the dreary and unrewarding existence of a private tutor in Paris.[61] From a political perspective, the move to Geneva also presented new opportunities. After the suppression of *L'Avenir* by the imperial authorities Barni had continued to collaborate with the *Revue de Paris*, but this publication was also banned in 1858 in the wake of Orsini's assassination attempt on Napoleon III.[62]

By the end of the 1850s, in other words, Barni was effectively reduced to public silence in Paris; Geneva therefore afforded him a welcome chance to 'resume public speaking'.[63] Indeed he greatly resented the authoritarian Empire's strict censorship of the press, and was eager to pursue his intellectual contributions to republican political thought: 'I am not of those who get accustomed to despotism.'[64] Most depressing of all for Barni was the state of public opinion in France in the late 1850s and early 1860s. During a visit to his mother in Amiens he remarked to Quinet that he had found the same 'despondency, cowardice, or inertia' as when he had left France.[65] Writing from Geneva to his friend Jules Simon in 1862 Barni confessed: 'I have often felt so sad when I have thought of the state of our poor France.'[66] The republican intellectual was dismayed by the apparently overwhelming public support for the imperial regime, and the Kantian thinker bitterly condemned 'these blind masses who live on legends and hardly think about history and morality'.[67] France had become too small and petty for him; he needed the fortifying air of republican Geneva to firm up his convictions and broaden his intellectual horizons, and to join the ranks of a community of exiles which was highly active in developing republican propaganda.[68]

Barni's years in Switzerland marked the apogee of his development as a moral philosopher and political thinker, and they also saw the beginnings of his involvement in the turbulent arena of practical politics. At first, however, his focus appeared exclusively philosophical. It was from his lectern at the Geneva Academy and in the evening courses he delivered at the Hôtel de Ville that he established his reputation as one of the foremost secular moralists of his generation. His various audiences heard him lay open his views on a broad range of applied ethical subjects: at the Academy he lectured on general historical topics before 1789, the philosophy of history, the history of moral and political ideas in antiquity, and the history of freethinking.

---

[60] Dide, *Jules Barni*, 73.   [61] Barni letter to Edgar Quinet, 10 November 1860, BN 20781.
[62] Dide, *Jules Barni*, 63.
[63] 'reprendre la parole.' Barni letter to Edgar Quinet, 15 January 1860, BN 20781.
[64] Barni letter to Edgar Quinet, 31 October 1859, BN 20781.
[65] Barni letter to Edgar Quinet, 10 October 1862, BN 20781.
[66] Letter from Barni to Simon, 20 June 1862. Archives Nationales, Papiers Jules Simon, 87 AP 1.
[67] Barni letter to Edgar Quinet, 5 September 1861, BN 20781.
[68] On this theme see the study of Marc Vuilleumier, 'L'impression et la diffusion de la propagande républicaine à Genève au temps du Second Empire (1852–1856)', in Jean-Daniel Candaux and Bernard Lescaze (eds), *Cinq siècles d'imprimerie genevoise* (Genève: Société d'histoire et d'archéologie, 1981), 273–96.

At his municipal evening classes he denounced the immorality of the reign of Napoleon Bonaparte and outlined his conception of the history of ethics in modern times.[69] Although he lectured mainly in Switzerland Barni's intellectual reputation rapidly crossed back over the Alps to his native land, partly through word of mouth—many exiled and visiting French republicans came to hear him[70]—and partly through print.[71] Many of his lectures were published in book form, and by 1870 Barni's list of titles included *Les martyrs de la libre pensée* (1862), *Napoléon et son historien M.Thiers* (1865), *Histoire des idées morales et politiques en France au XVIIIe siècle* (two volumes, 1865 and 1867), and *La morale dans la démocratie* (1868).

Barni's explorations of the history of moral and political ideas in the eighteenth century, which eventually yielded three published tomes,[72] have to be read at several levels. In their most immediate sense they represented a scholarly exegesis of the moral philosophy of the Enlightenment, depicted through the main intellectual figures of the eighteenth century. Barni's writings offered thorough and at times challenging views on such luminaries as Saint-Pierre, Voltaire, Diderot, Montesqieu, and Rousseau, as well as lesser figures such as Vauvenargues and Duclos. But as one reads through this portrait gallery of Enlightenment moral philosophers it becomes plain that Barni's main purpose was not to dwell on the past but rather to look to the present and immediate future. He was in effect also thinking, and writing, about his own condition; the three volumes presented Barni's views on the moral and political basis upon which the intellectual should lead his life in the city.

From this point of view the eighteenth century provided a model for modern times because it was 'the century of ideas';[73] it was an age in which philosophy was a practical rather than speculative discipline, committed 'to reform man and society through reason'.[74] But philosophical reason was not to be found everywhere; Barni's aim was also to pinpoint moral truths and uncover errors wherever they were to be found. His cast of writers was thus partly chosen for negative reasons; in the third volume Barni concluded that men such as Helvétius, Saint-Lambert, and Volney were intellectually interesting precisely because their conceptions of morality were flawed.[75] Barni had also not lost his taste for provocation, as was evidenced by his discussion of the case of Michel Servin, the Swiss 'martyr' who was persecuted and eventually sentenced to death at the instigation of Calvin. Predictably this condem-

---

[69] Many of Barni's lecture notes, covering the period 1862–70, are kept in the Bibliothèque Municipale of Amiens. See MS 930 C, 934 C, 935 C, and 936 C.

[70] Quinet regularly attended Barni's lectures whenever he was in Geneva. Du Pasquier, *Edgar Quinet en Suisse*, 227.

[71] For an account of Barni's years in Switzerland see Henry Fouquier, *Au siècle dernier* (Brussels, n.d.). Bib.Nat.8-Z–10014.

[72] A third volume was published in 1873, titled *Les moralistes français au XVIIIe siècle* (Paris: Germer Baillère, 1873).

[73] Barni, Jules, *Histoire des idées morales et politiques en France au XVIIIe siècle,* Vol. 1 (Paris: Germer Baillière, 1865), 5.

[74] Ibid., 14.   [75] Barni, *Les moralistes français*, 234.

nation of local religious intolerance caused outrage among Calvinist groups in Geneva;[76] one of Barni's lectures was interrupted by indignant Swiss hecklers.[77] Barni's relations with the Academy cooled noticeably after the incident.[78]

But Barni chose most of these figures, and the wider cast of 'martyrs' of free thought, for positive reasons. They were his personal heroes, as the author readily confessed: 'I love and admire heroism, whatever the form it takes.'[79] Indeed so strong was his sense of identification with some of his characters that they became completely entangled in his own persona. When told, for example, that Socrates was not a parochial thinker but a citizen of the world; that he had no aspiration to rule but sought instead to define the moral and practical principles of politics for the rest of society; and that he had lived his life as an 'enemy of all tyranny and apostle of justice and humanity',[80] Barni's readers could be forgiven for thinking that the author was talking as much about himself as about the Greek sage.

Similarly, it was no accident that Barni chose to dwell on the painful nature of exile in his chapter on Madame de Staël; for these purposes she effectively became the mouthpiece of his innermost feelings.[81] The poignancy with which he wrote about Rousseau's flight from political persecution and its dele- terious impact on his physical and mental health also carried strong autobio- graphical connotations.[82] But the broader purpose behind his study of Enlightenment morality and the history of free thinking was to present prin- ciples and values which could inspire collective action in the present day. Contemporary political themes and messages were constantly woven into the fabric of all his moral writings in the 1860s. The Stoics were thus victims of 'Caesarism', a phenomenon which not only corrupted society but also engen- dered madness among the rulers who suffered from it—this was an echo of the common French republican view that Napoleon III was mentally deranged.[83] The great value of eighteenth century philosophical thought was its capacity to escape from the clutches of religion and superstition and define morality on a secular basis.[84]

Rousseau's writings were interesting not in their literary or philosophical dimensions but because they were concerned with challenging despotism in all its forms.[85] Indeed philosophy itself was presented as a militant weapon whose main purpose was to lead the battle against 'established order'.[86] Behind its abstract and sometimes opaque formulations, in other words,

[76] Dide, *Jules Barni*, 111–30.

[77] See Archives d'État, Genève, Instruction Publique, BA–19 (1861): 'Résumé des désordres qui ont eu lieu au cours d'histoire de M.Barni.'

[78] Borgeaud, Charles, *Histoire de l'Université de Genève, Vol. 3 (1814–1900)* (Genève: Georg & Cie., 1934), 422.

[79] Barni, Jules, *Les martyrs de la libre pensée*, 2nd edn (Paris: Germer Baillière, 1880), 3.

[80] Ibid., 15.   [81] Ibid., 264.   [82] Ibid., 253–4.

[83] Ibid., 35. It was certainly allusions of this kind which led to the book being banned in France.

[84] Barni, *Histoire des idées morales*, Vol. 1, 11–12.

[85] Barni, *Histoire des idées morales*, Vol. 2, 208.

[86] Barni, Jules, *Histoire des idées morales*, Vol. 1 (Paris: Germer Baillière, 1865), 15.

Barni's moral philosophy was really throwing down the gauntlet at the Second Empire. It was largely for this reason that he hastened to publish his lectures, believing that they might contribute to re-awakening the public spirit in France.[87] And the final message of *Les Martyrs* was in this sense clearly pitched at his contemporary audiences: those who fought for freedom often had to risk all, and even make the ultimate sacrifice, in defence of their ideals. But this was a worthy battle, which had to be pursued 'even if we were to succumb in the struggle'.[88] Barni was also intent upon using his book as a vehicle for challenging Catholicism. In a letter to the translator of the Italian edition of *Les Martyrs* Barni drew out this point:

These lessons teach us something else: they prove that philosophy too knows how to inspire heroism and turn its followers into intrepid martyrs, just as admirable, if not more so, than those whose memory is invoked by Christianity to demonstrate the strength of its faith.[89]

As the political situation took a more liberal turn in France as from the mid-1860s Barni's writings, and indeed his actions, assumed a more explicitly political character. In particular his moral philosophy, which had until then dwelled on the eighteenth century—albeit as an allegorical representation of modern times—began to focus directly on establishing the proper theoretical foundations of the modern republican state. *La Morale dans la démocratie*, first published in 1868, represented the crowning achievement of this intellectual reorientation. It was one of Barni's most accomplished and creative pieces of writing, and was in many respects his single most successful work. It received glowing reviews in French republican circles and was highly influential among secular and idealist moralists; just as importantly the work provided the intellectual basis for all of Barni's subsequent political writings in the last ten years of his life.[90] Based on lectures first delivered in Geneva in 1865, the book was divided into three closely related parts, each dealing with a distinct range of applied ethical questions pertaining to the individual, the state, and international politics.

Barni's aim in publishing *La Morale* was to contribute to the revival of public debate in France in the late 1860s. 'Our France is awakening',[91] he wrote excitedly to Quinet in December 1868. A year later, having just returned from a visit to Paris, he sounded an even more optimistic note: 'the republican idea is accepted today, and the thing itself is awaited. Sooner or later it will arrive, and it will be up to us to make it live.'[92] To this end the regime of Napoleon III needed to be brought down. Barni privately presented his book as a direct

[87] Barni letter to Edgar Quinet, 5 September 1861, BN 20781.

[88] Barni, *Les martyrs de la libre pensée*, 288.

[89] Barni letter to Frigyesi, Geneva, 12 March 1869, reproduced in *Les États-Unis d'Europe*, No. 12 (21 March 1869).

[90] A second edition was published in 1880; and in 1992 the work, together with the *Manuel Républicain*, was re-edited in France by the Parisian publisher Kimé.

[91] Barni letter to Edgar Quinet, 8 December 1868, BN 20781.

[92] Barni letter to Edgar Quinet, 4 December 1869, BN 20781.

ideological challenge to the Bonapartist regime, and he was pleasantly surprised that the imperial censors had allowed it to pass without any cuts or suggested amendments.[93] But behind this relative optimism lay serious concerns. Barni's most pressing task in publishing his book was to galvanize the republican party into thinking more seriously about its underlying principles, which he felt were being increasingly sacrificed at the altar of practical politics. It was all well and good to concentrate on winning elections, he grumbled to Quinet:

But what then? Must we then wait six long years until the following elections? In any event should we not be thinking a little harder about the practical means of making republican democracy live, when its turn will come? But this is not something which our friends seem to be thinking about.[94]

La Morale was thus Barni's attempt to make his friends in France reflect upon the ethical premises of their republicanism and in particular to think about the social and moral conditions under which democratic institutions could flourish. The first key theme of the book was a defence of republican individualism. Barni began by distinguishing among different types of democracy: a 'demagogic' form, which represented the reign of brutal force; a 'Caesarian' model, in which society abandoned itself to one ruler; a 'collectivist' strand, associated somewhat misguidedly with Rousseau, which tended to privilege unduly the rights of the community over the individual; and a truly 'republican' democracy, which was founded on the respect of individual rights and the promotion of political freedoms. This distinction was itself an acknowledgement of the seriousness of the problem: democratic forms were more likely than not to tend towards despotism than towards political liberty.

For this reason republicans had to understand that no democracy could be genuine unless it enshrined individual rights: 'democracy is not equality in servitude, but freedom in equality.'[95] Democratic liberty was not merely a matter of building political institutions 'from above', however. It required the cultivation of a sense of citizenship and especially civic virtue among the people, and this goal could be achieved only though moral education. Politics and morality were indeed inseparable: 'to build a democratic edifice which does not become either demagogical, anarchic, tyrannical, or indeed despotic in any form, we must build on the moral ground.'[96]

Building on Barni's philosophical writings in the 1850s, *La Morale dans la démocratie* provided a comprehensive list of the republican virtues. The republican citizen was a man who respected himself, cultivating his rationality at all times and never allowing himself to be guided by baser instincts. Temperance was in this sense a key quality, enabling the virtuous man to live a sober and chaste life and to eschew hedonism.[97] In economic matters self-respect also dictated a clear line of conduct, which Barni characterized as 'disinterestedness'. This was not an absolute renunciation of worldly possessions, which

---

[93] Barni letter to Edgar Quinet, 20 March 1868, BN 20781.
[94] Barni letter to Edgar Quinet, 5 March 1869, BN 20781.
[95] Barni, *La morale dans la démocratie*, 3.   [96] Ibid., 13.   [97] Ibid., 24–5.

could after all deny man the means of leading a comfortable and dignified existence, but rather a refusal to make the achievement of wealth the principal criterion of the good life.[98]

Moderation was not a virtue, however, when it came to facing up to adversity. In Barni's account special emphasis was placed on strength of character,[99] and indeed moral and physical courage were presented as one of the supreme qualities of the citizenry. Courage was necessary to work hard and to avoid idleness, but it was also the key quality which allowed man to overcome private and public hardship. Here again there was little doubt that Barni's moral philosophy was steeped in his own personal experience: 'courage has other opportunities to be revealed: against physical suffering, which is a condition of our nature; against moral suffering, to which it is no less condemned; against the disgraces of all kind, especially those of public life.' He added, again evidently from an autobiographical inspiration: 'it is perhaps there that courage is the most difficult to practice.'[100]

The foundation of Barni's individualist moral philosophy lay in the proposition that public and private values were indissociably linked. The strength of this connection was manifested in several ways in *La Morale*. First, as noted above, Barni's entire ethical system was in many respects an extrapolation of the personal values according to which he had lived his own life: temperance, detachment, and courage were qualities which he constantly attempted to uphold, and would have occasion to display even more in the final years of his life. Furthermore, Barni constantly stressed that civic virtues were embedded in private social morality. An alcoholic who neglected his family and dissipated all his earnings in the tavern could not be a good republican no matter how paradigmatically he behaved in his 'public' life. Indeed it was almost certain that such internal corruption would manifest itself externally: 'bad husband, bad father, bad son, how could he not also be a bad citizen ?'[101]

But the reverse proposition was also true: there had to be a perfect conjunction between public values and private social life. Republican elites could not lead corrupt existences away from the public eye but had to give 'the example of the most scrupulous probity and the most pure morality'.[102] Equally important, finally, was the need for consistency in the values espoused by public elites. Barni was particularly keen that republicans should not be perverted by false values, and for this reason he repeatedly attacked monarchist decorations such as the Legion of Honour. Distinctions of this nature were mere instruments of despotic rule, and men who were lured by such honours were simply acting on misguided moral principles;[103] Barni was appalled that even some republicans should allow themselves to be led by vanity.[104] A good citizen thus had the duty not only to lead a virtuous existence publicly and privately but also to ensure that there was no contradiction between these two spheres. Ultimately, however, it was clear for Barni that the source of

---

[98] Barni, *La morale dans la démocratie*, 27.
[99] 'Force d'âme'.
[100] Barni, *La morale dans la démocratie*, 29.
[101] Ibid., 25.
[102] Ibid., 177.
[103] Ibid., 27–8.
[104] Ibid., 120.

ethical behaviour in all matters was individual morality; in this sense private ethics constituted for him the source of all republican virtues.

La Morale dans la démocratie also provided a theory of republican politics in which Barni spelled out his conception of the ideal polity. Many of its core elements were drawn from the traditional framework of nineteenth-century French republican political theory. There was a notable emphasis on the duty of the state to maintain and uphold the principles of liberty and equality, especially freedom of expression and the rights of property.[105] Also very much in line with mainstream republicanism were his attachment to mass education and his vehement opposition to the death penalty.[106] But unlike many of his fellow-republicans, especially those with Jacobin and centralist leanings, Barni's notion of individual freedom was applied well beyond the political sphere. In the name of economic liberty he categorically rejected any notion of 'governmental socialism' which might give the state a leading role in the organization of labour; such practices would not only destroy the sacrosanct principle of 'freedom of labour'[107] but also potentially lay the foundations for the worst form of despotism.[108]

Similarly, Barni applied the principle of liberty to the religious sphere, where he advocated a separation of Church and State but also strongly upheld the autonomous rights of religious schools.[109] To make clear the distance that separated him from his anticlerical colleagues Barni even pointed out that Christianity had been a positive influence in the moral history of mankind.[110] Barni's attachment to freedom extended even to the advocacy of greater equality in the treatment of women, although this was clearly an issue which caused him considerable discomfort. His bourgeois instincts told him that the real place of women was in the 'domesticity of home',[111] but his Kantian principles of natural law suggested that republican anti-feminist and conservative conceptions of gender inferiority were deeply flawed. Women were not meant to be condemned to a purely passive and contemplative role in society, and indeed it was in his view imperative that they should take an interest in politics. Barni also strongly denounced the chauvinism of the Napoleonic Civil Code, which had given legal grounding to the social and political inferiority of women in France.[112]

But even such examples of extreme injustice did not move Barni to embrace the positions of Condorcet and Mill, who had argued the case for the comprehensive equality of women.[113] In a republican polity women could look forward to more active roles in society, even in the public domain; but for Barni politics had to remain a masculine preserve because men were the 'natural representatives' of women,[114] even though he readily conceded that they had not discharged this representative function particularly well so far. Barni's failure to reconcile these contradictory views on feminine emancipation in his writings earned him many rebukes from republican reviewers.[115]

---

[105] Ibid., 144, 150.   [106] Ibid., 179–96.   [107] Ibid., 148.   [108] Ibid., 86, 167.
[109] Ibid., 155–6, 164.   [110] Ibid., 36–7.   [111] Ibid., 128.   [112] Ibid., 136–7.
[113] Ibid., 126–7.   [114] Ibid., 128.
[115] See for example Charles Renouvier's views in *Critique Philosophique*, 1 (1872), esp.157–9.

Barni's International Political Theory and Practice

The third section of *La Morale dans la démocratie* focused on the achievement
of peaceful relations among states. Barni's interest in the issue of peace was
prompted by his earlier readings of Kant, who, with Saint-Pierre and Rousseau,
had attempted to define the propitious conditions for international peace in
the late eighteenth century. Revisiting Barni's theoretical endeavours on the
anti-militarist front will prove a rewarding exercise both for general and particular reasons.

In broader terms there remain several misconceptions about the 'pacifist'
leanings of French republicans in the Second Empire, and through Barni's
public and private utterances and concrete practice the complex reality of
French republican anti-militarism emerges more clearly. The most common
misunderstanding here is the belief that the republican commitment to international peace, and the 'Kantian' approach more generally, was an essentially
idealist phenomenon, inspired by confused irenicist dreams rather than defi-
nite political objectives. Barni's writings will demonstrate that this notion is
contestable on at least two grounds. His project for building international
peace was specifically political in the sense that its attainment was predicated
upon a specific set of transformative goals, most notably the republicanization
of European politics. Furthermore, Barni was no idle dreamer: a powerful
underlying stimulus for his plans was the desire to work towards the overthrow of Napoleon III; and there was nothing vague or confused about this
aspiration among French republicans during the 1850s and 1860s. In a private
letter to his friend and mentor Edgar Quinet, Barni explicitly spelled out this
point: *La Morale* was not merely a general treatise about republicanism and
international peace but also had to be read as 'a perpetual attack against the
imperial regime'.[116]

Barni's thoughts on international peace represented an extension of the
framework laid down in Kant's political writings in the late eighteenth century. In *La Morale* Barni paid a handsome tribute to Kant's predecessors Saint-
Pierre and Rousseau for taking seriously the issue of peace, the former by his
elaborate project for a 'perpetual' peace among European sovereigns and the
latter by his critical commentary on Saint-Pierre's work. But neither of these
two thinkers could offer a valid starting-point for advancing the project of
international peace in nineteenth century Europe, Saint-Pierre because he did
not take sufficient account of its domestic political preconditions and
Rousseau because he was pessimistic about its very possibility.[117] Kant, in contrast, had offered a doctrine of peace which was 'moral, luminous, irre-
sistible'.[118] As long as international relations remained in a state of nature, war
would be both a natural and an inescapable phenomenon. It was therefore

---

[116] Barni letter to Quinet, 20 March 1868, BN 20781.
[117] Barni, *La morale dans la démocratie*, 237–8.   [118] Ibid., 245.

imperative to replace war with international law so as to create the conditions for a peaceful resolution of conflicts among states.

In Kant's view there was a duty to work towards this goal even if it could never be fully achieved:

In light of the absolute veto which reason opposes to the state of war, there are no more any grounds to worry whether a universal or perpetual peace is a condition which might one day be accomplished; we must act as if this thing, which may never come to pass, should be, and make it our goal.[119]

This pragmatic utopianism, based on firm moral principles but equally conscious of the obstacles which lay ahead on the road to peace, was also the defining premise of Barni's own approach. His purpose in writing about the issues of war and militarism was to bring the question of peace to the forefront of public attention and in particular to encourage discussion of Kant's preliminary conditions for international peace: an agreement on the desirability of ending war; the rejection of any forcible acquisition or exchange of states; the abolition of permanent armies; the elimination of national debt as a source of funding military expeditions; and a respect for the principle of non-interference in the internal affairs of states.[120]

Once these preliminaries were agreed, the two central pillars of the Kantian edifice could then be constructed: a free alliance of pacific states and, most importantly, the establishment of 'free governments' with republican constitutions.[121] For Barni, peace could not be achieved merely through diplomatic agreements among existing states because many governments were bellicose by nature. 'Caesarian' states were inherently militarist and expansionist, and in their internal arrangements always sacrificed political liberty to despotic rule. Peace could therefore emerge only when all military monarchies were replaced by truly republican democracies, freely united in an international pacific confederation. This would be a gradual process in the course of which the republican democracies forming an alliance would spread their influence across the international system:

A union which would make a universal republic of all nations cannot, in all likelihood, be established at one fell swoop; but suppose that some free peoples were to give an example of such a peace alliance, such as reason demands; this alliance would gradually spread and would eventually encompass all the peoples of the world.[122]

The grounding of peace in domestic republican politics was the most striking element in Barni's conception of international order and also its most controversial neo-Kantian element. At the same time Barni's doctrine of democratic peace clarified, and in many respects went beyond, Kant's own formulations in the late eighteenth century. Thus Barni rejected Kant's endorsement of the early French revolutionary distinction between active and passive

---

[119] Ibid., 239.
[120] Although the latter principle would be qualified by Barni. *La morale dans la démocratie*, 241.
[121] Ibid., 242–3. [122] Ibid., 244.

citizenship, and stressed that nothing less than full civic equality could serve as the basis for a republican polity.[123] He also highlighted the ambiguities in Kant's conception of republican government, in particular his acceptance of a constitutional monarchy and his belief that a separation of powers between executive and legislature was sufficient to define a regime as republican.[124] For Kant's French disciple this formal distinction was inadequate: indeed republican government was incompatible not only with all varieties of monarchy but also with any substantive restrictions on political freedom. In this sense republican institutions had to be fully democratic in character, a point which Kant had not adequately appreciated and which implicitly vitiated his entire conception of international peace.[125]

The root of the problem here was Kant's failure to identify the locus of sovereignty in the state. Blinded by his 'monarchical prejudices' and his horror at the radicalization of the French Revolution after 1792, Kant's doctrine of peace had failed to embrace the republican axiom that sovereignty ultimately rested in the people.[126] In Barni's judgement, Kant's obsession with the preservation of order, both domestic and international, also led him to adopt unduly conservative positions on issues of justice. Barni did not share Kant's ambivalence about the right to overthrow unjust or despotic rulers. As a good anti-Bonapartist he believed that if all other avenues had failed the people were entitled to reclaim the sovereignty which had been unjustly snatched from them. This was one of the many place where Barni's Kant was—silently—superseded by Rousseau:[127]

It is indeed a right inherent in every human being to resist any power which wishes to oppress him; but it is furthermore a duty of the citizen to overcome oppression by all legal means available, and in the absence of any other means, by the use of force.[128]

The reverse side of the proposition that peoples had rights against their own states was that states, in their turn, had duties towards other peoples. Barni went much further than Kant on the question of intervention in the internal affairs of other states. He accepted the Kantian precept that under normal circumstances states had a duty to respect each other's sovereignty and territorial integrity; this was one of the essential principles of a democratic peace.[129] But non-intervention was not, for Barni, a valid justification for what he termed 'international egoism'. The international community had a moral obligation to prevent strong states from subjugating weaker ones; and, in particular cases, such as the great-power partition of Poland in the late eighteenth century, states would even have been entitled to form a 'holy league to pull away the oppressed from the hands of the oppressor'.[130] This was a decisive departure from Kant, who, haunted by the spectre of revolutionary wars in the

---

[123] Barni, 'Kant et la Révolution Française', 490–1.   [124] Ibid., 496.
[125] Barni, *La morale dans la démocratie*, 242–3, n. 1.
[126] Barni, 'Kant et la Révolution Française', 500.
[127] I am grateful to Karma Nabulsi for bringing this point to my attention.
[128] Barni, *La morale dans la démocratie*, 116.   [129] Ibid., 227.
[130] Ibid., 228.

1790s, had frantically insisted that the principle of non-intervention should be rigidly and unconditionally upheld.[131]

La Morale's theory of international peace was thus inspired by Kant's writings but also—consistent with the *libre penseur*'s hostility to intellectual 'fetishism' of any kind—critical of them. However, this criticism was in essence creative rather than negative; Barni used the Kantian framework to develop a highly original vision of international peace. In a number of central areas—the definition of citizenship, the conception of the Republic in substantive rather than procedural terms, the rights of peoples to resist oppression, and the justification of collective intervention—Barni elaborated a theory of democratic peace which fortified the liberal vision of Kant with elements drawn from Rousseau and the nineteenth-century French republican tradition of war.[132]

It is thus all the more important to reiterate that Barni's version of democratic peace was not a free-standing ideological construct. In *La Morale* the principles of a pacific republican community emerged as the logical culmination of a series of reflections about individual and state morality; indeed peace was in many senses the extension to the international system of the *same* principles which were deemed to hold in the first two spheres. His moral hostility to the taking of human life by the state, which was demonstrated in his commitment to the abolition of the death penalty, naturally drove Barni's campaign to abolish inter-state killing;[133] core freethinking principles such as the importance of free discussion and human rationality were translated into his belief that peace had to be achieved at the systemic level through dialogue and the exchange of ideas; and his definition of 'fraternity' as a moral rather than a legal concept likewise informed Barni's view that international peace could not be imposed on states but had to be freely accepted by them.

La Morale also firmly rejected narrow and parochial conceptions of nationalism, and echoed Rousseau's warning that without proper 'regulation' patriotism could easily degenerate into a sentiment which was 'narrow, jealous, exclusive, unjust, barbaric'.[134] Barni condemned the sort of xenophobic nationalism 'which gives itself a duty to detest foreign peoples, which takes pleasure in denigrating and mocking them, and which, horrible to admit but alas too frequently the case, cannot be satisfied except at the cost of their blood'.[135]

In addition to his continuing commitment to an open conception of patriotism, Barni remained strongly attached throughout this period to the classical republican ideal of 'martial' citizenship. In *La Morale* there was a strong

---

[131] Even though he was moved by the plight of the Poles. See Gallie, W. B., *Philosophers of Peace and War* (Cambridge: Cambridge University Press, 1978), 8.

[132] See Nabulsi, *Traditions of War*.

[133] Barni was strongly influenced here by the work of the republican publicist Charles Lucas. See for example his *Civilisation de la guerre, observations sur les lois de la guerre et l'arbitrage international* (Paris: Cotillon, 1881), which picks up on many of the themes which Lucas had campaigned on during the 1860s and 1870s.

[134] Barni, *La morale dans la démocratie*, 123.   [135] Ibid., 135.

emphasis on physical and political vigour. Thus an essential component of civic education in his eyes was the practice of gymnastics, which the republics of antiquity had used to telling effect as a means of keeping the body in a supple and robust state; in Barni's view this also had to be the goal of modern republics.[136] Furthermore citizens should always be prepared to defend their country, and Barni approvingly cited Diderot's model of the nation in arms, practised in Switzerland, in which 'every citizen has two outfits, that of his occupation and that of the military'.[137] Every citizen, in other words, was a potential soldier.

In his popular study of Bonaparte, published in 1870—before the outbreak of the Franco-Prussian war—Barni went out of his way to commend the patriotic responses of European peoples to the Napoleonic invasions of the early nineteenth centuries; Spain in particular had provided the shining example of an entire nation rebelling against an unjust military occupation.[138] *La Morale* also stressed the importance of 'civic courage', which was a virtue ranked higher even than military courage because it allowed citizens to remain vigilant about their rulers and not to succumb to despotism.[139] In his catalogue of natural and inalienable rights, finally, Barni explicitly included 'resistance to oppression'. As mentioned earlier, he believed that political violence was entirely justifiable if citizens were faced with unjust rule. Barni's irenism in the 1850s and 1860s was thus strongly tempered by an appreciation of the necessity of violence in an unjust world and the corresponding importance of cultivating martial values among peoples.

In sum, Barni's notion of international peace was strongly predicated upon a distinct vision of republican democracy. Through his critique of 'Caesarian' and collectivist democratic forms, and his emphasis on the protection of individual political rights in a republican state, Barni effectively highlighted not only the domestic preconditions of international peace but also its institutional characteristics. He had stressed, as we noted earlier, that true republican states had to be built on secure moral foundations—hence the importance he attached to education and civic virtue; also that such states had to uphold the rule of law, without which there could be no real freedom; and finally that republican democracies had to allow their citizens the greatest degree of decentralized liberty consistent with the preservation of a unified state. Seen from this perspective, the principles governing peace among states—morality, law, and confederalism—were nothing less than an application of the institutional design of the ideal—French—republican state to the international system. Thus at many levels the connection between Barni's domestic and international political theories, and between achieving the good life at the inter-state level and within the state itself, was not contingent but absolutely necessary.

---

136 Barni, *La morale dans la démocratie*, 32.   137 Ibid., 165.
138 Barni, Jules, *Napoléon Ier* (Paris: Germer Baillière, 1870), 115–32.
139 Barni, *La morale dans la démocratie*, 118.

Institutionalizing Peace: The Ligue Internationale pour la Paix et la Liberté

In one of his scathing attacks on Napoleon Bonaparte Barni outlined his over-all philosophical objective—a formula which anticipated the notion of mutual assured destruction: 'that the art of war be advanced so far as to make war itself an impossibility.'[140]

The avoidance of war was not merely a theoretical concern for republican, liberal, and progressive thinkers during this period. After the end of the Napoleonic wars a large number of peace societies were established in the United States, Britain, France, and Switzerland; and from the early 1840s inter-national anti-war and anti-militarist gatherings began to be held on a regular basis in Europe.[141] Indeed by the time *La Morale dans la démocratie* was first published in 1868 Barni had already become an established figure in the world of European anti-militarism, largely through his prominent public role in founding the Ligue Internationale pour la Paix et la Liberté (LIPL), which held its first Congress at Geneva in September 1867.[142]

The Ligue was a landmark in the history of nineteenth-century peace move-ments, being the first significant organization of its kind explicitly to posit a necessary connection between international peace and the achievement of republican democracy within states. This radical stance singled out the LIPL from the somewhat tame humanitarianism of the philanthropic organizations operating elsewhere in Europe at the time. Barni's central role in this organi-zation is of interest for both specific and general reasons. His leadership of the Ligue presented him with the opportunity to institutionalize his doctrine of republican peace and to develop his skills as a practical politician. At the same time, as we shall see, the problems raised by this operationalization of repub-lican internationalism shed an important light on the practical and ideologi-cal fault lines in the Kantian project.

Barni was the first president of the Ligue, and his intellectual leadership of the organization between 1867 and 1870 represented a crucial phase in his political career. His years as an anti-militarist activist marked his transi-tion from a committed republican intellectual to a full-time 'professional' politician, which he would become upon his return to France in September 1870. At a personal level, Barni's duties as the first president of the Ligue required a consummate display of tact and diplomacy. The three Congresses held in Switzerland between 1867 and 1869 saw the arrival of many distin-guished international guests, not all of whom were renowned for their

---

[140] Barni, Jules, *Napoléon et son historien M. Thiers* (Geneva, 1865), 377.

[141] Beginning with the meeting held in London in 1843, these gatherings were held in Brussels (1848), Paris (1849), Frankfurt (1851), and London again (1851, 1856). See Cooper, Sandi, *Patriotic Pacifism: Waging War on War in Europe 1815–1914* (New York: Oxford University Press, 1991).

[142] For further analysis see Molnar, Miklos, 'La Ligue de la Paix et de la Liberté: ses origines et ses premières orientations', in Jacques Bariéty and Antoine Fleury (eds), *Mouvements et initiatives de Paix dans la politique internationale 1867–1928* (Berne: Peter Lang, 1987), 24–6, 27–33.

sense of modesty. Although the activities of the Ligue took up a great deal of his time, Barni deliberately shied away from the limelight, leaving open the stage for such eminences as Garibaldi—the acclaimed guest of honour at Geneva in 1867—and Victor Hugo, who presided over the 1869 Lausanne Congress. Barni's letter of invitation to Hugo, which has been preserved among the poet's private papers, is a model of republican cordiality and deference.[143]

But even such exemplary self-effacement was sometimes insufficient. Not especially known for his sense of modesty, Edgar Quinet threw a tantrum when Barni wrote asking him to endorse the initial programme of the 1867 Congress; the old republican patriarch was deeply offended at having been left out of the initial manifesto published in France calling for the convocation of the Congress.[144] Quinet's petulance was smoothed over by several letters and a personal visit to his Swiss residence by Barni. The operation's success can be measured by the fact that within a few months Quinet had not only endorsed the Congress but was eagerly discussing its organization with Barni.[145] At one meeting in Veytaux in August 1867 the two men discussed the programme of the Congress for eight hours.[146]

Even more daunting was the ideological challenge posed to Barni by the founding and development of the Ligue. It was one thing to write a learned treatise about international peace on the basis of Kantian principles, but quite another to get these principles endorsed by a large, complex, multi-national organization which by the late 1860s had representatives in England, Russia, Poland, Sweden, Italy, Austria, Spain, Switzerland, and Prussia. This 'opera-tionalization' of Barni's personal ideology was in many senses a remarkable success. Although, as we shall see, the debates of the First Congress revealed the existence of deep and enduring divisions among delegates about the pre-conditions of international peace, the 1867 Geneva gathering was a personal triumph for Barni in two key respects. First, the emerging orientation of the Ligue was largely influenced by his conceptions, and second, he was able to prevent the adoption of principles which would have significantly narrowed—and radicalized—the organization's ideological profile.

Thus in his opening speech at the Geneva Congress Barni began by wel-coming the fact that hostility to war was now a matter of concern not just to a small activist elite but to independent publicists, industrialists, students, and workers.[147] He went on to define the main threat to peace as emanating from 'Caesarism'—one of the organizing concepts of *La Morale dans la démocratie*—and ended by urging delegates to work towards the achievement of the kind of liberal republican democracy he had always championed:

---

[143] Barni to Victor Hugo, letter of 24 August 1869, Bibliothèque Victor Hugo, Paris.

[144] Barni, letter to Edgar Quinet, 17 June 1867, BN 20781.

[145] Barni, letter to Edgar Quinet, 8 August 1867, BN 20781.

[146] Du Pasquier, *Edgar Quinet en Suisse*, 218. The meeting took place on 11 August 1867.

[147] Barni, speech of 9 September 1867, quoted in appendix, *La Morale dans la Démocratie*, 260.

Let us strive to oppose the republican spirit to the Caesarian spirit, the civic spirit to the militarist spirit, the spirit of federation to the spirit of centralization, in one word the spirit of liberty and peace to the spirit of despotism.[148]

The Ligue, in Barni's conception, was thus the organizational embodiment of the distinct ideological purpose set out in *La Morale dans la démocratie*: the republicanization of international politics through domestic political change. This objective was to be pursued by appealing to as wide an international audience as possible—hence the reference to the diverse groups enumerated above; by specifying the enemy as autocratic and militaristic monarchies; by limiting the programmatic objective of the Ligue to political change at the domestic level; and by stressing the need to achieve these goals by peaceful rather than violent means. None of these basic objectives proved uncontroversial, and indeed Barni had to wage a spirited ideological battle within the Ligue's leadership structures to maintain these positions against the claims of more radical republican elements.

The minutes of a meeting of the permanent Central Committee of the Ligue, held in Berne in October 1867, demonstrate both the range of difficulties Barni encountered and the extent of his successes in responding to them. Twenty seven delegates were present on this occasion, representing six countries: Switzerland, Germany, France, Italy, Poland, and Russia, one of whose delegates was Bakunin.[149] A preliminary discussion of the Ligue's programme immediately opened up fundamental divergences. Bakunin proposed that the organization's name should be changed to Ligue Démocratique et Républicaine de la Paix. This apparently innocent semantic shift was loaded with significance: in the republican ideological context replacing 'liberty' with 'democracy' represented a clear signal that the organization was committed not merely to institutional change but also to radical economic and social transformation.

Indeed the Russian anarchist leader spelled this out with a proposed amendment specifying that in the current state of economic inferiority experienced by European populations 'there is no possibility of political and intellectual emancipation'.[150] The achievement of peace, in other words, was not simply a matter of changing the political constitutions of states: it also necessitated a full-scale economic and social revolution. At a later stage in the meeting, when the organization and readership of the Ligue's newspaper *Les États Unis d'Europe* were being discussed, this transformative goal was again stressed: 'the newspaper is aimed not at the powerful but at the humble folk.'[151] Supported by the liberal republican majority on the Committee, Barni was able to fend off these radical challenges. The Ligue retained its original name; its primary objective remained confined to institutional change, even though the significance of the

---

[148] Ibid.
[149] 'Procès-verbal de la séance du Comité Central permanent de la Ligue de la Paix et de la Liberté, tenue à Berne (Hôtel du Faucon) dimanche et lundi 20 & 21 Octobre 1867'. Bibliothèque Publique et Universitaire de Genève, Papiers Bosak-Hauké, FACS 10/3.
[150] Ibid., 8.   [151] Ibid., 11.

'social question' was recognized; and the readership of its official newspaper was specified in the following terms: 'the newspaper is aimed not only at the enlightened readers but also at the masses'[152]—a crucial distinction which highlighted Barni's belief that the key ideological terrain on which the struggle for peace had to be conducted was not socio-economic inequality but moral equality and cultural autonomy.

In the latter context a further challenge rapidly emerged over the issue of religion. At the Geneva Congress of 1867 there were sharp exchanges between republican and militant anti-clerical delegates, the latter insisting that international peace required not only a transformation of internal political institutions but also a vigorous battle against (Catholic) religion. For the benefit of those who did not immediately appreciate the connection between peace and the elimination of religion, a delegate from the Association of French Workers spelled out the argument:

Every religion is a despotism which also has its permanent armies, the priests. Have these armies not inflicted upon the people wounds deeper than any of those it has received on the battle-field? Of course! these armies have distorted legality, atrophied reason. Do not clear out the barracks in order to turn them into Churches. Raze them both to the ground![153]

Throughout his active anti-militarist phase—essentially from 1867 until his return to France in September 1870—Barni was concerned about the activities of the 'extreme tendencies'[154] within the movement, by which he meant both radical socialists and anti-clericalist elements. But, consistently with his cherished values of *libre pensée*, he stoutly defended the rights of free speech of those with whom he disagreed, on both social and religious matters.[155] At the same time he successfully saw off the Bakuninist challenge and held the organization to a distinct and intellectually coherent position: a firm attachment to republican democracy as a precondition of peace, but a cautious approach to the issues of social change and religion.[156] At the 1869 Lausanne Congress Barni defended the Ligue against accusations of insensitivity to issues of social and economic reform, and urged delegates to debate fully the questions of 'pauperism' and social equality.

His proposed solution to these problems, however, fell well short of socialist and anarchist aspirations:

If we wish to make all class antagonism disappear let us first be fair towards each other, and let the principle of humanity enter our habits and soften, like a soothing balm, the friction of the different elements of the social engine. Workers and employers, let us moralize and humanize the factory, and the economic problem will be resolved.[157]

---

[152] Bibliothèque Publique et Universitaire de Genève, Papiers Bosak-Hauké, FACS 10/3.

[153] Eugène Dupont, quoted in *Annales du Congrès de Genève*, ed. Jules Barni (Geneva, 1868), 171.

[154] Barni, letter to Edgar Quinet, 14 September 1868, BN 20781.

[155] Barni, Jules, 'Preface', *Annales du Congrès de Genève*, xii, xiii.

[156] Bakunin and a number of his followers, including Elisée Reclus, resigned from the *Ligue* after its Bern Congress of September 1868. See *Les États Unis d'Europe*, No. 39 (30 September 1868).

[157] Quoted in *Notice biographique sur M.Jules Barni*, 25.

This belief that individual education and moral action could assuage and even ultimately eradicate class conflict was very much in line with the social philosophy of republican elites in France in the 1860s and 1870s. It was also one of the consistent weaknesses of the liberal and constitutionalist strand of republicanism, which often drew sharp criticisms even from sympathetic sources.[158]

The most difficult issue for Barni was the extent to which the Ligue could publicly endorse the use of force as a desirable, or indeed necessary, instrument for achieving international peace. In a sense this issue was indirectly raised in the course of Barni's arguments with Bakunin and his followers over the necessity of social revolution: one sensed that the republican constitutionalist's opposition here was not merely to the goal but also to the implied manner of its realization. But in the European republican movement in the nineteenth century there were many voices which emphatically rejected the claim that anti-militarism could offer any solution to the problem of war. In 1867, for example, Barni invited Mazzini to attend the Geneva Congress; the Italian revolutionary nationalist leader not only declined but also wrote back a blistering defence of war:

The aim, in a world exposed to oppression, to moral anarchy, to the corruptions of privilege, to the whims of individuals and to the brute force which sustains them, our duty reveals it to us: it is the triumph of the moral law, the suppression of everything which stands in the way of its accomplishment, the reorganization of Europe, the sovereignty of free nations, equal and in partnership, the mutual assistance of all to all for the emancipation of those who are oppressed, for the relief of all those who suffer, for the education of all, the independence of all, the armament of all.[159]

This conception of a republican 'just war' was emphatically rejected by Barni during his years in Geneva. However, the problem was rendered considerably more complex by the fact that the advocacy of force as a means of achieving peace also emanated from a broad range of Ligue members and sympathizers, many of whom had no immediate sympathy with the Bakuninist and Mazzinian positions. A case in point was the approach of Joseph Bosak-Hauké, an influential figure in the (republican) Polish emigration in Switzerland and one of the members of the Ligue's Central Committee after 1867. Bosak argued that verbal propaganda in favour of a democratic and republican peace would not suffice to achieve the transformative political goals of the Ligue. In the face of autocratic governments which were backed by strong military power and oppressed their peoples, and other peoples, it was very likely that the only method of founding a durable peace was through encouraging public opinion to respond to autocracy and militarism by force. In such circumstances, indeed, a war of liberation would not only be acceptable but positively desirable:

---

[158] For example the positivist J. de Bagnaux's review of *La Morale dans la Démocratie*, in which he welcomed the book warmly and stressed that in overall terms he was 'entirely favourable' to Barni's approach. However, he regretted Barni's timidity on the issue of social reform. *La Philosophie Positive* (March-April 1869), 217, 236–7.

[159] Quoted in Dide, *Jules Barni*, 161.

If war were to become the only means of salvation, and if the strength of public opinion were to decree war, ah then! such a war would not be a calamity or a disaster—oh
no! A war sanctioned by the peoples of Europe would not bring death but life, our future
and our civic virtues.[160]

This positive endorsement of 'republican war' went much further than Barni's
neo-Kantian republicanism seemed to allow for. As we saw earlier he had no
difficulty accepting that peoples had a right to resist oppression, and likewise
he recognized that states—and peoples—had a duty to intervene to prevent
'Caesarist' states from oppressing other peoples. But there was a considerable
conceptual gap between these two propositions and Bosak's view that the best
way of furthering the goals of the Ligue was through the active promotion of
war. Indeed in the controversy which erupted within Switzerland after the
holding of the Geneva Congress Barni went to considerable lengths to stress
that the programme of the Ligue was not 'insurrectionary'.[161] Although hotly
debated among the membership, this issue remained unresolved during
Barni's years in Switzerland. Its emergence highlighted what was probably the
most serious practical problem posed by the Kantian project: the implementation of its propositions in a world in which ignorance, oppression, and injustice remained the norm.

From Cosmopolitanism to Patriotism:
The Challenge of the Franco-Prussian War

'I believe that unless war sweeps us away one of these days our League can
become a great thing. It is still a child, but a child which is in good health.'[162]
Barni was cautiously optimistic about the future of the Ligue, but also very
much aware of the increasing fragility of the European balance of power after
1866. Yet although it did not come as a complete surprise, the outbreak of the
Franco-Prussian war in the summer of 1870 represented an enormous blow to
his hopes for turning the 'armed truce' of Europe into a lasting peace, let alone
a 'perpetual' one.

The war had a profound impact on Barni's life. After the fall of the Second
Empire in September 1870 he abandoned his life as a Swiss exile and returned
to France, where he immediately became an adviser to the new republican
Government of National Defence. After France's military defeat in 1871 Barni
decided to remain in France and offer his services, both political and intellectual, to the struggle to build republican institutions. His return to France thus
brought an end to his active anti-militarist phase. Between 1871 and his death

---

[160] Bosak-Hauké, Joseph, *Une motion faite à la réunion constitutive du Comité Permanent de la Ligue
de la Paix et de Liberté relative à la question la paix ou la guerre* (Geneva, 1867), 14–15.
[161] See for example Barni's open letter to Pasteur Munier, *Les États Unis d'Europe*, No. 7 (16
February 1868).
[162] Barni letter to Edgar Quinet, 5 October 1868, BN 20781.

in 1878 Barni made his mark on French politics as a member of the National Assembly, as a key figure in local republican politics in Amiens, and, perhaps most importantly, as one of the leaders of the Société d'Instruction Républicaine, a propaganda association which actively promoted the republican cause in provincial France in the 1870s.

The Franco-Prussian war constituted a probing test of Barni's character and convictions: it challenged his innermost feelings, shook his fundamental thoughts on issues of peace and war, disturbed his working relationship with the Ligue, threatened his conception of republican patriotism, and ultimately appeared to force him to question his overall commitment to the ideals of 'cosmopolitanism'. The outbreak of the war was in a theoretical sense a challenge to Barni's writings—and the Ligue's proclamations since 1867—about the sources of military conflict in the international system. The short-run events which led to the war—Napoleon III's opposition to the Hohenzollern candidacy to the Spanish throne and his declaration of war against Prussia—seemed to Barni a confirmation of the Kantian contention that wars were caused by the insatiable ambitions of monarchist states. As he wrote in a manifesto of the Ligue in July 1870:

The disaster which has just occurred without warning confirms yet again, in the most glaring manner, the truth of the principles which our League is working to establish. As long as the peoples continue to live under this monarchical regime which they are supporting at their expense, there can be no peace guaranteed for them.[163]

According to the organization's statutes the Ligue was committed to holding an extraordinary Congress in the event of an outbreak of war. In his opening speech at this gathering, held at Bâle in late July 1870, Barni, however, sounded a less triumphalist note. The Franco-Prussian war was clearly a blow to those who believed that international relations could irreversibly escape from the horrors of violence and inter-state conflict: 'it is enough to cast doubt on progress.'[164] Barni also acknowledged that, although the war was the product of a clash between two 'Caesarisms', both Prussia and especially France possessed representative institutions. Indeed by the late 1860s the Second Empire had effectively become a parliamentary monarchy, and Barni was implicitly forced to recognize that even a political system with male universal suffrage could be led into war: a concession which had significant repercussions for his theory of the causes of war.[165] Barni could not fail to notice that the course of events had contradicted the widespread pacifist and anti-militarist beliefs, which he had to some extent shared, that a declaration of war would be categorically opposed by the people. Barni railed against the 'old leaven of chauvinism which is too easily fermented' and lamented the apparent enthusiasm of the French and Prussian peoples for this fratricidal war.[166]

---

[163] 'Manifeste du Comité Central de la Ligue de la Paix et de la Liberté', 15 July 1870; *Les États Unis d'Europe*, No. 3 (July 1870).
[164] Barni speech at Bâle Congress, 24 July 1870, in *Les États Unis d'Europe*, No. 8 (August 1870).
[165] Ibid.   [166] Ibid.

In the months of July, August, and early September 1870 Barni was especially disappointed with the attitude of his French compatriots. With the
development of parliamentary institutions under the liberal Empire he had
hoped that the republican voice would become both more prominent and
more effective in France. However, the Second Empire seemed to have been
politically strengthened by the development of parliamentary government,
and the regime appeared to continue to enjoy mass support even as French
armies suffered defeats on the battleground. In a letter written in August 1870
to his friend Viardot, the news that the government had declared a state of
siege in Paris elicited the following frustrated tirade from Barni:

I had had the illusion that upon hearing this news the whole of Paris would take to the
streets to proclaim the downfall of the Empire and the establishment of the republic.
Instead of this it allows itself to be placed under martial law by the government of
Bonaparte! Will it at last have the strength to undertake the great revolution which alone
can save and rebuild our country? I still hope so, but I would no longer dare affirm it.[167]

In its early months the Franco-Prussian conflict thus forced Barni to reconsider
many of his core assumptions and beliefs about peace, war, and republicanism. The need for this reappraisal was exacerbated by the vexed question of
how far and on what terms France should continue to wage war against
Prussia. This issue was highly contentious within France and among European
members of the Ligue, and its development created serious tensions between
Barni and his more overtly pacifist and anti-militarist colleagues in the Ligue.
In the early months of the war, while he was still in Geneva, Barni privately
adopted a position of 'revolutionary defeatism'. This stance was based on several considerations: his instinctive opposition to violence, which led him to
hope for a rapid end to the war; his belief that having started an unjust war
France should not be allowed in any way to benefit from it; his profound dislike of the French army, which had played a considerable role in the 1851 *coup
d'état* and the repression which followed it; and a prayer that a comprehensive
defeat of Napoleon III's French forces would provoke the downfall of the
Second Empire.[168]

However, when the Sedan disaster forced out the Bonapartist regime and
replaced it with a republican government in early September 1870, Barni's
position began to shift. In a manifesto dated 5 September 1870 the Ligue welcomed the advent of the Republic and called on both Prussia and France to lay
down their arms and sue for an 'honourable' peace, based on the preservation
of the national sovereignty and territorial integrity of both states:

Let us put down our weapons, extend to each other a fraternal hand, and, respecting our
mutual independence, let us carry our rivalries and our struggles over into the fertile
fields of peace.[169]

[167] Barni letter to Louis Viardot, Geneva, 10 August 1870, Bibliothèque Nationale, Papiers Louis
Viardot, NAF 16274.
[168] Ibid. Barni mentions to Viardot that he 'approved the defeat of the French'.
[169] 'Le Comité Central de la Ligue Internationale de la Paix et de la Liberté. Au Peuple Français et
au Peuple Allemand.' Geneva (5 September 1870).

But with one of the key arguments for his defeatism—the overthrow of the Second Empire—now overtaken by events, Barni began a more fundamental reappraisal of his position. France, he recognized, could not make peace while Prussia occupied her territory: 'your soil is invaded, and the monarch who occupies it will almost certainly not agree to turn back after the victories he has just won.'[170] He therefore acknowledged that peace was not an end in itself but could be overridden by more fundamental considerations such as the preservation of French territorial integrity. In his August 1870 letter to Viardot, Barni expressed the hope that the war would bring about the re-emergence of the 'spirit of 1792' in France: a historical reference traditionally invoked by nineteenth-century French republicans to describe a justified defensive war against foreign invasion.[171]

At this point Barni left Geneva and returned to France, where he immediately joined the entourage of the republican leader Léon Gambetta, the Minister of War in the new Government of National Defence.[172] As the prospects for an honourable peace rapidly disappeared—the Prussians categorically refused the 'republican' terms offered by Foreign Minister Jules Favre on 17 September—the republican government's position hardened. In their efforts to rally the French population to the cause of national defence, Gambetta and his colleagues adopted a language which had strong martial overtones and was thus increasingly at odds with the even-handed proclamations of the Ligue.

In the absence of Barni, the Ligue's Geneva representatives issued a proclamation on 24 September condemning those on both sides of the conflict who sought to escalate the war. The text singled out those 'enemies of fraternity among peoples' in France who were advising 'a war of extermination' against Prussia.[173] Even more troubling was a Ligue manifesto published a month later, which after recognizing the moral legitimacy of France's patriotic resistance against the invading Prussians went on to argue that an immediate peace could be more beneficial to the republican cause than an indefinite prosecution of the war. The latter might in any event lead to a French defeat, which would be hugely costly in terms of human and material resources and would severely hamper the construction of republican institutions in France. The better alternative was to make an immediate peace, which would allow these institutions to flourish rapidly and would very soon inspire other European countries to follow the French model. The Kantian goal of a republican community of peaceful states could thus be achieved without conflict. Then came the crucial paragraph:

As compared with such a great favour which you would carry out for Europe, or rather the whole world, and for which you yourselves would reap the main rewards (and which

---

[170] Ibid.

[171] Barni letter to Louis Viardot, Geneva, 10 August 1870, Bibliothèque Nationale, Papiers Louis Viardot, NAF 16274.

[172] Archives de la Préfecture de Police, Paris (hereafter APP) Dossier 946 (Barni) (undated report).

[173] 'Concitoyens de France et d'Allemagne.' Manifesto of the Ligue Internationale de la Paix et de la Liberté (Geneva, 24 September 1870).

would make your own happiness), what is the payment of one or two billions for the costs of war, the dismantling of a few fortresses *and even, in the event of extreme necessity, a few other sacrifices consistent with your honour?* This would be a small price for the liberty which you would have acquired through this war.[174]

References to unspecified 'other sacrifices'—clearly the authors had French territory in mind—starkly underlined the pacifist position: an immediate peace, even if its terms were fundamentally unjust, was preferable to the high costs of war. To Barni, and to all French republicans in the Government of National Defence, such a proposition was unacceptable. Barni responded swiftly to the manifesto of his former colleagues by restating the official French position, which he now fully endorsed: 'honourable peace or war to the death until French soil has been completely cleansed, such is the task which the very nature of things has placed in the hands of the republic.'[175] He had come a considerable way from his earlier position whereby he perceived a defeat of the French army as the best possible outcome for France.

How far was his overall scheme of values transformed by the Franco-Prussian war, though? It is important not to exaggerate the impact of the conflict on Barni's thinking. After 1871 many republicans completely dismissed any notion of cosmopolitanism from their conception of international politics. A typical case in point was Gambetta, who spelled out his position in September 1871 in a letter to the organizers of the Lausanne Peace Congress:

I have never been a very strong advocate of the ideas and principles of cosmopolitanism . . . In the present state of our country, it is on the contrary necessary that our souls should be tied more strongly than ever to the principles of national allegiance and that they should find their sustenance in the French idea.[176]

This sort of language went completely against Barni's political and emotional instincts. It is true that his public utterances became somewhat more belligerent in tone after the end of the Franco-Prussian war. At a series of public meetings in the Somme he declared that the lost provinces of Alsace-Lorraine needed to be taken back from Prussia by peaceful means if possible. But if diplomatic instruments proved unsuitable France was entitled to reorganize its army and fight a 'great war'.[177] Perhaps carried away by the bitterness he felt after France's defeat he even evoked the necessity of 'revenge'.[178] And yet the scale of this transformation is not to be exaggerated. It should be emphasized that in the very same speech in which Barni discussed the desirability of 'revenge' against Prussia he insisted on the continuing validity of the Kantian ideal of an international confederation of pacific states. France had a duty to

[174] 'Concitoyens de France et d'Allemagne.' Manifesto of the Ligue Internationale de la Paix et de la Liberté (Geneva, 21 October 1870); emphasis added.

[175] Jules Barni, 'La République', *Les États-Unis d'Europe*, No.9 (25 October 1870).

[176] Gambetta letter of September 1871, quoted in Barral, *Les fondateurs de la Troisième République*, 203.

[177] Barni, Jules, *Ce que doit être la République* (Union Républicaine de la Somme, 1872), 33.

[178] Ibid., 34.

work towards 'the reign of peace, this ideal of humanity which must be pursued, even if we were never able to accomplish it fully'.[179]

In other words there was no place in Barni's value system after 1871 for the kind of aggressive nationalism displayed by many of his compatriots after the Franco-Prussian war and the loss of Alsace-Lorraine. Nor was there any display of chauvinism on his part. On the contrary, in response to Gambetta's plea to his fellow-republicans to give priority to France, Barni upheld the importance of fraternity among peoples[180] and derided the typical Gallic tendency to regard France as the beacon of world civilization:

By constantly repeating and persuading ourselves that we were marching at the head of civilized peoples, we have ended up placing ourselves at their rear.[181]

His attitude remained very much in step with the sober conception of patriotism outlined in *La Morale dans la démocratie*: a strong civic sentiment tempered by an identification with the principles of justice and humanity. Barni also kept in very close touch with his former colleagues of the Ligue in Switzerland; a police report of 1875 thus noted that he still held a subscription to its newspaper *Les États-Unis d'Europe*.[182]

Barni's Contributions to the Founding of the Third Republic: The Theory of Municipalism

'The Republic will change the face of things'.[183] Despite the humiliating defeat at Sedan in September 1870 and the menacing advance of enemy troops into French territory—his own town of Amiens would be occupied by the Prussians in late November 1870—Barni reacted to the downfall of the Second Empire with jubilation. The abdication of Napoleon III put an end to a regime to which Barni had remained implacably opposed and which he believed had been deeply damaging to France's integrity and international reputation.

From a broader perspective the restoration of republican government, even in the tentative and somewhat shambolic shape assumed by the Government of National Defence, gave Barni an immediate opportunity to participate in the intellectual elaboration and practical construction of the emerging political order. After he joined Gambetta's staff Barni was given the task of editing the *Bulletin de la République Française*, the official organ of the new government which was posted in every municipality of France—a measure of the extent to which he was immediately co-opted into the Gambetta leadership's inner circle.[184] Barni also assumed explicitly political functions during the war,

---

[179] Ibid., 35.
[180] Barni, Jules, *Les principes et les moeurs de la République* (Paris: Société d'Instruction Républicaine, 1873), 12.
[181] Ibid., 13.   [182] APP, BA—946 (Barni), report dated 1 June 1875.
[183] Barni letter to Edgar Quinet, 8 September 1870, BN 20781.
[184] Grévy, *La République des opportunistes*, 14, 360 n.104.

traces of which can be gleaned from official documents printed in the Commission of Enquiry on the Government of National Defence. Thus a telegram of Clément Laurier to Gambetta dated 19 January 1871 mentions Barni's appointment as 'Inspector General of Public Instruction'.[185] The following day Barni was despatched on a 'mission' to a number of southern departments, where he was asked to ensure the implementation of Gambetta's instruction that all schoolteachers should be up to their task 'from the political and republican points of view'.[186] Indeed Barni clearly played an important role in reviewing the appointments of public functionaries who depended on the Ministries of Interior and War until the end of the Franco-Prussian war.[187]

With the advent of peace in 1871 and the difficult beginnings of democratic politics, Barni chose to abandon the republic of letters and to devote himself fully to public life. Between the summer of 1871 and his death in July 1878 he remained an ardent champion of the republican cause, and in many ways these years marked the apogee of his career as a public figure. In this period he became one of the leaders of the republican party in Amiens, a member of the National Assembly in Paris, and an influential personality in republican intellectual circles across France. As we shall see below, he also made decisive contributions to the development of republican political sociability during these years. He was thus in a paradigmatic sense one of the 'founders' of the new order which gradually emerged in France during the 1870s.

He was also typical in that his personal experiences epitomized the difficulties faced by the first generation of men and women who made the Third Republic. As a former exile Barni did not find things easy upon his return to France, and he had to battle hard to make any headway. He also sometimes had to cope with betrayal and intense personal disappointments. And the sheer strain of it all took a serious toll on his health, eventually causing his untimely death, ironically just as the republicans were securing their hold on power at national and local levels. Like many republicans whose lives were broken by the Second Empire, Barni did not live to see the promised land of a fully fledged Republic in France.

Barni's contribution to the emergence of the Republic after 1871 can best be traced by examining his endeavours in three related but distinct spheres: as an advocate and leading theorist of the paradigm of republican 'municipalism'; as a political activist and representative of the people, notably in his capacity as a member of the National Assembly in Paris (1872–7) and the Amiens municipal council (1874–8); and finally as an architect of republican political sociability, particularly through his organization and leadership of the influential Société d'Instruction Républicaine.

---

[185] *Enquête Parlementaire sur les Actes du Gouvernement de la Défense Nationale*, Vol. 4, 134.
[186] Ibid., 126.   [187] Ibid., 539.

Barni and the Notion of Republican Municipalism

Like his comrades Littré, Dupont-White, Vacherot, and Pelletan, Barni took an active interest in theorizing about the territorial conditions of republican citizenship. His own views on local liberty first developed during the 1860s. In *La morale dans la démocratie* Barni cited Turgot's views on municipal government as a way of highlighting the principle of local economic self-reliance. The civic properties of self-rule were hinted at but not developed into a positive doctrine; the main point of the argument was that local populations should not expect everything from the state.[188] And although his interests during this decade were mainly focused on the issue of international peace rather than on the political and territorial structures of the future republican state, he explicitly endorsed the principle of decentralization in two articles written in *Les États-Unis d'Europe*.

In the first article, written shortly after the establishment of a Commission of Decentralization by the liberal Empire, Barni carefully distinguished his commitment to greater local liberty from that offered by Napoleon III and Emile Ollivier, who were merely attempting in his view to dupe French opinion into supporting a more democratic version of Bonapartism.[189] He also rejected the version of decentralization advocated by legitimists and Orleanist liberals, both of which groups were seeking to reinforce their social and political domination over local populations.[190] But for Barni these flawed versions of decentralism did not vitiate the quality of the genuine article. On the contrary, a true republic could only be decentralized:

> It is no less evident that the establishment of a republican democracy necessarily presupposes decentralization, and that without the latter the former will always more or less evoke memories of the monarchy and remain unstable. In truth let us not forget that centralization and monarchy are correlated terms, for centralization in France was the accomplishment of the *ancien régime* before being taken up by Napoleon. In contrast a democratic republic, that is to say the government of the people by themselves, necessarily means decentralization, that is to say the development of municipal, provincial, or departmental freedoms. What indeed could signify the government of a people by themselves if a country was hemmed by an administrative network all of whose powers proceeded from one central point, not allowing any of the groups which made up the people to manage their own affairs? Where such a state of affairs were to exist, we could conclude that even if the government called itself republican, the republic would exist only in name.[191]

Barni's Genevan years played a crucial role in shaping his later views on local self-government. First, and obviously, he was residing in a city—and indeed a country—where municipal power was a deeply rooted and celebrated feature of the political culture. Barni developed close personal links with the

---

[188] Barni, *La morale dans la démocratie*, 168–169.
[189] Barni, Jules, 'La Décentralisation en France', *Les États-Unis d'Europe*, No. 3 (March 1870).
[190] Ibid.   [191] Ibid.

Genevan municipality— he delivered many courses of evening lectures in the city hall—and he often referred admiringly to the considerable proportion of the Genevan budget allocated each year to primary education.[192] It is also possible that during his years in Geneva Barni became a member of the Freemasonry; at the very least there is little doubt that he moved in Masonic circles.[193] Through such links Barni was exposed to an organization whose constitutional philosophy strongly affirmed the autonomy of local lodges within the framework of a national organization: essentially the same principle which he would later apply to relations between central government and local territorial units. It is also worth remembering that Barni kept in touch with events in Amiens throughout these years, notably through his close friend Frédéric Petit, the future mayor of Amiens and already a passionate champion of the republican notion of communal freedom during the 1860s.

But there can be no doubt that his anti-militarist endeavours also directly influenced Barni's later thoughts on the vertical structure of the republican state. In his critique of 'Caesarism' he identified a strong correlation between domestic despotic rule and the pursuit of militarism at the international level. But 'Caesarism' was also a term used to characterize centralized government, and Barni was well aware that for many anti-militarists the abolition of war was a matter of replacing not only political authoritarianism by republicanism but also centralized government by local autonomy and even federalism.[194] Even if Barni himself did not espouse this solution at the domestic level, he explicitly propounded 'confederalism' as the basis for the future union of pacific states in international politics. Furthermore he clearly came to understand the domestic implications of despotic rule more fully as a result of his exposure to the arguments of radical anti-militarists; and in the early 1870s his use of the term 'Caesarism' in a somewhat more sociological sense[195] suggested that their message had not been entirely lost upon him.

If the seeds of his ideas about local liberty were evidently sown in Switzerland, the plant blossomed only upon his return to France in 1870. Barni arrived at his conclusions on municipalist politics largely on the basis of his participation in the republican war effort between September 1870 and February 1871, and his evaluation of the political situation in France thereafter. After the end of the Franco-Prussian war and the bloody suppression of the Commune in Paris, he

---

[192] Barni, *Ce que doit être la République*, 11.

[193] Barni was accused of membership of the Masonry in the 1870s, a charge commonly directed at republican intellectuals who had lived abroad during the Second Empire. It is true that some of his close friends in the republican party—for example, Frédéric Petit—and in the international peace movement—Bosak-Hauké—had Masonic affiliations. During the 1850s and 1860s Geneva also served as a refuge and operational base for French Masons. The only direct reference of Barni's Masonic activities to emerge so far is a reference to his membership of the Grande Loge Nationale in 1874. For a further examination of the political affiliations of French free-masons during this period, see Hazareesingh and Wright, *Francs-Maçons sous le Second Empire*.

[194] At the 1867 Geneva Congress the interventions of Bakunin and Charles Longuet focused explicitly on the link between political centralization and war. See *Annales du Congrès de Genève*, 248, 250–7.

[195] In 1871 Barni defined Caesarism as 'the suppression of intelligence by brute numbers'. *Ce que doit être la République*, 10.

was keen that republicans should draw the appropriate political and ideological lessons from recent events. In his public speeches in July and August 1871 he stressed the irreversibility of the abolition of monarchical government in France and the need for the French nation to rally to the republican banner. Like his mentor Gambetta, Barni was particularly eager to appeal to the 'intelligent conservatives' in France, for whom there would always be a place in the republican political system alongside the 'progressive party'. Indeed it was necessary in a healthy democracy for the forces of order and movement to influence and mutually restrain each other.[196] But in a sense his main priority in the summer of 1871 was the reform of republican political culture, which needed to take on the qualities of flexibility, realism, and what he termed 'wisdom'.[197]

Without ever explicitly calling them Jacobins, Barni launched a fierce attack on his republican colleagues who still subscribed to variants of Jacobin doctrine; its very existence continued in his eyes to damage the political and electoral interests of the republican movement. It was imperative, he asserted, that republicans should abandon 'this spirit of intolerance and exclusion, the preserve of sectarians, which was perhaps natural in the struggle, but which is contrary to any true spirit of government'. To remove any possible doubt as to the objects of his remonstrations, Barni added that republicans should cease to cultivate a sterile fetishism of the revolutionary past; those who admired and indeed had recently sought to emulate the deplorable practices of the 1790s had proved to be the worst enemies of the republican cause.[198]

In a pamphlet published a few years later the same hostility to Communard ideological dogma and Jacobin revolutionary violence was apparent: 'a true love of liberty rejects fanaticism from wherever it might come.'[199] The Republic, in Barni's eyes, could not be true to its ideals unless it subscribed unambiguously to the principles of political liberty and civic equality. Both of these principles found their natural expression in an open and tolerant democratic polity and in universal suffrage, the institution through which the people exercised their inherent right to participate in the life of the city.[200] On the basis of all this Barni was able to define republicanism as the supreme doctrine of self-government: it was a political system which allowed individuals to develop a sense of self-mastery,[201] and it was also a theory of collective life in which the people as a whole exercised sovereign power over themselves.[202] Consistent with the principle of self-rule and with all the other notions outlined above, such as flexibility, inclusivity, and democracy, republicanism also offered a public philosophy of territorial government in which the principle of local autonomy was widely practised.

In his first public speeches delivered in France in the summer of 1871 Barni thus explicitly endorsed the principle of decentralism. Citizens, he asserted, had to be offered every opportunity to involve themselves in public life:

---

[196] Ibid., 27–8.   [197] 'sagesse'. Ibid., 30–1.   [198] Ibid., 29–30.
[199] Barni, *Les principes et les moeurs de la République*, 21.
[200] Barni, Jules, *L'instruction républicaine* (Paris: Société d'Instruction Républicaine, 1872), 5.
[201] Barni, *Les principes et les moeurs de la République*, 5.   [202] Ibid., 7.

This, in passing, presupposes a broad measure of decentralization which, instead of leaving all political power concentrated in one central point and in a small number of hands, on the contrary disseminates it, divides it, and in so doing divides the effective responsibilities in all points of the territory.[203]

This municipalist position was spelt out at greater length in Barni's *Manuel Républicain*, whose chapters initially appeared separately in the *Bulletin Officiel de la République* during the Franco-Prussian war. Completed and first published in December 1871, the book was acclaimed in republican circles throughout France. In the *Manuel* Barni described the commune as 'the alveolus of the State'.[204] Despotic governments would always attempt to suppress communal freedoms; in republican polities, in contrast, 'municipal freedoms constitute the very foundation of public freedoms. Each commune governs itself, it is like a small republic in a great one'. However, this principle of communal self-rule was not unqualified:

Being itself a full component of the whole of which, while keeping its own life and autonomy, it forms only a part, it belongs, for all that which bears upon the general interests of the association of which it is a member, to the mass of the people as a whole, and it is subject, in this capacity, to the laws and public authorities which it imposes upon itself.[205]

The commune was therefore the paradigm of republican political freedom, 'a free group in a free society'.[206] Rejection of Jacobinism and an acceptance of federalist principles qualified by the necessity of a central state to uphold the general interest: Barni not only signed up to the doctrine of republican municipalism but, by publishing it in one of the most successful pamphlets of the 1870s, he contributed significantly towards its dissemination and wider acceptance in France. This theoretical achievement was compounded by his activities as a political agent and architect of republican political sociability during the 1870s, when Barni successfully put his own municipalist principles into practice.

Barni as an Agent of Republicanism in the 1870s

'Political ambition is legitimate and salutary . . . We must not only allow but even encourage wise men, provided of course they are fit to do so, to take part in public affairs.'[207] Those reading these lines in 1868 could not have suspected that barely three years later Barni would have become a fully committed activist in France, both in the republican politics of Amiens and eventually as his town's elected representative in the National Assembly in Paris. Barni's political career in France proved relatively brief; his national and local mandates lasted only five years before he was forced to abandon them because of his failing health.

---

[203] *Ce que doit être la République*, 18–19.
[204] Barni, Jules, *Manuel Républicain* (Paris: Germer Baillière, 1872), 23.   [205] Ibid., 24.
[206] Ibid., 25.   [207] Barni, *La morale dans la démocratie*, 124–5.

Yet the significance of these years, in both personal and political terms, was enormous. Politically Barni was the 'spiritual guide'[208] of a very small elite who planned and organized the republicanization of Amiens—and more broadly the penetration of republicanism into the department of the Somme—in the crucial years between 1871 and 1877. In national politics he witnessed the difficult years of Ordre Moral between 1873 and 1877, and played his part in the parliamentary battle against monarchist, imperialist, and clerical forces in the National Assembly. The outcome of this struggle, which the republicans won in the elections of the summer of 1877, was decisively influenced by a municipalist propaganda organization conceived by Barni in 1870, the Société d'Instruction Républicaine. In each of these respects Barni's activities thus demonstrated the practical value of his intellectual approach to politics. In personal terms, finally, these years represented the culmination of Barni's long and often painful battle against political authoritarianism. He was able to satisfy his individual ambitions to some extent, and emphatically demonstrated that a 'sage' could play a positive role in public life. Most importantly, perhaps, Barni's public activities also displayed considerable congruence with his own philosophical conception of integrity. When put to the test, the neo-Kantian philosopher's public life remained entirely true to his moral theory of republican action.

Barni's return to political and intellectual activity in France in fact pre-dated the downfall of the Second Empire. In late 1869 his name appeared in Paris among a list of future contributors to the *Revue Républicaine*, edited by the radical republican publisher Lucien Le Chevalier; the names announced also included such prominent left-wing figures as Louis Blanc, Flourens, Lissagaray, and Ranc.[209] Barni was clearly well-connected in the radical circles of the republican movement, and in the immediate aftermath of the Franco-Prussian war he helped found the extreme left-wing group in the National Assembly, along with other glorious exiles such as Hugo, Quinet, Louis Blanc, Schoelcher, and Ledru-Rollin.[210] After 1871 Barni became one of the leading figures in the 'Union Républicaine' parliamentary group, which eventually became the dominant voice of Gambettist opportunism in the 1870s.[211] His letters to his friend Frédéric Petit, the future mayor of Amiens, indicate that he was in frequent and regular contact with Gambetta between 1871 and 1876.[212]

But it was Amiens which offered the real launching-pad for his return to French public life. Again in the final years of the Second Empire Barni, although still nominally based in Geneva, became closely involved with a

---

[208] Pierre Lenormand, 'Le mouvement républicain dans la Somme au début de la IIIe République (1870–1877)', *Revue Historique* (January–March 1946), 10.

[209] A copy of the notice announcing the publication of the *Revue Républicaine*, dated December 1869, is in the Bibliothèque Nationale, LC2 3240.

[210] Grévy, *La République des opportunistes*, 102.   [211] Ibid., 221.

[212] For example, his letter to Petit of 31 January 1872; in Archives Frédéric Petit, Correspondance Barni. I am very grateful to Monsieur Lucien Debary (Auberchicourt), the custodian of the Petit family archives, for supplying me with copies of Barni's letters to his friend Frédéric Petit.

small group of influential republican leaders, most notably René Goblet and Frédéric Petit, both of whom would serve as mayors of Amiens in the early decades of the Third Republic. In February 1869 Petit launched *Le Progrès de la Somme*, a newspaper which provided the intellectual focal point of republican activism in the department in the early decades of the Third Republic.[213] Barni was among the initial set of shareholders, and wrote the occasional column on national and international political issues; more importantly he made regular financial contributions to keep the newspaper alive in its infant years.[214] *Le Progrès de la Somme* was suspended by the Ordre Moral authorities in 1874, despite vigorous protests from Barni and Goblet. When publication was allowed to resume in January 1876, Barni was again one of the leading financial contributors.[215]

Amiens also provided the immediate focus for Barni's activism on the front of republican political sociability. In October 1869 he founded the Cercle de l'Union Ouvrière, which under the name of 'Circle of the Don' became the leading agent and promoter of working-class republicanism in the Somme. Issues of the *Progrès de la Somme* were regularly read out and discussed at the Circle's meetings, along with pamphlets and propaganda material produced within the republican movement. Barni again assumed the role of spiritual leader in the early stages, even though his attendance of meetings tailed off after he assumed his local and national electoral mandates in Amiens and Paris. The Circle's activities provoked the concern and hostility of conservative forces in the department throughout the 1870s, and the association was officially banned by the Prefect of the Somme in the summer of 1877.[216]

His prominence as a republican intellectual in both Paris and Amiens made it extremely likely that Barni would be drawn into the electoral field during the 1870s. The opening up of democratic politics in the early Third Republic, and particularly the progressive shift in effective institutional power from the executive to the 'republican' legislature, provided opportunities for ambitious and well-connected figures like Barni to make their mark on the local and national scene. Indeed in a way the Genevan sage was a typical representative of the 'new social strata' whose advent Gambetta heralded in the 1870s. But success in the electoral arena was no easy matter, as Barni appreciated only too well; he had not forgotten his humiliating experiences at the hands of universal suffrage under the Second Republic. While he still firmly believed that the mass vote was the best guarantee against social revolution, the years of the Second Empire had inoculated him against automatically assuming a correlation between universal suffrage and republican political outcomes.

This prudence was to be further justified in the 1870s with the electoral revival of Bonapartism under the banner of the 'Appeal to the People'. After May 1873 republican electoral successes were also frustrated by the successive Ordre Moral governments which, until the fateful elections of summer 1877,

[213] Lenormand, 'Le mouvement républicain dans la Somme', 11.
[214] Letter of Barni to Frédéric Petit, 21 December 1876, in Archives Frédéric Petit.
[215] Ibid., 28.   [216] *Le Progrès de la Somme* (25 June 1877).

deployed a battery of repressive measures to prevent republican candidates from being returned in national and local elections.[217] But some of the problems faced by the republicans were of their own making. Gambetta's strategy of drawing conservatives and liberals into the republican camp, when successful, provoked tensions between opportunist converts to the republican cause and established—and often long-suffering—loyalists such as Barni himself. A further source of intra-republican division was the personal and ideological differences among republican leaders; when not adequately reconciled such tensions could provoke serious and politically damaging rifts within local republican leaderships across France.

At a personal level Barni was aware of his limitations as a candidate. Although he was brought up in Amiens he had not lived there since the days of the Second Republic, and he well appreciated that he needed to work hard to establish himself among the voters of the Somme.[218] In this context he also understood that his ideological profile needed to be re-adjusted in light of the changed political circumstances of the early 1870s; this particularly required placating the conservative instincts of the French electorate. At the same time, however, this shift had to be accomplished while remaining true to the core republican principles cherished by the party faithful. Police surveillance records of the Circle of the Don's discussions in 1871 and 1872 illustrate how Barni succeeded in this delicate balancing act.

During his election campaigns in Amiens in late 1871 and summer 1872 the former Genevan exile was generally supported by the Circle. At a meeting held in January 1872 the presiding officer praised Barni and stressed: 'we must support him'; the local candidate was especially commended for his active presence on the ground.[219] After his successful election in June 1872 a special meeting of the Circle was held to celebrate Barni's victory; the 'calumnies' against him in the local conservative press were vigorously denounced.[220] His image as a member of the republican left was still sufficiently strong in early July 1872 for one member of the Circle to assert that 'Louis Blanc and Barni were wonderful men and we need many like them in the Chamber'.[221]

By August, however, the honeymoon had apparently ended. At a meeting of the Circle one radical activist lambasted the attitude of the republican leadership in Paris and Amiens: 'Gambetta, Goblet and Barni are all just scoundrels and this is typical of the race of lawyers.'[222] Another activist even suggested putting out an article in the *Progrès de la Somme* against Goblet and Barni, 'given that since they are in the Chamber they have not stopped betraying the

[217] See Grubb, Alan, *The Politics of Pessimism* (Newark: University of Delaware Press, 1996).

[218] Barni letter to Edgar Quinet, 11 January 1872, BN 20781.

[219] Report of Police Commissioner to Prefect of Somme, 4 January 1872; Archives Départementales de la Somme (hereafter ADS), 99 M 80952.

[220] Report of Police Commissioner to Prefect of Somme, 13 June 1872, ADS 99 M 80952.

[221] Report of Police Commissioner to Prefect of Somme, 5 July 1872, ADS 99 M 80952.

[222] Report of Police Commissioner to Prefect of Somme, 9 August 1872, ADS 99 M 80952. Unlike the other two republicans named Barni was not a lawyer, but he had clearly sounded like one to some members of the Circle.

people'.[223] Barni's position had recovered sufficiently by September 1872, however, for a member of the Circle to suggest that he should be put forward as the next republican candidate for the mayorship of Amiens.[224] A month later the records of all the republican deputies of the Somme were reviewed by the president of the Circle. One man was especially singled out: in the president's estimate of all the elected representatives 'there is only one of them who is good, a true and loyal friend, and that is Barni'.[225] The Amiens deputy had clearly secured the allegiance of local republican enthusiasts, and the Circle remained entirely devoted to him thereafter until his political retirement in 1877.

Ultimately the real problem was not whether he would be appealing enough for republican activists—his credentials as a victim of Bonapartism could hardly be bettered—but whether he would appear sufficiently moderate and pragmatic for the Somme electorate. Barni's leadership of the anti-militarist Ligue in the late 1860s, and his known connections with radical republicans in Paris in the final years of the Second Empire, provided his conservative opponents with ample material to challenge his candidacy for the National Assembly in the early 1870s. During his unsuccessful campaigns in the Seine in July 1871 and the Somme in January 1872, Barni faced strong criticism from anti-republican quarters for his 'radical' political sympathies in the Second Empire era. Particularly wounding was the allegation that he had been a member of the First International; the Ligue was frequently, and often deliberately, lumped together with Marx's organization. As his accomplice Goblet explained to his somewhat discouraged friend in early 1872: 'it is clear that your opponents have very cleverly used against you this slanderous confusion.'[226]

Barni's strategic response to this line of attack was to suppress any reference to his anti-militarist activities in his own campaigning material. In his election posters in 1871 and 1872 he described himself not as a professor of philosophy, although he had held this position for ten years in Geneva, but as 'former Inspector General of Public Instruction': a post he had occupied for barely a month in early 1871.[227] The point was clearly to stress his 'French' roots, tenuous as they were, in contrast with his 'internationalist' experiences and affiliations. Indeed his long years in Switzerland were mentioned only in so far as they had allowed him to sample the 'living reality' of republican institutions in Geneva.[228] Barni also went out of his way to emphasize his attachment to 'republican order'. Workers had to be turned away from 'these deceptive theories which today mislead so many minds: communism, or what we now call collectivism'.[229]

---

[223] Report of Police Commissioner to Prefect of Somme, 9 August 1872, ADS 99 M 80952.

[224] Report of Police Commissioner to Prefect of Somme, 30 September 1872, ADS 99 M 80952.

[225] Report of Police Commissioner to Prefect of Somme, 4 October 1872, ADS 99 M 80952.

[226] Letter dated 26 January 1872, quoted in Lenormand, 'Le mouvement républicain dans la Somme', 19.

[227] Barni election poster for January 1872 election to National Assembly. ADS, 99 M 80768.

[228] Election poster issued by the electoral committee of the Union Républicaine de la Somme, 25 December 1871. ADS, 99 M 80768.

[229] *Ce que doit être la République*, 23.

But his republicanism was not merely a defence of the economic status quo. It offered wide-ranging change, but this change was defined in terms of cultural transformation, especially in the field of education, rather than political innovation. One of his principal election slogans in 1872 was thus 'to enlighten, moralize, pacify'.[230] Ideological temperance, in sum, was presented as a key virtue but by no means at the expense of republican justice. The election brochure put out by the Union Républicaine de la Somme for the June 1872 legislative by-election in Amiens, which would see Barni finally win his seat in the National Assembly, described the republicanism of the former Genevan exile in these terms: ' a man of principles, he has always shown himself to be both moderate and determined in the defence of republican ideas.'[231]

Even though he enjoyed a number of successes as a parliamentarian, most notably his appointment to the presidency of the parliamentary Commission on Higher Education in 1876, Barni's legislative career in Paris never entirely took off after 1872. This was mainly because political conditions at the centre long remained inimical to a man of his political loyalties and ideological inclinations. He also suffered from increasingly long bouts of illness which kept him away from Versailles, for example during much of 1875.[232] Although he recovered sufficiently to contest again, and comfortably win, his Amiens seat in February 1876, his personal health began to decline seriously just at the moment when the republicans were preparing their final assault on conservative forces in the summer of 1877. During his first spell as a legislator (1872–6) the government was in the hands of Ordre Moral administrations which were deeply hostile to republican activists such as himself. Indeed Barni spent most of his early years as a deputy campaigning against Albert de Broglie government's energetic attempts to restrict republican political activities, notably by curbing freedom of expression. In late 1872 Barni thus protested against the government's refusal to allow a public meeting of the Union Républicaine in Amiens.[233]

Despite such problems these difficult years were put to effective use by Barni, and it was during this period that his republican municipalist doctrine assumed a concrete shape in Amiens. Along with his accomplices Petit and Goblet, Barni clearly appreciated that the republicanization of the town, and eventually the department, was contingent upon the development of political and associational activity at grass-roots level. To this end they regularly organized meetings of the Somme republican leadership with mayors of the department who were sympathetic to the republican cause.[234] Barni also systematically campaigned against the Ordre Moral government's attempts to control the nomination of mayors. The republican position across France was that mayors should be elected by their municipal councils and not centrally

---

[230] Ibid.   [231] *Notice biographique sur M. Jules Barni*, 34.
[232] Barni letter to Mme.Edgar Quinet, 22 November 1875, BN NAF 15511.
[233] *Le Progrès de la Somme* (5 November 1872).
[234] For an account of one such meeting, see *Le Progrès de la Somme* (13 May 1873).

appointed; and although he failed to prevent the adoption and implementation of the Broglie law on the appointment of mayors, in 1874 Barni took this
opportunity to reaffirm his political commitment to 'the most absolute decentralization'.[235]

Most crucially, Barni was one of the architects, along with Frédéric Petit, of
the capture of the Amiens municipal council by a republican majority in 1874.
In the elections of November 1874 the republican list won 22 of the 34 seats
on the council. Goblet and Petit were among those candidates who received
the most votes, and Barni came in fourth position, another sweet revenge for
a man who had so often been humiliated by universal suffrage.[236] Barni's
attendance of council meetings after 1874 was not assiduous but he played a
distinct role in the development of secular education in Amiens. In August
1875 his proposal to increase the salaries of primary schoolteachers in Amiens
and its suburbs was adopted; a year later he initiated and presided over the first
prize-giving ceremony for local state primary schools.[237] However, he did not
live to see the implementation of his dream of an equivalent public ceremony
to the Genevan 'Schools' Festival' in Amiens; it was left to his friend Petit to
inaugurate the first such gathering in 1880.[238]

Creating the Republic from Below: Barni's Leadership of The Société d'Instruction Républicaine

Asked to highlight the main aspects of Barni's character during their years of
exile in Geneva, Edgar Quinet stressed his friend's stoicism and apparent
placidity:

He resembles in every way the philosophers in the times of the Caesars. He would never
compromise on his duty; but do not expect from him either enthusiasm, or activism, or
warmth of sentiments. Calm and honest by nature he endures, he resigns himself, like
the philosopher under the Roman emperors.[239]

Quinet was entirely mistaken—and more than a touch churlish—to portray
Barni as an impractical fatalist. On the contrary, the neo-Kantian philosopher
believed in the necessity of intellectual intervention in the political arena and
indeed also thought that such actions could yield positive changes. Although
his local and national electoral mandates yielded concrete and durable
results, it was probably through his leadership of the Société d'Instruction
Républicaine (SIR) during the 1870s that Barni made his most telling, and least
acknowledged, contribution to the political and intellectual founding of the
Third Republic. This organization was established by Barni during the Franco-
Prussian war as a means of promoting republican and patriotic values in the
provinces. Evidence of its close association with the new republican order was

---

[235] *Le Progrès de la Somme* (16 December 1873).
[236] *Mémorial d'Amiens* (23 November 1874).   [237] Dide, *Jules Barni*, 227.
[238] Ibid., 230.   [239] Quoted in Du Pasquier, *Edgar Quinet en Suisse*, 92.

the insertion of the SIR's statutes in the *Bulletin Officiel de la République Française*, the official publication of the provincial delegation of the Government of National Defence.[240]

Briefly interrupted by the French capitulation and the Paris Commune, the association's activities resumed in November 1871 in Tours. The war having ended, its main aim was to promote public awareness of republicanism by the organization of public conferences; the publication of a regular journal; and the production and dissemination of brochures and pamphlets.[241] Under Barni's direction the association soon moved its headquarters to Paris, first to Rue Saint-Jacques, then to Rue Sainte-Catherine d'Enfer; another office was later opened at the Rue des Saint-Pères. Alongside its President Barni, the SIR bureau consisted of Vice-President Jules Cazot, one of the leaders the republican movement in the Midi,[242] and two Secretaries, Narcisse Leven and Auguste Marais.

A Central Committee of ten to fifteen members also functioned through most of the 1870s; among the initial group were republican notables such as Henri Martin, Pierre Joigneaux, Henri Brisson, Eugène Despois, and Eugène Spuller. Eugène Pelletan was also a member. General Assemblies were regularly held in Paris, normally under the presidency of an eminent figure of the republican party.[243] The SIR forged links with a number of leading republican associations across France; indeed one of the keys to its effectiveness was its willingness to cooperate with, and benefit from the resources of, like-minded political, cultural, and civic organizations. Thus in the early 1870s the SIR merged its assets and distribution networks with those of the *Bibliothèque Démocratique*, an alliance which gave its publications an immediate opening into the audience of its older and more established partner.[244] In addition, close links were set up with departmental branches of the Société pour l'Instruction Elémentaire, an older republican society set up by Lazare Carnot in the Revolutionary era and later presided over by his son Hippolyte; its distribution networks also proved effective in conveying SIR brochures across provincial France.[245] A similar relationship was forged with the influential Ligue de l'Enseignement;[246] its founder Jean Macé later served on the SIR

---

[240] See *Bulletin Officiel de la République Française* (Bordeaux, 4 January 1871), which noted that 'the society we are referring to has no official character, but it pursues an objective which is of such importance for the future of the French Republic that we feel we should publish its statutes'.

[241] For further details, see the 1872 circular letter of the Central Committee of the SIR, and the statutes of the organization, in Barni, *L'instruction républicaine*, 27–35.

[242] Jules Cazot was Secretary-General at the Ministry of the Interior in the Government of National Defence (1870–1), also serving as representative of the Ministry at the delegation of Tours. Between 1871 and 1876 he represented the department of the Gard in the National Assembly, after which he was elected to the Senate. In 1879 he served as Minister of Justice and took an active role in justifying republican policy against religious congregations.

[243] For a report on the 1876 meeting, held at the Cirque d'Hiver, see *Le Patriote* (13 August 1876), 44.

[244] The director of the *Bibliothèque Démocratique* collection was Victor Poupin; leading republican patrons included Arago, Barthélémy Saint-Hilaire, Michelet, Quinet, Simon, Gambetta, and Ferry.

[245] Archives de la Préfecture de Police, Paris, BA–1497 (Société d'Instruction Républicaine), (hereafter APP–1497), report dated 2 March 1874.

[246] APP–1497, report dated 21 August 1877.

Central Committee.[247] Provincial republican newspapers were also regularly used to carry advertisements of SIR pamphlets; orders were addressed to the Paris office, where the bulk of the society's literature was kept.[248]

Until the end of 1876 Barni was the driving force behind the SIR's activities. As he put it in a letter to Frédéric Petit in early 1872, he was 'very busy with the affairs of the Société d'Instruction Républicaine'.[249] He directly oversaw the development of the organization in his own department after 1871, not merely by setting up local branches but also by securing approval of the SIR's political and civic objectives by the Union Républicaine of the Somme. Partly on the basis of his experiences with Gambetta during the Franco-Prussian war, Barni saw that the development of political agitation and propaganda across France was a critical factor in the construction of a republican civic consciousness;[250] indeed the development of popular political education was viewed by Barni as 'a question of life or death'.[251] Although hampered considerably by military authorities—many departments remained under martial law in France for several years after the Franco-Prussian war—as well as by local administrative and judicial institutions, which sometimes prosecuted its members, the SIR was able to establish an effective network of offices and correspondents throughout France by the mid-1870s.

According to a police report in September 1874, many republican deputies and general councillors were affiliated to the national organization, and a sizeable number of offices had opened at departmental and local levels; the Versailles branch was seen as one of the most active. The Central Committee also kept up a regular correspondence with local organizations, notably in such departments as the Somme, Aisne, Côte d'Or, Vosges, Seine-et-Oise, Oise, and Allier. The same report also gave details of booksellers which stocked SIR publications; in the department of the Oise alone seven such suppliers were identified.[252]

Barni himself kept in close touch with these developments through his personal correspondence with local republican leaders and intellectuals, notably Louis Mie, Edmond Hugues, Edmond Magnier, Courdaveaux, Louis Bresson, Eugène Véron, Ballue, and Eugène Garcin.[253] At the same time the national political climate initially made it very difficult for the SIR to achieve some of its primary goals. For example, due to adverse political circumstances between 1873 and 1876, the SIR was unable to organize public conferences to spread the republican gospel; local prefects almost invariably denied permission for such meetings to be held. Furthermore, its newspaper Le Patriote was banned several times between November 1871 and June 1873, at which point a ruling of the Seine administrative tribunal decreed its definitive suppression.[254]

[247] APP–1497, report dated 1 August 1881.
[248] In a ground-floor room at the Rue Sainte-Catherine d'Enfer office, which was on the second floor, according to a well-informed police report; APP–1497 3 July 1877.
[249] Letter of Barni to Frédéric Petit, 4 February 1872, in Archives Frédéric Petit.
[250] Barni, L'instruction républicaine, 13–14.   [251] Ce que doit être la République, 16.
[252] APP–1497, report dated 18 September 1874.   [253] Dide, Jules Barni, 217.
[254] APP–1497, report dated 3 August 1876.

The only avenue left open to the SIR for the development of republican propaganda activities, therefore, was the publication of its own brochures and pamphlets.[255] Barni assumed this intellectual and ideological challenge with relish. Between 1872 and 1877, 71 pamphlets were issued by the SIR in two separate series: 32 publications of 25–35 pages each and a series of 39 shorter brochures of approximately half that length.[256] This entire literary project was conceived by Barni; he not only wrote many of the pamphlets himself but also commissioned and often directly oversaw the production of the others.[257] There were three particular strengths to the SIR literature: the detail and sophistication of its attacks against the enemies of republicanism, most notably the Bonapartists;[258] the sober and moderate tone with which the concerns of the peasants were addressed; and finally, and perhaps most significantly, the strong emphasis on the local political underpinnings of the republican civic order, notably the role of communal and municipal institutions.[259]

The doctrine of republican municipalism, which Barni had done much to promote in practice through his political activities in Amiens, was thus also given a wider ideological platform in France through the literary output of the SIR. Indeed in broader terms the organization's contribution to the dissemination of republicanism in provincial and rural France in the 1870s was enormous. The SIR's elasticity allowed its political aims and propaganda literature to be adopted by other institutions of republican sociability. It was thus frequently the case that a meeting of a republican association would begin or conclude with a discussion of a 'democratic pamphlet'; many of the SIR's pamphlets became widely known in local republican circles through this practice. But the SIR literature did not merely preach to the converted. It was also used by local republican leaders to spread their political message and most importantly to stigmatize their religious, monarchist, and imperialist opponents.[260]

After 1875 this role was accentuated and formalized, and in the campaigns for the legislative elections of 1876 and 1877 the SIR's propaganda material was used extensively throughout France. In 1876 *Le Patriote*, which resumed publication after the republican victory in the legislative elections, announced that more than a million of its brochures had been distributed throughout France during the parliamentary election campaign.[261] In the crucial political battle of the summer 1877, when the republicans challenged President MacMahon's attempt to assert his authority over the National Assembly, the

[255] Grévy, *La République des opportunistes*, 132–3.

[256] Almost the entire collection of pamphlets is held at the Bibliothèque Nationale in Paris, LB57–1300.

[257] A point made at Barni's funeral by his friend and colleague Auguste Marais, the SIR secretary. See *Le Progrès de la Somme* (10 July 1878).

[258] Barni, Jules, *L'Appel au Peuple* (Paris: Le Chevalier, 1874).

[259] This literature is more extensively analysed in Hazareesingh, Sudhir, 'The *Société d'Instruction Républicaine* and the Propagation of Civic Republicanism in Provincial and Rural France 1870–1877', *Journal of Modern History*, 71 (1999), 271–307.

[260] For the example of Sadi Carnot in the Côte d'Or, see Harismendy, *Sadi Carnot*, 164–5.

[261] APP–1497, report dated 3 August 1876.

SIR's propaganda and organizational networks again proved crucial, indeed, so much so that the Minister of the Interior banned the Parisian organization in August 1877.[262] It was not surprising, in the light of such developments, that a police report later conceded that the organization could legitimately claim to have rendered 'the most eminent services to the republican cause' during these critical years.[263] The conservative press agreed with this evaluation while of course deploring the outcome. An article in *Le Gaulois* in the early 1870 thus denounced Barni and the SIR which 'under the disguise of conferences and education is but a vast and most dangerous political society'.[264]

By a cruel irony Barni was unable directly to witness the political climax of all his efforts to promote the republican cause in France. Already seriously ill by the end of 1876, he was forced to abandon his Amiens parliamentary seat in the elections of 1877. He retired from active political life in the summer of that year, and left Paris for the peace and tranquillity of Mers-les-Bains, where he died in July 1878. His funeral in Amiens, which had just witnessed the triumphant re-election of the republican list in the municipal elections of February 1878, was the occasion of a remarkable display of civic and patriotic fervour. A true freethinker and Kantian republican to the last, Barni explicitly forbade any attempt to tempt him into a late conversion to Catholicism on his deathbed. No religious rites were performed at his burial in the Madeleine cemetery;[265] despite the pleas of some of Barni's relatives, Barni's wife honoured his wishes to be given a civil burial.[266]

Conclusion: Barni's Multiple Contributions to French Republicanism

'He passes for a moderate and sensible republican but he is not a bashful one.'[267] Barni's personal courage and integrity earned him the affection of his friends, won the admiration of his colleagues, and, always a mark of stature in an intellectual, forced the respect of many of his adversaries. Indeed the first epithet which springs to mind when summing up his life and political itinerary is integrity. The different elements of his republican politics blended together almost seamlessly, as we shall note below; but what made Barni a particularly compelling figure was the extent to which he strove to remain faithful to the entire range of republican values he cherished. Thus his public stances, both in opposition and when the republicans were in power, remained broadly congruent with his theoretical conceptions of politics. The republican ethical code which he publicly professed was also broadly respected in his own private life. When this stern sense of integrity made it necessary for hard choices to be made, Barni unfalteringly made them. This

---

[262] APP, BA—946 (Barni) Minister of Interior to Prefect of Police, letter dated 22 August 1877.
[263] APP–1497, undated report (probably late 1878/early 1879).
[264] *Le Gaulois* (31 August 1872).   [265] *Le Progrès de la Somme* (10 July 1878).
[266] *Le Gaulois* (8 July 1878).   [267] APP–946, police report dated 3 January 1872.

was perhaps more than anything else what earned him the admiration of his fellow republicans. When, in typically understated fashion, the positivist review *La Philosophie Positive* described him as an 'honest man',[268] it was in this respect giving voice to a widely shared view among French republicans.

Barni was driven by an implacable sense of the justness of his cause, a feeling which often helped him in times of political difficulty. As he prepared for the electoral campaign which was to lead to his election to the National Assembly in the early 1870s he wrote to his friend Petit:

Our opponents will wage a relentless war against me, and they are as powerful as they are wicked. Never mind, we must face up to the struggle and not despair of victory.[269]

At the same time his commitment to his principles often caused Barni great personal difficulties. His decision to refuse the oath of allegiance to Napoleon III cost him his academic post in France after the Bonapartist coup; similarly his belief in the overriding value of truth and integrity eventually damaged his relations with the Geneva Academy during the 1860s and compromised his political career in the immediate aftermath of the Franco-Prussian war. But the reverse was also the case. Barni's integrity often proved a source of strength. For example, there was no doubt that his successful political entrenchment in Amiens after 1872 was largely due to the overwhelming sense of respect he enjoyed among local republican activists and voters. Unlike some republicans of the 'opportunist' variety, Barni achieved this privileged position without reneging on his moral and political values: an achievement in itself for an elected republican politician during these troubled and volatile years.

A further distinctive feature of Barni's republicanism was the central position occupied by ethical principles within its theoretical framework. There was a strong moral underpinning to all varieties of French republicanism during the nineteenth century, but the notable characteristic of its idealist strands was that their entire theory of politics was anchored in moral intuitions about human nature and society. As a neo-Kantian Barni very much epitomized this approach. His belief that moral considerations lay at the heart of politics shone through in two key ways: in his own intellectual construction of republicanism, which developed from a moral theory in the 1840s, 1850s, and early 1860s into a full-blown conception of political action in the late 1860s and 1870s; and in his repeated emphasis on individual rights and duties as the defining pillar of republican politics.

As with his sense of integrity, Barni's philosophical individualism could at time prove a source of weakness. Thus it is hard to deny that his social philosophy, although progressive in its inspiration, was undermined by his consistent reluctance to treat the issue of working-class poverty as a collective problem. Like most of his liberal republican contemporaries he believed that the solution to the problem of worker alienation would come through

[268] J.de Bagnaux, review of *La Morale dans la Démocratie*, *La Philosophie Positive* (March–April 1869), 218.

[269] Barni letter to Petit, 19 January 1872; Archives Frédéric Petit.

education and enlightened paternalism; and in this respect even the events of 1870–1 in Paris did not cause a fundamental reappraisal of this thinking. His limited views on the role of women were also inconsistent with his emphasis on the republican value of equality. In all probability his attitude on this question was shaped more by his bourgeois instincts, not to say prejudices, than by his critical intellectual faculties. But Barni's individualism, and indeed his moralism more generally, was on balance a greater source of strength. It allowed him successfully to articulate the central messages in the republican ideological platform in the late Second Empire and early Third Republic and in particular to stress that republican politics was above all a matter of cultivating and adhering to moral principles: developing individual education, promoting patriotism and respect for the law, and protecting individual rights. This moralism was arguably the defining element in the republicans' political triumph over their monarchical and imperialist rivals during the 1870s, and in this sense it might be said that Barni's explicitly articulated political moralism, with its weaknesses and inconsistencies no less than in its strengths, spoke for the entire republican mainstream.

In more general terms Barni's political thought is striking for its attempt to synthesize different intellectual elements into a coherent whole. Of the different forces which cemented his republicanism, the most significant by far, as well the most original and creative, was his neo-Kantianism. Personally Barni closely identified with Kant, and the latter's austere moralism was a decisive influence on many specific choices he made throughout his life. Kant's stoicism also provided a constant source of comfort when events took a disobliging turn; Barni's French visitors thus often noticed how precious a companion Kant proved during the difficult years of his Genevan exile. More broadly, the writings of the German idealist philosopher provided his French disciple with the intellectual foundations upon which the latter's political thought came to rest. It was through Kant that Barni became a freethinker and eventually a republican; it was Kant also who helped him define the public and private virtues which were the essence of the republican good life; Kant still who reinforced Barni's sense that republicanism was a doctrine concerned primarily with individual empowerment rather than the collective good; and Kant above all who spurred his thinking about the democratic underpinnings of international peace. This Kantian bedrock also provided the essential element of continuity between the different phases of Barni's political thought; it was the link which held together his early preoccupations with individual morality, the later development of his systematic moral philosophy, and his transition to a fully fledged theory of politics by the late 1860s.

It is in this particular respect that the claim that Barni was a follower of Victor Cousin's 'eclecticism' has to be decisively rejected. Barni, it is true, drew from a wide range of intellectual influences in assembling his political thought, and was in this superficial sense a disciple of his former *maître* at the Ecole Normale. But Barni was never as shallow as Cousin and was always at the same time much more consistent; he also never showed the craven adoration of power which was Cousin's hallmark. Unlike Cousin, finally, Barni also went beyond the philosophy of those from whom he borrowed. Kant may have been his intellectual master, but Barni was no slavish devotee. As we saw earlier, his own writings on international peace clarified and developed the lines of argument laid down by the author of *Perpetual Peace* and fortified his message with many elements borrowed from Rousseau. In this context another important element of unity in Barni's political thought is worth underlining again: the congruence between his 'international' political theory and his conception of the republican good life within France. Not only was there no fundamental discontinuity between the two, but Barni drew on each sphere in order to develop his views on the other. His ethical principles and his theory of republican democracy reinforced his irenic views, and the notion of an international federation of peaceful states helped him to crystallize his thoughts about decentralization and republican citizenship.

Another way in which Barni was representative of his republican generation was through his years away from France during the 1860s. Like his republican colleagues who were scattered around the cities of Europe during the 1850s and 1860s, most notably London and Brussels, he experienced the full range of trials and tribulations of exile during his stay in Geneva. Unlike most French exiles, however, Barni was materially very comfortable in Geneva. At the same time the place aroused rather mixed emotions in him; he loved the physical environment, for example, but did not seem to have been especially enamoured of the local inhabitants. Professionally his relations with the Geneva Academy began well enough but soon deteriorated to a level of frosty formality; his Swiss hosts probably did not relish the presence in their midst of a man who became one of the leading figures in European anti-militarism by the late 1860s.

The most intriguing aspect, and also the most difficult to evaluate, of Barni's years away from France was their intellectual influence on him. At one level he was already well prepared to lead a cosmopolitan cultural existence before 1860: Geneva was perhaps even a natural home for a Frenchman of Italian descent who also happened to be fluent in German. It is clear that his Genevan exile provided a welcome opportunity to open Barni's thoughts in new directions and to test his theories and intuitions about politics against a novel range of experiences. Indeed his years in Switzerland proved fertile for his ideological development despite the fact that he had to underplay them after 1871 for political reasons.

It was in Geneva that his political thought matured into a comprehensive ethical system by the late 1860s; in Geneva that he learned his first real lessons in political activism as President of the Ligue; and in Geneva that he saw the practical demonstration of the ideals of republican education and decentralized citizenship. Finally, it is clear that the Swiss context was crucial to the elaboration of Barni's greatest practical contribution to French politics in the 1870s, the Société d'Instruction Républicaine. The SIR was the domestic French equivalent of the Ligue in terms of its broad aims—the republicanization of politics; constitutional structure—a loose confederal alliance of like-minded groups; and organizational methods—most notably the vital part played by propaganda activity. It is even arguable that the synthetic and open conception of republicanism which the SIR advocated during the 1870s was largely derived from Barni's appreciation of Swiss republican practice, in which federal unity was well reconciled with local diversity and all social groups were included in the ideological mythology of the republican state. The Swiss model of patriotism, with its emphasis on civic rather than ethnic or nationalistic values, was also clearly one of the principal inspirations for the SIR's conception of French patriotism in the 1870s.

Ultimately, however, one of the key measures of an intellectual's life is the extent to which his voice carried not only conviction but also influence. Barni's writings enjoyed uneven success. Although his translations of Kant had become authoritative in French philosophical circles by the late Second Empire, some of his scholarly works reached only a very small audience; his translation of Fichte's work thus sold only a few hundred copies. But Barni's intellectual influence was considerable in two distinct spheres. His mature writings shaped and often entirely anticipated the works of renowned French neo-Kantians such as Massol and especially Renouvier. The main themes in the latter's *Science de la Morale* (1869) thus offered striking parallels with Barni's own *Morale*, published a year earlier. In addition Barni's writings aimed at popular audiences were generally very well received. *La Morale dans la démocratie*, but also *Napoléon Ier* and especially the *Manuel Républicain*, not only drew widespread critical attention but were favourably commented upon well beyond the broad confines of the republican intellectual community and also beyond France.

But in sheer numerical terms it was probably the works Barni authored under the auspices of the Société d'Instruction Républicaine which enjoyed the largest readership; and as we have seen it was also through his leadership of this organization that Barni made his most decisive practical contribution to the emergence of republican institutions in France in the 1870s. His political life was not of course a catalogue of successive triumphs. Barni had his fair share of failures and even disasters, from his electoral routs under the Second Republic to the collapse of his anti-militarist crusade in the late 1860s in the wake of the Franco-Prussian war. Even after the Republic was constitutionally proclaimed in 1875 Barni was not spared; his attempt to secure election to the indirectly elected Senate foundered on the reefs of cynical political manipulation, a rejection which bitterly disappointed the republican philosopher.

Yet in his successes as well as his failures Barni always attempted to remain true to himself and to his ideals. Perhaps he should best be remembered as a model of republican civic virtue, not in any hagiographical sense but as a reminder that for all nineteenth-century republicans politics and morality were indissociable activities.

Conclusion:
The Origins of the Third Republic
Reconsidered

THROUGH its examination of the political thinking and practices of five founders of the Third Republic, this book is a tribute to the ideological breadth, creativity, and potency of nineteenth century French republicanism. It also highlights, from a historical point of view, the fact that the edifice of Third Republic was built with a variety of bricks and stones, and not of uniform material as many of its later historians claimed.

Breadth, above all: the conventional distinction between a rationalist, progressive, optimistic republicanism, and a religious, conservative, and pessimistic anti-republicanism—the mantra of all orthodox accounts of the origins of the Third Republic—appears misleading. Within the overall republican political tradition, within the same constitutionalist undercurrent or political generation, and even within the same individual, we have found not consensus, coherence, and linear teleological thinking, but instead tensions, conflicts, agonizing reappraisals, open-endedness, and uncertainty. But this diversity and complexity were both sources of strength; they suggest that republicanism was a powerful force in nineteenth century French and European politics through its capacity to hold together, in a potent synthesis, a range of ideological concepts and values whose coexistence might not at first sight have been thought possible.

Let us briefly examine some examples of this ideological range as it emerges from this book. Consider the case of liberalism and its interface with republicanism. John Gray has recently identified two liberal traditions in modern Western political thought. The first is the liberalism which pursues an ideal and universal form of life, embedded in human rights and rationalism; this is a tradition associated with Locke and Kant, and more recently with Rawls. The second is the liberalism of peaceful coexistence, diversity, and value pluralism, which originates in Hume and Hobbes and whose recent champions have included Michael Oakeshott, Isaiah Berlin, and Gray himself.[1] With its rhetorical claims to represent *la civilisation universelle* French republicanism has

---

[1] Gray, John, *Two Faces of Liberalism* (Oxford: Polity Press, 2000).

typically seen itself, and been seen, as a variant of the first liberalism and an emphatic adversary of the second, as illustrated by its continuing resistances to 'multiculturalism'.

But our portrayal of its nineteenth-century variants makes it much less obvious that French republicanism falls squarely within the first of these liberal traditions. Our five thinkers were ardent champions of the principle of diversity: in their multi-layered conception of territorial citizenship—local, national, and European; in their respect for, defence of, and in some cases conversion to religion; in their belief that culture was advanced by interaction and *mélange* rather than isolation and exclusion; and in the eclectic range of ideological sources, both within and outside France, which inspired their intellectual *démarche*. They refused, in short, to confuse their political thinking with the centralist, nationalist, and often parochial intellectual values of Jacobinism. Modern French republicanism, too, should not be reduced to the latter; and in its current quest for accommodating greater notions of diversity and toleration need not look to the American east coast for inspiration. It should rather seek to rediscover its own roots in the theorizations and practices of the republican good life in the nineteenth century.

The same sense of breadth—and creativity—comes across if we examine how our five thinkers made sense of a key concept such as 'progress'. Here too nineteenth-century French republicanism appears to reach across an apparently wide divide. In his *History of the Idea of Progress* Robert Nisbet makes a helpful distinction between two ways of thinking about progress in Western political thought between the mid-eighteenth and late nineteenth centuries. The first equates it with the development of individual freedom and has as both its means and ultimate end a state of peace: this notion of 'progress as freedom' underpins the writings of Condorcet, the American founding fathers, Adam Smith, Kant, and John Stuart Mill. The second strand sees progress in terms of conflict, and has as its end the legitimization of power and the creation of new political communities: this line begins with Rousseau and flourishes in a variety of ways in the nineteenth century with Saint-Simon, Comte, Hegel, and Marx.[2] As the nineteenth century drew to a close, both of these notions were to some extent undermined by the emergence of irrationalist doctrines which questioned the possibility and desirability of progress.[3]

Our five intellectuals were intimately familiar with all these different aspects of the problematic of progress, and sought to trace original solutions to the dilemmas it posed. The most creative in this respect was Littré, who took Comtian positivism's progressive laws of history-as-conflict and welded them to a narrative of the triumph of republicanism-as-freedom. In the case of Barni, too, opposing notions of progress were dialectically reconciled by transcending the dichotomy between Kant and Rousseau and positing a conception of

---

[2] Nisbet, Robert, *History of the Idea of Progress* (New York: Basic Books, 1980).

[3] On this theme see Burrow, John, *The Crisis of Reason: European Thought 1848–1914* (London and New Haven: Yale University Press, 2000).

republican progress which married the imperatives of peace with a realistic appreciation of the necessity of struggle, if necessary violent, to secure its achievement. Dupont-White maintained a lifelong belief in political progress despite the pessimistic mood which increasingly held sway among his conservative liberal friends in the 1860s and 1870s and his own scepticism about human nature, education, and the value of 'science'. Progress, for him, was essentially a matter of promoting law in society; his creativity was reflected in his championing of Mill's work while at the same time believing that individual freedoms should be promoted through the state rather than despite it. With Pelletan, in contrast, progress became a metaphor for the defence of individual political and intellectual rights against an oppressive and overbearing public authority. The only exception to this general trend was Vacherot, who seemed more disillusioned with progress, and some of his late writings in many ways anticipated the criticisms of 'rationalism' which had become commonplace in Western political thought by the early twentieth century, most notably a scepticism of the value of mass democracy and a yearning for the return to some form of 'elite' rule.

If we were to carry out the same exercise in relation to the concept of liberty, finally, we would again find that nineteenth century French republicanism contained elements of both 'negative' freedom—the absence of external interference on an agent—and 'positive' freedom—the ability of the agent to act. Despite the problems with its original formulation, Isaiah Berlin's classical distinction still offers an excellent basis for thinking about the problems of political liberty.[4] Our intellectuals were broadly united in thinking that freedom required on the one hand the definition of spheres of public and private life which the state could not encroach upon—for example, the institutions of the press and private property—and on the other hand the release of the talents and capacities of members of society in order to promote their self-realization. This synthesis between different notions of freedom broadly underpinned the foundation of the Third Republic and has remained at the heart of French public law ever since. In general terms it saw freedom as a substantive, as opposed to a merely formal, quality; in intellectual terms it tended to define freedom in the Kantian terms of autonomy rather than merely taking individual wishes as its premise; and above all for this republican tradition freedom was something to be achieved through the public sphere and particularly through political action. This was in contrast with the liberal view, defended by Constant and later Tocqueville, that freedom was an essentially 'private' notion. In all these respects the political thought of our five intellectuals helped to forge the decisive French republican synthesis of the later nineteenth century.

Perhaps the most striking illustration of the ideological breadth of nineteenth century French republicanism has come through our examination of

---

[4] Berlin, Isaiah, 'Two Concepts of Liberty', in *Four Essays on Liberty* (Oxford: Oxford University Press, 1969).

the intellectual influences which shaped our five thinkers. We all know that behind the disciple Littré was the towering figure of his master Auguste Comte. But this was just one example: Kantianism was the bedrock of Barni's political thought; early socialist influences continued to linger in the later political thinking of Littré, Pelletan, and Dupont-White; the Doctrinaires, especially Guizot, re-emerge as powerful prompts in the republicanism of Dupont-White and Vacherot; and Pelletan's thought was constantly permeated with the principles of Saint-Simonianism. Ideologically, this was very much a Republic open to all talents.

Real Worlds and Possible Alternatives

Living as we do in an age when politics seems to be much more concerned with interest than ideology—although this is of course an ideological position in itself—and where Marxist and post-modernist accounts have succeeded in instrumentalizing and relativizing the significance of political thought, it is perhaps hermeneutically difficult for us to recapture a political world in which concepts, principles, and symbols were defining sources of political identities. But it is incumbent upon us to try, for such indeed was the world to which our intellectuals belonged.

From this angle this book is a modest celebration of the potency of intellectual history. Through the lives and thoughts of our five thinkers we have witnessed how ideas could make a difference: to the lives of the intellectuals themselves, who all showed a willingness to sacrifice themselves to uphold them; to wider political communities, not only in France but in Europe, which were on many critical occasions mobilized and influenced by them; and above all to the very actions of the political elites who founded the Third Republic. Although their philosophical baggage was considerable, Thiers, Gambetta, Ferry, and the republican political leadership of the 1870s and 1880s were not systematic political thinkers in the sense that they did not attempt to devise comprehensive accounts of republican ideology. But Barni, Dupont-White, Littré, Pelletan, and Vacherot did, and the political founders of the Third Republic relied heavily on their works—and those of other intellectuals like them—to define their conceptions of the good life. Reading the works of our five thinkers provides critical insights into republican elite thinking at a key moment in the political history of modern France.

In its emphasis on period sources—books, articles, pamphlets, public and private utterances, and letters, as well as administrative sources held in public archives—the book has sought to reconstitute the authentic voices of the intellectuals and to make sense of their discourse in the precise political and ideological contexts of the time. It was particularly important not to allow the meaning of their writings to be distorted by ascribing values, intentions, and aspirations which were drawn from later periods or by philosophical frameworks which might reflect preoccupations other than their own. Immensely valuable in many other respects, contextuality thus also proved a useful barrier against teleology. This comes out very forcefully in what our analysis suggests about the principles which held the French political community together. The continuing allegiance of many republican thinkers to ideas of internationalism and cosmopolitanism indicates that the significance of 'nationalism' in the political thought of early Third Republic republicanism should be greatly relativized.

In the same spirit, the book suggests that the Third Republic could have developed in many different ways. The point has been very well made by Quentin Skinner: one of the key functions of the history of political thought is to highlight the existence of alternatives.[5] The variety of republicanisms on offer among our five intellectuals, and the connections and overlaps among them, point to a multiplicity of possible political outcomes after 1870. For example, the marginalization of 'socialist' concerns from early Third Republic republicanism was not an ideological a priori but rather a consequence of political actions on both sides of the socialist-republican divide in the period between 1870 and 1900. Put differently, there was nothing in the ideological value system of opportunism and radicalism which represented an intrinsic barrier to 'socialism'. Even a moderate figure such as Littré continued after 1871 to have, and to articulate publicly, strong sympathies for a certain evolutionary and pragmatic conception of 'socialism'. The divorce between socialists and republicans in the early Third Republic was thus essentially a matter of political contingency, not ideological necessity. John Plamenatz underscored the point in a wonderful little book written half a century ago: socialists and republicans, in his view, quarrelled 'for reasons that political theory cannot guess at, reasons that only the historian can discover'.[6]

The same point about possible alternatives can be made about the relationship between religion and republicanism. Like their fellow-republicans Barni, Dupont-White, Littré, Pelletan, and Vacherot can broadly be described as secular intellectuals in the sense that their overall project was to provide the intellectual foundations of a new morality of *laïcité* which was not grounded in Catholicism.[7] However these principles and sentiments have too often been presented through the oversimplifying prism of the battle between 'clericalism' and 'anticlericalism'. Behind the general philosophical attachment to secularism among republicans lurked a wide range of views and attitudes on religious questions, most notably the separation of Church and State, the erosion of religion and its progressive replacement by science, and indeed the very existence of God. And within this diversity there was also much appreciation for the historical role

---

[5] Skinner, *Liberty before Liberalism*, 116–17.

[6] Plamenatz, John, *The Revolutionary Movement in France 1815–1871* (London: Longmans, 1952), 170.

[7] The classic work on this subject is Weill, Georges, *Histoire de l'idée laïque en France au XIXe siècle* (Paris: Alcan, 1925). For good recent overviews of this question see Stock-Morton, Phyllis, *Moral Education for a Secular Society: The Development of Morale Laïque In Nineteenth Century France* (Albany: State University of New York Press, 1988); Mayeur, Jean-Marie, *La question laïque* (Paris: Fayard, 1997).

of the Church and a strong sense that republicans should respect and tolerate the religious beliefs of their fellow-citizens.

Anticlericalism, in sum, was simply one of the possible configurations of the relationship between republicans and Catholics, and the battles of the 1870–1905 period should not be represented as the logical conclusion of a polarized conflict between secular and religious views of the world in the nineteenth century. This polarization was a later—ideological—invention of the republicans themselves and of a French historiographical tradition which sought to play down the influence of spiritual and deist undercurrents within the republican movement.

The Relationship between Individual Lives and Political Trajectories

How far was the nineteenth-century republican intellectual a product of such variables as private morality, temperament, family background, occupation, professional networks, and territorial cultures? At the most personal level, of course, biographical differences can have very little impact on political thinking. That Littré led an ascetic existence, Vacherot dressed poorly, Pelletan was garrulous, Dupont-White a man of eccentric tastes and habits, and Barni loved cats and mountain walks might matter greatly to the historian's reconstruction of individual narratives but not at all to a quest to uncover connections between biography and political thought. At the same time, a number of possible links between the two spheres seem to suggest themselves at the end of this book.

One is the possible cross-over between social and political elitism. Dupont-White was aristocratic in manner and in temperament, and spent most of his life confined within the relatively narrow circles of Parisian bourgeois sociability; in a slightly different way, Vacherot did the same, although his elitist circles were more intellectual than social, being confined to the milieu of the Parisian academies and later the Comte de Paris. In contrast, Barni and Pelletan were more archetypal 'men of the people' who thrived in contact with the masses—and the provinces—and were the object of genuine adulation among the republican rank and file in the Somme, the Seine, and the Bouches-du-Rhône. Littré pulled off a typically neo-Comtian synthesis by combining institutional—and political—elitism with a genuine sense of empathy with people.

What of family background? Our five intellectuals were very different in terms of their origins, upbringing, and social, professional, and intellectual affiliations. Dupont-White's father Jean-Théodore moved in noble circles and identified with the monarchy before 1789, and his son Charles-Brook was brought up in a strictly traditionalist setting which profoundly marked his character and style. At the other end of this social spectrum, which in the late eighteenth and early nineteenth centuries was also a political one, was Etienne Vacherot, born of humble peasant stock and related through his wife to the revolutionary leader Georges Danton, and Emile Littré, whose bourgeois parents were devout Jacobins who worshipped the Revolution and especially the memory of Robespierre. Protestantism imbued the familial atmosphere in which the young Eugène Pelletan grew up, whereas Jules Barni's parents displayed few overt inclinations towards religiosity. Dupont-White's mother was English and Barni's family originated from the Italian peninsula, while the other three were of solid French descent. Is there any evidence to suggest that these social variations had significant political translations?

Not a great deal: Dupont-White's comfortable inheritance enabled him to give up paid employment in 1843 and devote himself fully to a life of research and writing. Vacherot and Barni went to the École Normale Supérieure and eventually became professional philosophers; Pelletan studied law and then rapidly abandoned it to embrace a career in journalism and letters; Littré prepared himself to practise medicine but was then forced by circumstances—the death of his father—to earn his living by writing and scholarly research. In an age in which political affiliation was partly defined in terms of 'family tradition', we found echoes of this form of political socialization, most notably in the political choices of Littré and Vacherot. But overall our five examples point to the acquisition of political views by our intellectuals outside the framework prevailing in their home setting.

In fact the most interesting differences among our five thinkers stemmed from the variety of networks of sociability with which they were affiliated. Through their various professional activities and textual productions they came to be associated with a range of institutional and cultural networks, to which must be added their membership of various social organizations. Taken together these 'structures of sociability' defined the physical spaces within which they operated, providing the principal sites where they exercised their *magistère intellectuel*. A small example may illustrate this point. Although there was some overlap among them, it was interesting that these five thinkers brought out their books, journals, and pamphlets with different publishers. Pelletan remained loyal to Pagnerre; Dupont-White to Guillaumin; Barni generally stayed with Germer-Baillière and with Ladrange for his translations of Kant; Vacherot ranged among Chamerot, Calmann-Lévy, and Hachette, while Littré spread his literary tentacles across a broad range of *maisons d'édition* including Hachette, Guillaumin, and Didier; on occasion he also used the resources of his own press at the offices of the *Philosophie Positive*. What was being expressed in these different preferences was a complex mixture of personal friendships, tribal loyalties, and overt but subtle signalling of an individual's identification with specific intellectual communities and political sensitivities. Pagnerre and Hachette, for example, were republican houses, while Calmann-Lévy was more commercially oriented; Ladrange specialized in the publication of philosophical works.[8]

---

[8] For further discussion of the publishing world during this period see Debauve, Jean-Louis, 'Un éditeur républicain: la maison Pagnerre et Eugène Pelletan', in Paul Baquiast and Georges Touroude (eds), *Une dynastie républicaine charentaise: les Pelletan* (Meudon-la-Forêt: Association des Amis d'Eugène et Camille Pelletan, 1998), 28–38.

Too much should not be made of five examples. But the personal circumstances of our thinkers can tell us a little about how political allegiances were shaped, maintained, and abandoned among nineteenth century French intellectuals. Above all our findings invite us to be extremely cautious about proposing sociological generalizations about the social preconditions of republican affiliation. In strictly socio-economic terms, for example, Dupont-White did not belong to the republican world: the overwhelming majority of the upper-middle-class strata from which he hailed explicitly sided against the Republic in the political struggles of the Second Empire and early Third Republic. Conversely, everything in Vacherot's modest background suggested that he should not only become a republican but should remain steadfast in his allegiance. The outcomes in both cases, as we have seen, inverted this 'sociological' logic: Dupont-White stayed throughout his life a firm, if somewhat unconventional, republican, whereas after the 1870s Vacherot, despite hailing from Gambetta's 'new social strata', abandoned the fold to align himself with the monarchists.

Ideology, as noted earlier, was a defining element in the formation of republican identities, but our narratives have also uncovered the precise institutional mechanisms through which these ideas could be acquired and maintained: among the key 'public' variables here were education, which brought our intellectuals into contact with the speeches and writings of key republican figures; professional networks, which created and sustained close political links among them; intellectual associations such as learned societies, journals and newspapers—and, as we have just mentioned, publishing houses—which possessed specific cultural norms and tacitly agreed political orientations. Barni's embrace of republicanism was significantly facilitated by the influence of republican freethinking philosophical circles in Paris; conversely, Vacherot's exit was to some extent determined by his professional frequentation of the Académie des Sciences Morales et Politiques, a majority of whose members were Orleanist. Ideas, we may thus conclude rather predictably, matter—but in an institutionally bounded context.

But republican ideas were not shaped purely by interactions in the 'public' sphere. What has also emerged is the importance of the private realm in the making—and unmaking—of republican thought. We have seen throughout the book that specific forms of private sociability such as the *salon* acted both as a site where republicans could gather in troubled times and as a forum within which arguments about the good life could be exchanged. To give one critical example, Pelletan's alignment into the republican camp was greatly facilitated by the influence of George Sand and her entourage. But the most critical 'private' determinant of republican affiliation to emerge from this book is religion. In the cases of Pelletan and Dupont-White, it is striking to note the extent to which the social world in which they evolved was suffused with Protestantism. Pelletan worshipped the *pasteur* Jarousseau and in many respects modelled his republican persona on his distinguished ancestor—a figure venerated by the Pelletan clan until well into the twentieth century—

while Dupont-White's close circle of friends largely consisted of leading figures in the liberal Protestant community.

The most remarkable case, however, was that of Vacherot, who not only returned to the Catholic faith towards the end of his life but took this return as the starting point of his ideological re-examination of his republican affiliation itself, a process which eventually led him to abandon the Third Republic and side with its monarchist adversaries. In all three cases, but especially in the third, public politics were not only shaped but defined by private beliefs.

The Ideological Origins of the Third Republic

Some of the classical fault lines of republican thinking emerge in very clear light through the works of our five intellectuals. Thus, elitism and republicanism quite often went hand in hand. There is a strong element of cultural superiority in certain articulations of French republicanism; and in the writings of Littré and Dupont-White in particular we see an explicit belief in the superiority of European civilization and a vindication of its right to rule over 'lesser' peoples—a philosophy which would partly underpin the colonial expansion of the early Third Republic. Whether this republican 'racialism' should be connected to the later degeneration of the Third Republic into the closed, aggressive, and intolerant nationalism of Vichy is a question which has been posed very lucidly by Gérard Noiriel in a well-documented and provocative critique of the cultural assumptions and nationality practices of the Third Republic.[9]

Furthermore, none of our intellectuals pushed their thinking very far on issues of social reform and especially working class political integration. Somewhat paradoxically, given that how unconventional a republican he was, the intellectual who went furthest in this area was Dupont-White. Perhaps it was the very absence of the baggage that encumbered his more orthodox republican colleagues which proved helpful here. Vacherot and Littré did not consider the issue deeply, while Barni and Pelletan stayed broadly within the ideological framework of liberal republicanism, stressing their commitment to the idea of alleviating working class suffering while at the same time pinning their ultimate hopes on education and philanthropy.

The attitude of our intellectuals to the civic and political integration of women in society also left much to be desired. This was one respect in which they were not especially distinctive: the thinking of the first generation of (male) elites of the Third Republic was notoriously clouded over the issue. Particularly when seen in light of recent scholarship, which has done much to reconstitute the range and power of feminist voices in nineteenth century France,[10] the weaknesses of our intellectuals—and their republican contemporaries—appear

---

[9] Noiriel, Gérard, *Les origines républicaines de Vichy* (Paris: Hachette, 1999).

[10] See most notably Joan W. Scott's wonderfully titled work *Only Paradoxes to Offer* (Cambridge, MA: Harvard University Press, 1996) and the collective study edited by Corbin, Alain, Lalouette, Jacqueline, and Riot-Sarcey, Michèle, *Femmes dans la cité 1815–1871* (Grâne: Créaphis, 1997).

striking here. At some point in their long careers, each of our five thinkers confronted the issues raised by the integration of women into public life, but always remained on the defensive, struggling to reconcile their commitment to the principles of equality and universality with their practical refusal to accord full membership of the political community to their sisters. The full political integration of women, at least in procedural terms, was achieved only after the Second World War: an outcome to which the Third Republic remained resolutely hostile.[11]

These blind spots appear especially extraordinary in the case of women. It might plausibly be argued that nineteenth-century republican intellectuals were largely ignorant of the social conditions in which workers lived; but the same could hardly be said about their relationship with women. Indeed our five intellectuals were close friends of such remarkable republican figures as George Sand, Daniel Stern, and Juliette Adam. What, then, might explain their relative absence of engagement with the project of feminine empowerment? Three possible types of explanation could be run here. One would be broadly ideological and would stress that, since the Revolutionary era, moderate republicans had always taken a restrictive view of equality, always defined in civil as opposed to social or physiological terms. Another would rest on a contingent account, highlighting the fears of working-class revolts after 1848 and 1871 and elite republican concerns—probably well-founded—that enfranchising women would give an enormous boost to the Catholic Church and its political allies. Finally a socio-cultural argument could be offered, drawing out the 'bourgeois' nature of republicanism and identifying the normative constraints on the equalization of gender roles.

While they may each tell us something about nineteenth century republican anti-feminism, these accounts do not altogether carry conviction. The first does not explain the particular intensity of some manifestations of republican anti-feminism, for example, Proudhon; the second does not work completely because the Third Republic's hostility to the enfranchisement of women lasted throughout the regime and thus long after the events of the mid- and late nineteenth century had been forgotten; and the socio-cultural account ignores the fact that anti-feminism was also strongly in evidence among other social classes and groups, most notably the aristocracy. Republican anti-feminism thus arose through a combination of these factors together with the fact that many powerful women in nineteenth century France deliberately eschewed a robust form of feminism, the most emblematic example being George Sand, a resolute defender of the rights of women but in overall terms an advocate of feminine difference rather than feminine equality.[12]

To turn now to the positive side, one of the key features of this book has been the attempt to take a much wider temporal view of the formation of modern republicanism. One overall conclusion which emerges is the limited

---

[11] See on this subject Smith, Paul, *Feminism and the Third Republic* (Oxford: Clarendon Press, 1996).
[12] See Jack, Belinda, *George Sand, A Woman's Life Writ Large* (London: Vintage, 2001), 363–4.

heuristic value of the conventional distinction between the '1848' generation and that of the 1860s and 1870s. Despite their reputation as dreamy idealists, *quarante-huitard* thinkers such as Pelletan were also hard-headed and pragmatic republicans; and conversely the political thought of Littré in the 1870s underlined that positivism did not rest on 'facts' alone. The self-images of the age should not lead us uncritically to accept formulations which were arguably more to do with inter-generational conflicts of ambition than with genuine ideological differences.

Our intellectuals' writings and political lives also draw attention to the fundamental importance of the local political sphere in nineteenth-century republicanism. On this theme, the book may be viewed as a confirmation of one of the key hypotheses in our earlier 1998 work *From Subject to Citizen*. In the present book this theme appears as a dialogue—and a tempestuous one—between the Jacobin centralism of Dupont-White on the one hand and the 'municipalism' of Littré, Barni, and Pelletan on the other. Vacherot, for his part, perfectly symbolizes the ideological readjustment of his republican generation, which began with strong centralist assumptions in the 1840s and 1850s and became converted by the late Second Empire to the virtues of greater local self-government. The ideological battle lines were drawn around the notion of citizenship. Dupont-White's liberal *étatiste* tradition regarded the state as the agent of civic consciousness, while the municipalists argued that republican citizenship had to be embedded in a considerable measure of autonomy to territorial units. This self-government was seen as a necessary form of political education and also as a means of drawing members of the political community into active participation in public life. The 'municipalist' approach won the day, and the Third Republic's conception of citizenship was largely drawn around the commune, the territorial sphere which up to this day continues to constitute the primary source of the political identity of French men and women.

At the same time this commitment to municipalism should not be regarded as a vindication of petty local concerns over substantive matters of 'national interest'. Posing the problem in these terms is a category mistake which derives from the application of modern conceptions of civic identity to nineteenth century political agents. What emerges from our study in terms of the political self-definition of republican intellectuals is the constant interface among three levels: the local, the national, and the European. Barni was in this respect an archetype. His theoretical and practical contributions to republican politics spanned across the entire range: in Geneva during the 1860s he promoted the value of internationalism and cosmopolitanism; in Paris after 1870 he worked in the National Assembly to found the new republican order; and in the municipality of Amiens and across the whole of France through his work in the Société d'Instruction Républicaine he highlighted the importance of local political activism in the making of the Third Republic. And although he was much less active politically, Littré's life and political thought can be made sense of in exactly the same terms. As a member of the National Assembly and the Conseil Général of the Seine in the 1870s, he worked to promote the victory of republicanism at a national and local level; and *La Philosophie Positive* was explicitly framed as a journal which addressed itself to 'European' concerns, not merely French ones. The point made earlier is therefore worth repeating: to regard the republicanism of the early Third Republic exclusively through the prism of the 'nation state' is to miss out a great deal of the constitutive features of nineteenth-century republican identity.

Ideological Filiation and its Complexities

One of the most striking findings of this book is the sheer weight and variety of diachronical influences on republican thinking in the later nineteenth century. This provides us with an opportunity to revisit the influences of earlier generations on the intellectual foundation of the Third Republic and more generally what might be described as the process of ideological 'filiation': the passing of a collective heritage from fathers to sons and how the latter set about constructing a republican 'canon' in honour of the former.

The first theme which appears across the output of our five thinkers is a strong sense of respect for their forefathers. At one level, Littré remained devoted throughout his life to Comte; Pelletan likewise defended the memory of his mentor Lamartine; Dupont-White and Vacherot used key concepts drawn from the writings of the Doctrinaires; and Barni celebrated the ideological potency of Kant. They were thus respectful of their ideological guides without being deferential. Indeed their esteem did not preclude criticism, which at times could go so far as the complete rejection of certain aspects of their thought. But in overall terms they strove to tread a path between fidelity and intellectual autonomy, a moral posture which was in marked contrast to the cruelty with which some republicans of the 1870s and 1880s attacked their *quarante-huitard* predecessors.

What also emerges is a contrast between explicit and implicit borrowings, and changes over time in the manner in which particular heritages were viewed. Littré explicitly cited Comte, and throughout his life claimed to be his heir and true disciple: a proposition vigorously contested by the 'orthodox' positivists. Pelletan, for his part, did not overtly refer to his Saint-Simonianism in his later years, even though it clearly shaped his thinking; the same absence is notable in Vacherot's later intellectual relationship with the Doctrinaires. These different strategies were partly a function of the potency of the 'dominant' republican discourse in France after 1870, whose ideological exclusivism made it difficult for a mainstream political thinker to acknowledge his intellectual debts to figures such as Guizot and Saint-Simon. Another taboo here was the evaluation of the Second Empire's legacy. After 1870 it was extremely rare to find republicans making positive references to the regime of 'Badinguet' and in this sense the black legend of the imperial era was largely a product of the ferocity with which republican historians and intellectuals attacked Napoleon III's reign in the later nineteenth century.

But this was a matter of political expediency. Littré and Dupont-White in the 1850s and 1860s, and Vacherot later in his life, had many positive things to say about the Second Empire. In this respect they were probably much more representative of the republican mainstream than history seems to have recorded. To be clear, the republican hatred of the Second Empire after 1870 was not entirely fabricated. But while its intensity had real roots in the violence of December 1851 and the debacle of the Franco-Prussian war, this virulent republican anti-Bonapartism was essentially a function of the need of all new regimes in France ideologically to demonize their immediate predecessors: a common enough trait in the nineteenth century. By the 1860s, however, a significant number of republicans found it very easy to accommodate themselves to the existence of a regime which was progressively democratizing and liberalizing its institutions, and which, had it not been distracted by a futile conflict with Prussia, may well have lived on much longer: another important example of a possible historical alternative to the Third Republic.

How did republican memory come to assume its specific content? When the republican canon came to be constructed by the late nineteenth century, it included the likes of Michelet, Quinet, and Hugo but none of our five thinkers—except Littré perhaps. Offering an explanation for their exclusion is difficult, for it involves counter-factual reasoning, which is never an entirely satisfactory exercise. However, elements of an explanation can be found by looking at the process of inclusion and exclusion in the very writings of our five thinkers. Rousseau is the most obvious example of systematic exclusion. Pelletan was the only intellectual who referred to him explicitly and in positive terms; Littré, Dupont-White, and Vacherot tended not to mention him at all or to be highly critical of his political thought; and Barni was evidently enormously influenced by him but preferred to hide behind the 'safer' figure of Kant. For most of the nineteenth century, Rousseau's status among constitutionalist republicans remained ambiguous; even as late as 1878 the commemoration of the centenary of his death was largely a matter for the republican left and extreme left; the moderates and opportunists preferred to celebrate Voltaire.[13] Rousseau's deism and political radicalism were much less appealing in the political context of the 1880s and 1890s than the sceptical anticlericalism of the author of *Candide*. It was only in the early twentieth century that Rousseau's stature was finally recognized across the political and intellectual spectrum; but this was a Rousseau who had been divested of most of his political radicalism. Thus the official committee for the commemoration of the bicentenary of his birth in 1912 stressed that by far the most important aspect of Rousseau's work was 'his exceptional literary genius'.[14]

The irony of history was that most our thinkers, except Littré, ended up being treated by posterity much in the same way as they—and their predecessors in

---

[13] Goulemot, Jean-Marie and Walter, Eric, 'Les centenaires de Voltaire et de Rousseau', in Pierre Nora (ed.), *Les lieux de mémoire* (Paris: Gallimard, 'quarto' edition, 1997), 372–3.

[14] Comité Francais, *Deuxième centenaire de Jean-Jacques Rousseau*. Bulletin bi-mensuel du Comité Francais, Samedi 8 Juin 1912, 1. Bibliothèque Nationale, 4 LN 27 58294.

the nineteenth century—had treated Rousseau. Like all ideological constructs, republican memory was selective, and there was no place in its Pantheon for those figures whose profile threatened the edifice of republican 'nation-building'. Dupont-White was too eclectic, Vacherot too heterodox, Pelletan too spiritual, and Barni too much of an internationalist to fit into the narrowly 'nationalist' republican mould which came to be constructed in the late nineteenth century. But while it reveals much about the selectiveness of republican memory, this exclusion should not diminish in our eyes the critical roles, both theoretical and practical, performed by our intellectuals in the establishment of the Third Republic. Memory and history are two distinct enterprises: the flaws of the former should not be allowed to impinge upon the serenity of the latter.

Republican Memory and the Potency of the 1789 Myth

Two overlapping conclusions about nineteenth century French political thought thus emerge: first, the republicanism of the Third Republic was not the exclusive preserve of one philosophical doctrine or undercurrent, least of all positivism; and second, many ideological structures which appeared during the Restoration and July Monarchy continued to exercise powerful influences on the French intellectual community well into the late nineteenth century and even beyond. The 'long' intellectual histories of the influences of the Doctrinaires and the Saint-Simonians, from this point of view, remain to be written. Our book has hopefully done enough to show that such exercises could prove singularly rewarding.

This book also sought to investigate the 'long' transformation of republican political culture across the eight decades separating the Revolutionary era from the founding of the Third Republic. What were the intellectual mechanisms of this transformation and what was the significance of this change for the eventual political success of the republicans in the 1870s? As François Furet has shown, nineteenth century republicans constantly invoked the 'principles of 1789' and in some of their writings the Revolution appears as a fixed point of reference for later generations, defining the broad philosophical principles—liberty, civil equality, sovereignty, active citizenship—that were eventually codified in the Third Republic.[15] This ideological lineage between the 1790s and the 1870s is also frequently identified by modern intellectual historians of republicanism.

But we should be careful not to overplay the elements of continuity between the First and the Third Republics, for several reasons. By the late 1860s these 'principles of 1789', as broadly defined above, were no longer the exclusive property of the republican party but were shared by Bonapartists, Orleanist liberals, and even liberal legitimists. If the republicans were success-

---

[15] Furet, *La Révolution*.

ful in their ideological battle against their competitors in the 1860s and 1870s, it could not therefore have been a result of these principles. Furthermore the meaning of many of these key concepts shifted over time as the political context within which they were deployed evolved. 'Sovereignty', for example, took on an entirely new meaning in the nineteenth century with the introduction of male universal suffrage.

It is sometimes asserted, especially by historians of the French Revolution, that the political contexts of the late eighteenth and late nineteenth centuries were so different as to rule out any meaningful overlaps between the political cultures of the First and the Third Republics. The republicanism of the 1789 revolution, according to this view, was rooted in the Enlightenment myth of human perfectibility and was obsessed with classical analogies and the promotion of virtue. None of these Promethean sounds is echoed in the sober and pragmatic republicanism of the Third Republic, which was primarily concerned with order and the cultivation of rationality.

This point is too important to be pursued here, although we should bear in mind—and Karma Nabulsi's work on the republican tradition of war in the 1830s is there to remind us of it—that the belief that republicanism was essentially about virtuous and heroic action was still thriving among many variants of European republicanism well into the nineteenth century. Indeed there was a heroic quality to the republicanism of the early Third Republic, and it came largely from their identification with the Revolution through their self-definition as not only the descendants of the First Republic but also as those who would complete its 'mission'. In this sense 1789 mattered much more to nineteenth-century republicans as an idealized construct than as a practical model for political emulation: in other words, as a myth rather than as an historical reality. Myths are double-edged political instruments, serving as creative but also constraining elements within a political culture. In the latter sense, they can weigh down a political tradition by insisting on a rigid and unconditional respect for the past; in the former, they can help a collectivity to make sense of its present concerns through a reconfiguration of its recent history. Creative myths, in short, do not simply situate political agents spatially and temporally; they also have a capacity to mobilize individual and group action, and lead political movements towards the fulfilment of their goals.

This is precisely where 1789 played a crucial role in the political imagination of nineteenth century French republicans. Between 1830 and 1870 their historians and pamphleteers passionately debated the meaning and interpretation of the events of the 1790s, and sought to make sense of them in the context of the future republican order. This was not simply a debate among a small group of Parisian thinkers about religion and the Terror and against the use of political violence, in which 'liberal' republicans triumphed over their 'Jacobin' colleagues. During the decades which preceded the establishment of the Third Republic republican intellectuals all over France formed their own individual views about the meaning and significance of the 1790s, and in this way appropriated the events in a wide variety of ways. Here is Barni, for example, responding to the proposition that centralization was a product of the republicans in 1790s and for that reason should not be touched by their successors:

I would reply first that, however legitimate it might be, the cult of the Revolution should not be blind, and that we the men of the nineteenth century should only accept its legacy after taking clear stock; and that if we found it to have taken a false route (as it did for example in its early stages over the relationship between Church and State) it would be unfortunate that a misguided sense of respect, inspired by some sort of revolutionary superstition, should prevent us from correcting its mistakes and thus repairing the damage which might have resulted from it.[16]

This passage brings out two equally significant features of the political thought of the intellectual founders of the Third Republic. The first is that their minds instinctively harked back to the 1790s whenever confronted with a specific situation or general problem; the second is that this framework was on balance more liberating than constraining. Through their creative re-interpretations of the events of the 1790s, each intellectual redefined his own conception of the good life and prepared the ground for the new republican order to come. The French Revolution of 1789 was in this sense an essentially creative myth: it provided the ammunition for Barni, Vacherot, and Littré to articulate their hostility to revolutionary republicanism; it enabled Pelletan to celebrate through the Girondins the importance of a localized and decentralized conception of citizenship; and it gave Dupont-White an opportunity to highlight the value of strong individual leadership and the rule of law. There was much else of substance, but the point to emphasise here is the inventive and dynamic nature of the 1789 myth and, by implication, the pivotal role played by intellectuals in the process of redefining the meaning and significance of the Revolution for their own political generations.

Well and good, it might be said. But so what? Surely these subtle intellectual distinctions did not go beyond the complex and sometimes byzantine world of republican groups and undercurrents. But this ideological reorientation had a much wider significance. If we are correct in ascribing to the 1789 myth the centrality we have given it in the political imagination of nineteenth century French republicanism, the *droit d'inventaire* deployed by the intellectual founders of the Third Republic performed a critical function in the battle which divided France between 1814 and 1877. There was from the Restoration onwards a common recognition among political elites that the Revolution had brought a number of irreversible changes to French politics and society. But this minimalist consensus on such principles as civil equality and national sovereignty left open the unfinished business of the 1790s and raised the issue of how much further the Revolution's programmatic objectives, explicit and assumed, could be taken. In nineteenth-century political argument '1789' thus became a contested ideological object which divided Bonapartists,

---

[16] Barni, Jules, 'La décentralisation en France', *Les États-Unis d'Europe*, No.4 (April 1870).

Orleanists, legitimists, and republicans from each other and within themselves. Bonapartists celebrated in the Revolution the birth of the modern French nation, the refounding of centralized government, and, through its Napoleonic episode, the provision of strong charismatic leadership. Orleanists and liberal legitimists stressed the importance of civil equality and law-based government, and the principle of national sovereignty; and radical republicans saw the 1790s as the launching-pad for the revolutionary transformation of French society along more egalitarian and fraternal lines.

In other words, all had 'their' myth of 1789. Why did the moderate, municipalist republican version eventually prevail over the others? Because in the course of the nineteenth century its thinkers creatively redefined the Revolutionary epic in such a way as to retain its heroic qualities but at the same time provide it with an aura of inclusivity and benevolence. 'In order to govern France', Gambetta said after 1871, 'we need violent words and moderate deeds'. This was a political version of what the intellectual founders of the Republic had already worked through, namely, that the republican idea had to capture the imagination of the French people and appeal to their sense of grandeur while at the same time reassuring them that the excesses of the 1790s would never be revisited. This was the programme of the Third Republic which our five intellectuals did so much to define, and in their successful reinvention of the myth of 1789 they also remind us that in politics myths can sometimes be just as important as reality itself.

BIBLIOGRAPHY

Primary sources

Académie Royale de Belgique, Bruxelles

Correspondence Laveleye: letters of Émile Laveleye to Charles Dupont-White (1860–77).

Archives d'État, Genève

Instruction Publique Cc3: correspondence concerning Barni appointment to Geneva Academy (1860).
Instruction Publique Ba19: 'résumé des désordres qui ont eu lieu au cours d'histoire de M.Barni.'
Instruction Publique Q49: letter of Wartmann to Conseil d'État on Barni lectures (January 1861).
Étrangers Dg9: residence permit for Mr and Mrs Barni (1862).
RC421 decree of Conseil d'État confers title of 'Professeur Honoraire' to Barni (1868).

Archives Carnot, Chateau de Presles (private collection)

Cecile Carnot papers:
letters from Charles Dupont-White to Cécile Carnot (c.1845–75);
letters from Charles Dupont-White to Gustave de Thou (late July Monarchy/Second Republic).

Archives Frédéric Petit, Auberchicourt (private collection)

Correspondance Barni. Letters from Jules Barni to Petit (early Third Republic).

Archives Nationales, Paris

417 AP Papiers Georges Coulon:
417 AP2 (dossier 4) 'Les Pelletan': contains some letters of Eugène Pelletan to George Sand (1837) and a collection of letters to his neighbours M. et Mme. Pironneau (1876–84).
417 AP7 Letters received by Coulon (1868–72).
417 AP8 Letters received by Coulon 1873 (includes one from Jules Barni).
87 AP Papiers Jules Simon.
87 AP 7 Vacherot letters to Jules Simon: (1864–80).
87 AP 7 Barni letters to Jules Simon: (1862–5).

Archives de la Préfecture de Police, Paris

BA–1 917 dossier Léon Gambetta.
BA–1 946 dossier Jules Barni.
BA–1 1158 dossier Émile Littré.
BA–1 1216 dossier Eugène Pelletan.

BA–1 1232 dossier Edgar Quinet.
BA–1 1270 dossier Jules Simon.
BA–1 1289 dossier Étienne Vacherot.
BA–1 1497 dossier *Le Patriote, Société d'Instruction Républicaine*.

Archives Départementales de la Somme, Amiens

99 M 95212 letters and notes from Ministry of Interior to Prefect of Somme (1859–62).
99 M 702 correspondence received by Prefect of Somme from departmental agents (early Third Republic).
99 M 80952 police reports on republican political activities in the Somme (1871–77).
99 M 80767 and 80768 electoral posters, Union Républicaine de la Somme (1871–72).

Bibliothèque de l'Arsenal, Paris

Fonds Enfantin 7769/68: letter from Eugène Pelletan to Enfantin.

Bibliothèque de l'Institut de France, Paris

Manuscript collection.
Ms. 1989: letter from Littré dated 2 August 1876.
Ms. 2565: Vacherot letter to Charles Levêque, Professor at the Collège de France (30 March 1861).
Ms. 2655: Maury correspondence (includes four letters from Littré between 1863 and 1869).
Ms. 3747: 'Les Académiciens de mon temps'. Various documents on members of the Académie Française, including some pieces on Littré, and a range of material on his funeral in June 1881.
Ms. 4490: Halévy letters (includes letter from Vacherot).
Ms. 7330: Eugène Pelletan letters to his editor Pagnerre.
Fonds Lovenjoul D.605: Sainte-Beuve correspondence with Littré.

Bibliothèque Nationale, Paris

Manuscripts collection:
Vacherot letters:
NAF 12929 Vacherot letter to Auguste Gefroy (n.d.)
NAF 21597 Vacherot letter to Henri Martin (1 February 1871).
NAF 22869 Vacherot letter to Mazet (18 January 1870).
Barni letters:
NAF 14113 Barni to Edgar Quinet (undated).
NAF 15551 Barni to Mme. Quinet (22 November 1875).
NAF 15517 Barni to Mme. Quinet (28 March 1875).
NAF 16274 Barni to Louis Viardot (10 August 1870).
NAF 20781 Barni letters to Edgar Quinet (October 1859–January 1872).

Bibliothèque du Protestantisme, Paris

Ms. 816 (20a) Correspondance Charles Read: letter from Dupont-White to Read (1878).

Bibliothèque Universitaire de Genève, Geneva

Manuscripts collection.

FACS 10/1, 10/2, 10/3 and 10/4: Papiers Bosak-Hauké (correspondence, including one letter from Jules Barni to Bosak, 9 September 1870; material relating to activities of *Ligue de la Paix*).

Archives Francis Chaponnière, C1 folio 18: newspaper articles concerning Jules Barni.

Archives de Belles-Lettres, Vols 52, 67: Barni letters to President of *Société de Belles-Lettres*, Geneva (1864–7).

Ms. 2807: letter from Jules Barni to J.B.G.Galiffe, professor at Académie de Genève (October 1862).

Ms. fr.6131 Papiers Henri Bordier: letter from Barni to Bordier (January 1860).

Ms. fr.4673 Papiers Jules Vuy: letter from Barni to Vuy (March 1866).

Ms. var.15/19 Correspondance Burillon: letter from Barni to Burillon (April 1863).

Bibliothèque Victor Hugo, Paris

Letter from Jules Barni to Hugo (24 August 1869).
Letter from Émile Littré to Hugo (17 February 1863).
Letters from Eugène Pelletan to Hugo (1862–79).

Nineteenth-century newspapers, reviews, and journals consulted

L'Avenir
Le Bien Public
Bulletin du Grand Orient de France
Bulletin Officiel de la République Française
Le Clairon
Le Correspondant
Le Courrier de la Somme
Critique Philosophique
La Démocratie Pacifique
Les États-Unis d'Europe
Le Figaro
La Gazette de France
Le Gaulois
L'Impartial
Journal de Genève
Journal des Débats
Journal des Économistes
La Liberté de Penser
Mémorial d'Amiens
Le Moniteur Universel
La Nouvelle Minerve
Le Patriote
La Philosophie Positive
La Politique Nouvelle
Le Progrès de la Somme
La République Française
Revue Britannique

Revue Contemporaine
Revue de France
Revue de l'Instruction Publique
Revue de Paris
Revue des Deux Mondes
Revue Indépendante
Revue Politique et Parlementaire
Le Siècle
Le Soleil
Le Temps
L'Union
L'Univers

Secondary sources

ADAM, JULIETTE, *Mes premières armes littéraires et politiques* (Paris: Lemerre, 1904).

—— *Mes sentiments et nos idées avant 1870* (Paris: Lemerre, 1905).

—— *Mes illusions et nos souffrances pendant le siège de Paris* (Paris: Lemerre, 1906).

—— *Nos amitiés politiques avant l'abandon de la revanche* (Paris: Lemerre, 1908).

AGOULT, COMTESSE MARIE D' (Daniel Stern), *Mémoires 1833–1854* (Paris: Calmann-Lévy, 1927).

AGULHON, MAURICE, *La République au village* (Paris: Plon, 1970).

—— *1848 et l'apprentissage de la République* (Paris: Seuil, 1973).

—— *Les quarante-huitards* (Paris: Gallimard, 1992).

ALEXANDRE, CHARLES, *Souvenirs sur Lamartine* (Paris: Charpentier, 1884).

ALLAIN-TARGÉ, HENRI, *La République sous l'Empire. Lettres (1864–1870)* (Paris: Grasset, 1939).

ANDLER, CHARLES, *Les origines du socialisme d'État en Allemagne* (Paris: Alcan, 1897).

ANDRÉOLI, ÉMILE, *Le Gouvernement du 4 Septembre et la Commune de Paris* (Paris: Bocquet, 1871).

ANON. *Un projet de décentralisation* (Nancy: Vagner, 1865).

ANON. *De la décentralisation. Objections au projet du comité de Nancy par un ancien préfet* (Paris: Librairie Centrale, 1866).

APRILE, SYLVIE, 'La République au salon: vie et mort d'une forme de sociabilité politique (1865–1885)', *Revue d'Histoire Moderne et Contemporaine*, 38 (1991), 473–87.

AQUARONE, STANISLAS, *The Life and Works of Émile Littré 1801–1881* (Leyden: Sythoff, 1958).

ARDAILLOU, PIERRE, *Les républicains du Havre au XIXe siècle (1815–1889)* (Rouen: Publications de l'Université de Rouen, 1999).

D'ARDEUIL, FUMERON, *La décentralisation* (Paris: Plon, 1866).

AROUX, FÉLIX, *Ce que c'est que le socialisme. Projet de discours à un Congrès* (Paris: Germer Baillière, 1870).

AUCOC, LÉON, 'Les controverses sur la décentralisation administrative', *Revue Politique et Parlementaire* (May 1895).

AUDOIN-ROUZEAU, STÉPHANE, *1870: la France dans la guerre* (Paris: Armand Colin, 1989).

AUGÉ, PAUL (ed.), *Larousse du XXe siècle* (Paris: Larousse, 1929).

AZOUVI, FRANÇOIS and BOUREL, DOMINIQUE, *De Köenigsberg à Paris: la réception de Kant en France (1788–1804)* (Paris: Librairie Philosophique Vrin, 1991).

BAKER, ALAN R. H., *Fraternity Among the French Peasantry: Sociability and Voluntary Associations in the Loire Valley, 1815–1914* (Cambridge: Cambridge University Press 1999).

BAQUIAST, PAUL, *Une dynastie de la bourgeoisie républicaine. Les Pelletan* (Paris: L'Harmattan, 1996).

—— and TOUROUDE, GEORGES, *Une dynastie républicaine charentaise: les Pelletan* (Meudon-la-Forêt: Association des Amis d'Eugène et Camille Pelletan, 1998).

BARNI, JULES, *Discours prononcé à la distribution des prix du Collège Royal de Charlemagne par M. Barni, professeur agrégé de philosophie* (Paris, 1842).

—— 'Des beaux-arts dans la philosophie de Kant', *La liberté de penser*, No. 9 (August 1848).

—— 'Le suffrage universel et l'instruction primaire', *La liberté de penser*, No.14 (January 1849).

—— *Philosophie de Kant. Examen de la 'Critique du Jugement' par Jules Barni* (Paris: Ladrange, 1850).

—— 'Terre et Ciel', *L'Avenir*, No. 2 (13 May 1855).

—— 'Le Mensonge', *L'Avenir*, No. 5 (3 June 1855).

—— 'Du rôle de la morale dans la société', *L'Avenir*, No. 9 (1 July 1855).

—— 'Idées de Kant sur l'éducation', *L'Avenir*, No.12 (22 July 1855); No.14 (5 August 1855); No.15 (12 August 1855).

—— 'Kant et la Révolution Française', *Revue de Paris* (15 March 1856).

—— 'La Religion Naturelle par Jules Simon', *Revue de Paris* (1 August 1856).

—— *Histoire des idées morales et politiques en France au XVIIIe siècle*, 2 Vols (Paris: Germer Baillière, 1865).

—— *Napoléon et son historien M. Thiers* (Geneva, 1865).

—— 'Preface', *Annales du Congrès de Genève* (Geneva, 1868).

—— 'La Décentralisation en France', *Les États-Unis d'Europe*, No. 3 (March 1870).

—— 'La Décentralisation en France', *Les États-Unis d'Europe*, No. 4 (April 1870).

—— 'La République', *Les États-Unis d'Europe*, No. 9 (25 October 1870).

—— *Napoléon Ier* (Paris: Germer Baillière, 1870).

—— *Ce que doit être la République* (Amiens : Union Républicaine de la Somme, 1872).

—— *L'instruction républicaine* (Paris: Société d'Instruction Républicaine, 1872).

—— *Manuel Républicain* (Paris: Germer Baillière, 1872).

—— *Les principes et les moeurs de la République* (Paris: Société d'Instruction Républicaine, 1873).

—— *Les moralistes français au XVIIIe siècle* (Paris: Germer Baillière, 1873).

—— *L'Appel au Peuple* (Paris: Le Chevalier, 1874).

—— *Les martyrs de la libre pensée*, 2nd edn (Paris: Germer Baillière, 1880).

—— *La morale dans la démocratie*, 2nd edn (Paris: Alcan, 1885).

BARRAL, PIERRE, *Les fondateurs de la République* (Paris: Armand Colin, 1968).

—— 'Ferry et Gambetta face au positivisme', *Romantisme*, 21–22 (1978).

BARROT, ODILON, *De la centralisation et de ses effets* (Paris: Didier, 1870).

BASDEVANT-GAUDEMET, BRIGITTE, *La Commission de Décentralisation de 1870* (Paris: Presses Universitaires de France, 1873).

BÉCHARD, FERDINAND, *Du projet de décentralisation administrative annoncé par l'Empereur* (Paris: Gazette de France, 1864).

BEN-AMOS, AVNER, *Funerals, Politics and Memory in modern France 1789–1996* (Oxford: Oxford University Press, 2000).

BERLIN, ISAIAH, *Four Essays on Liberty* (Oxford: Oxford University Press, 1969).

BERSTEIN, SERGE (ed.), *Les cultures politiques en France* (Paris: Seuil, 1999).

BERSTEIN, SERGE and RUDELLE, ODILE (eds), *Le modèle républicain* (Paris: Presses Universitaires de France, 1992).

BERTOCCI, PHILIP, *Jules Simon: Republican Anticlericalism and Cultural Politics in France 1848–1886* (Columbia: University of Missouri Press, 1978).

BILLARD, JACQUES, *De l'école à la République: Guizot et Victor Cousin* (Paris: Presses Universitaires de France, 1998).

BLANC, ELIE, *Un spiritualisme sans Dieu. Examen de la philosophie de M. Vacherot* (Lyon: Librairie Générale Catholique et Classique, 1885).

BLANC, LOUIS, *La République une et indivisible* (Paris: Naud, 1851).

BONNEFONT, GASTON, 'Dupont-White, un penseur contemporain', in *Revue Britannique*, 6 (1889).

BORGEAUD, CHARLES, *Histoire de l'Université de Genève Vol. III (1814–1900)* (Genève: Georg & Cie., 1934).

BOSAK-HAUKÉ, JOSEPH, *Une motion faite à la réunion constitutive du Comité Permanent de la Ligue de la Paix et de Liberté relative à la question la paix ou la guerre* (Geneva, 1867).

BOUTROUX, ÉMILE, *Notice sur la vie et les oeuvres de M. Étienne Vacherot* (Paris: Firmin-Didot, 1904).

BRISBARRE, J., *Discours prononcé à la distribution des prix du Lycée Impérial d'Amiens* (Amiens, 1857).

DE BROGLIE, GABRIEL, *MacMahon* (Paris: Perrin, 2000).

DE BROGLIE, VICTOR, *Vues sur le gouvernement de la France* (Paris: Michel Lévy, 1872).

BROOKS, JOHN III, *The Eclectic Legacy: Academic Philosophy and the Human Sciences in Nineteenth-Century France* (Newark: University of Delaware Press, 1998).

BURDEAU, FRANÇOIS, *Libertés, Libertés locales chéries* (Paris: Cujas, 1983).

BURROW, JOHN, *The Crisis of Reason: European Political Thought 1848–1914* (London and New Haven: Yale University Press, 2000)

CAUBET, JEAN MARIE LAZARE, 'Réception d'Émile Littré dans la Franc-Maçonnerie', *La Philosophie Positive* (September–October 1875), 161.

CAUWES, PAUL, *Cours d'Économie Politique* (Paris: Larose et Forcel, 1893).

Le Centenaire de l'École Normale 1795–1895 (Paris: Hachette, 1895).

CHARLE, CHRISTOPHE, *Naissance des 'intellectuels' 1880–1900* (Paris: Éditions de Minuit, 1990).

—— *Les intellectuels en Europe au XIXe siècle* (Paris: Fayard, 1996).

CHARLETY, SÉBASTIEN, *Histoire du Saint-Simonisme 1825–1864* (Paris: Hartmann, 1934).

CHARLTON, D. G., *Positivist Thought in France During the Second Empire 1852–1870* (Oxford: Clarendon Press, 1959).

—— *Secular Religions in France 1815–1870* (London: Oxford University Press, 1963).

COHEN, WILLIAM B., *Urban Government and the Rise of the French City: Five Municipalities in the Nineteenth Century* (London: Macmillan, 1998).

COMBES, ANDRÉ, *Histoire de la Franc-Maçonnerie au XIXe siècle*, 2 Vols (Paris: Éditions du Rocher, 1999).

COMITÉ FRANCAIS, *Deuxième centenaire de Jean-Jacques Rousseau*. Bulletin bi-mensuel du Comité Francais, Samedi 8 Juin 1912. Bibliothèque Nationale, 4 LN 27 58294.

COMTE, AUGUSTE, *Correspondance*, Vol. 6 (1851–2) (Paris: Vrin, 1973).

CONKLIN, ALICE, *A Mission to Civilize: The Republican Idea of Empire in France and West Africa 1895–1930* (Stanford: Stanford University Press, 1997).

COOPER, SANDI, *Patriotic Pacifism: Waging War on War in Europe 1815–1914* (New York: Oxford University Press, 1991).

CORBIN, ALAIN, GÉROME, NOELLE, and TARTAKOWSKI, DANIELLE (eds), *Les usages politiques des Fêtes aux XIXe–XXe siècles* (Paris: Publications de la Sorbonne, 1994).

CORBIN, ALAIN, LALOUETTE, JACQUELINE, and RIOT-SARCEY, MICHELE (eds), *Femmes dans la cité 1815–1871* (Grâne: Créaphis, 1997).

COUSIN, VICTOR, *Cours d'histoire de la philosophie morale au XVIIIe siècle Vol. IV. Philosophie de Kant* (Paris: Ladrange, 1842).

—— *Oeuvres de M. Victor Cousin. Discours Politiques* (Paris: Didier, 1851).

CROSSLEY, CERI, *French Historians and Romanticism. Thierry, Guizot, the Saint-Simonists, Quinet, Michelet* (London: Routledge, 1993).

DABOT, HENRI, *Souvenirs et impressions d'un bourgeois du quartier Latin* (Paris: Quentin, 1899).

DATTA, VENITA, *Birth of a National Icon: The Literary Avant-Garde and the Origins of the Intellectual in France* (Albany: State University of New York Press, 1999).

DAVID, MARCEL, *Le printemps de la fraternité: genèse et vicissitudes 1830–1851* (Paris: Aubier, 1992).

DEBAUVE, JEAN-LOUIS, 'Un éditeur républicain: la maison Pagnerre et Eugène Pelletan', in Paul Baquiast and Georges Touroude (eds), *Une dynastie républicaine charentaise: les Pelletan* (Meudon-la-Forêt: Association des Amis d'Eugène et Camille Pelletan, 1998).

DELACROIX, Eugène, *Journal 1822–1863* (Paris: Plon, 1996).

DELAROA, JOSEPH (ed.), *Le Duc de Persigny et les doctrines de l'Empire* (Paris: Plon, 1865).

DÉLOYE, YVES, *École et citoyenneté: l'individualisme républicain de Jules Ferry à Vichy* (Paris: Presses de la Fondation Nationale des Sciences Politiques, 1994).

DERFLER, LESLIE, *Paul Lafargue and the Founding of French Marxism 1842–1882* (Cambridge, MA: Harvard University Press, 1991).

—— *Paul Lafargue and the Flowering of French Socialism 1882–1911* (Cambridge, MA: Harvard University Press, 1998).

DIDE, AUGUSTE, *Jules Barni, sa vie et ses oeuvres* (Paris: Alcan, 1892).

DIETZ, JEAN, 'Jules Ferry et les traditions républicaines', *Revue Politique et Parlementaire* (1934–5).

DIGEON, CLAUDE, *La crise allemande de la pensée française (1870–1914)* (Paris: Presses Universitaires de France, 1959).

DU CAMP, MAXIME, *Souvenirs Littéraires* (Paris: Hachette, 1883).

DU PASQUIER, MARCEL, *Edgar Quinet en Suisse. Douze années d'exil (1858–1870)* (Neuchâtel: Éditions de la Baconnière, 1959).

DUPONT-WHITE, CHARLES, *Essai sur les relations du travail avec le capital* (Paris: Guillaumin, 1846).

—— *L'Individu et l'État* (Paris: Guillaumin, 1857).

—— *La centralisation, suite à L'Individu et l'État* (Paris: Guillaumin, 1861).

—— 'Introduction', John Stuart Mill, *Le Gouvernement Représentatif* (Paris: Guillaumin, 1862).

—— 'L'administration locale en France et en Angleterre: De l'Esprit des Races', *Revue des Deux Mondes* (15 August 1862), 884–6.

—— 'Centralisation et Liberté', *Revue des Deux Mondes* (1 February 1863), 581–3.

—— 'Préface', John Stuart Mill, *La liberté* (Paris: Guillaumin, 1864).

—— 'Le Positivisme: A Propos d'Un Livre de M. Littré', *Revue des Deux Mondes* (1 February 1865).

—— *La liberté de presse et le suffrage universel* (Paris: Douniol, 1866).

—— *De l'équilibre en Europe* (Paris: Revue Contemporaine, 1867).

—— *Le progrès politique en France* (Paris: Guillaumin, 1868).

—— *Des candidatures officielles* (Paris: Guillaumin, 1868).

—— *Ce qui pourrait tenir lieu d'une Constitution* (Paris: Revue Britannique, 1872).

—— *La République Conservatrice* (Paris: Guillaumin, 1872).

—— *Le suffrage universel* (Paris: Douniol, 1872).

—— 'Impuissance politique de la philosophie', *Revue de France*, 17 (February 1876).

—— 'Perspectives Politiques I', *Revue de France*, 32 (December 1878).

—— 'Perspectives Politiques' II, *Revue de France*, 33 (January 1879).

—— *Politique Actuelle* (Paris: Guillaumin, 1875).

—— *Mélanges philosophiques* (Paris: Guillaumin, 1878).

DUPUY, ROGER (ed.), *Pouvoir Local et Révolution* (Rennes: Presses Universitaires de Rennes, 1995).

ELWITT, SANFORD, *The Making of the Third Republic: Class and Politics in France 1868–1884* (Baton Rouge: Louisiana State University Press, 1975).

Enquête Parlementaire sur les Actes du Gouvernement de la Défense Nationale (Paris: Librairie des Publications Législatives, 1876).

FAGUET, ÉMILE, *Le libéralisme* (Paris: Société Française, 1902).

FAURE, ALAIN (ed.), *Le XIXe siècle et la Révolution Française* (Paris: Éditions Créaphis, 1992).

FERRY, JULES, *La lutte électorale en 1863* (Paris: Dentu, 1863).

FLOURENS, GUSTAVE, *Paris Livré* (Paris, 1871).

FOUILLÉE, ALFRED, *La science sociale contemporaine* (Paris: Hachette, 1880).

La France des années 1870: naissance de la IIIe République. Actes du Colloque de la Fondation Singer-Polignac, 27 April 2000 (Paris, 2000).

FOUQUIER, HENRY, *Au siècle dernier* (Brussels, n.d.).

FREEDEN, MICHAEL, *Ideologies and Political Theory* (Oxford: Oxford University Press, 1996).

DE FREYCINET, CHARLES, *Souvenirs 1848–1878* (Paris: Delagrave, 1912).

FURET, FRANÇOIS, *Le passé d'une illusion. Essai sur l'idée communiste au XXe siècle* (Paris: Robert Laffont, 1995).

—— *La gauche et la révolution au milieu du XIXe siècle. Edgar Quinet et la question du Jacobinisme 1865–1870* (Paris: Hachette, 1986).

—— *La Révolution*, 2 Vols (Paris: Hachette, 1988).

—— 'Révolution Française et Tradition Jacobine', in Colin Lucas (ed.), *The French Revolution and the Creation of Modern Political Culture*, Vol. 2 (Oxford: Pergamon, 1988).

—— and OZOUF, MONA (eds), *Le siècle de l'avènement républicain* (Paris: Gallimard, 1993).

GALLIE, W. B., *Philosophers of Peace and War* (Cambridge: Cambridge University Press, 1978).

GARRIGUES, JEAN, *La République des hommes d'affaires (1870–1900)* (Paris: Aubier, 1997).

GELINEAU, PIERRE, *Pour l'Idée. Fêtes du centenaire d'Eugène Pelletan 1813–1913* (Saint-George de Didonne, 1913).

GEORGE, JOCELYNE, 'Mémoire révolutionnaire et tradition municipale républicaine. Le cas du Var au XIXème siècle', in Michel Vovelle (ed.), *Révolution et République: l'exception française* (Paris: Kimé, 1994).

GERBOD, PAUL, *La condition universitaire en France au XIXe siècle* (Paris: Presses Universitaires de France, 1965).

—— *Paul-François Dubois, universitaire, journaliste et homme politique 1793–1874* (Paris: Klincksieck, 1967).

—— *La vie quotidienne dans les lycées et collèges au XIXe siècle* (Paris: Hachette, 1968).

GERSON, STÉPHANE, 'Town, Nation, or Humanity? Festive Delineations of Place and Past in Northern France, ca.1825–1865', *Journal of Modern History*, 72 (2000), 628–82.

GIRARD, LOUIS, *La Seconde République* (Paris: Calmann-Lévy, 1968).

—— *Les libéraux français* (Paris: Aubier, 1985).

DE GOBINEAU, ARTHUR, *Essai sur l'inégalité des races humaines*, in Jean Boissel (ed.), Arthur de Gobineau, *Oeuvres*, Vol. 1 (Paris: Gallimard, 1983).

GONCOURT, EDMOND and JULES, *Journal* (Paris: Fasquelle & Flammarion, 1956).

GOULEMOT, JEAN-MARIE and WALTER, ERIC, 'Les centenaires de Voltaire et de Rousseau', in Pierre Nora (ed.), *Les lieux de mémoire* (Paris: Gallimard, 'quarto' edition, 1997).

Grand Dictionnaire Universel, Supplément (Geneva-Paris: Slatkine, 1982).

Grand Larousse Encyclopédique, Vol. 4 (Paris: Larousse, 1961).

GRATRY, A., *Étude sur la sophistique contemporaine ou lettre à M. Vacherot* (Paris: Gaume, 1851).

GRAY, JOHN, *Two Faces of Liberalism* (Oxford: Polity Press, 2000).

GRÉVY, JEROME, *La République des opportunistes 1870–1885* (Paris: Perrin, 1998).

GRUBB, ALAN, *The Politics of Pessimism: Albert de Broglie and Conservative Politics in the Early Third Republic* (Newark: University of Delaware Press, 1996).

GUIONNET, CHRISTIANE, *L'apprentissage de la politique moderne: les élections municipales sous la monarchie de Juillet* (Paris: l'Harmattan, 1997).

GUIRAL, PIERRE, *Prévost-Paradol 1829–1870. Pensée et action d'un libéral sous le Second Empire* (Paris: Presses Universitaires de France, 1955).

—— *Adolphe Thiers* (Paris: Fayard, 1986).

HALÉVY, DANIEL, *La fin des notables* (Paris: Grasset, 1930).

—— *La République des Ducs* (Paris: Grasset, 1937).

HANOTAUX, GABRIEL, *Histoire de la Fondation de la Troisième République 1870–1873* (Paris: Plon, 1925).

HARISMENDY, PATRICK, *Sadi Carnot, l'ingénieur de la République* (Paris: Perrin, 1995).

HARRIS, RUTH, *Lourdes: Body and Spirit in the Secular Age* (London: Penguin, 1999).

HARRISON, CAROL, *The Bourgeois Citizen in Nineteenth-Century France: Gender, Sociability and the Use of Emulation* (New York: Oxford University Press, 1999).

HARTMANN, MAX, *Sismondi und Dupont-White als Begrunder des sozialen interventionismus in Frankreich* (Zurich, 1943).

HAZAREESINGH, SUDHIR, *Political Traditions in Modern France* (Oxford: Oxford University Press, 1994).

—— *From Subject to Citizen: The Second Empire and the Emergence of Modern French Democracy* (Princeton: Princeton University Press, 1998).

—— 'The *Société d'Instruction Républicaine* and the Propagation of Civic Republicanism in Provincial and Rural France 1870–1877', *Journal of Modern History*, 71 (1999), 271–307.

—— and WRIGHT, VINCENT, *Francs-Maçons sous le Second Empire. Les loges provinciales du Grand-Orient à la veille de la Troisième République* (Rennes: Presses Universitaires de Rennes, 2001).

HIGONNET, PATRICE, *Goodness Before Virtue* (Cambridge, MA: Harvard University Press, 1998).

HOLMES, STEPHEN, *Benjamin Constant and the Making of Modern Liberalism* (New Haven: Yale University Press, 1984).

HUARD, RAYMOND, *Le mouvement républicain en Bas-Languedoc* (Paris: Presses de la Fondation Nationale des Sciences Politiques, 1982).

—— *La naissance du parti politique en France* (Paris: Presses de la Fondation Nationale des Sciences Politiques, 1996).

HUBBARD, ARTHUR, 'Les franchises communales', *La Philosophie Positive* (January–February 1877), 133.

—— 'Les franchises communales' (suite), *La Philosophie Positive* (March–April 1877), 228–44.

—— 'Les franchises communales' (suite et fin), *La Philosophie Positive* (May–June 1877), 425.

HUGO, VICTOR, *Histoire d'un crime* (Paris: Hetzel, 1884).

IHL, OLIVIER, *La fête républicaine* (Paris: Gallimard, 1996).

JACK, BELINDA, *George Sand, A Woman's Life Writ Large* (London: Vintage, 2001).

JANET, PAUL, *Victor Cousin et son oeuvre philosophique* (Paris: Calmann Lévy, 1885).

JANICAUD, DOMINIQUE, *Une généalogie du spiritualisme français* (The Hague: Martinus Nijhoff, 1969).

JARDIN, ANDRÉ, *Histoire du libéralisme politique* (Paris: Hachette, 1985).

JAUME, LUCIEN, *L'Individu effacé ou le paradoxe du libéralisme français* (Paris: Fayard, 1997).

—— (ed.), *Coppet, creuset de l'esprit libéral* (Paris: Economica, 2000).

JENNINGS, JEREMY, *Intellectuals in Politics: From the Dreyfus Affair to Salman Rushdie* (London: Routledge, 1997).

JOANA, JEAN, *Pratiques politiques des députés français au XIXe siècle: du dilettante au spécialiste* (Paris: L'Harmattan, 1999).

JOHNSON, MARTIN PHILIP, *The Paradise of Association: Popular Culture and Popular Organizations in the Paris Commune of 1871* (Ann Arbor: University of Michigan Press, 1996).

JONES, STUART (ed.), *Comte. Early Political Writings* (Cambridge: Cambridge University Press, 1998).

KANT, IMMANUEL, *Critique du Jugement: Observations sur le beau et le sublime*, ed. Jules Barni, 2 Vols (Paris: Ladrange, 1846).

—— *Critique de la raison pratique; Fondements de la métaphysique des moeurs*, ed. Jules Barni (Paris: Ladrange, 1848).

—— *Métaphysique des moeurs I; Essai sur la paix perpétuelle*, ed. Jules Barni (Paris: Ladrange, 1853).

—— *Métaphysique des moeurs II; Traité de pédagogie*, ed. Jules Barni (Paris: Ladrange, 1855).

—— *Critique de la raison pure*, ed. Jules Barni (Paris: Germer Baillière, 1869).

KELLY, GEORGE ARMSTRONG, *The Humane Comedy: Constant, Tocqueville and French Liberalism* (Cambridge: Cambridge University Press, 1992).

KRIEGEL, BLANDINE, *Philosophie de la République* (Paris: Plon, 1998).

DE LA GORCE, PIERRE, *Histoire du Second Empire*, Vol. 2 (Paris: Plon, 1894).

LALOUETTE, JACQUELINE, *La libre pensée en France 1848–1940* (Paris: Albin Michel, 1997).

LAROUSSE, PIERRE, *Grand Dictionnaire Universel du XIXe Siècle* (Geneva-Paris: Slatkine, 1982).

DE LAVELEYE, ÉMILE, *Du progrès des peuples anglo-saxons* (Bruxelles: Guyot, 1859).

—— *Un précurseur, Charles Dupont-White* (Paris: Imprimerie Nationale, 1878).

LAVERTUJON, ANDRÉ (ed.), *Gambetta inconnu* (Bordeaux: Gounouilhou, 1905).

LAVISSE, ERNEST, *Souvenirs* (Paris: Calmann-Lévy, 1988).

LE BRAS-CHOPARD, ARMELLE, 'Les premiers socialistes', in Pascal Ory (ed.), *Nouvelle histoire des idées politiques* (Paris: Hachette, 1987).

LEFEVRE, ANDRÉ, *La renaissance du matérialisme* (Paris: Octave Doin, 1881).

LEGRAND, LOUIS, *L'influence du positivisme dans l'oeuvre scolaire de Jules Ferry* (Paris: M. Rivière, 1961).

LENORMAND, PIERRE, 'Le mouvement républicain dans la Somme au début de la IIIe République (1870–1877)', *Revue Historique* (January–March 1946).

LEPENIES, WOLF, *Between Literature and Science: The Rise of Sociology* (Cambridge: Cambridge University Press, 1988).

LEROY-BEAULIEU, PAUL, *L'État moderne et ses fonctions* (Paris: Guillaumin, 1890).

Levallois, Jules, *Milieu de siècle, Mémoires d'un critique* (Paris: Librairie Illustrée, n.d.)

Lévêque, Pierre, *Histoire des forces politiques en France 1789–1880* (Paris: Armand Colin, 1992).

Leverdays, Émile, 'La centralisation', in *Œuvres posthumes*, Vol. 3 (Paris: G.Carré, 1893).

Une lignée républicaine: les Carnot sous la IIIe République, Actes du Colloque de Limoges (Limoges: Lucien Souny, 1989).

Ligou, Daniel, *Frédéric Desmons et la Franc-Maçonnerie sous la Troisième République* (Paris: Gedalge, 1966).

Littré, Émile, *De la Philosophie Positive* (Paris: Librairie Philosophique de Ladrange, 1845).

—— *Application de la philosophie positive au gouvernement des sociétés et en particulier à la crise actuelle* (Paris: Librairie Philosophique de Ladrange, 1850).

—— *Conservation Révolution Positivisme* (Paris: Ladrange, 1852).

—— *Circulaire de M. Émile Littré, faisant connaître aux disciples de feu M. Comte qu'il ouvre une souscription afin de continuer à Mme. Comte, sa veuve, la pension que lui faisait son mari* (Paris, 1857).

—— *Paroles de philosophie positive* (Paris: Delahays, 1859).

—— *Fragments de philosophie positive et de sociologie contemporaine* (Paris: Bureaux de la Philosophie Positive, 1876).

—— *Auguste Comte et la Philosophie Positive*, 3rd edn (Paris: Bureaux de la Philosophie Positive, 1877).

—— *Dictionnaire de la langue française*, 5 Vols (Paris: Hachette, 1877).

—— *Étude sur les progrès du positivisme* (Paris: Germer Baillière, 1877).

—— *Conservation Révolution Positivisme*, 2nd edn (Paris: Bureaux de la Philosophie Positive, 1879).

—— *De l'établissement de la Troisième République* (Paris: Bureaux de la Philosophie Positive, 1880).

—— *Comment j'ai fait mon dictionnaire de la langue française* (Paris: Delagrave, 1897).

—— *Du devoir de l'homme envers lui-même et envers ses semblables* (Paris: Loge La Clémente Amitié, 1906).

—— and Paulin, J.-B. Alexandre (eds), *Oeuvres politiques et littéraires d'Armand Carrel*, Vol. 1 (Paris: Chamerot, 1857).

Logue, William, *Charles Renouvier, Philosopher of Liberty* (Baton Rouge: Louisiana State University Press, 1993).

Lucas, Charles, *Civilisation de la guerre, observations sur les lois de la guerre et l'arbitrage international* (Paris: Cotillon, 1881).

MacIntyre, Alasdair, *After Virtue* (London: Duckworth, 1981).

Marmier, Xavier, *Journal 1848–1890*, Vol. 1 (Geneva: Droz, 1968).

Martin, Maurice, 'Essai sur les doctrines sociales et économiques de Dupont-White' (Ph.D. thesis, Université de Grenoble, 1899).

Martin-Fugier, Anne, *La vie élégante ou la formation du Tout-Paris 1815–1848* (Paris: Seuil, 1990).

Maurras, Charles, *L'idée de décentralisation* (Paris: Revue Encyclopédique, 1898).

Mayeur, Jean-Marie, *Les débuts de la Troisième République* (Paris: Seuil, 1973).

—— *La question laïque* (Paris: Fayard, 1997).

Mélonio, Françoise, *Tocqueville et les Français* (Paris: Aubier, 1993).

Michel, Henry, *L'Idée de l'État* (Paris: Hachette, 1898).

Michelet, Jules, *Journal*, 2 Vols (Paris: Gallimard, 1959).

Mineka, F. and Lindley, D. (eds), *The Collected Works of John Stuart Mill* (University of Toronto Press, Routledge Kegan and Paul, 1972).

MOLNAR, MIKLOS, 'La Ligue de la Paix et de la Liberté: ses origines et ses premières orientations', in Jacques Bariéty and Antoine Fleury (eds), *Mouvements et initiatives de Paix dans la politique internationale 1867–1928* (Berne: Peter Lang, 1987).

MORIN, FRÉDÉRIC, *Les idées du temps présent* (Paris: Michel Lévy, 1863).

NABULSI, KARMA, *Traditions of War* (Oxford: Oxford University Press, 1999).

NAPOLÉON, JÉROME, *Choix de discours et de publications du Prince Napoléon* (Paris, 1874).

NAPOLÉON, LOUIS, *Discours, messages, et proclamations de l'Empereur* (Paris: Plon, 1860).

—— *Oeuvres de Napoléon III*, Vol. 5 (Paris: Plon, 1869).

NICOLET, CLAUDE, 'Jules Ferry et la tradition positiviste', in François Furet (ed.), *Jules Ferry fondateur de la République* (Paris: EHESS, 1985).

—— *L'Idée républicaine en France* (Paris: Gallimard, 1983).

—— 'Littré et la République', in *Actes du Colloque Littré, 7–9 Octobre 1981* (Paris, 1983).

—— *Histoire, Nation, République* (Paris: Odile Jacob, 2000).

NISBET, ROBERT, *History of the Idea of Progress* (New York: Basic Books, 1980).

NOIRIEL, GÉRARD, *Les origines républicaines de Vichy* (Paris: Hachette, 1999).

NOLEN, DÉSIRÉ, *Kant et la philosophie du XIXe siècle* (Montpellier: Martel, 1877).

NORD, PHILIP, *The Republican Moment: Struggles for Democracy in Nineteenth-Century France* (Cambridge, MA: Harvard University Press, 1995).

Notice biographique sur M. Jules Barni, candidat républicain (Amiens: Publications de l'Union Républicaine de la Somme No. 6, 1872).

OLLÉ-LAPRUNE, LÉON, *Étienne Vacherot* (Paris: Perrin, 1898).

OLLIVIER, ÉMILE, *L'Empire Libéral*, Vol. 12 (Paris: Garnier, 1908).

—— *Journal 1846–1860*, Vol. 1 (Paris: Julliard, 1961).

ORY, PASCAL (ed.), *Nouvelle histoire des idées politiques* (Paris: Hachette, 1987).

—— and SIRINELLI, JEAN-FRANÇOIS, *Les intellectuels en France de l'Affaire Dreyfus à nos jours* (Paris: Armand Colin, 1992).

OZOUF, MONA, 'Entre l'esprit des Lumières et la lettre Positiviste: les républicains sous l'Empire', in François Furet and Mona Ozouf (eds.), *Le siècle de l'avènement républicain* (Paris: Gallimard, 1993).

DE PARIS, COMTE, *Instructions de Mgr. le Comte de Paris aux représentants du parti monarchique en France* (Paris: Librairie Nationale, 1887).

—— 'Lettre-Manifeste aux maires sur le projet de réorganisation des communes de France' (Sheen House, 4 July 1888).

PELLETAN, EUGENE, 'Des religions nouvelles', *La Nouvelle Minerve* (1836).

—— 'Le Tombeau de Napoléon', *Revue Indépendante* (1 December 1841).

—— 'Histoire de Dix Ans par M.Louis Blanc', *Revue Indépendante* (1 February 1842).

—— 'Comment les dogmes se regénèrent. Le Catholicisme', in Eug. Pelletan, Aug. Colin, Hipp.Morvonnais, Victor Hennequin, *Les dogmes, le clergé et l'État. Études Religieuses* (Paris: Librairie Sociétaire, 1844).

—— *Histoire des trois journées de Février 1848* (Paris: Louis Colas, 1848).

—— *Profession de Foi du XIXe Siècle* (Paris: Pagnerre, 1852).

—— *Heures de Travail*, 2 vols (Paris: Pagnerre, 1854).

—— *Le Monde Marche. Lettres à Lamartine* (Paris: Pagnerre, 1857).

—— *Droits de l'Homme* (Paris: Pagnerre, 1858).

—— *Qu'allons-nous faire? Conférence de Zurich* (Paris: Librairie Nouvelle, 1859).

—— *Une étoile filante* (Paris: Dentu, 1860).

—— *La comédie italienne* (Paris: Pagnerre, 1862).

—— *La tragédie italienne* (Paris: Pagnerre, 1862).

—— *Le droit de parler. Lettre à M.Imhaus* (Paris: Pagnerre, 1862).

PELLETAN, EUGENE, *A Mm. les électeurs de la première circonscription des Bouches-du-Rhône* (1863). Bibliothèque Nationale, Le77–724.

—— *Aide-toi le ciel t'aidera* (Paris: Pagnerre, 1863).

—— *Le Crime* (Paris: Pagnerre, 1863).

—— *Le 31 Mai* (Paris: Pagnerre, 1863).

—— *Les fêtes de l'intelligence* (Paris: Pagnerre, 1863).

—— *L'Ombre de 89. Lettre à M. le duc de Persigny* (Paris: Pagnerre, 1863).

—— *La charte du foyer* (Paris: Pagnerre, 1864).

—— *Discours d'un député* (Paris: Pagnerre, 1864).

—— *Le Termite* (Paris: Pagnerre, 1864).

—— *Qui perd gagne* (Paris: Pagnerre, 1864).

—— *La mère* (Paris: Lacroix, 1865).

—— *Aux électeurs de la IXe circonscription de la Seine* (Paris, 1869) Bib.Nat.Le 77–2483.

—— *La femme au XIXe siècle* (Paris: Pagnerre, 1869).

—— *Le travail au XIXe siècle* (Paris: Pagnerre, 1869).

—— *Nouvelles Heures de Travail* (Paris: Pagnerre, 1870).

—— *Les uns et les autres* (Paris: Pagnerre, 1873).

—— *Le 4 Septembre devant l'enquête* (Paris: Pagnerre, 1874).

—— *La naissance d'une ville* (Paris: Germer Baillière, 1876).

—— *Première aux électeurs. Est-ce la République?* (Paris: Leroux, 1876).

—— *Élisée. Voyage d'un homme à la recherche de lui-même* (Paris: Germer Baillière, 1877).

—— *Jarousseau le pasteur du désert* (first published 1855) (Paris: Germer Baillière, 1877).

—— *Dieu est-il mort?* (Paris: Degorce-Cadot, 1883).

—— and MAURY, ALFRED, *Histoire universelle des religions*, Vol. 1 (Paris, 1844).

PETIT, ÉDOUARD, *Eugène Pelletan* (Paris: Quillet, 1913).

PETTIT, PHILIP, *Republicanism: A Theory of Freedom and Government* (Oxford: Oxford University Press, 1997).

PIETRZYKOWSKI, C., 'Jules-Romain Barni 1818–1878'. Mémoire de maîtrise (Université de Jules-Verne Picardie, 1995).

PILBEAM, PAMELA, *Republicanism in Nineteenth-century France 1814–1871* (London: Macmillan, 1995).

PLAMENATZ, JOHN, *The Revolutionary Movement in France 1815–1871* (London: Longmans, 1952).

POCOCK, JOHN G. A, *The Machiavellian Moment* (Princeton: Princeton University Press, 1975).

—— *Virtue, Commerce, and History* (Cambridge: Cambridge University Press, 1985).

PRÉVOST-PARADOL, LUCIEN-ANATOLE, *Quelques pages d'histoire contemporaine*, 2 Vols (Paris: Michel Lévy, 1864).

—— *La France Nouvelle* (Paris: Calmann-Lévy, 1868).

PROUDHON, PIERRE-JOSEPH, *La pornocratie ou la femme dans les temps modernes* (Paris: Lacroix, 1875).

QUINET, EDGAR, *La Révolution*, 2 Vols (Paris: Lacroix, 1865).

—— *Lettres d'exil*, 2 Vols (Paris, Calmann-Lévy, 1885).

RAUDOT, CLAUDE-MARIE, *L'administration locale en France et en Angleterre* (Paris: Douniol, 1863).

RÉMOND, RENÉ, *Les droites en France* (Paris: Aubier, 1982).

DE RÉMUSAT, CHARLES, 'De la Centralisation en France', in *Revue des Deux Mondes* (15 October 1860).

RENAN, ERNEST, Speech at the Académie Française, 27 April 1882, quoted in *La Philosophie Positive* (July–August 1882), 142.

RENAN, ERNEST, *La réforme intellectuelle et morale* (Bruxelles: Complexe, 1990).

RENOUVIER, CHARLES, *Manuel républicain de l'homme et du citoyen* (Paris: Imprimeurs-Unis, 1848).

République Occidentale. Ordre et Progrès. Rapport à la Société Positiviste, par la Commission chargée d'examiner la nature et le plan du nouveau gouvernement révolutionnaire (Paris, 1848).

REY, ALAIN, *Littré l'humaniste et les mots* (Paris: Gallimard, 1970).

DE RIBBES, CHARLES, *La nouvelle école libérale et la décentralisation* (Marseille : Imprimerie de Vve. Olive 1859).

ROBB, GRAHAM, *Victor Hugo: A Biography* (New York: Norton, 1997).

ROBERT, ADOLPHE; BOURLOTON, EDGAR, and COUGNY, GASTON (eds), *Dictionnaire des parlementaires français* (Paris: Bourloton, 1891).

ROLDAN, DARIO, *Charles de Rémusat: certitudes et impasses du libéralisme doctrinaire* (Paris: l'Harmattan, 1999).

ROSANVALLON, PIERRE, *Le moment Guizot* (Paris: Gallimard, 1985).

—— *Le sacre du citoyen. Histoire du suffrage universel en France* (Paris: Gallimard, 1992).

—— *L'État en France* (Paris: Seuil, 1990).

—— *Le peuple introuvable. Histoire de la représentation démocratique en France* (Paris: Gallimard, 1998).

ROTH, FRANÇOIS, *La guerre de 1870* (Paris: Fayard, 1990).

ROTHNEY, JOHN, *Bonapartism after Sedan* (Ithaca: Cornell University Press, 1969).

DE RUGGIERO, GUIDO, *The History of European Liberalism* (London: Oxford University Press, 1927).

DE SAINT-SIMON, HENRI, *Le Nouveau Christianisme et les écrits sur la religion*, ed. Henri Desroche (Paris: Seuil, 1969).

SAND, GEORGE, *Correspondance*, 26 Vols, ed. Georges Lubin (Paris: Garnier, 1980–95).

—— *Histoire de ma vie* (Paris: Stock, 1993).

SCHATZ, ALBERT, *L'individualisme économique et social* (Paris: Colin, 1907).

SCHEURER-KESTNER, AUGUSTE, *Souvenirs de jeunesse* (Paris: Charpentier, 1905).

SCOTT, JOAN W, *Only Paradoxes to Offer* (Cambridge, MA: Harvard University Press, 1996).

SIMON, JULES, *Le Devoir* (Paris: Hachette, 1854).

—— *Souviens-toi du Deux-Décembre* (Paris: Havard, 1889).

—— *Mémoires des autres* (Paris: Testard, 1890).

SIMON, WALTER MICHAEL, *European Positivism in the Nineteenth Century: An Essay in Intellectual History* (Ithaca: Cornell University Press, 1963).

SIX, JEAN-FRANÇOIS, *Littré devant dieu* (Paris: Seuil, 1962).

SKINNER, QUENTIN, 'The Republican Ideal of Political Liberty', in Gisela Bock, Quentin Skinner, and Maurizio Viroli (eds), *Machiavelli and Republicanism* (Cambridge: Cambridge University Press, 1990).

—— *Liberty before Liberalism* (Cambridge: Cambridge University Press, 1998).

SMITH, PAUL, *Feminism and the Third Republic* (Oxford: Clarendon Press, 1996).

SOLTAU, ROGER, *French Political Thought in the Nineteenth Century* (New Haven: Yale University Press, 1931).

SPRIET, HENRI, *Dupont-White: étude sur les origines du socialisme d'État en France* (Paris: Giard et Brière, 1901).

SPULLER, EUGENE, 'Eugène Pelletan', in *Figures disparues*, 2nd series (Paris: Alcan, 1891).

Statuts de la Ligue Nationale contre l'Athéisme (Paris: Rue de Richelieu, 1887).

STEARS, MARC, 'Beyond the Logic of Liberalism', *Journal of Political Ideologies*, 6 (2001), 215–30.

STERN, DANIEL, *Mémoires, souvenirs et journaux de la Comtesse d'Agoult*, 2 Vols (Paris: Mercure de France, 1990).

STOCK-MORTON, PHYLLIS, *Moral Education for a Secular Society: The Development of Morale Laïque in Nineteenth Century France* (Albany: State University of New York Press, 1988).

STONE, JUDITH, *Sons of the Revolution* (Baton Rouge: Louisiana State University Press, 1996).

TAINE, HIPPOLYTE, *Les philosophes français du XIXe siècle* (Paris: Hachette, 1857).

—— 'Psychologie du jacobin', *Revue des Deux Mondes* (1 April 1881).

—— *Carnets de Voyage: Notes sur la Province 1863–1865* (Paris: Hachette, 1897).

—— *Hippolyte Taine. Sa vie et sa correspondance* (Paris: Hachette, 1902).

TAITHE, BERTRAND, *Defeated Flesh: Welfare, Warfare and the Making of Modern France* (Manchester: Manchester University Press, 1999).

TARGET, P. F., *Élections du 21 Août 1881* (Paris, 1881).

—— *Élections du 4 Octobre 1885* (Paris, 1885).

TCHERNOFF, IOUDA, *Le parti républicain au coup d'état et sous le Second Empire* (Paris: Pedone, 1906).

THÉPOT, ANDRÉ, 'Michel Chevalier', in Jean Tulard (ed.), *Dictionnaire du Second Empire* (Paris: Fayard, 1995).

THOMSON, DAVID, *Democracy in France* (London: Oxford University Press, 1946).

THUILLIER, GUY, 'Aux origines du radicalisme: "La Démocratie" d'Étienne Vacherot', *Revue Administrative*, 254 (March–April 1990), 117–26.

THUREAU-DANGIN, PAUL, *Le parti libéral sous la Restauration* (Paris: Plon, 1876).

TOUCHARD, JEAN, *La gloire de Béranger* (Paris, Armand Colin, 1968).

TOUROUDE, GEORGES, *Deux républicains de progrès, Eugène et Camille Pelletan* (Paris: L'Harmattan, 1995).

TRIDON, GUSTAVE, 'Gironde et Girondins', in *Oeuvres diverses de Gustave Tridon* (Paris: Allemane, 1891).

TRUESDELL, MATTHEW, *Spectacular Politics: Louis-Napoleon Bonaparte and the Fête Impériale, 1849–1870* (New York: Oxford University Press, 1997).

VACHEROT, ARSÈNE, 'Les rapports du pouvoir municipal avec l'État', *Revue des Deux Mondes* (1 July 1876).

VACHEROT, ÉTIENNE, *Histoire critique de l'école d'Alexandrie* (Paris: Librairie Philosophique de Ladrange, 1846–51).

—— 'La doctrine du progrès', *Revue de Paris* (15 September 1856).

—— *La Métaphysique et la Science*, 2 Vols (Paris, Chamerot, 1858).

—— *La Démocratie* (Paris: Chamerot, 1860).

—— 'M.Damiron', *La Réforme Littéraire* 16 February 1862

—— *Essais de philosophie critique* (Paris: Chamerot, 1864).

—— 'La situation philosophique en France', *Revue des Deux Mondes* (15 June 1868).

—— 'La crise religieuse au XIXe siècle', *Revue des Deux Mondes* (15 October 1868).

—— *La Religion* (Paris: Chamerot, 1869).

—— 'La situation politique et les lois Constitutionnelles: II', *Revue des Deux Mondes* (1 and 15 December 1874).

—— *Notice sur Paul-François Dubois* (Paris: Picard, 1875).

—— 'Les difficultés de la situation politique', *Revue des Deux Mondes* (15 October 1876).

—— 'La République constitutionnelle et parlementaire', *Revue des Deux Mondes* (15 November 1879).

—— 'La République libérale', *Revue des Deux Mondes* (1 March 1880).

—— 'Les nouveaux Jacobins', *Revue des Deux Mondes* (1 July 1880).

—— 'Les trois états de l'esprit humain', *Revue des Deux Mondes* (15 August 1880).

—— *La politique extérieure de la République* (Paris: Germer Baillière, 1881).

—— 'La révision des lois constitutionnelles', *Le Correspondant* (10 March 1883).

—— *Le Nouveau Spiritualisme* (Paris: Hachette, 1884).

—— 'Lettre-Manifeste aux maires sur le projet de réorganisation des communes de France', Sheen House (4 July 1888), Bib.Nat.Rés.Lb57–9615.

—— 'La Démocratie', *Le Correspondant* (10 April 1887).

—— *La Démocratie Libérale* (Paris: Calmann-Lévy, 1892).

—— 'La question sociale', *Le Soleil* (9 December 1893).

VALLES, JULES, *L'insurgé* (Paris: Gallimard, 1975).

VERLY, HIPPOLYTE, *Essai de biographie lilloise contemporaine 1800–1869* (Lille: Leleu, 1869).

VIALLANEIX, PAUL, *Michelet, les travaux et les jours* (Paris: Gallimard, 1998).

VILLEY, DANIEL, *Charles Dupont-White, sa vie, son oeuvre, sa doctrine* (Paris: Alcan, 1936).

—— 'Sur la traduction par Dupont-White de "La Liberté" de Stuart Mill', *Revue d'Histoire Économique et Sociale*, 24 (1938).

VIVIER, NADINE, *Propriété collective et identité communale: les biens communaux en France 1750–1914* (Paris: Publications de la Sorbonne, 1998).

VUILLEUMIER, MARC, 'L'impression et la diffusion de la propagande républicaine à Genève au temps du Second Empire (1852–1856)', in Jean-Daniel Candaux and Bernard Lescaze (eds), *Cinq siècles d'imprimerie genevoise* (Genève: Société d'histoire et d'archéologie, 1981).

WEBER, EUGEN, *Peasants into Frenchmen* (London: Chatto, 1977).

WEILL, GEORGES, *L'école Saint-Simonienne* (Paris: Alcan, 1896).

—— *Histoire du parti républicain en France de 1814 à 1870* (Paris: Alcan, 1900).

—— 'Les Saint-Simoniens sous Napoléon III', *Revue des Études Napoléoniennes*, 3 (1913), 391–406.

—— *Histoire du mouvement social en France* (Paris: Alcan, 1924).

—— *Histoire de l'idée laïque en France au XIXe siècle* (Paris: Alcan, 1925).

—— *Histoire du catholicisme libéral en France* (Genève: Slatkine, 1979).

WELCH, CHERYL B., *Liberty and Utility: The French Idéologues and the Transformation of Liberalism* (New York: Columbia University Press, 1984).

WHATMORE, RICHARD, *Republicanism and the French Revolution: An Intellectual History of Jean-Baptiste Say's Political Economy* (Oxford: Oxford University Press, 2000).

WILLARD, CLAUDE, *Les Guesdistes* (Paris: Éditions Sociales, 1965).

WILLIAMSON, EDWIN, *The Penguin History of Latin America* (London: Penguin Press, 1992).

WINOCK, MICHEL, *Les voix de la liberté. Les écrivains engagés au XIXe siècle* (Paris: Seuil, 2000).

WRIGHT, JOHNSON KENT, *A Classical Republican in Eighteenth-century France: The Political Thought of Mably* (Stanford: Stanford University Press, 1997).

WRIGHT, VINCENT, 'Le Conseil d'État et l'affaire de la confiscation des biens d'Orléans en 1852', *Études et Documents*, No. 21 (1968), 231–49.

—— 'The coup d'état of December 1851: Repression and the Limits to Repression', in Roger Price (ed.), *Revolution and Reaction: 1848 and the Second French Republic* (London: Croom Helm, 1975).

ZELDIN, THEODORE, *Émile Ollivier and the Liberal Empire of Napoleon III* (Oxford: Clarendon Press, 1963).

ZÉVAÈS, ALEXANDRE, *L'Histoire de la Troisième République* (Paris: Georges-Anquetil, 1926).

INDEX